IMAGINING WORLD ORDER

IMAGINING WORLD ORDER

LITERATURE AND INTERNATIONAL LAW IN EARLY MODERN EUROPE, 1500–1800

CHENXI TANG

CORNELL UNIVERSITY PRESS
Ithaca and London

Copyright © 2018 by Cornell University

All rights reserved. Except for brief quotations in a review, this book, or parts thereof, must not be reproduced in any form without permission in writing from the publisher. For information, address Cornell University Press, Sage House, 512 East State Street, Ithaca, New York 14850. Visit our website at cornellpress.cornell.edu.

First published 2018 by Cornell University Press

Printed in the United States of America

Library of Congress Cataloging-in-Publication Data

Names: Tang, Chenxi, 1968– author.
Title: Imagining world order : literature and international law in early modern Europe, 1500–1800 / Chenxi Tang.
Description: Ithaca : Cornell University Press, 2018. | Includes bibliographical references and index.
Identifiers: LCCN 2018025257 (print) | LCCN 2018025998 (ebook) | ISBN 9781501716935 (e-book pdf) | ISBN 9781501716928 (e-book epub/mobi) | ISBN 9781501716911 | ISBN 9781501716911 (cloth ; alk. paper)
Subjects: LCSH: Law in literature. | International relations in literature. | European literature—Early modern, 1500–1700—History and criticism. | European literature—18th century—History and criticism. | International law—History.
Classification: LCC PN56.L33 (ebook) | LCC PN56.L33 T36 2018 (print) | DDC 809/.933554—dc23
LC record available at https://lccn.loc.gov/2018025257

For Paul and Klaus

Contents

Acknowledgments xi

Introduction 1
International Law 3
Literary Approaches to International World Order 9
A Dual History of International Law and European Literature 20

1. The Old World Order Dissolving 25
Universal Laws in Flux (Neoscholastic Jurisprudence) 28
Cosmic Order Disturbed (Camões's *Os Lusíadas*, Reason of State) 37
The Beginnings of Public International Law (Gentili, Suárez, Grotius) 54

2. The Poetics of International Legal Order 66
Treaty and Allegory in the Renaissance 68
The Founding Narratives of International Legal Personality (Grotius, Hobbes, Leibniz) 75
The Founding Narratives of International Society (Grotius, Leibniz) 87
Spectacles of International Order 97
The Drama of International Society 103

3. **International Order as Tragedy** 107

   The Renaissance of Tragedy and the Problem of International Order   107

   The Sovereign Will and the Tragic Form (Marlowe's *Tamburlaine*, Shakespeare's *King John*)   113

   A Tragicomic Intermezzo: The Shapes of World Order in Shakespeare's Romances   128

   The Tragedy of Reason of State (Lohenstein)   140

   The Tragedy of Marriage Alliance (Corneille)   152

   International Order Through Tragic Experience   167

4. **International Order as Romance** 170

   The Romance Form and World Order (The Greek Romance, Barclay's *Argenis*)   172

   The Crisis of Political Romance in the Mid-Seventeenth Century (Herbert)   191

   The Apotheosis and Extinction of Political Romance (Anton Ulrich, Leibniz)   197

5. **The Divergence between International Law and Literature around 1700** 205

   The Depersonalization of the State (Gryphius, Milton)   206

   The Birth of the Private Individual (Milton, Racine)   213

   International Law as a Field of Expert Knowledge   218

   Literature and the Private Individual   229

6. **The Novel and International Order in the Eighteenth Century**   231

    The Fictional Construction of Society: *Ius Naturae et Gentium*   233

    The Fictional Construction of Society: Poetics of the Novel   238

    Transnational Commercial World Order (Defoe)   244

    Sentimental World Order (Gellert, Sterne)   255

    Cosmopolitan World Order (Wieland, Goethe, Kant)   266

Epilogue   281

Notes   283
References   307
Index   335

ACKNOWLEDGMENTS

The present book owes its origin to my research on a period in the history of European literature and thought that lies beyond its scope—the tumultuous decades between the French Revolution and the Congress of Vienna. Trained as a Germanist, I have a standing interest in this period, as it coincided with the heyday of German literature generally known as the classical-romantic age. Almost a decade ago, I made a discovery in studying this period: there seems to be a close connection between international law and poetic literature. As the law between states, international law was supposed to ensure a normative order for the world. But it had none of the institutions at its disposal that would make a legal order possible—neither a legislative nor a jurisdictional authority, let alone centralized law enforcement. International law was intrinsically fragile and ineffective. As such, it provoked interventions by poetic literature. International world order seemed to be as much a literary as a legal problem. Excited by this finding, I decided to write a book on international law and literature in the eighteenth and nineteenth centuries. However, in order to give some historical depth to the study, I thought it necessary to go back to the beginning of public international law in the Renaissance. This step led to the reconception of the whole project as two books, with the one dealing with the early modern period and the other with the time from the French Revolution to the First World War. The present volume is the first of the two books.

The first draft of this book was written during the years between 2011 and 2015. I thank my Berkeley colleagues Timothy Hampton and Victoria Kahn for helping me to get acquainted with the early modern period and Niklaus Largier for writing one letter of recommendation after the other for my grant and fellowship applications. The strategic working group "Law and Humanities" run by Berkeley's Townsend Center for the Humanities in 2014 opened up many new perspectives for me. My Berlin colleagues Ethel Matala de Mazza and Joseph Vogl hosted me a number of times at Humboldt University when this book was in the process of gestation. My sojourn in

Berlin in 2014 was funded by the Alexander von Humboldt Foundation. The Mellon Foundation provided a generous grant to defray all kinds of research expenditure, while a University of California President's Faculty Fellowship in the Humanities (Fall 2013) and a faculty fellowship at Berkeley's Townsend Center for the Humanities (Spring 2014) gave me the much-needed time to write. Rüdiger Campe, Andreas Huyssen, Dorothea von Mücke, and Daniel Purdy supported my grant applications.

After the completion of the first draft in 2015, a dozen or so anonymous outside reviewers for my promotion case at Berkeley offered general assessments of the strengths and weaknesses of the book manuscript (at that time much longer than the final version), as well as detailed comments on specific arguments. Their suggestions served as the basis for a thorough revision. Simon Stern read the manuscript from a legal scholar's perspective. His leads helped me make a number of necessary adjustments to the manuscript. Finally, the anonymous peer reviewers' generous comments, constructive criticism, and valuable suggestions for further research and structural improvement enabled me to undertake another round of revision. Many imperfections remain, but fortunately this is not the end of the story. The imperfections marring this book goad me to do things differently in working on the question of international world order in the nineteenth and twentieth centuries.

Unless otherwise noted, all translations are mine. Verse is translated in prose.

IMAGINING WORLD ORDER

Introduction

International world order—the normative order among states—is today most often discussed in terms of international law or international politics. As a historical phenomenon, it is usually framed in terms of successive transformations of international law and international relations.[1] The key finding of the present book is that it is as much a literary as a legal or political problem. The scene of our story is Europe, and the period under consideration is roughly the three centuries from 1500 to 1800, the classical period of international law. The book shows how poetic literature contributed to the emergence of international law, how it worked on the problems besetting international law and imaginatively rehearsed various models of world order, and how in the process a set of literary forms common to major European languages—a European literature—evolved.

The normative order between political communities, rulers, and individuals outside of their native communities had been a concern in all parts of the world since ancient times.[2] The articulation of this concern in legal terms may be broadly called international law. The form of international law that emerged in Europe from the sixteenth to the eighteenth century as the law between sovereign states—so-called modern international law—represented one particular approach to world order. It was initially designed to regulate the system of states on the European continent as well as the overseas expansion of European states, but it turned out to have global consequences: its language, its normative propositions, and its modus operandi eventually spread around the world, either imposed on other peoples through colonialism and imperialism, or consciously appropriated by other peoples for their own purposes.[3] In awareness of such far-reaching consequences, the present book turns to the formative period of modern international law. (Its worldwide diffusion—a torturous process that occurred mostly after 1800—lies outside of the purview of this book.) Yet what follows is no conventional legal history, but a rarely told story of international law in relation to poetic literature, showing how the aspiration of international law to establish a normative order of the world depended on and called for the literary imagination.

Poetic literature may prepare the ground for international law by exposing certain problems waiting for legal solutions or by creating certain symbolic resources that feed into the law. For example, the Renaissance epic as exemplified by Luís Vaz de Camões's *Os Lusíadas* (1572) indicates the collapse of the cosmic order and the triumph of the idea of reason of state, anticipating the rise of public international law around 1600 (discussed in chapter 1). Tragedies in the late seventeenth century bespeak the depersonalization of the state as well as the separation of the public and the private in the world of states or international world, anticipating the development of international law into a field of expert knowledge on affairs of the state (discussed in chapter 5). The *Bildungsroman* of the late eighteenth century enabled Immanuel Kant's cosmopolitanism by creating a cosmopolitan subject (discussed in chapter 6). The poetic imagination may play a constitutive role in the making of the discourse of international law. For example, the theory and practice of international law in the sixteenth and seventeenth centuries deployed poetic operations in various media—pictorial allegories, narratives, performance—to figure a universal normative order (discussed in chapter 2). Finally, and most important, poetic literature may diagnose and offer remedies for the insufficiency, fragility, and uncertainty of international law. For example, the genre of tragedy, which flourished during the century spanning the English Renaissance, French Classicism, and the German Baroque, staged the impotence, collapse, or sheer absence of international law. Plays by Christopher Marlowe (1564–93), William Shakespeare (1564–1616), Pierre Corneille (1606–84), Andreas Gryphius (1616–64), and Daniel Casper von Lohenstein (1635–83), to name just a few towering tragedians, displayed scene after bloody scene of irresolvable conflicts in the international arena, evoking a normative world order as something that inexorably comes to naught (discussed in chapter 3). By contrast, the political romance, beginning with John Barclay's *Argenis* (1621) and culminating in the turgid volumes of Anton Ulrich von Braunschweig-Lüneburg (1633–1714), affirmed an international legal order—mostly in the form of royal marriage alliances—by means of the magic of plotting (discussed in chapter 4).

The entwined history of European literature and international law began with the political reality of the rise of the sovereign state and the ensuing imperative to establish a normative order for the international world. International law—the law between sovereign states—was a response to this imperative. Literature also responded to this imperative, doing so mainly by engaging with international law, occasionally affirming it, often contesting it, always uncovering its problems and rehearsing imaginary solutions. If there was a normative world order—or what Carl Schmitt called "the *nomos* of the earth"— it was perhaps above all a product of the literary imagination.[4] Some key literary works in the European tradition can be read as part of the great enterprise of answering the pressing question of modern times: How is international world order possible? This great enterprise, as we shall see, prompted the making of key generic forms common to the literary production in major European languages—the epic, the tragedy, the romance, and the novel, among others. The plurality of states on the European continent and their need to get along with each other on a normative basis contributed significantly to the development of a European literature.

International Law

The term "international law" was coined by Jeremy Bentham (1748–1832) towards the end of the eighteenth century as a "new though not inexpressive appellation" to designate the "principles of legislation in matters betwixt nation and nation."[5] International law in this sense had existed since at the latest the decades around 1600 under the name of *ius gentium* (in the vernacular, the "law of nations," "droit des gens," "Völkerrecht," "derecho de gentes," or "diritto delle genti"). In Roman law, *ius gentium* is one of the three sources of private law, referring to the law that natural reason establishes among all humans. It is distinguished, on the one hand, from *ius naturale* or the law that nature teaches to all living beings, including animals, and, on the other hand, from *ius civile* or the law that a particular commonwealth sets up for itself.[6] The criterion of distinction is the scope of application. In a consequential breakthrough of jurisprudence, *ius gentium* was radically redefined in the late sixteenth and early seventeenth centuries as the law regulating the dealings of states with one another—that is, as international law. This new *ius gentium* overlapped with the older form in certain areas, for instance with regard to such issues as war, peace, and legation.[7] But it acquired an entirely new significance, defined no longer as a source of private law, but as a law with a distinctive subject—the sovereign state. As the law between states, it figured as a branch of public law.[8] We call it public international law today.

The emergence of public international law was all of piece with the rise of the sovereign state. In Europe, the state—or, as historians tend to term it, the modern state—evolved from the late Middle Ages to the sixteenth century. The state was a kind of political community characterized by centralized power structures wielding exclusive authority over people in a large territory, with England, France, and Spain standing as its prime examples.[9] Although political realities may have looked different from country to country, the state was conceptualized in these distinctively modern terms by the end of the sixteenth century—as a separate legal and constitutional order, as a compulsory organization with a territorial basis, and as the sole source of legitimate force.[10] This concept of the state, we know further from historians, was bound up with the concept of sovereignty.[11] Sovereignty, in its classic definition by Jean Bodin, means above all the supreme power of creating and applying laws: "The first prerogative (*marque*) of a sovereign prince is to give law to all in general and to each in particular [. . .] without the consent of any other, whether greater, equal, or below him."[12] In addition, the sovereign may "annul, change, or correct the laws according to the exigencies of situations, times, and persons."[13] It is, of course, also in the sovereign that the power of interpreting and enforcing the laws is vested.[14]

The rise of the sovereign state as the dominant political form made it necessary to reconceive world order. If the state is the primary or the most important mode in which people are grouped, and if it figures as the sole appropriate object of individuals' allegiances, then the relations among states make up a predominant dimension of the society of humankind as a whole. What should be the normative basis of such relations? The question of international order proved to be a question about its possibility. Instead of ensuring international order, the Christian religion became in the wake of the Protestant Reformation a proximate cause for bloody strife among states. Ethical norms seemed hardly applicable to states as abstract, impersonal entities. Even on a personal level they proved woefully inadequate for regulating the mutual behavior among rulers who were intent on pursuing the interests of the states embodied or represented by them. In fact, all traditional normative models seemed to collapse if it came to the relations between sovereign states. Even cosmological ideas, wherever they had not yet been challenged or abandoned, were enlisted in the sixteenth and seventeenth centuries to justify the absoluteness and perpetuity of the individual state, thus militating against rather than facilitating a normative order among states.[15]

International law was an attempt to establish a normative order among states by legal means. States sometimes behaved like neighbors in a small community, settling their disputes by informal rules, thus maintaining what a legal scholar calls "order without law."[16] As a legal and constitutional order, however, the modern state could not help drawing on the language, practices, and even institutions of law in dealing with one another. The rise of the modern state necessitated international law. Conversely, international law was also an integral dimension of the modern state, for the domestic order of the state, ensured by the sovereign authority, presupposed an outside—the space of other states, or the space of international relations—and the law governing this outside space was international law.[17]

From the outset, international law was a problem child of jurisprudence. It was supposed to provide a corpus of legal norms governing sovereign states in their dealings with each other, but the sovereign, by definition, did not submit to any higher laws. Equally troubling was that international law did not constitute a unified normative order: a normative order requires a common source of authority that integrates disparate norms into a coherent whole, but sovereign states have no acknowledged common authority that would promulgate, apply, and enforce laws. International law was thus intrinsically fragile and ineffective. Indeed, even its existence was sometimes questioned. Hugo Grotius (1583–1645), often called the founding father of public international law, identified three sources for international law: the law of nature, customs, and treaties. His contemporary Thomas Hobbes (1588–1679) cast doubt on the validity of all of them. As to the law of nature, Hobbes points out in *Leviathan* (1651), "The Interpretation of the Law of Nature, is the Sentence of the Judge constituted by the Soveraign Authority, to heare and determine such controversies, as depend thereon; and consisteth in the application of the Law to the present case."[18] Custom, at one time binding on a community as a matter of course, was now considered to have no force unless it was formally validated by the sovereign authority.[19] In the words of Hobbes, "Custom does not constitute law in its own right," and the so-called customary laws "are to be accepted among the written laws, not because they are customary [. . .] but because of the will of the sovereign, which is declared in the fact that he has allowed the opinion to become customary."[20] Finally, an agreement based on explicit consent is null and void if there is no sovereign power "set up to constrain those that would otherwise violate their faith": "If a Covenant be made wherein neither of the parties performe presently, but trust one another; in the condition of meer Nature, (which is a condition of Warre of every man against every man,) upon any reasonable suspicion, it is Voyd: But if there be a common Power set over them both, with right and force sufficient to compel performance; it is not Voyd."[21] Since there is no sovereign authority between states, no part of international law—whether derived from the law of nature or mutual consent—could have any force. It is, therefore, doubtful whether international law is law at all.

Hobbes was the ancestor of the so-called deniers of international law who usually base their arguments on the lack of a sovereign authority ensuring compulsory jurisdiction and enforcement. By contrast, the "idealists" insist that international law is law in spite of this lack because it is mandated by higher principles—morality, justice, and the like. There is a wide spectrum of positions between these two extremes. For the "apologists," the lack of a sovereign authority does not disqualify international law as law, for compliance does not always require compulsion. States actually comply with international law on a regular basis, because it provides them with a useful tool for solving their problems. There are then the "reformists," who seek to elevate international law to the standards of domestic law. And finally, there are the "critics," who see in international law one of the tools employed by powerful nations to dominate others.[22] The legal positivism of Hans Kelsen (1881–1973) and H. L. A. Hart (1907–92) offers useful insights into the special status of international law as law.

For Kelsen, international law is not mere "opinions current amongst nations," but law proper. His "pure theory of law," or *reine Rechtslehre*, approaches international law as a specific kind of positive law, as susceptible to structural analysis as the law of any individual state. Yet there is a fundamental difference between international law and domestic law: whereas domestic law, be it the law of the United States, France, or Mexico, makes up a unified legal order, international law consists of a multitude of legal norms without cohering into a unified legal order. An "order," Kelsen writes, "is a system of norms whose unity is constituted by the fact that they all have the same reason for their validity; and the reason for the validity of a normative order is a basic norm, [. . .] from which the validity of all norms of the order are derived. A single norm is a valid legal norm, if it corresponds to the concept of 'law' and is part of a legal order; and it *is* part of a legal order, if its validity is based on the basic norm of that order."[23] The legal order thus understood is nothing other than the state. Against the background of "the identity of state and law," international law looms as a special problem.[24] In the international world, there is neither an effective constitution that could be considered the empirical counterpart to the transcendental-logically presupposed basic norm, nor are there legislative, judicial, and administrative organs that could create and apply norms according to specific procedures.

Consequently, the multitude of norms meant to regulate the mutual behavior of states that makes up international law does not constitute a unity. If there is any international legal order to speak of, it is a "primitive legal order": international law "shows a certain similarity with the law of primitive, i.e. stateless society in that international law (as a general law that binds all states) does not establish special organs for the creation and application of its norms. It is still in a state of far-reaching decentralization. It is only at the beginning of a development which national law has already completed."[25]

Hart's *The Concept of Law* (1961), another milestone in legal positivism, also features an extensive discussion of international law. Hart proposes understanding a functioning legal system as the union of primary and secondary rules. Primary rules are the rules of obligation, concerned with the actions that people must or must not do, while "the secondary rules are all concerned with the primary rules themselves. They specify the ways in which the primary rules may be conclusively ascertained, introduced, eliminated, varied, and the fact of their violation conclusively determined."[26] Hart distinguishes three kinds of secondary rules: the rules of recognition, which determine the validity and ensure the systematic unity of primary rules; the rules of change, which regulate the introduction, modification, or elimination of primary rules; and finally the rules of adjudication, which regulate the application of primary rules. In light of the conception of law as the union of primary and secondary rules, the status of international law requires clarification, for "it is indeed arguable," Hart concedes, "that international law not only lacks the secondary rules of change and adjudication which provide for legislature and courts, but also a unifying rule of recognition specifying 'sources' of law and providing general criteria for the identification of its rules."[27] The lack of secondary rules distinguishes international law from the fully-fledged legal order characteristic of the state, but Hart does not deny that international law is law. His jurisprudence is more consistently descriptive than Kelsen's. Instead of prescribing what international law should or must do, he points out some interesting facts about international law: the absence of centrally organized sanctions does not lead to lawlessness all the time, for wars are costly and risky, and in most cases it is simply more convenient to abide by the rules than to violate them by military means; the sovereign state as the subject of international law is actually flexible enough to accept many kinds of legal arrangement; despite the absence of secondary rules, the rules of international law are "very unlike those of primitive society, and many of its concepts, methods, and techniques are the same as the modern municipal law"; and finally, the set of rules in international law, which do not constitute a systematic unity for lack of a rule of recognition, can be effective in their own way. In sum, international law represents a legal order that is uncertain and inefficient in comparison to domestic law, but intermittently effective and constantly changing.[28]

From the perspective of legal positivism, then, international law is law, but a deficient law. It is undeniable that international law sets great store by the language, techniques, and trappings of the legal system developed by the modern state over centuries. But it lacks an effective constitution that could stand in for the basic norm ensuring a unified legal order. Or, from Hart's perspective, it lacks the secondary rules that could remedy the uncertainty and inefficiency of mere primary rules. International law is law insofar as it comprises a collection of legal norms, but these norms do not really cohere into a legal order. "In a normative order," in the words of the German legal theorist Christoph Möllers, "the element of order itself is normative. Here norms are created, which stem from a common source of authority, and which therefore are connected with one another."[29] What international law lacks is a common source of authority that ensures an order of norms.

In sum, one can either say that international law is law but does not constitute a legal order, or one can say that it is an incomplete, uncertain, and unstable legal order. Taking domestic law to be the standard of civilization, Kelsen, Hart, and others characterize international law as "primitive." Of course, international law does not have to be measured by the standards of domestic law. One can just accept it as a law in its own right, a law fundamentally different from domestic law. In this view, the uncertainty, instability, and incompleteness of international law are more unsettling still, for now international law gestures towards a normative order without even being able to specify what this order is like. One way or another, international law is obviously not a legal order that is already constituted, but one constantly in the process of being constituted. International law may be "a primitive law of a primitive community," as Hersch Lauterpacht (1897–1960) puts it.[30] But the "primitive community" called international society is certainly not one frozen in time. It is rather what the anthropologist Claude Lévi-Strauss (1908–2009) calls a "hot society"—a society "resolutely internalizing the historical process and making it the moving power of [its] development."[31] What this book aims to study is certain aspects of the historical process that international society has internalized and taps into as a source of energy to power its development.

How to remedy the uncertainty, instability, and incompleteness of international law? Or, to put it in slightly different words, how to turn the collection of norms making up international law into a normative order? One answer to the question is the doctrinal discourse. In contrast to legal dogmatics—the interpretation and systematization of positive legal norms—doctrines are learned opinions or theories that not only establish particular legal norms, but may also provide a unifying principle for all legal norms. Formulated by jurists and philosophers in a public space of legal argumentation and debates, doctrines intervene in the world of states from the vantage points of *communis opinio*, legal knowledge, reason, and conscience. The Kantian cosmopolitanism, based on a "transcendental principle of publicness," epitomizes the doctrinal discourse in international law.[32] Another answer to the question is poetic literature. In engaging with international law, poetic literature operates mostly on the level of what Kelsen calls basic norms and what Hart calls secondary rules. But it lays down neither a basic norm nor a secondary rule. Rather it opens up an imaginary space, a fictional laboratory as it were, in which to explore the consequences of the lack of basic norms or secondary rules, and to experiment with some kind of basic norm or secondary rule. Or poetic literature may open up a fictional forum for deliberating and adjudicating international legal issues, standing in for legislative and judicial institutions, or offer norms and normative order beyond the law. These two answers are related, for the doctrinal discourse often deploys poetic devices or draws on literature, while literature may test out doctrines.

Literary Approaches to International World Order

The attempts of poetic literature to cope with the uncertainty, instability, and incompleteness of international law lead, in varying ways, to the figuration of a normative world order that international law is incapable of realizing. Poetic literature engages with international law mainly in the following four modes:

- poetic constitution of international law, i.e. the poetic operations deployed by the legal discourse to turn disparate international legal norms into a normative order;
- poetic lawmaking, i.e. the making of a normative world order by means of fictional experiments;
- poetic jurisdiction, i.e. the evocation of a normative world order through the judgment of the reader or audience;
- poetic contestation of international law, i.e. the questioning of the adequacy of the legal approach in the international world and the figuration of a normative world order beyond the law.

Poetic Constitution of International Law

That law deploys poetic operations is not news. The interdisciplinary study of law and literature is concerned not only with literary texts as legal texts, but also with legal texts as literary texts. Interpreting contracts, statutes, and constitutions may involve procedures and techniques of literary criticism, while judicial opinions can be treated as literary writing.[33] Poetic operations also form an integral dimension of international law. In the present context, those poetic operations are especially worth mentioning which marshal heteroclite norms into a coherent international legal order. There are poetic operations that elevate a particular norm to the symbol of international legal order as such, and there are those by which the doctrinal discourse constructs an international legal order.

International law is not a unified, systematically operative legal order, mainly because of the peculiarity of the creation of norms in the international world. States as subjects of international law participate directly in lawmaking by signing bilateral or multilateral treaties, by giving consent to customs, or by accepting general principles. This gives rise to a set of incoherent norms with varying material and personal scope, as well as with varying levels of normativity. Yet it is not uncommon that a particular treaty is declared to seal the eternal friendship between the signatories and thereby to serve as the foundation of world order at large. Nor is it unheard of that a particular principle set forth by one state is declared to ensure a new world order. In rhetorical terms, what is at work in such cases is synecdoche. But as Quintilian (c. 35–100 CE) observed with regard to synecdoche, "liberior poetis quam oratoribus," poets are freer than orators.[34] Poetic imagination is so unconstrained and so capacious as to transform a part into a whole, expanding one particular norm into a general normative order, condensing norm into normativity. Poetic imagination may exercise its power in the medium of writing. And it may be also at work in visual media as well as in performance. In chapter 2, we will see visual images that portray a particular peace treaty as a symbol of eternal peace. We will also see ritual and ceremonial performances in the international world, which refer customary norms of conduct to a mythic ground of universal world order.

That international law comprises a heteroclite set of norms without cohering into a normative order is a view of legal positivism. The doctrinal discourse does envisage a normative order. Ever since the days of the medieval Commentators on civil law, learned opinions have been held in high esteem in the European legal tradition. Especially in international law learned opinions have pride of place, if only because there are no other acknowledged common authorities in the world of states. To the authors of the great doctrinal systems in the classical age of international law—from the neoscholastic Francisco Suárez (1548–1617) and the humanist Grotius to the Enlightenment savants Christian Wolff (1679–1754) and Emer de Vattel (1714–1767)—there was never a doubt about the existence of an international legal order, in which each norm, whatever its source, would find its place. As well as laying down specific norms pertaining to war, peace, or any other aspect of the dealings of sovereign states, the doctrinal discourse offers an organizing principle that connects and orders these specific norms into a coherent whole—a principle that is normative itself. It can do so because it commands an authority beyond the state—the authority of legal learning, reason, and conscience, which comes into its own in a public space of debates and legal argumentation.[35]

In constructing an international legal order, the doctrinal discourse makes use of poetic operations.[36] To a certain extent, every legal order involves poetic operations. Within the legal order of a state, every norm can be derived from other norms by virtue of a certain principle, as analyzed by Kelsen, Hart, and other legal positivists. But what is the legitimizing ground, the authorizing origin of a legal order as a whole? This is a pressing question, for actors in a legal system need to believe that there is an ultimate normative foundation for legal decision-making and determination of order.[37] Legal positivism, however, leaves this question unaccounted for, since the authorizing origin of a legal order necessarily lies outside of the legal order itself, and is thus not accessible to legal discourse.[38] It exists only in or as a mythical narrative. Philosophers speak of the "mythical foundation of authority" or "mythical justification of the [normative] system as a whole."[39] Indeed, legal systems are often undergirded by mythical narratives that explain their foundation and purpose.[40] Just think of the myth of the divine gift of the Ten Commandments and the legends of Solon and Lycurgus, as well as the numerous mythic narratives in Livy and beyond that explain the origin and evolution of Roman law.[41] As Robert Cover puts it, "No set of legal institutions or prescriptions exists apart from the narratives that locate it and give it meaning. For every constitution there is an epic, for each Decalogue a scripture."[42]

As much as the legal system of a state is predicated on narratives of its foundation, it tends, in modern times at least, to emphasize its rationality and mask the poetic operations constitutive of it. In the international legal order constructed by the doctrinal discourse, poetic operations leave more visible traces. To begin with, particular legal norms often come with a narrative that explains their cause, basis, or genesis. Displaying their humanistic erudition, the founding fathers of international law such as Alberico Gentili (1552–1608) and Grotius often trace the specific doctrines they espouse back to ancient sources, including ancient poetry.[43] More important, the doctrinal discourse tends to assume the existence of an international legal order at the outset, prior to setting forth particular legal norms. For instance, Grotius's *De jure belli ac pacis* (1625) and Wolff's *Jus gentium methodo scientifica pertractatum* (1749), two of the most important works in the doctrinal discourse of international law, begin with the assumption of a *magna universitas* (a great society of states) and a *civitas maxima* (the supreme state) respectively.[44] Both are fictive entities embodying international legal order. They fit the classic definitions of legal fiction developed by medieval Commentators on the *Codex Iuris Civilis*. The great jurist and poet Cino da Pistoia (1270–1336), for instance, stated, "Ficto est in re certa contraria veritati pro vertitate assumptio."[45] Cino's definition was echoed by Baldus de Ubaldis (1327–1400): "Fiction is an assumption contrary to truth in a matter known with certainty; and it is to be noted that wherever something can be said properly to be asserted, or properly to exist, there is truth; and wherever something cannot be said properly to be asserted, or properly to exist, there is fiction."[46] As the assumption of something obviously not true (*contraria veritati*), however, fiction promotes truth (*pro veritate*), for it serves the purposes of utility (*utilitas*) and equity (*aequitas*) and corresponds to natural law—that is, the objective truth and norms prior to civil law.[47] As Andrea Alciato (1492–1550) bluntly put it, "fictio naturam imitatur," fiction imitates nature.[48] Grotius and Wolff may have conceived of natural law in different terms, but they certainly assumed *magna universitas* and *civitas maxima* to be an imperative of nature.

The fiction of international legal order in Grotius and Wolff epitomizes what the philosopher Kendall Walton calls make-believe.[49] The doctrinal discourse invites us, or at least the participants in international affairs, to play the game of make-believe, to pretend that there is a legal order in the international world. The specific norms about war, embassy, and treaty function as the props by means of which the participants go along with this game of make-believe. Grotius's *magnum opus* was dedicated to the French king Louis XIII, and the Swedish king Gustavus Adolphus was reported to carry Grotius's heavy tome on his campaigns during the Thirty Years' War.[50] The two kings were serious players of the game of make-believe devised by the doctrinal discourse of international law. It was not for nothing that Louis XIII bore the sobriquet "le juste." To play a game, however, presupposes the participants' consciousness of the difference between the game and the real world in which it takes place. It is this consciousness, suspended during the game yet nonetheless always present, that makes playing a game so much fun. To be immersed in a fictional world, to be emotionally invested in the fictional characters, presupposes the reader's secret knowledge that he sojourns only temporarily in the fictional world and that he will return sooner or later into his own world. In moving back and forth between the worlds, enacting the difference between the two worlds, the experiences of the fictional world transform into aesthetic gratification. By the same token, however seriously King Louis XIII or King Gustavus Adolphus played the game of make-believe and pretended that there was an international legal order, they were always aware of how different the world inhabited by them actually was: the chaos of the Thirty Years War, fomented at least in part by the Swedish king himself, was anything but the lawful order of a *magna universitas*. It was perhaps precisely this awareness that made the kings appreciate the doctrines of international law. But the pleasure afforded by reading Grotius amidst the carnage of the Thirty Years War was presumably an aesthetic one.

The doctrinal discourse creates a make-believe world governed by a perfect normative order, be it called *magna universitas*, *civitas maxima*, or something else. Like other fictional worlds, this world is fleshed out by narratives. As the examples of Hugo Grotius and Gottfried Wilhelm Leibniz (1646–1716) analyzed in chapter 2 indicate, there are narratives about what fictive persons act in a such world, where they originate, how they are recognized, and how they relate to each other and to things. Together these narratives legitimize the assumption of an international legal order, just as mythical narratives of foundation legitimize the legal system of a state.

Poetic Lawmaking

Pistoia's definition of legal fiction—"Ficto est in re certa contraria veritati pro vertitate assumptio"—may double as a definition of poetic fiction.[51] For Aristotle, poetic fiction—the representation of fictive persons doing fictive things—reveals more truth about the human world than history does, because it brings to light probable and necessary connections, whereas historians merely reproduce particular facts.[52] The Aristotelian notion of poetic fiction as a nonfactual but all the more profound kind of truth was emphasized in the Renaissance by Philip Sidney: "And therefore, as in History looking for truth, they go away full fraught with falsehood, so in Poesy looking but for fiction, they shall use the narration but as an imaginative ground-plot of a profitable invention."[53] In the words of the twentieth-century literary critic Frank Kermode, poetic fictions "are for finding things out."[54] Given its extraordinary capacity for promoting truth, poetic fiction is well equipped to institute a normative order for the international world.

The affinity of the poet with the legislator is a topos dating back to antiquity. Lycurgus, the lawgiver of Sparta, found inspiration in the poetry of Thales and Homer, and the Athenian lawgiver Solon was himself a noted poet.[55] In the Renaissance, theories of art invested the artist with the same kind of sovereignty as jurisprudence imputed to the princely lawgiver.[56] This line of thought culminated in the theory of poetic production in the romantic era. The Kantian aesthetic conception of the genius as "the inborn predisposition of the mind (*ingenium*) through which nature gives the rule to art" turns the genius-artist into the prototype of the lawgiver.[57] The revolutionary painter Jacques-Louis David, in his monumental *Le Serment du Jeu de Paume*, let the "jeune et divine Poésie" preside spiritually over the assembly of legislators.[58] The English poet Percy Bysshe Shelly, in the meantime, added a touch of romantic pathos to the image of the poet as legislator in his "Defence of Poetry" (1821): "Poets [. . .] are not only the authors of language and of music, of the dance and architecture and statuary and painting; they are the institutors of laws and the founders of civil society and the inventors of the arts of life [. . .]." In short, "poets are the unacknowledged legislators of the World."[59]

Especially in the international world of states, which lacks a central legislative body, the poet aspires to the role of the legislator. The poet's legislative ambition, however, cannot be to make particular international legal norms, for he neither signs treaties as a sovereign ruler does, nor clarifies customary rules and sets forth general principles as a learned jurist would do. What the poet can accomplish is rather something different from—indeed something higher than—making particular norms; it is to figure out the mechanism that organizes particular norms into a whole, to envision a possible normative order. Poetic fiction, Aristotle tells us, represents "people doing things (*prattontōn*)."[60] As such, it may deal with the handling of norms—treaties, customs, general principles, and the like—by certain agents in the international arena, who pursue certain goals by certain means in certain settings. By the art of plotting, which orders actions into temporally and causally patterned sequences, poetic fiction reveals a mechanism underlying the creation and application of norms. The seventeenth-century political romance in the manner of John Barclay's *Argenis*, for instance, typically shows how a marriage treaty comes into being—a treaty that, leavened by the magic of love, stands for the lawful concord between sovereigns in general. The genre of high tragedy in the same century, for its part, usually uncovers the causes and consequences of the violation of norms. Poetic lawmaking thus operates on the level of what Hart calls secondary rules—the rules that "specify the ways in which the primary rules may be conclusively ascertained, introduced, eliminated, varied, and the fact of their violation conclusively determined."[61] Responding to the lack of such secondary rules in the international world, poetic fiction experiments with various possibilities of ascertaining, introducing, eliminating, and modifying norms, as well as of determining the violation of norms. In so doing, it constructs various models of normative order. Poetic fiction, in the words of Jerome Bruner, "subjunctivizes" reality; that is, it constructs an alternative world in the subjunctive mode: "To be in the subjunctive mode is [. . .] to be trafficking in human possibilities rather than in settled certainties. An 'achieved' or 'uptaken' narrative speech act, then, produces a subjunctive world."[62] A model of international world order constructed by poetic fiction is subjunctive, indicating what is possible, what might be or might have been. As such, it holds up an aesthetically corrective mirror to reality, in which legal norms do not cohere into a normative order.

Poetic fiction deals with human or human-like actions taking place in time and space, whereas international world order is a normative order among states. The fictional construction of models of international order—poetic lawmaking—is predicated on politico-legal theories that establish equivalence between human agents and states. In the seventeenth century, the doctrine of royal absolutism that equates the king's person with the state provided the basis of the poetic lawmaking undertaken by political romance and tragedy. Both genres feature royal persons as protagonists. On the basis of the doctrine of royal absolutism, they can negotiate problems pertaining to the state, including the problem of normative order between states, by representing actions of royal persons. The eighteenth-century novel, on the other hand, depends on the modern natural-law theory of political authority, which postulates a homology between the state and the natural individual person, between interstate relations and interpersonal relations in the state of nature. In light of this theory developed by Hobbes and Samuel von Pufendorf (1632–94), the novel can construct models of international bonds by representing the actions and interactions of private individuals. Poetic lawmaking, then, presupposes, extends, and complements political-legal theory.

Poetic Jurisdiction

One of the most vexing problems of international law is the lack of compulsory jurisdiction. States, the subjects of international law, double as its interpreters. And for the longest time, there was hardly any other means against the breach of law than self-defense. The lack of a judicial court authorized to speak the law in the last resort is perhaps the surest sign of the deficiency of international law. The institution of the judicial court is sometimes traced to divine intervention in the mythic past, as Aeschylus wanted his fellow Athenians to believe through the tragic reenactment of the foundation of the Areopagus in the *Oresteia* trilogy. Or it results from the conscious, rational decision of a community, as was the case with the establishment of the Supreme Court of the United States.[63] With a view to ensuring peace and order in the international world of states, generations of self-appointed world improvers—from Eméric Crucé (1590–1648) to Charles-Irénée Castel de Saint-Pierre (1658–1743) and Jeremy Bentham—called for "the establishment of a common court of judicature for the decision of differences between the several nations."[64] But this was all to no avail. Prior to the twentieth century, there was nothing even remotely resembling a court in the international world. In the course of the twentieth century, international courts of justice and other dispute settlement bodies were set up. But they solve the problem only to a limited degree, as they are not compulsory. Without a court speaking the law, jurisdiction fell to poetic literature.

There is a close affinity between juridical and poetic judgment. Ancient Greeks saw many similarities between the court of law and the tragic stage, drawing an analogy between forensic persuasion and poetic mimesis, the judge and the theatrical audience.[65] Today, it is widely recognized that the court operates by means of storytelling.[66] A court poised to adjudicate a case needs first to establish the facts and then to find the appropriate norms for assessing the facts. This process shares much with the production and the reception of literary texts.

However different the court proceedings for establishing facts may be in different times and in different legal traditions, they always involve reconstructing who has done what to whom and under what circumstances. Or, in other words, they involve representing people doing things. "People doing things" is for Aristotle the object of poetic mimesis.[67] There are usually many voices in the courtroom to tell what has happened—plaintiff, defendant, prosecutor, and attorneys, as well as witnesses. The differences among these voices draw attention to a distinction that literary critics have made since the Russian Formalists: between the plot—the order and the manner in which events are presented in the narrative discourse—and the story—the order of events as they take place in the world referred to by the narrative discourse. A court hearing first gathers the plots or narrative discourses produced by the many voices in the courtroom, which reorganize the story by means of more or less sophisticated techniques of narrative presentation—manipulation of the narrative time, the artful use of perspectives, modulation of the narrative voice, and so on—all for the purpose of making certain points and having a certain effect on the judge or jury. The judge infers the story from the narratives told to him or her, reconstructing the sequence and causality of events as they might have actually taken place. Already in establishing the facts of a case, the court follows the same logic as literary communication on the basic level—communication in which the reader or audience tries to figure out the story by working through the presentation of events in the vehicle of narrative or dramatic discourse.

After the facts are established, the judge needs to find out what the law is for the case at hand, thereby making a decision. To make a ruling on the basis of available legal material—law codes, statutes, precedents, and the like—is an act of interpretation. This is especially true in hard cases where the existing rules and rulings are insufficient to settle a dispute, either because the existing rules conflict and so suggest competing answers, or because they are incomplete and offer few clues on the case at hand. Legal interpretation follows similar principles as literary interpretation. Ronald Dworkin argues, "We can usefully compare the judge deciding what the law is on some issue [. . .] with the literary critic teasing out the various dimensions of value in a complex play or poem."[68] The paramount principle of adjudication, for Dworkin, is integrity. Integrity demands that judges do their best as community officials to construct a rule that would fit best within the law as a whole and make the whole body of law coherent, and that would best defend the moral and political aspirations that the law is supposed to serve. This is a demand for articulate consistency. This is also a demand for justification, for to administer the law as a whole means also to account for the grounds and the purpose of law. In similar ways, integrity is the principle of literary interpretation as well. A literary critic should strive to construct an interpretation that makes the whole text or a whole body of texts as coherent as possible, while also accounting for the purposes of literature in doing so. Dworkin carries his analogy between law and literature even further by observing that a judge is not merely a critic but also an author, for a judge's ruling, once made, becomes part of the law that will be interpreted. He compares judges to an imaginary group of writers working on a chain novel. On the basis of their interpretations of previous chapters, the novelists form their own views about the novel in progress and develop working theories about its characters, plot, thoughts, and diction. The individual novelists, in writing their own chapters, endeavor to make the novel formally as coherent as possible so that it could be construed as the work of a single author. At the same time, each novelist seeks to make the work in progress the best novel possible in accordance with "his more substantive aesthetic judgments, about the importance or insight or realism or beauty of different ideas the novel might be taken to express."[69] Like novelists participating in the project of the chain novel, judges must think of their decisions as part of a long story that is interpreted and then continues, according to the formal criterion of fit and the substantive criterion of justification. Along a similar line of argument, Jerome Bruner points out that in appealing to precedents legal interpretation "is akin to locating a story in a literary genre, and lawyers (like literary critics) often exercise learned ingenuity in choosing their precedents."[70]

While adjudication in a court of law has a pronounced literary quality, literature may serve as an imaginary court. Friedrich Schiller (1759–1805) famously argued that "the jurisdiction of the stage begins where the domain of earthly laws reaches its limit."[71] What Schiller said about theater applies to fictional literature in general: literature assumes the function of a court when the law fails for any reason—either because the law is by its very nature powerless in certain areas of human life, or because it is deficient in certain other areas. Representing human conflicts of all kinds, literature calls upon its readers to make judgments and find solutions. The jurisdiction of literature as an imaginary court is voluntary, in contrast to the compulsory nature of adjudication in a real court. And it does not incur violence as decisions in a real court do.[72] The voluntary and purely symbolic nature of literary jurisdiction gives it many advantages. For instance, without having to worry about the drastic, indeed violent effects of its interpretive acts, literature can test out all the possibilities of interpretation and judgment. It has the capacity for transcending the generality and severity of the law and promoting equity, as defenders of poetic literature have argued since antiquity.[73] As such, literary jurisdiction can be regarded as complementary to the jurisdiction of the court. At times when the legal system is uncertain or in crisis, literary jurisdiction may play a more important role.[74] In the international world of states, which has no compulsory jurisdiction to speak of, it takes on the greatest importance, for in the absence of a real court of law, the imaginary court of literature may be the only recourse.

Indeed, beginning in the Renaissance, the contest between states became a main concern of poetic literature. Evoking the theatricality of the courtroom, the tragic stage unrolled scene after scene of agonistic struggle in the international arena, investing the audience with the role of the judge over those who consider themselves sovereigns and therefore defy jurisdiction. In the meantime, in books rivaling the weighty tomes of jurisprudence, fictional and historical narratives about the ever-turbulent international world challenged their readers to pass judgment. Throughout the centuries, ideas of the state changed. So did state practices. But conflicts between states seemed as inexorable as ever, for there was no jurisdictional authority that could resolve them and enforce a peaceful order. The absence of a court of law fomented conflicts, and conflicts generated ever more literary representations. Literary representations in turn prompted the reader to adjudicate on the conflicts. The lack of compulsory jurisdiction in the international world necessitated literary jurisdiction.

The imaginary court of literature is a protean institution, for the audience or readership of literature is constituted and reconstituted under ever-changing historical conditions. The commercial theater audience in Shakespeare's London differed from the audience recruited from the *cour* and the *ville* that assembled to watch the tragedies of Pierre Corneille and Jean Racine (1639–99).[75] The audience of German baroque tragic plays—the Gymnasium students and burghers of Silesian towns—was something else altogether. From the eighteenth century onwards, theater audiences were made up mainly of educated city dwellers. Literary readership underwent dramatic transformations as well. Seventeenth-century political romance was read by aristocrats, the eighteenth-century novel by the middle class, and nineteenth-century historiography by academics or highly educated members of the middle class (*Bildungsbürger*). While literary jurisdiction over international affairs is unlikely to lead to any definite, incontrovertible verdicts, it entails rehearsing the act of judging again and again in varying circumstances. Through the iterations of the act of judging, literary jurisdiction moves from one particular conflict to all possible conflicts in the international world, testing out all possible interpretations of its laws and thereby keeping alive an imaginative vision of international world order.

In an attempt to explicate integrity as an adjudicative principle, Dworkin invents an imaginary, indeed mythic judge, whom he calls Hercules: "Law as integrity [. . .] requires a judge to test his interpretation of any part of the great network of political structures and decisions of his community by asking whether it could form part of a coherent theory justifying the network as a whole. No actual judge could compose anything approaching a full interpretation of all of his community's law at once. That is why we are imagining a Herculean judge of superhuman talents and endless time."[76] In a certain sense, only literary readership could be this mythic Herculean judge. Unlike an actual judge who must reach a decision within a limited period of time in order to reinstate the legal order, a reader of literature does not have to decide under the pressure of time. Readers also have the luxury of being able to revise their decisions again and again. Last but not least, literary readership is immortal in the sense that literary texts, once fixated in the form of a book, can reach generations after generations of readers. As a "Herculean judge of superhuman talents and endless time," literary readership is poised

Literary Contestation of Law

Through poetic lawmaking and poetic jurisdiction, literature remedies and compensates for the insufficiencies of international law. Literature may also contest international law outright, taking on the task of developing alternative, nonlegal models of world order. It may help promote religion and morality as the normative anchor of the world. Equally important, it fashions new models of normative order that are applicable to the international world. For instance, the eighteenth-century novel creates a social world with the commercial or emotional bonds between private individuals as its warp and woof. Such a social world can be held up as a model for international order, insofar as relations between states are homologous to relations between private individuals in the state of nature according to modern natural law theory.

Perhaps the most remarkable alternative offered by poetic literature to international law is the aesthetic vision of world order. Particularly in the decades after the French Revolution, the aesthetic worldview came to the fore. Amid calls for a new mythology—for turning the world into a work of art—international law, along with the state, was sacrificed on the altar of aesthetics.[77] The idea of the "aesthetic state" (Schiller) went hand in hand with the idea of an aesthetic world of states. The aesthetic vision of world order elaborated particularly by German romanticism is not discussed in the present book, but it haunts every page of it, for the literary texts that are discussed embody it in one way or the other. Compared to law, poetic literature is removed from decisions impinging directly on someone's life—removed, that is, from the "imposition of violence on others."[78] This remove vouchsafes it, from the outset, the status of the work of art, an intrinsic aesthetic quality. The literary approach to international order ultimately implies the displacement of international law by aesthetics.

A Dual History of International Law and European Literature

In the period covered by this book, international law emerged as a law between sovereign states and formed its own jurisprudential canon. It was the classical age of international law.[79] Compared to conventional histories of international law, the following chapters are preoccupied neither with explicating doctrines nor with documenting state practice; rather, they approach international law in relation to the literary imagination. They show how the literary imagination constitutes it, responds to it, complements it, contests it. Their common thrust is to tell a story of how international law imaginatively could have been.

It should be noted that only international law in the European tradition is being considered here. Peoples in other parts of the world had their own ideas about lawful relations between political communities, and these ideas had their own chronology and followed their own logic of historical change. Recently, there have been calls for a global history of international law, a history that takes into account not only the legal tradition in Europe, but also those in other regions; not only Europe's own perspective on its encounters with other peoples, but also the perspectives of the peoples on the receiving end of colonial and imperial domination.[80]

As a history of literature, the present book shows how literary texts in major European languages from the Renaissance to the end of the eighteenth century engaged with the emerging public international law and performed the functions of poetic lawmaking, poetic jurisdiction, and poetic contestation, and how in the process a set of generic forms common to all European languages—a European literature—evolved.[81] Initially, the epic, a poetic form serving to evoke and affirm cosmic order in archaic Greece and Augustan Rome, was revived to figure a normative world order in a new reality shaped by the exploration of new territories overseas and the rise of the sovereign state on the European continent. But this ancient poetic form proved to be inadequate indeed for the task at hand. The Renaissance recreation of the epic manifested instead the need for a legal approach to the new reality, an approach that conceived of world order in terms of legal arrangement between states. Along with the emergence of public international law, two other forms of ancient Greek literature—tragedy from the classical period and romance from the time of the Roman Empire—were revived to deal with the problems raised by the legal approach to world order. The one was deployed primarily to experiment with possibilities of adjudicating conflicts in the international world that lacked a formal jurisdiction; the other primarily to experiment with possibilities of creating a lawful order between sovereigns by the magic of plotting. In so doing, they developed into major genres in seventeenth-century Europe: tragedy and political romance. Around 1700, in the wake of the separation of the private from the public—a process that can itself be traced in tragic poetry, the generic form designed to figure division—international law and poetic literature bifurcated. Literature began to occupy itself primarily with private persons. A main indicator of this development was the rise of the novel in the eighteenth century. Yet by virtue of the homology between the state and the individual person postulated by the modern natural law theory, the novel could develop fictional models of normative order for the world of states precisely by representing the lives, values, and communities of private individuals.

The epic, the tragedy, the political romance, and the novel were the principal generic forms that evolved concurrently in the main literary languages in Europe from the Renaissance to the eighteenth century. Together they formed the backbone of what can be called a European literature. European literature, if considered a unity at all, has usually been defined in terms of the classical and medieval traditions shared by different national languages, as can be seen, for instance, in Ernst Robert Curtius's *European Literature and the Latin Middle Ages*. The present book demonstrates that the formation of a European literature also owed at least some part to the politico-legal imperative for the competing states on the European continent to come to terms with one another, to institute a normative order between one another.

Literary genres themselves, of course, have a normative character insofar as they bundle together a set of formal standards and principles by which to guide, even to regulate, literary production and reception.[82] In this sense, the generic forms examined in this book constituted a system of poetic and aesthetic norms—that is, a normative order of literature. By engaging with international law and imagining a normative order for the international world, literature developed its own normative order. This is the story I tell over the next six chapters.

The first chapter investigates the fundamental reorientation in the conceptions of the normative order between political communities in the sixteenth century, which eventually led to the rise of public international law. Against the backdrop of the cataclysmic transformations of the political world in the wake of the discovery of the New World, the Reformation, and the rise of the sovereign state, jurists and poets turned to the traditional models of world order, particularly the ancient natural law and the classical epic. Yet the attempts to revive the traditional models of world order just served to prove their obsolescence. In explicating the universal laws of nature, the Neoscholastic jurist Francisco de Vitoria (1483–1546) elaborated the concepts of subjective right and voluntary consent. In emulating the epic figuration of cosmic order by Homer and Virgil, Luís Vaz de Camões's epic *Os Lusíadas*, the first Renaissance epic, brought the political doctrine of reason of state to the center of attention. Subjective right, voluntary consent, and reason of state—all of these notions undermined the universal laws of nature as well as the cosmic order envisioned by the classical epic. At the same time, they also lay the conceptual groundwork for conceiving of world order in a new way, namely in terms of public international law.

With the emergence of public international law in the decades around 1600, world order became a matter of international legal order. The second chapter investigates the poetic operations constitutive of international legal order in a variety of media—pictorial allegory, narration, and performance. Even during the century preceding the emergence of public international law, princes big and small, laying claim to sovereignty, tried increasingly to regulate their relations by means of legal instruments. Yet because they were less and less willing to acknowledge any superior authority—that was precisely what the claim to sovereignty was about—legal instruments had little, if any, force. For this reason, legal instruments were often coupled with ingenious allegories that served to anchor them to some fictive supernatural agent. In the meantime, elaborate ceremonial rituals and sumptuous spectacles were invented to accompany interactions between sovereigns, referring their legal arrangements to a mythic ground. The doctrinal discourse of public international law, which gained traction in the course of the seventeenth century, operated with narratives. Most notable were the narratives of the origin and the status of international legal persons, as well as the narrative construction of an international legal community. Despite their obvious difference, the poetic operations analyzed in this chapter all served to assure the emerging international society of its integrity, origin, and purpose. As such, they contained the germ of the various arts and poetic literature that negotiated the problems besetting international society. In the seventeenth century, the principal forms of poetic literature concerned with international society were tragedy and political romance. Given the royal absolutist identification of the king's person with the state, these two generic forms could tackle international affairs by representing the actions of royal characters.

The third and fourth chapters uncover the intrinsic connections between the forms of tragedy as well as romance and international order. Based on detailed readings of exemplary tragic dramas from the English Renaissance to the German Baroque and French Classicism, chapter 3 demonstrates how tragedy represents the fragility and inevitable failure of international law and thereby conjures up, through tragic experience, a normative world order as something that is persistently unavailable. Chapter 4 is concerned with the connections between the romance form and international order. Drawing on the plot pattern of the Greek romance, political romance represents sovereign persons moving towards concord in spite of mishaps and adversities, indeed in spite of themselves. By examining John Barclay's *Argenis*, the prototype of political romance, and by reconstructing the rise and fall of the genre over the course of the seventeenth century, chapter 4 demonstrates how the romance form epitomizes the power and ultimately also the limitations of the literary imagination in figuring international world order.

Chapter 5 argues that international law and literature diverged from one another in the decades around 1700. In the wake of the English Revolution and at the height of royal absolutism in the age of Louis XIV, both political thought and poetic literature testified to the separation of two spheres in the international world: the sphere of the depersonalized state to be managed by means of governmental knowledge, and the sphere of private individuals with their desires, conscience, and domestic life. Nowhere can this process be more clearly seen than in the great tragedies of the time—Andreas Gryphius's *Carolus Stuardus* (1657), John Milton's *Samson Agonistes* (1671), and Jean Racine's plays. The separation of these two spheres—whether or not one calls it the separation between the public and the private—led to the divergence between international law and poetic literature. In the early decades of the eighteenth century, international law established itself as one of the increasingly specialized fields of knowledge concerned with affairs of the state, while poetic literature turned to affairs of private persons.

The development described in the fifth chapter, however, does not mean that literature ceased to concern itself with the problem of international order. It means rather that the relationship between international law and literature was reconfigured. In particular, precisely by representing the affairs of private individuals, the novel—a new kind of prose fiction emerging in the eighteenth century—became a key player in the literary figuration of international order. The final chapter of the book is concerned with the eighteenth-century novel. The poetics of the novel corresponded closely to Samuel Pufendorf's natural jurisprudence, which provided the dominant theoretical paradigm for international law from the late seventeenth to the late eighteenth century. Informed by this correspondence, the novel form developed three distinctive models of international order: transnational commercial world order in Daniel Defoe's novels early in the century, sentimental world order in the novels of the mid-century, and cosmopolitan world order in the German *Bildungsroman* later in the century.

Chapter 1

The Old World Order Dissolving

At the time around 1500, a new world—in multiple senses—opened up for Europeans. There was, of course, the discovery of a new continent on the other side of the Atlantic as well as the exploration of the African coasts and the East Indies. There was also the Protestant Reformation, which would in due time divide, convulse, and transform Christian Europe. Last but not least, the rise of principalities on the Italian peninsula, the concomitant power struggle, and the intervention of the big powers France and Spain in Italian politics created a political space populated with self-interested, power-seeking rulers who would soon insist on nothing less than their sovereignty. Under the pressure of these cataclysmic events, traditional models of normative order, particularly those concerning the relations between political communities, crumbled. The time around 1500 has often been considered to be the great divide between an old, medieval world order and a new, modern world order. In his *Nomos der Erde* (1950), the twentieth-century German legal thinker Carl Schmitt sees the 1494 Treaty of Tordesillas (the treaty by which Spain and Portugal, under the auspices of the Pope, divided up the recently discovered lands in the New World, as well as those yet to be discovered) as the beginning of a "global linear thinking" (*globales Liniendenken*) that underpinned a modern world order called *jus publicum europaeum*. This world order, according to his grand narrative, lasted until the First World War.[1] Drawing on the work of generations of historians, the legal historian Wilhelm Grewe also dates the beginning of the modern world order to 1494, although he emphasizes another event taking place in that year, namely the invasion of Italy by Charles VIII of France. That event, he maintains, inaugurated a European state system on which modern international law depends.[2] Some other scholars, leery of the neat division of European history into medieval and modern eras, consider the time around 1500 to be not a rupture but a phase in the long-term transformation of "the canonistic-papal conception of world order" into "a secularized world order" as articulated by Grotius's system of international law. This transformation was not marked by "a clear, bright line," but stretched over "a zone several centuries in length."[3]

Instead of interpreting the cataclysmic events around 1500, this chapter tracks the general disorientation and reorientation that they triggered during the following century. The conceptual reformulation of natural law theory and the renaissance of epic poetry serve as good examples in this regard. The ancient tradition of natural law postulated a universal, immutable, and objective order of the world in the form of a set of commands and prohibitions supposed to be immediately valid in all human societies, within a particular political community as well as between political communities. The tradition culminated in Thomas Aquinas (1225–74). In the sixteenth century, a new wave of Thomism known as Spanish Neoscholasticism recalibrated its conceptual makeup. The first important representative of Spanish Neoscholasticism, Francisco de Vitoria (1483–1546), raised a new question about natural law in response to the legal challenges posed by the Spanish conquest of the Americas: who can be considered the subject of natural law? Such a question led to the idea of subjective natural right. Accordingly, the normative order of the world seemed not so much to be objectively given once and for all as to be a provisional result of the negotiations between the subjects of natural law in pursuing their respective rights. Vitoria used the term *ius gentium*, known from Roman law, to designate the law that does justice to subjective rights. Understood in this sense, *ius gentium*, or the law of nations, may or may not have a universal scope as the traditional natural law does. It certainly does not remain the same all the time, for it depends on the voluntary consent of the subjects of natural law, which in turn depends on the vagaries of circumstances. The universal laws of nature fell into a state of flux.

While the ancient natural law theory was debated and reformulated, the epic poetry of classical antiquity was revived. The classical epic portrays a cosmic order in action, setting forth, in particular, a lawful order between political communities under the auspices of the divine. The first serious attempt to emulate the classical epic in the Renaissance was the Portuguese poet Luís Vaz de Camões's *Os Lusíadas* (1572), a poem about Vasco da Gama's first voyage to India from 1497 to 1499. In spite of all the formal trappings of the epic—narrative *in media res*, divine council, and the like—the cosmic order breaks down. No longer are strangers and natives governed by the law of Zeus/Jupiter in their encounter, as can be seen in the Homeric or Virgilian rituals of hospitality and descriptions of just war. Instead, the natives try desperately to fend off the threat of strangers, while the Portuguese try to aggrandize their country and their ruler. Even the poet's repeatedly proclaimed ambition to surpass Homer and Virgil turns out to be part of the endeavor to redound upon the greatness of Portugal. Showing self-interest, self-preservation and self-aggrandizement to be the motive forces of action, Camões's epic poem proves to be a purveyor of the political doctrines of reason of state. Formally, it bears the traits of advice book for princes as well as those of annals—two main genres in the literature of reason of state. The discourse of reason of state, inaugurated by Niccolò Machiavelli (1469–1527) and Francesco Guicciardini (1483–1540) and culminating in the works of Giovanni Botero (1544–1617) and Justus Lipsius (1547–1606), is concerned with the efficiency and technical rationality of statecraft rather than with the normative foundation and purpose of the state. As regards the relations between states, it is concerned with the techniques of diplomacy and warfare rather than with a normative order. With a plot illustrating the maxims of reason of state, *Os Lusíadas* describes diplomatic intrigues and bellicose skirmishes between strangers and natives, displaying the absence of any higher law capable of bridging their differences. If the classical epic exhibits a lawful order of the human world under divine auspices, *Os Lusíadas* demonstrates its impossibility in an age under the sway of reason of state.

Precisely by trying to reinvigorate the ancient theory of natural law and the classical epic, Neoscholastic jurisprudence and the Renaissance epic testified to their obsolescence. In Vitoria's legal thought and Camões's epic poem, the universal, immutable world order disintegrated, falling victim to the legal concepts of subjective natural right and voluntary consent, as well as to the political doctrines of reason of state. These concepts and doctrines, for their part, prompted a new way of conceiving of world order—public international law. Francisco Suárez (1548–1617), the last significant representative of Spanish Neoscholasticism, radicalized the concepts of subjective natural right and voluntary consent. A member of the Society of Jesus founded in 1534 as part of the Catholic effort to counter the Protestant Reformation, Suárez set much store by the free will. The overarching voluntarist approach enabled him first to develop a theory of the state as a *corpus mysticum* brought into being by the consent of individual persons. Ascribing a free will to the state, he then argued that the free consent of states gave rise to a law regulating their relations to each other—international law. In the meantime, Alberico Gentili (1552–1608), a jurist in the tradition of *mos italicus*, realized the necessity of legalizing reason of state. If reason of state is amenable to any law, it can only be one that facilitates the pursuit of interest, for example the law of embassy that helps channel the communication between states, or the law of war that helps states settle their conflicts in an orderly fashion. Finally, Hugo Grotius (1583–1645) synthesized the concept of subjective natural right and the concept of interest, turning them into the principle of the natural right to life and property. Deducing the laws of nature from this principle, he inaugurated modern natural jurisprudence. Applied to states, the laws of nature become international law. According to Grotius, the voluntary agreements between states—treaties and customs— also belong to international law, and they depend, to an even higher degree, on the subjective rights and interests of the parties involved. With Suárez, Gentili, and Grotius, world order became a matter of legal order between states.

Universal Laws in Flux (Neoscholastic Jurisprudence)

The Birth of the Subject of Natural Law in the New World

Beset by political turmoil at home, unceasing wars across Europe, and brutal conquests overseas, jurists in the sixteenth century turned to the ancient tradition of natural law to affirm a normative order for a time out of joint. Their arguments, however, bore testimony to the inadequacy of the ancient tradition. World order ceased to be guaranteed by the universal, immutable laws of nature.

Inspired by Stoic ideas, Cicero (106–43 BCE) conceived of the world as a "civitas communis deorum atque hominum," a well-ordered community abiding by an unchanging law—a law that issues from the divine, yet is recognized by the human, because the human is endowed with the divine faculty of reason.[4] This law animating the world as a whole is the law of nature: "Law in the proper sense is right reason in harmony with nature. It is spread through the whole human community, unchanging and eternal, calling people to their duty by its commands and deterring them from wrong-doing by its prohibitions."[5] Because the only true law is the law of nature established by right reason, laws enacted by a particular polity, as well as laws obtaining among polities, must be consistent with it: "We cannot be exempted from this law by any decree of the Senate or the people; nor do we need anyone else to expound or explain it. There will not be one such law in Rome and another in Athens, one now and another in the future, but all peoples at all times will be embraced by a single and eternal and unchangeable law."[6] In the Christian era, church fathers found the Stoic idea of natural law so amenable to Christian dogmas that they integrated it into their theological considerations without much difficulty. For St. Augustine (354–430 CE), when man grows and approaches the years of reason, "he knows the natural law which all have fixed in their hearts: what you do not wish to be done to you, do not do to another. Is this learned from the pages of [books] and is not read, in a way, in nature itself?"[7] Meanwhile, natural law was not only a philosophical and theological theorem, but also an integral part of jurisprudence. The Roman jurist Ulpian spoke of *ius naturale* as "that which nature has taught to all animals; [. . .] Out of this comes the union of man and woman which we call marriage, and the procreation of children, and their rearing."[8]

Thomas Aquinas consummated the ancient tradition of natural law, not only by weaving together the various strands of this tradition—pagan and Christian, philosophical, theological, and juristic—into a whole, but also by setting off, in his true Scholastic manner, natural law against other kinds of law. Law, according to his *Summa Theologica*, is "a kind of rule and measure of acts, by which someone is induced to act or restrained from acting."[9] Its purpose is to order things in such a way as to secure the common good. Insofar as ruling and measuring is proper to reason, law can be best defined as the rational ordering of things. By means of law (*lex*), a rational order—an objective relationship of equality or reciprocity—is instituted, called right (*ius*) or "the just thing itself" (IIaIIae, q. 57, a. 1). The rational pattern of all things in the universe, laid down by God as the omnipresent ruler, is the eternal law. The participation of the rational creature in the eternal law is called the natural law. It comes in a variety of commands and prohibitions, which are supposed to be in force in all human societies regardless of faith (because it is not the divine law) and local particularities (because it is not human laws), which cannot be changed (IaIIae, q. 94, a. 5), and which are ingrained in the hearts of men (IaIIae, q. 94, a. 6). This conception of natural law epitomizes the idea of *ordo* at the heart of medieval thought.[10] Aquinas spoke of a twofold order: "The one, whereby a created thing is directed to another, as the parts to the whole, accident to substance, and all things whatsoever to their end; the other, whereby all created things are ordered to God" (Ia, q. 21, a. 1). As well as designating the ordered relation of creatures with one another, the natural law instantiates the ordered relation to God, for it is grounded in the eternal law. The order of the human world is predicated upon divine order.

As Giorgio Agamben points out with regard to Aquinas, "Things are ordered insofar as they have a specific relation among themselves, but this relation is nothing other than the expression of their relation to the divine end. And, vice versa, things are ordered insofar as they have a certain relation to God, but this relation expresses itself only by means of the reciprocal relation of things. The only content of the transcendent order is the immanent order, but the meaning of the immanent order is nothing other than the relation to the transcendent end."[11] This point is worth keeping in mind, because world order in modern times—the subject matter of this book—becomes increasingly problematic as the transcendent end loses self-evidence and certainty.

The Scholastic conception of the rational, natural order of the human world was put to the test in the Age of Discovery. In the face of the events across the Atlantic, the Spanish theologians and jurists trained in the Thomist tradition were initially at quite a loss. In a lecture held in 1535, Domingo de Soto (1494–1560) addressed the question of the legal title of the Spaniards to the newly discovered overseas territories, but had to admit that he had no answer: "Re vera ego nescio." Unable to reach a judgment on so perplexing a matter, he referred, with patent resignation, to the inscrutability of God's plan: "nam iudicia Dei abyssus multa."[12] Since the law of nature is evident to reason, there should actually be no serious difficulty in assessing the lawfulness of particular actions. There was, however, no consensus about the applicability of the natural law to Amerindians. To be sure, the law of nature is a rational pattern universal in scope and application, but are the people discovered on the new continent human beings? Indeed, what is a human being from the perspective of natural law? Confronted with such questions, Neoscholastic jurists, especially Francisco de Vitoria, worked out an elaborate definition of human agency by which to evaluate the qualification of the natives of the New World for natural law. In so doing, he constructed the subject of natural law to complement the Thomist conception of natural law as an objective rational order.

The definition of human agency developed by Vitoria takes the form of a series of distinctions. The most basic distinction is between the human and all other beings, especially the animal. According to Aquinas, man is master of his own actions, whereas the animal is not (IaIIae, q. 1, a. 1). This Thomist distinction was elaborated and modified in significant ways by sixteenth-century natural law theorists, becoming the basis of a general theory of ownership.[13] Man owns his actions because he cognizes and wills an end, for the sake of which he acts. Acting towards an end involves using other things and persons. By contrast, driven by natural instincts rather than actively pursuing a rationally and freely chosen end, the animal is incapable of using one thing for the sake of another. Vitoria concluded, "Wild animals have no rights over their own bodies (*dominium sui*); still less then can they have rights over other things."[14] The distinction between the human and the animal also leads to a theory of the origin of the commonwealth. For Vitoria, "In order to ensure the safety and defence of animals, Mother Nature endowed them all from the very beginning with coats to fend off the frost and the weather." By contrast, "to mankind Nature gave only reason and virtue, leaving him otherwise frail, weak, helpless, and vulnerable, destitute of all defence and lacking in all things, and brought him forth naked and unarmed like a castaway from a shipwreck into the midst of the miseries of this life."[15] Because of his natural deficiency, man has no other choice than to join hands with other men to form a political community that affords him security and protection. Consequently, the commonwealth is not a human invention, but a kind of armature provided by nature: "Public power is founded upon natural law."[16] In sum, in contrast to the animal, the human being is the master of his actions, owns property, and lives in a political community.

Another distinction drawn by Vitoria to define the human is between normal and abnormal human beings. Dominion over one's own actions or free judgment requires both reason and will. Although these faculties are the same in all human beings, they are not always used in the same way. First, "the defect and imperfection of the sensory-cognitive part" may lead to "the defect, imperfection or absence of the use of reason."[17] Second, "sensual appetite (*appetitus sensitivus*) could be a cause of the lack of the use of reason."[18] Third, the use of reason might be damaged by certain modifications of the will—for instance, hatred or love, as well as certain habits impressed on the will; finally, education and instruction contribute significantly to the use of reason. For instance, well-educated, civilized men are more capable of using reason than peasants. Consequently, it is necessary to distinguish the normal human being capable of the use of reason or free judgment from the abnormal human being deprived, wholly or partly, of this capability—for instance, children, madmen, dreamers, and the like.

Vitoria distinguishes further between the human and the believer. Aquinas defines the natural law as the participation of rational creatures in the eternal law. In Europe, rational creatures turned out to be identical with believers in Christ. But the use of reason, according Vitoria, has no necessary relation to faith. On the one hand, "every man can act morally, as soon as he has reached the use of reason, even if he does not know or is not able to know God."[19] On the other hand, "not everyone who has reached the use of reason is obliged to turn to God explicitly, distinctly, and formally."[20] If someone recognizes that he has to live in accordance with right reason, he qualifies himself as a rational being capable of carrying out the natural law regardless of faith.

Vitoria's construction of the subject of natural law was inextricably intertwined with the vexing legal situation created by the discovery and conquest of the New World. The definition of the human in contrast to the animal, revolving around the concept of dominion as it did, was bound up with the question about the property rights and political self-rule of the Amerindians and, consequently, with the question about the legitimacy of the Spanish conquest. The distinction between the normal human being and children, madmen, dreamers, and the like addressed the doubts about the presence and sufficiency of the natives' rational faculty. Finally, the distinction between the human and the believer engaged with the prevalent attempts at the time to justify the conquest on the ground of the barbarians' lack of Christian faith. Thus we can speak of the birth of the subject of natural law in the New World. It needs to be noted, however, that along with the conquest of the New World, there was another impetus for the subjective turn of natural law: the Protestant Reformation. The Lutheran insistence on the fallen and sinful nature of man and the primacy of grace moved the question of human agency into the center of theological and, in the same breath, juristic debates. Juristic reasoning in the service of the Counter-Reformation converged with that in the context of Spanish overseas expansion.[21] In any case, these distinctions combine to make up a set of criteria by which to assess the human quality, hence the qualification for natural law, of a living being. They construct a rational, normal, secular human being as the subject of natural law. Without jettisoning the Thomist notion of the objective order of nature, Vitoria made it possible to conceive of normative order in terms of voluntary agreements reached by rational subjects.

The import of the subjective approach to natural law came to the fore at the conference convened by Charles V in Valladolid in 1550 to assess the justice of Spanish conquests. The two main opponents at the conference, Juan Ginés de Sepúlveda (1490–1573) and Bartolomé de las Casas (1474–1566), both invoked natural law, the former to defend the Spanish conquest, the latter to condemn it. A humanist, Sepúlveda adhered to the ancient tradition of natural law that posited an objective order of nature. By contrast, Las Casas, a Dominican as Vitoria was, adopted the Neoscholastic subjective approach.[22] Since the Amerindians are "barbaric, uninstructed in letters and the art of government, and completely ignorant, unreasoning, and totally incapable of learning anything," Sepúlveda argued, "for their own welfare, people of this kind are held by natural law to submit to the control of those who are wiser and superior in virtue and learning, as are the Spaniards (especially the nobility), the learned, the clergy, the religious, and, finally, all those who have been properly educated and trained."[23] Underlying this argument is the notion of an objective order of nature, in which the inferior is subordinate to the superior, the less perfect to the more perfect. Las Casas, by contrast, argued from the standpoint of the subject of natural law. In one of his theoretically most lucid moments, he pointed out, "The less perfect yield naturally to the more perfect as matter does to form, body to soul, sense to reason. I do not deny this at all. Nevertheless, this is true only when two elements are joined by nature in first act, as when matter and the form that gives being to the thing unite in one composite, [for example] when body and soul are joined to each other and make an animal, and when the senses and reason exist in the same subject. But if the perfect and the imperfect are separated and inherent in different subjects, then imperfect things do not yield to the more perfect, but they are not yet joined in first act."[24] Here the objective and the subjective approaches to natural law clashed with each other head-on. Whereas from the objective standpoint human beings are unequal insofar as they occupy different positions and exhibit different qualities in a preexisting normative order, from the subjective standpoint they are equal insofar as they are all subjects of natural law. Whereas from the objective standpoint there is and has always been one overarching order, from the subjective standpoint order is created through the joining together of the multitude of subjects.

The Rise in Prominence of *Ius gentium*

The claims of the subject of natural law are natural rights. The Neoscholastic reconceptualization of natural law in terms of its subject went hand in hand with the elaboration of late medieval conceptions of subjective right—that is, conceptions of *ius* in terms of faculty (*facultas*), power (*potestas*), and *dominium*.[25] The leading question of Vitoria's *De Indis*—"whether these barbarians, before the arrival of the Spaniards, had true dominion"—is, in fact, a question about the subjective rights of the Amerindians, for "dominion is a legal right (*dominium est ius*)," and legal right has something to do with the power of the subject: "We do not speak of anyone being 'the owner' of a thing (*dominium esse*) unless that thing lies within his control."[26] Consequently, legal norms are now supposed to do justice to, and to mediate between, the natural rights of different subjects. As such, they cease to be the laws of nature immediately evident to reason, but have to be established by legal reasoning. Vitoria's determination of "the just title" of the Spanish rule over the Amerindians perfectly illustrates this point.[27]

Vitoria establishes first the right of the Spaniards to travel (*ius peregrinandi*), and then pleads the Spaniards' right to preach the gospel (*ius praedicandi*). Should the Amerindians resist or even violently oppose the Spaniards' traveling and preaching activities, they are actually violating their rights granted by nature, so that Spaniards are allowed, indeed obliged to fight against them. In such a just war, Vitoria argues in *De jure belli* (1539), it is lawful to kill innocent people if necessary, just as it is lawful to plunder, to enslave, and to keep the booty.[28] If the Amerindians lose the just war waged by the Spaniards, they must pay reparation—for instance by offering their lands. These norms ascertained by Vitoria, along with a number of others such as the right to free the innocent Amerindians from their tyrannical masters—humanitarian intervention *avant la lettre*—and the right to build alliances with some Amerindians in their internecine wars, can be read as a retroactive legal justification of the Spanish imperial expansion.[29] Whatever their merits, they are obviously not universally recognized precepts of natural law, but the product of a juristic reasoning aimed at mediating between the subjective rights of two opposing parties. Vitoria refers to them as belonging to *ius gentium* or the law of nations.

In Roman law, *ius gentium* belongs to private law.[30] According to Ulpian, "*Jus gentium*, the law of nations, is that which all human peoples observe. That it is not co-extensive with natural law can be grasped easily, since this latter is common to all animals whereas *jus gentium* is common only to human beings among themselves."[31] In terms of content, Hermogenian said, "As a consequence of this *ius gentium*, wars were introduced, nations differentiated, kingdoms founded, properties individuated, estate boundaries settled, buildings put up, and commerce established, including contracts of buying and selling and letting and hiring."[32] Produced by Rome's military and commercial contacts with other peoples, and considered a law common to all *gentes*, *ius gentium* stood Vitoria in good stead in his grappling with the new legal situation created by the Spanish overseas expansion. He adhered to the Roman typology of laws, discussing *ius gentium* as part of private law. In his handling, *ius gentium* connotes the legal order of the whole world:

> The law of nations (*ius gentium*) does not have the force merely of pacts or agreements between men, but has the validity of a positive enactment (*lex*). The whole world, which is in a certain sense a commonwealth, has the power to enact laws which are just and convenient to all men; and these make up the law of nations. From this it follows that those who break the law of nations, whether in peace or in war, are

committing mortal crimes, at any rate in the case of the graver transgressions such as violating the immunity of ambassadors. No kingdom may choose to ignore this law of nations, because it has the sanction of the whole world.[33]

The law of nations, then, is the law made by the whole world for the whole world, superseding the time-honored notion of the immutable lawful order of nature.

But how could the whole world make and enact laws, since it does not have a government to do so? There are two possible answers to this question: laws making up *ius gentium* are either instituted a priori by reason and therefore apply to the world of rational beings in general, or they are instituted by certain people as provisions for particular human affairs but then adopted by mankind in its entirety. In the former case, *ius gentium* would be tantamount to, or at least derivable from, natural law. In the latter case, it would be a function of positive legislation accepted worldwide by consent. Vitoria seems to embrace both possibilities. In connection with the putative right of Spaniards to travel to and dwell among the Amerindians, he sought to ground the law of nations in natural law, citing Gaius's definition in *Institutiones*: "[*ius gentium*] is or derives from natural law, as defined by the jurist: 'what natural reason has established among all nations is called the law of nations.'"[34] But in his commentary on Aquinas's conception of the law of nations as derivable from the natural law, Vitoria dissented from the master, arguing that it could not reside in nature itself, but must have issued from human consent. Accordingly, *ius gentium* must be classified as positive law rather than natural law: "Quod jus gentium potius debet responi sub jure positivo quam sub jure naturali."[35] Vitoria vacillated between two options, sometimes stressing the one, sometimes the other.[36] At still other times, he suggested that certain portions of *ius gentium* were derived from natural law while other portions were instituted by humans in particular circumstances: "And there are certainly many things which are clearly to be settled on the basis of the law of nations (*ius gentium*), whose derivation from natural law is manifestly sufficient to enable it to enforce binding rights. But even on the occasions when it is not derived from natural law, the consent of the greater part of the world is enough to make it binding, especially when it is for the common good of all men."[37]

With regard to Gaius's definition and Hermogenian's list in *Digesta*, the great Commentator Bartolus (1314–57) distinguished between *ius gentium primaevum* and *ius gentium secundarium*, with the former proceeding from natural reason and the latter from the "usage of peoples (*vsu gentium*)."[38]

The Bartolist distinction was elaborated in the sixteenth century. For instance, in his *Controversiarum illustrium* (1564), Fernando Vázquez de Menchaca (1512–69) offers the following scheme of classification: natural law consists of norms applicable to animals and humans alike; *ius gentium primaevum* or the "natural law of nations" consists of norms applicable to humans but not to animals, and *ius gentium secundarium* consists of norms that originated with certain peoples at a certain time and in a certain place, but gradually spread around the world in the course of time.[39] Vitoria may or may not have known the Bartolist distinction, but the mere admission that it contains elements extraneous to natural law implies that the normative order of the world is no longer assured once and for all by natural reason, but is subjected to the consent of men. Consent depends on the vagaries of circumstances. A norm may command the consent of some but not all subjects. A consent given may also be revoked. The normative order instituted through consent, then, is necessarily limited in scope and subject to renegotiation and alteration.

Vitoria's handling of *ius gentium* empowers juristic reasoning. If this law consists partly of general norms extrapolated from natural reason and partly of particular norms reached through voluntary consent, it depends on juristic reasoning for its unity. It is up to the jurist to ascertain whether human laws originating in certain circumstances have won the consent of the whole world, or at least "the consent of the greater part of the world," or perhaps have won no consent at all. And it is up to the jurist to adjudicate whether they actually serve "the common good of all men." It is also up to the jurist to establish whether these human laws are consistent with the norms putatively established by natural reason. If the whole world is "in a certain sense a commonwealth," then its legislator and judge seem to be neither God nor natural reason, but the jurist. To claim that certain human laws command the consent of the world requires evidence, to judge whether laws instituted by one or a few polities serve "the common good of all men" requires interpretation, and to reconcile particular human laws with general norms of natural reason requires dialectical argumentation. Involving empirical evidence, interpretation and argumentation, *ius gentium* is likely to be variable and open to contestation.

In sum, as little as Vitoria seemed willing to leave behind the comforting natural-law conception of a universal, objective order of the world, he inaugurated, by way of an at times equivocal discussion of *ius gentium*, a conception of world order as fundamentally open to change. After Vitoria, discussions about the status of *ius gentium* intensified and became more systematic in the second half of the sixteenth century.⁴⁰ But they hardly moved beyond the parameters he had set. A statement by Soto, Vitoria's disciple and colleague in Salamanca, was typical: "Natural law is inscribed in our mind without argumentation. *Ius gentium* is deduced from natural law by argumentation and hence long deliberation without, however, requiring the assembly of all humans. Municipal law (*ius civile*) is constituted by the will of some men assembled in a council."⁴¹

Cosmic Order Disturbed (Camões's *Os Lusíadas*, Reason of State)

Along with the ancient natural law theory, the classical epic presented the sixteenth century with another traditional model of world order. Recounting events in a bygone age closed unto itself, an age in which the divine intervenes directly in human affairs, the classical epic depicts a cosmic order at work. This cosmic order has a politico-legal dimension, as the elaborate rituals of hospitality in the *Odyssey* as well as the conduct of war in the *Aeneid* make manifest. As the first large-scale attempt to revive the classical epic in the Renaissance, Luiz Vaz de Camões's *Os Lusíadas* seeks to represent the Portuguese expansion in the East as part of the cosmic economy. Yet instead of the Homeric rituals of hospitality and the Virgilian code of war, *Os Lusíadas* is full of disorderly scenes of encounter, scenes that display the absence, indeed the impossibility, of a lawful order. Camões's poem is too concerned with the interest and the greatness of the Portuguese to bother with higher normative principles that would connect all the peoples of the world. It proffers narratives that illustrate the valor and prudence of the Portuguese as well as other qualities purportedly enabling them to maximize their interests and achieve greatness, while buttressing these narratives with specific advice on the techniques of government. In so doing, *Os Lusíadas* participated in the production of practical knowledge about government, which involved genres ranging from advice books for princes around 1500 to the flourishing literature on reason of state around 1600. The purpose of practical knowledge about government was to preserve and expand the power of a state in its competition with other states, thus militating against ethical, juridical, or any other norms transcending the interests of particular states. However emphatically Camões's poem tries to assume the formal trappings of the classical epic, it nonetheless dismantles the epic vision of cosmic order. When it finally conjures up such a vision in the end, it also hastens to debunk it as a figment of fantasy.

The Epic Form and World Order

The classical epic is a poetic form designed to figure cosmic order. According to the famous definition by Goethe and Schiller, the epic poet presents events as completely past.[42] Mikhail Bakhtin rephrased this definition in terms of the "absolute conclusiveness and closedness" of the epic world or cosmos.[43] The Homeric and Virgilian cosmos consists of the divine and the human, the living and the dead, the perfect and the monstrous, as well as their mixtures in varying measure. Crucial to epic representation is the ordering of all these beings, among themselves and in relation to one another. In particular, the epic is concerned with the bond between strangers, as well as that between political communities.

The prototype of the narrative of voyage, *The Odyssey* is structured around a complex web of intertwined scenes of encounter in foreign lands. These scenes encapsulate the Homeric vision of human relations outside of a local political community. Consider the first of such scenes, in which Telemachus and his companion Athena in the guise of Mentor land on Pylos (book 3). It is remarkable, first of all, that neither the foreign traveler nor the natives of Pylos expresses any surprise at their chance encounter. Before they even ask for the stranger's name, the Pylians invite him and his companion to join them right away in their feast. Communication at the moment of encounter depends not on the identities of the parties involved, but on their immediately recognizable humanity. In the Homeric epic, this initial act of communication has a ritual character. The welcome ritual usually takes the form of bathing the guest, dressing him in fresh clothes, and putting on lavish feasts in his honor. Here in Pylos the religious ritual that is taking place at the time of Telemachus's arrival doubles as a welcome ritual. In fact, the ritual of hospitality always has a religious dimension. Under the gaze of the divine, the host and the guest recognize each other's humanity. This mutual recognition finds expression in the constantly repeated reminder that the stranger is protected by Zeus. The welcome ritual thus enacts the bonding of humans in general, staging a community of humanity as a whole, which transcends the borders and differences of local communities. Rituals are communal. In the welcome ritual and, by the same token, also in the farewell ritual that usually culminates in exchange of gifts, the local community that constitutes itself through the performance of rituals merges into the greater community of humankind.

As an expression of the mutual recognition of the shared humanity of the host and the guest, the ritual of hospitality in the Homeric epic implies a specific norm of encountering and relating to the other. Any deviation from this norm on the part of the host necessarily compromises his humanity. In stories of his voyages, Odysseus tells the Phaeacian king that whenever he lands on a foreign shore, the first thing he does is to ascertain whether the inhabitants of this place are human or not. The main criterion that he uses is the mode of welcome proffered by them. Either they greet the stranger with the proper welcome ritual, thus proving to be human and ceasing to be the other; or they fail to greet the stranger with the proper welcome ritual, thus proving to subhuman beasts (such as the Cyclops) or superhuman immortals (like Circe). Homer makes a point of noting the dangerously close relationship between the hospitable Phaeacians and the beastly Cyclops, who were once neighbors and both related to Poseidon. It was a mythic king who led the Phaeacians off in a vast migration and civilized them, leaving behind the Cyclops in their brute savagery.[44] For legal thinkers like Grotius and Rousseau, the Cyclops stand as figures of lawlessness, while in literary works they become a prototype of poetic characters—such as Marlowe's Tamburlaine and Shakespeare's Caliban—who precisely through their savagery reveal the nature of the law.[45] Of course, in the human world hospitality is every so often violated. The reckless behavior of the suitors during Odysseus's absence is exactly the opposite of hospitality. The narrative of the *Odyssey* as a whole is designed to contain and rectify this egregious violation of the normative order of the human world.

Hospitality was not a poetic invention of Homer, but a legal institution in antiquity meant to regulate human intercourse outside of a polity. As a historian of international law puts it, "The process of making foreign friends in antiquity was largely one of legal process. The highly refined forms of friendship statuses observed within Greek city-states, and the elaborately articulated vassalage relationships practiced by the cultures of the ancient Near East and by the Romans, were all conceived as *legal* relationships, governed by pre-conceived notions of rights and responsibilities. The actors, whether they were the alien resident in a foreign city or a polity in political association with another, were controlled by the rule of law."[46] Rudolf von Jhering (1818–92) also pointed out, "The understanding of law determines the knowledge of hospitality, and the understanding of the latter determines the knowledge of the former." As a practice that ensures the rule of law also outside of the *polis*, "the exercise of hospitality figures as a mark of civilization, whereas the lack thereof figures as a mark of the barbarity of a people."[47]

In Homeric scenes of encounter, the welcome ritual is followed by the telling of stories, either by the host as is the case after Telemachus's arrival in Pylos and Sparta, or by the guest as is the case after Odysseus's arrival on

Phaeacia, or by a professional bard who regales both the guest and the host with tales of the past. The figure of the bard makes his appearance at a number of key junctures in *The Odyssey*, including Ithaca, Sparta, and Phaeacia.[48] Bardic performance of epic poetry makes up an integral part of the ritual of hospitality, through which a universal bond of humanity is forged. Not only does the epic represent the making of a normative world order through rituals of hospitality, but in the form of tales performed at such rituals, it also participates in the making of a normative world order.

The Homeric ritual of hospitality continues in Virgil's *Aeneid*. Landing at Carthage after the storm caused by Juno, the hero Aeneas is welcomed by the Carthaginian queen Dido with a feast rivaling the one given by the Phaeacian king Alcinous in honor of Odysseus. Hospitality is now explicitly invoked as a law instituted by Jupiter, as Dido lifts a prayer: "Jupiter, you, they say, are the god who grants / the laws of host and guest."[49] The Carthaginian episode is but a brief one. Compared to the *Odyssey*, the *Aeneid* is less concerned with hospitality towards individual strangers than with the encounter between peoples—the ferocious war between the Trojans and the Latin tribes. Like the ritual of hospitality, the war in the *Aeneid* is carried out under the aegis of Jupiter, meant to institute a universal order of the human world transcending the boundary of local political communities. Virgil's epic figuration of war bears on the justification of war, as well as the lawful conduct of war.

Long before the Trojans actually clash with the Latins, Jupiter, "unrolling the scroll of Fate," already prophesies the war and its purpose:

Aeneas will wage
a long, costly war in Italy, crush defiant tribes
and build high city walls for his people there
and found the rule of law. (I. 313–16)

The rule of law is to be administered by an "empire without end" (I. 334). The empire will fight more wars, but all for the sake of making and enforcing laws. In other words, war is a requisite for a peaceful world order based on the imperial rule of law. This divine vision of world order is affirmed again and again at key junctures of the epic poem—by Aeneas's father Anchises in the underworld, and by the shield made by Vulcan for Aeneas. In what can be seen as a reprise of the Ciceronian argument made in *De Re Publica*, that the universal law of nature finds realization in Rome, Jupiter's prophecy, Anchises's vision, and the Shield of Aeneas envisage a cosmic order to be enforced by Roman rule and governance.[50] All three episodes, it must be noted, figure as set pieces of the epic form, exemplifying respectively divine council, journey through the underworld, and ekphrasis. The conception of war in terms of cosmic justice is no mere accidental ingredient in Virgil's epic, but is inscribed in the epic form itself.

With such a cosmic justification of war, the savage warfare between the Trojans and the Latins can be nothing else but an enactment of justice. First, the war is occasioned by the hellish injustice of Turnus. After reaching the Tiber River, Aeneas immediately signs a peace treaty with King Latinus. It is the Fury Allecto—enlisted by Juno under the motto "if I cannot sway the heavens, I'll wake the powers of hell!" (VII. 365)—who instigates Turnus to war. Second, Aeneas allies himself with Evander, the paragon of piety and righteousness, whereas Turnus allies himself with the tyrant Mezentius who, after committing unspeakable crimes against man and nature, has been driven out by his own people. Third, in conducting the war, Turnus resorts to nefarious tactics, for instance by attacking the Trojan camp unannounced and setting the Trojan ships on fire. Fourth, as the conclusion to the war, Aeneas proposes a treaty that ensures a lasting peace grounded on the rule of law (VII. 223–228). Attending thus to all aspects of a war—beginning, alliance, conduct, and conclusion—the *Aeneid* formulates nothing less than a code of war. Together with the cosmic justification of war, this code affirms an objective justice that underpins eternal peace, either positively or *ex negativo*.

The cosmic justice that the war between Trojans and Latin tribes enacts is identified, of course, with the imperium of Rome, with *pax romana*.[51] A central purpose of the *Aeneid* was the celebration of the foundation of Augustan Rome. The glorification of the imperial rule of Rome as cosmic justice leaves no room for facts. Indeed, it at times contradicts the actual history of Rome. For instance, the image of the amicable brothers Romulus and Remus in Jupiter's prophecy—"And Romulus flanked by brother Remus will make the laws" (I. 350)—belies the fact that one murdered the other.[52] In this sense, the epic narrative of the foundation of Rome is "an ideology of empire."[53] The obverse of glorification is mourning—mourning for what is sacrificed in the imperial pursuit of Rome. The "pessimistic" readers of the *Aeneid* draw attention to the coexistence of the public voice of victory and the private voice of sorrow, to the juxtaposition of the celebratory narrative of achievement and the melancholic narrative of defeat and loss, and to Aeneas's slaying of Turnus at the end as tragic victory.[54] Cosmic justice comes with a price.

World Order Impossible: Scenes of Encounter in Camões's *Os Lusíadas*

In the course of the sixteenth century, at a time when Europeans managed to venture much further than Odysseus or Aeneas had done, the epic as a poetic form for representing voyage and world order was resuscitated. The first great epic based on the classical model was Camões's *Os Lusíadas*, a poem celebrating Vasco de Gama's exploratory voyage to India. The opening verse, "Arms are my theme, and those matchless heroes" (1, 1) echoes the *Aeneid*'s opening, "Arma virumque cano," and the poet solemnly announces that he "would take Homer's lyre to commend" Portuguese heroes (1, 12).[55] Indeed, Camões goes to great lengths to reproduce a classical epic by deploying some of its key formal devices: narrative *in medias res*, divine council—despite the evident incongruity between the pagan divinities and the Christian God—and supernatural prophecy, to name just a few salient examples. As befits an epic of voyage, *Os Lusíadas* features many scenes of encounter, one of which—Malindi—furnishes the occasion for the epic hero himself to narrate the prehistory of his voyage, serving as the analogue to Phaeacia in the *Odyssey* and Carthage in the *Aeneid*. As elaborately and as self-consciously as Camões seeks to recreate the epic form, the scenes of encounter in his poem look disconcertingly different from those in its classical predecessors. Both Homeric rituals of hospitality and the Virgilian just war are gone. Rather than staging a lawful order of the human world under the auspices of the divine, they display the disorderliness of the world, indeed the impossibility of world order.

There are four major scenes of encounter in *Os Lusíadas*: Mozambique, Mombassa, Malindi, and Calicut. They share a similar communicative structure. Whereas in Homer and Virgil the strangers and the natives encounter each other under the overarching law of Zeus/Jupiter, the two parties of every encounter in *Os Lusíadas* are invariably beholden to different laws. In Mozambique, after an initially friendly interaction, the Sheikh

> required to see
> The books of our laws, commandments, or faith,
> To judge if they matched his own (1, 63).

The travellers and the natives are separated by both political and religious allegiances. There is no higher law, no shared sense of justice that could bridge the gulf between the two parties. Indeed, there is so little sense of justice that the Portuguese usually use criminals to reach out to local peoples on first encounter. Da Gama's fleet carries on board prisoners who are "sentenced for gross crimes" and whose lives "could be hazarded" in dangerous situations. In Mombassa, da Gama sends "two of the cleverest, trained" from among these prisoners, "to spy on the city and defences / Of the resourceful Muslims" (2, 7). In Malindi, "one of the captives was dispatched to bring / Their landfall to the notice of the king" (2, 74). By using criminals to establish contact, the Portuguese place, from the outset, their relation to the other outside the law. The treaties that they hasten to offer upon arrival in a new place, then, seem to be less legal instruments than legalistic ploys to nail down local rulers to their schemes. The encounter inaugurated by criminals concludes, logically, with a criminal act. Along with spices, da Gama has some natives abducted as evidences of his "discovery" of India (9, 13–14).

As strangers and local peoples no longer recognize a higher law, they also cease to be transparent to each other. After inquiring about "the books of our laws, commandments, or faith," the Sheikh of Mozambique

> implored our captain to offer him
> Some demonstration of what arms we bore
> In the event we found ourselves in war (1, 63).

To the suspicion of the Sheik, da Gama responds with intimidation:

> I can satisfy this desire of yours;
> But view them as a friend, for well I know
> You'll never wish to see them as a foe (1, 66).

This exchange between the Sheik and da Gama is a prototypical scene of encounter in *Os Lusíadas*: the Homeric hospitality is replaced by latent hostility. This hostility manifests itself through various tactics.

First, there is simulation and dissimulation. After the Sheik has seen the arsenal of the Portuguese, "suspicion took root in his heart," but

> nothing showed in his face or gestures
> As, behind a cheerful mask, he continued
> Treating them with gentle condescension,
> Until he could find out his true intention (1, 69).

The double tactics of pretending to be what one is not and not to be what one actually is generate traps, plots, and schemes, all designed to take in the other. The narrator usually associates these tactics with native peoples, using them as proof of the nefariousness of infidels. But the Portuguese are certainly no less expert in simulation and dissimulation. When da Gama is detained in Calicut, he tries to come up with schemes to free himself from custody. At this juncture, the narrator remarks approvingly that a great captain must possess the quality of "knowing the enemy, and outwitting him / With strategy and subtle design" (8, 89).

Second, there is preemptive strike. Always suspecting the other of evil designs, each party attempts to destroy its opponent first. In Mozambique, the Sheikh tries to neutralize the Portuguese before they can put their dangerous arms to use. But the captain da Gama "knew the risk / of trusting in a dangerous rival" (1, 85). So he sets out well provided and strikes before the Sheik's men could attack, routing with cannonade the natives armed merely with spears and shields. Taken together, the tactics prompted by latent hostility make every encounter into psychological warfare, in which both parties become mirror images of each other.

Besides depicting the psychological mechanism of hostility, the scenes of encounter in *Os Lusíadas* provide perceptive political analysis of the play of interests, which forecloses the possibility of a lawful world order. For the Portuguese, the most important thing is to acquire fresh provisions and find local pilots who can guide them towards India. The places that do not satisfy these needs are simply uninteresting. Off the coast of Mozambique, da Gama sees "no reason to make landfall / On islands which looked uninhabited" (1, 44). As Malindi offers a good prospect in this regard, they have no qualms allying themselves with its Muslim sultan. This lends their crusading zeal against the infidels more than a touch of hypocrisy. In Calicut, the complex interplay of the interests of various local actors keeps the Portuguese on edge: the king's soothsayer fears that the newcomers would eventually "destroy the people and their power" (8, 46); the local Muslims resent the presence of Christians; the king's counselors, bribed by Muslim priests, persuade the king to resist the Portuguese; the king himself fears the Portuguese but is also eager to profit from trading with them; the local governors are gripped by greed in their dealings with the Portuguese. The narrator cannot help exclaiming, "Vile self-interest and the sordid thirst / For gold compels up to our very worst" (8, 96).

The only place where the Portuguese establish a good rapport with the local people is Malindi. As elsewhere, this encounter begins with mutual suspicions, as da Gama refuses to disembark, sending instead a criminal to probe the disposition of the local authority. Thereafter, however, Camões spares no effort in making the Malindi episode into an epic set piece complete with lavish feasts and storytelling. Regardless of the historical reality of the Malindi-Portuguese alliance, which had something to do with commercial rivalry in the western Indian Ocean, the relationship between the Sultan of Malindi and da Gama as depicted in *Os Lusíadas* is anything but Homeric hospitality.[56] Rather than recognizing the other's humanity under the gaze of the divine or honoring the universally valid law of host and guest, the Sultan extends warm welcome to the Portuguese because of "the great deeds they had performed" (2, 103). If Odysseus's stories told at the court of Alcinous and Aeneas's stories told at the court of Dido revolve around their respective voyages, da Gama's narrative at the court of the Sultan deals mainly with the "great deeds" of Portuguese kings, so that his own voyage becomes merely an exemplification and continuation of Portuguese "greatness." Chief among these "great deeds" are victories over the Moors. Implausible as it is that a sultan should be so impressed by stories about the defeat of Muslims, at the end of da Gama's narrative

> the Muslim king was at his wits' end
> How to entertain the brave mariners,
> To gain the Christian king's alliance
> And the friendship of such strong people (6, 1).

The good rapport between Malindi and the Portuguese, then, does not issue from any norms or shared sense of justice, but is entirely predicated upon one party's admiration for the "greatness" of the other. As well as being jejune wishful thinking, this concern with "greatness" testifies to the poet's indebtedness to the doctrine of reason of state, which counteracts normative order, as we shall see later.

The Crisis of the Epic Form: *Os Lusíadas* as Historical Writing and Advice Book

The various elements of the scenes of encounter in *Os Lusíadas*—the allegiance to different jurisdictions and faiths, latent hostility, psychological warfare, calculation of interests, and admiration for "greatness"—combine to indicate that the lawful world order as envisaged by the classical epic is no longer possible. If the representation of a lawful world order is a constitutive element of the epic form, the crisis of world order manifest in the scenes of encounter in *Os Lusíadas* suggests that the epic form may be in jeopardy. Indeed, Renaissance poets resuscitated the classical epic only to prove that it could no longer be recreated in its original form.[57] As the first serious, large-scale epic poem composed according to the classical model, *Os Lusíadas* also stands as the first testimony to the crisis of the epic form. The dedication to King Sebastião, with which the poem opens, indicates that Camões's reproduction of the classical epic is blended with two other genres current in the sixteenth century: historical writing and mirror-for-princes. Both prove to counteract the epic form.

While invoking Homer and Virgil as his predecessors, the poet proclaims in the dedication to the king, not too modestly, his intention to surpass the ancients: instead of the great voyages of Odysseus and Aeneas, he will "sing of the famous Portuguese / To whom both Mars and Neptune bowed" (1, 3). Such a poem about the "famous Portuguese" is superior because it tells of "true deeds" ("verdadeiras vossas são tamanhas," 1, 11). By "true deeds" he means history, in contrast to the mythological core of the *Odyssey* and the *Aeneid*.[58] First of all, the poet implies that his narrative of Vasco da Gama's voyage is based on historical records. Da Gama himself makes the same point after telling the Malindian Sultan of his voyage: his tale outshines those of Odysseus and Aeneas because of its naked and pure truth (5, 89). Second, the narrative of da Gama's voyage provides the occasion for recounting the historic deeds of many other "famous Portuguese." Vasco da Gama relates the "long descent" (3, 3) of the kings of Portugal in his speech at the court of Malindi; his brother Paulo tells the official of Calicut about the illustrious heroes of Portugal; the Nymph on the isle of love sings about Portuguese explorers and conquerors coming after da Gama; and the sea goddess Tethys prophesies the Portuguese discoveries around the world, both East and West.

When the narrator as well as his hero Vasco da Gama speaks of "truth" in *Os Lusíadas*, they refer to facts. The interest in the facticity of political actions rather than their normative principles—in politics as it is rather than as it should be—characterizes the most important historical writing of the sixteenth century, Francesco Guicciardini's *Storia d'Italia*. It was also this interest that fueled the widespread and sustained reception, in the sixteenth and early seventeenth centuries, of the Roman historian Tacitus (ca. 56–120 CE) known for his unblinking, brutally matter-of-fact account of the power play of political actors under the principate. Camões's turn to history reflects the concern of his age with the reality of political actions. Rather than enabling him to surpass Homer and Virgil, however, this vaunted turn actually goes against the epic form, as historical facticity undercuts the epic ideal. As mentioned above, Virgil's Rome has little to do with historical facts. It is rather an ideal, and it is this ideal that serves as the motive principle and the telos of the epic narrative. *Os Lusíadas* invokes what looks like an ideal in the very first stanza: a "new kingdom (*Novo Reino*)" (1, 1). Yet it endeavors to ground this "new kingdom" in facts—perilous voyages and military exploits of some "famous Portuguese"—rather than in divine providence, cosmic order, or any other transcendent principle.[59] Facts never add up to an ideal. After all the facts have been enumerated, the ideal "new kingdom" disappears from view, leaving behind no more than a faint echo of a hollow ideology. To be sure, the Virgilian ideal is also an ideology from the perspective of a latter-day critic who knows about the historical facts of Rome. But the Virgilian narrative itself takes care not to confront this ideal with compromising facts. In the case of Camões, by contrast, there is within the text itself a striking discrepancy between historical facts and the vision of the "new kingdom." The more facts about the "famous Portuguese" he adduces, the further he drifts away from an ideal that would lend his narrative direction and coherence.[60]

Os Lusíadas opens and closes with lengthy addresses to King Sebastião. Both addresses are more exhortatory than acclamatory. The dedication at the beginning first reminds him that his mission should be "to win for God much of the world again" (1, 6), and then recommends that he take the deeds of past kings and heroes celebrated in the poem as signposts: "Take up the reins of your kingdom / To furnish matter for another epic" (1, 15). The address at the end offers various concrete pieces of advice such as "Promote only men of experience" (10, 149) or

> Show favour in their professions to all
> As they bring their talents to bear:
> And let holy men make observances
> Of fasting and due penance (10, 150).

The addresses to the king at the beginning and the end frame *Os Lusíadas* as an advice book or mirror-for-princes, a prominent genre in the political literature of the sixteenth century. With roots in the antiquity and the middle ages, advice books for princes increased greatly in the late *quattrocento* when city republics gradually gave way to princely rule in Italy. This genre reached its first climax in Niccolò Machiavelli's *Il Principe* (1513).[61] In the course of the sixteenth century, along with the consolidation of monarchical states across Europe, advice books for princes mushroomed, mostly in reaction to Machiavelli.[62] If Machiavelli was still preoccupied with the acquisition of princely power and the techniques of maintaining it, authors of advice books in the second half of the century, including such prominent names as Botero and Lipsius, turned their attention to the preservation of the state itself through the art of government. With its hortatory suggestions and encouraging examples for the expansion and preservation of Portugal—this "small house of Christendom" (1, 6) perpetually threatened by powerful neighbors and annexed to Spain in 1580—*Os Lusíadas* at once reflected the Machiavellian preoccupation with maintaining princely power and prefigured the theoretical treatises on techniques of government published later in the century. The art of government, however, is contrary to the epic. The epic is concerned with foundation and end. Virgil sings at once of the founding of Rome by Aeneas and of the Augustan imperial reign as the final aim of Rome, a reign that realizes Jupiter's justice so completely as to return to the Golden Age of Saturn.[63] By contrast, in the art of government, as Michel Foucault once pointed out, "there is no problem of origin, of foundation, or of legitimacy, and no problem of dynasty either." Nor must "the problem of the endpoint [. . .] be posed."[64] All it cares about is the management of the affairs of the state as advantageously as possible.

Reason of State

Historical writing and advice books for princes in the sixteenth century were intertwined with one another. On the one hand, advice books for princes tended to stress the importance of *exempla* and *historia*. Machiavelli proffered his *Il Principe* to Lorenzo de' Medici as a gift crafted by "continual study of ancient history."[65] His *Discorsi* (1517) opens with an admonition against ignoring ancient history "in constituting republics, in maintaining states, in governing kingdoms, in forming an army or conducting a war, in dealing with subjects, in extending the empire."[66] Later in the century, Lipsius occupied himself intensively with Tacitus through editions and commentaries, before penning his famous *Politicorum sive civilis doctrinae libri sex* (1589).[67] In fact, Tacitus, the historian of the principate, represented a major source of topics and insights for almost all writers concerned with techniques of government in an age when most European peoples lived in monarchical rather than republican states, becoming in the process the name-giver for a main doctrine in early modern political thought: Tacitism.[68] On the other hand, political historians tended to focus on techniques of government. In contrast to the Virgilian extolment of the Augustan reign as the realization of the lofty ideal of Rome, Tacitus's sketch of the Augustan reign in the *Annals* spotlights Octavian's skills in governing: "Dropping the title 'triumvir,' Octavian presented himself as a consul, and as a man satisfied to hold tribunician authority in order to safeguard the people. Then, by seducing the military with donatives, the masses with grain allowances, and everybody with the pleasure of peace, he gradually increased his powers, drawing to himself the functions of Senate, magistrates, and laws."[69] In his *Storia d'Italia* (written in the 1530s), Guicciardini, a great admirer of Tacitus, describes in frightening detail the maneuvers of princes and their representatives in the tumultuous decades following the French invasion of Italy in 1494.

Taken together, historical writing and advice books for princes made up the core of a field of political knowledge concerned with the efficiency and technical rationality of statecraft. The rationality postulated, explicated, and advocated by this kind of political knowledge was encapsulated by the concept of reason of state. The term "reason of state" stemmed from Guicciardini. In *Dialogo del reggimento di Firenze* (written in 1521–25), he states dispassionately, "When I talked of murdering or keeping the Pisans imprisoned, I didn't perhaps talk as a Christian: I talked according to the reason and practice of states."[70] The "reason" here refers to the principles of political action, which aim exclusively at power and interest without regard for religious or moral pieties. In his *Della Ragion di Stato* (1589)—a book that turned "reason of state" into a catchphrase for European political thought for a long time to come—Botero equates reason of state with the practical knowledge of government: "State is a stable rule over a people and Reason of State is the knowledge of the means by which such a dominion may be founded, preserved and extended. Yet, although in the widest sense the term includes all these, it is concerned most nearly with preservation, and more nearly with extension than with foundation; for Reason of State assumes a ruler and a State (the one as artificer, the other as his material)."[71] Botero's "reason" means mainly the practical capability of administration.

In both its connotations indicated by Guicciardini and Botero, the concept of reason of state detaches the state from all ethical and religious moorings. The "reason" in reason of state is no longer the Ciceronian *recta ratio*, which teaches the universal principles of justice, but an instrumental reason for calculating the most efficient means of preserving and expanding the state.[72] Justice used to be considered the end of the commonwealth by political philosophers from classical antiquity to the civic humanism of the Renaissance. In the works of Botero and other contemporary theorists of reason of state, however, it became one of the many requisite means of preserving the state. Prudence, once upon a time understood as *recta ratio agibilium* and hence inseparable from justice, became a "code of governmental techniques."[73] Even Christian religion figured now merely as a pawn on the chessboard of a prince, to be deployed tactically for the sake of preserving and enlarging the state: "Religion makes subjects obedient to their ruler, brave in war, daring in moments of danger, liberal in time of want and ready in the event of public need."[74] With all ethical and religious norms disposed of, what remained was nothing more than naked interests to be protected and maximized by all means: "It should be taken for granted that in the decisions made by princes interest will always override every other argument; and therefore he who treats with princes should put no trust in friendship, kinship, treaty nor any other tie which has no basis in interest."[75] The state became a purpose in and for itself.[76]

One of the first political practices in which reason of state found expression was diplomacy. Ancient practice that it was, diplomacy gained a new momentum in fifteenth-century Italy, at a historical juncture when the rise of principalities at the expense of city republics eroded extant legal orders and transformed the political space into a "delegitimized world of the power-seekers."[77] For Machiavelli, a prince is bound by no laws in dealing with foreign powers, just as he cares little about the legitimacy of his rule over subjects. The most decisive factor in a prince's external relations is military force. But since force alone is hardly enough on all occasions, words and negotiation—in other words, diplomacy—may be useful as well. Concerned with powerbrokering as it was, diplomacy in the fifteenth and sixteenth centuries entailed juridically problematic activities that aimed to establish rapport among rulers in the absence of law or other binding norms.[78] Assuming the self-interested nature of rulers and the absence of any generally recognized norm among them, Machiavelli had actually only one technique of diplomatic negotiation to recommend: "one must be a great feigner and dissembler."[79] "A prince who wishes to do great things," he contends in *Discorsi*, must "learn to practice deceit." Even the Romans "did not fail to use fraud." Indeed, "force by itself [never] suffices, whereas instances can easily be found in which fraud alone has sufficed."[80] Guicciardini recommended simulation and dissimulation in equally unapologetic terms.[81] To be a "feigner and dissembler" means to introduce a difference between the self as representation and the self as the represented. While the self as representation accedes to norms (such as treaties), the self as the represented counteracts them. It is in this difference between representation and the represented that self-interest is to be realized.

Another consequence of the doctrine of reason of state for political practice was the competition between states, with each state striving for "greatness." Machiavelli's advice was meant for princes who wanted to achieve "great things." This term, which recurs throughout *Il Principe*, refers to the honor, glory, and fame that come with the establishing and securing of a princely state. Later in the century, with the consolidation of the monarchical state, authors on reason of state were more concerned with the measures needed to preserve and expand a state already established and secured. "Greatness," then, came to mean the sum total of positive qualities of an existing state. Botero's *Delle cause della grandezza e magnificienza delle città* (1588) emphasizes material power as the main criterion of greatness. His *Della Ragion di Stato* focuses on the greatness of the ruler. A state, for Botero, is preserved by the affection and the admiration of the people for the ruler. The qualities that win affection are justice and liberality, and those that win admiration are prudence and valor. The princes who demonstrate such qualities—for example, Alexander of Macedon and the Emperor Constantine—are called great. Insofar as reason of state is the knowledge of the means of preserving the state, greatness—the qualities that command admiration and thereby help preserve the state—falls within its remit. Since reason of state serves no other purpose than the pursuit of interest, the greatness based on it has no normative content. It merely elicits an affect, that of admiration.

The plot of *Os Lusíadas* revolves around these two practical manifestations of reason of state: diplomacy and the striving for greatness. The scenes of encounter between the traveling Portuguese and the peoples around the Indian Ocean bear the hallmarks of the sixteenth-century European understanding of diplomacy—the absence of law, the play of simulation and dissimulation, the dominance of self-interest. At the same time, the Portuguese quest for greatness informs the epic narrative from beginning to end. The poet's addresses to King Sebastião that frame the main narrative express his solicitude for the preservation and expansion of Portugal, offering practical advice to this end. The narrative of da Gama's journey and, to an even greater degree, the interpolated historical narratives of various "famous Portuguese" recount heroic deeds characterized by prudence and valor ("conselho e ousadia," 8, 29)—by qualities that, according to theorists of reason of state such as Botero, make up the greatness of rulers. Within such a macrostructure, the poem projects the greatness attested to by the narrated heroic deeds onto the young king: "Look kindly on my kindness so / This epic may become your own" (1, 18).

The core principle of reason of state is the interest of the prince and his state. Diplomacy is nothing else than the negotiation of interests, and the greatness of a state implies the maximization of interests. Given the divisive nature of interest, reason of state cannot provide for a normative order of the world. The narrator of *Os Lusíadas* does attempt to turn greatness—or rather the admiration elicited by greatness—into the foundation of a world order. Listening to the epic hero Vasco de Gama's story of Portuguese kings, the sultan of Malindi is so impressed by their greatness that he eagerly submits to the Portuguese:

> "He would be ready to sacrifice
> His country and his life at any time
> To a king so good, a people so sublime" (6, 4).

The poet certainly wishes to see the whole world follow the lead of the sultan. But he is doomed to disappointment—a disappointment so inconsolable that the poem as a whole takes on a desolate, melancholic tone. But it is a melancholic tone quite different from the one occasionally audible in the *Aeneid*. In Virgil, the voice of melancholy and sorrow bemoans the sacrifice and loss entailed by victory and imperium. In Camões, by contrast, it bemoans the failure to achieve universal victory and imperium. Greatness cannot serve as the foundation of world order, because it lacks normative validity and transcendent grounding. As Vasco da Gama's own historical narrative of Portuguese kings makes abundantly clear, deeds of valor and prudence, however extraordinary they may be, are mere contingent facts, liable to be compromised and canceled out by acts of weakness and evil, by unredeemed violence and unexpiated crimes. For instance, Alfonso the Fifth was just as "terrible" (4, 54) as Alfonso the First was great. Without a higher, normative point of reference, no great deeds can be sure to meet with universal approbation. Paulo da Gama's description of the deeds of Portuguese heroes in Calicut, presented in the mode of epic ekphrasis, seem to impress the local officials who are the willing audience: "So da Gama expounded the great deeds / [. . .] The Catual's eyes were spellbound" (8, 43). But this does not prevent these officials from plotting against the Portuguese. Finally, the deeds considered great are usually directed against other princes and peoples, chiefly military campaigns, so that they may help unite a state through the admiration of the subjects, but counteract any bonding between states or peoples.

The doctrine of reason of state in *Os Lusíadas* is, on the formal level, bound up with the generic affinity of this text to historical writing and advice books for princes. Yet the text aspires to be an epic after all. It does so by concluding with a vision of cosmic order that would remedy the disorderliness of the world. This vision manifests itself as an imaginary encounter in a phantasmic space: the encounter between Portuguese mariners and nymphs on the isle of love.

Poetic Justice

After having visited Calicut on the Western coast of the Indian subcontinent and abducted some natives as evidence of his "discovery" of India, Vasco da Gama and his fleet set sail for the return journey. Venus, the protector of the Portuguese, places a lush island on their homeward route and populates it with beautiful nymphs suitably prepared by Cupid's arrows. She decides to reward the Portuguese mariners with the highest possible pleasures. *Os Lusíadas* climaxes with the orgiastic lovemaking of ardent mariners and enamored nymphs on the isle of love. What looks like a fantasy of sexually starved mariners, however, turns out to be a vision of cosmic harmony.

Before the mariners arrive on the island, Cupid was

> Marshalling a force of lesser cupids
> For an expedition against mankind
> To punish the heresy, still prevalent
> In these present days, of expending
> All their passion (for so they were accused)
> On things intended merely to be used (9, 25).

The expedition of cupids stands in striking contrast to the expedition of the Portuguese. Whereas the latter serve the interest of Portugal in their endeavors of self-preservation and expansion, the former seek to fight against the pursuit of interests and infuse love into mankind. In particular, the god of love condemns princes driven by self-interest: "Whatever love they felt was for / Themselves and for others like them" (9, 27). He also condemns the clergy "fawning [. . .] on power and wealth" (9, 28). His arrows punish greed and fill all humans with love. His expedition, then, is supposed to merge the whole world in a loving union. The lovemaking of nymphs and mariners instantiates the universal bonding of the world under the auspices of Cupid and his mother Venus. After lovemaking, "the beautiful nymphs with their lovers, / Hand in hand and in happy accord," are summoned to "tables laden with exquisite dishes" (10, 2) and "smoky wines" (10, 4). Regardless of Camões's indebtedness to Plato's *Symposium* and Marsilio Ficino's commentary *De amore* (1466), which such imagery evokes, it is clear at this point that he envisions love as a cosmic principle. With all individuals united in love, time and space no longer matter. A nymph sings prophetically of what is going to happen in the future. Tethys, who as sea-goddess and queen of the nymphs has appropriately devoted herself to the captain, shows

Vasco da Gama the entire cosmos. In this cosmos—which is, incidentally, still Ptolemaic, as if Copernicus (1473–1543) had never existed—he can see not only the past and the future, but also where he wishes to be (10, 79). In contemplating it, he partakes of "the deepest and highest Wisdom, / Who is without beginning and end" (10, 80). Far from being mere satisfaction of carnal needs, what happens on the isle of love is the initiation into divine knowledge and the realization of cosmic harmony through love, which nullifies reason of state and redeems a world divided by interests.[82]

Yet the isle of love is by no means free of the practical concerns of the political world. Venus places it in the middle of the ocean to reward the Portuguese mariners for the hardship that they have endured. The nymph on the isle who sings about future Portuguese heroes prophesizes that "all the heroes, and others worthy / In different ways of fame and esteem / [. . .] / Will taste this island's pleasures," and that the "lovely nymphs, these tables richly furnished" will serve as the "glorious rewards for tasks accomplished" (10, 73). The isle of love, with its vision of cosmic harmony that transcends the pursuit of interest, ultimately serves the interest of the Portuguese in their quest for greatness. It resembles those fictions that practical men invent as antidotes to their worries and toils, and that precisely in this function serve practical purposes.

Indeed, the isle of love is marked by fictiveness. In presenting the cosmos to the Portuguese captain, the sea-goddess Tethys declares herself, along with "Saturn and Janus, Jupiter and Juno," to be "mere fables / Dreamed up by mankind in his blindness." She then continues:

> We serve only to fashion delightful
> Verses, and if human usage offers
> Us more, it is your imagination
> Awards us each in heaven a constellation (10, 82).

The vision of cosmic order meant to redeem the disorderliness of the world, to give voyages a direction and a purpose, and thereby to make the narrative into an epic, thus debunks itself as poetic fiction. With the vision declared a fiction, the epic form can be nothing more than "delightful verses" that offer their services to those eager to assert their own greatness.

The Beginnings of Public International Law (Gentili, Suárez, Grotius)

Instead of affirming the unchanging laws of nature, Neoscholastic jurisprudence unsettled them. Vitoria delivered natural law up to the rights and the will of the subject. Instead of recreating the cosmic order evoked by the classical epic, the Renaissance epic enacted its disruption. Camões's *Os Lusíadas* depicts a world riven with the disorderly pursuit of interest at the behest of reason of state.[83] Subjective right, free will, reason of state—all of these concepts and doctrines undermined traditional models of normative world order. At the same time, however, they served as the starting points for conceiving of normative world order in a new way—as international legal order. The Neoscholastic doctrines of subjective natural right and free will led to a concept of international law in the thinking of Francisco Suárez. The attempt to legalize reason of state led to the formulation of a law of embassy and a law of war by Alberico Gentili. Combining Neoscholastic jurisprudence with the doctrine of reason of state, Hugo Grotius devised a new theory of natural law, which, in turn, enabled him to elaborate a highly sophisticated theory of international law. Suárez, Gentili, and Grotius would be seen as the founders of public international law.

The Birth of the Concept of International Law in Neoscholastic Jurisprudence: Francisco Suárez

We have seen that *ius gentium* came to prominence as Vitoria directed attention to the subject of natural law in the wake of the Spanish conquest of the Americas, thus complementing the notion of objective natural lawful order with the notion of subjective natural right. It was in mediating the rights of different subjects—Amerindians and Spaniards—that he invoked *ius gentium*. In so doing, however, he also created the thorny problem of having to clarify its status vis-à-vis natural law as well as man-made laws. Francisco Suárez, the last important representative of Spanish Scholasticism, solved this problem by giving *ius gentium* a unique subject—the state.

Curcial to Suárez's redefinition of *ius gentium* is the concept of free will. Spanish Scholasticism had a general voluntarist tendency, as can be seen in Vitoria's conception of human agency as well as the emphasis on voluntary consent in his discussion of *ius gentium*. But the firm Jesuit belief in free will—theologically a reaction to the Protestant insistence on the fallen nature of man and the primacy of grace—enabled Suárez to concede to man a natural liberty outside of a political community. In *De legibus, ac Deo legislatore* (1612), he writes, "In the nature of things all men are born free; so that, consequently, no person has political jurisdiction over another person, even as no person has dominion over another" (3.2.3).[84] It is also through the exercise of free will, however, that man forms a political community: "[By] special volition, or common consent, [the multitude of mankind] are gathered together into one political body through one bond of fellowship and for the purpose of aiding one another in the attainment of a single political end. Thus viewed, they form a single mystical body which, morally speaking, may be termed essentially a unity; and that body accordingly needs a single head" (3.2.4). Because the exercise of free will is in the nature of things, the state founded on the "special volition" and "common consent" of people is also natural, even though it does not originate with nature.[85] Just as the freedom of will is given to individual persons by nature, it is also naturally given to the state as a corporate person. The corporate will of the state is articulated through the laws that it gives to itself. These laws are *ius civile*, by means of which the state regulates the relation of its members to each other. But the state as a corporate person exists alongside other states, in a similar way as individual persons exist alongside each other. The laws that states willingly observe in their relation to one another are *ius gentium*:

> For even though the whole of mankind may not have been gathered into a single political body, but may rather have been divided into various communities, nevertheless, in order that these communities might be able to aid one another and to remain in a state of mutual justice and peace (which is essential to the universal welfare), it was fitting that they should observe certain common laws, as if in accordance with a common pact and mutual agreement. These are the laws called *iura gentium*; and they were introduced by tradition and custom, as we have remarked, rather than by any written constitution. (*De Legibus* 3.2.6)

Proceeding from the natural liberty of man, Suárez thus arrives at a conception of *ius gentium* as the law between states. The free consent of the people gives rise to the state, and states, in turn, form a lawful community by free consent. This larger community, however, differs qualitatively from the individual state. Whereas Suárez regards the state, in his good Aristotelian and Scholastic manner, as the perfect community and sees its perfection in its legislative power, the community of states represents for him by no means a world state, but rather a conglomerate of separate entities coexisting with each other. Consequently, "there is in existence no legislative power with jurisdiction over the whole world, that is, over all mankind; and therefore, no civil law can be thus universal" (3.4.7). The law holding together the community of states—*ius gentium*—is not made by a political authority vested with legislative power, but established by custom.

Custom comes and goes. Suárez's conception of *ius gentium* as customary law obtaining between states surrenders the normative order of the world to the vicissitudes of time. This is all the more worrisome, as Suárez's conception turns out to be strained by a paradox. In book 7 of *De legibus, ac Deo legislatore*—the most systematic treatment of customary law in early modern Europe—Suárez argues that only a perfect community—the body politic "possessing the capacity for legislative authority over itself"—is capable of introducing custom (7.9.6). Furthermore, the will of the body politic is necessary for lending validity to a custom that has been introduced. If customs are not willed, "they are not properly legal customs carrying a binding obligation" (7.14.5). The custom, in short, depends on the will of the state. As customary law, *ius gentium* is thus subjected to the particular will of individual states, even though it has individual states as its subjects. World order seems to be taken hostage not only by time, but also by the contingency of the voluntary actions of individual states.

Yet Suárez is not willing to give up the traditional notion of the objective order of nature altogether. Again, the crux of the matter is the concept of free will. On the one hand, nature requires free will, for even though natural law is founded in reason, its binding force "is imposed *per se* (so to speak) and primarily upon the will" (2.10.4). On the other hand, free will is granted by nature. The state constituted through the voluntary consent of the people, as well as the law that it gives to itself—*ius civile*—originates from human nature. By analogy, if states voluntarily consent to certain unwritten norms—the customary *ius gentium*—to regulate their relations to each other, then these norms, however mutable in time, must be seen as lying in the nature of things as well. In other words, there is a lawful order of nature, but it is actualized only through free will—first the free will of individuals who congregate into a state, and then the free corporate will of the states in their dealings with each other. In a manner reminiscent of the Molinist reconciliation between free will and divine Providence—the omniscient God possesses not only knowledge of everything actually happening and to happen in the future, but can also foresee, by means of his *scientia media*, how humans will freely act or not act in any circumstance, thereby knowing in advance all future contingent events— Suárez mediates between free will and the objective order of nature.[86]

Whatever its theoretical merit, the order of nature as conceived by Suárez takes the form of a state-centered world legal order contingent upon the voluntary actions of individual states. Indicative of the general turn of jurisprudence towards the sovereign will as the main source of law in the seventeenth century, Suárez's Scholastic legal thought also heralded the paradox inherent in modern international law: as the law between sovereign states, it governs legal persons that recognize no law higher than their own will.

Legalizing Reason of State: Gentili's Conception of International Law

Camões recreated epic poetry to affirm a cosmic order in an age unsettled by overseas conquests and the rise of the sovereign state, only to demonstrate the triumph of the divisive force of reason of state. Gentili, a great lover of epic poetry, but above all a jurist immersed in the legal tradition cultivated in Italy for centuries—the so-called *mos italicus*—sought to give a legal form to the exercise of reason of state.[87] In his *De armis Romanis* (1599), the fictive defender of the Roman Empire points out that princes, in contrast to private persons, do not have to obey laws, as "for princes there is something which is considered greater—and actually is greater—something to which all other things are subordinated: rule."[88] If rule or *principatus* has any principle, it is necessity and expediency. For the sake of rule, war is necessary. Deception and theft are no less so. In an unapologetic affirmation of reason of state, he declares, "That which is not allowable according to the law necessity makes allowable. Necessity has no law, but it itself makes law. Necessity makes that acceptable which would otherwise be unacceptable. And because of necessity one justly departs from customary measures."[89] Law is displaced by reason of state. Yet paradoxically it is precisely by means of this displacement that law comes into its own. Rethinking law after its displacement by reason of state, Gentili devises a new kind of jurisprudence, one aimed at enabling states to pursue their respective interests and to manage their governmental affairs with greater security and efficiency.[90] Its key components are a law of embassy and a law of war, elaborated in *De legationibus libri tres* (1585) and *De jure belli libri tres* (1598) respectively.

Embassy and war were topics in the ancient *ius gentium*. Returning to these topics with the doctrine of reason of state in mind, Gentili began with installing the sovereign as the legal subject. The ambassador is sent by a sovereign: he is someone "who in the name of the state or of a person still more sacred has been sent [. . .] to say or do something in the interest of the state or sacred person by whom he has been sent."[91] War is waged by sovereigns: "The war on both sides must be public and official and there must be sovereigns on both sides to direct the war."[92] Persons other than the sovereign—rebels, brigands, and private individuals—are excluded from the right of embassy and right of war. Conversely, nothing, not even religion, disqualifies a sovereign for the right of embassy and that of war: "[The] rights of embassy ought not to be disturbed on account of religious differences," and "war is not waged on account of religion."[93] With legal subjectivity granted exclusively to sovereigns in the law of embassy and the law of war, both become parts of international law in the modern sense, namely as the law between states. Whereas Suárez arrived at the modern conception of public international law on the basis of a constitutionalist theory of the state, Gentili did so through the doctrine of reason of state.

With sovereigns as its subjects, international law is supposed to provide a legal framework for their pursuit of interests. The task of ambassadors consists in representing the interest of a state in relation to another state by words or action, thus freeing the embassy from any ethical requirements. Arguing against the poet Torquato Tasso's ethical view of the ambassador as the angelic man of peace (developed in his 1578 dialogue *Il Messagiero*), Gentili maintains that not lofty ideals, but "the mission which has been entrusted to the ambassador is the mark at which he should aim."[94] His discussion of the causes for making war indicates even more clearly the primacy of state interest. In the characteristic parlance of reason of state, he names necessity, expediency, and honor as the causes of both defensive and offensive warfare. This implies that a state may in principle start a war whenever its interest dictates. The justice invariably claimed by a belligerent state in starting a war can thus be nothing else than a cipher for its particular interest. For this reason, "war may be waged justly on both sides."[95] Justice that is divided and pluralized forfeits all universally binding material content, becoming instead variable subjective claims. If interest reigns supreme in both matters of embassy and those of war, law can do nothing more than specify the formal conditions under which a state may protect and enforce its interests.

As instantiations of formal justice, Gentili's laws of embassy and of war stipulate standardized diplomatic and military procedures—punctilious diplomatic ceremonials, rules regarding the conduct of war, and the like. A clear definition of the legal personality of the agents of embassy and war belongs to the procedural rationality of the diplomatic contest of words as well as the military contest of arms. The ambassador is a public person sent by one sovereign to another, and "the perfect ambassador is one who can accomplish efficiently the business and duties that have been assigned to him or that he himself has recognized the necessity of undertaking." This public personality of the ambassador must be strictly distinguished from his actions and beliefs as a private person: "The ambassador's personality is mixed."[96] A soldier has a similarly mixed personality, performing a designated role in a public war yet remaining at the same time a private person. In his designated role in war, he is an enemy or *hostis*, "a person with whom war is waged and who is the equal of his opponent." But an enemy also partakes of the common nature of mankind. If soldiers abandon their roles in war and become suppliants, they must be treated as members of the community of humankind rather than as enemies.⁹⁷ Because of this distinction between the enemy and the human, persons not engaged in the public contest of arms—women, children, civilians—must be protected in times of war.

In the fifteenth and sixteenth centuries, as discussed above in connection with *Os Lusíadas*, diplomacy consisted of juridically problematic activities. Gentili's law of embassy laid down a set of procedural rules for diplomatic action, lending it a predictability not possible merely by employing the psychological techniques of simulation and dissimulation as recommended by Machiavelli and Guicciardini. Similarly, his law of war laid down a set of procedural rules for the military contest among states. As such, it took the form of *ius i bello*, displacing *ius ad bellum* or the right to war that presupposed an objective justice determining who is in the right and who is in the wrong. A just war (*iustum bellum*) in the sense of a war governed by the law of war (*ius i bello*) meant henceforth a regular warfare, "war in due form," rather than a war grounded in justice.⁹⁸ For Gentili, there is an international legal order. It is procedural orderliness.

Synthesizing Subjective Natural Right and Reason of State: Hugo Grotius's Theory of Natural Law and International Law

Neoscholastic jurisprudence and the theory of reason of state were brought into a productive synthesis by Hugo Grotius. Grotius was born in 1583 in the Dutch town of Delft, in the midst of the long-lasting wars between the Low Countries and their erstwhile imperial master Spain, and he died three years before the Peace of Westphalia officially recognized the independence of the United Provinces. His life bore witness to the rivalry among European states that had been unfolding since the sixteenth century. Engaged in the high politics of the United Provinces early on in his life, he was appointed in 1601 the official historiographer and in 1607 the public prosecutor of the States of Holland. In these and other capacities, Grotius cultivated a political thought founded on doctrines of reason of state. A historian detects in Grotius "a stress on the need for warfare and the *grandezza* of empire, a deep dislike of mass politics, a craving for discipline and a strong sense of the importance of economics."⁹⁹ When he was asked to write an apology for the seizure of the Portuguese merchantman *Santa Catarina* in the Strait of Singapore in 1603 by a captain of the Verenigde Oostindische Compagnie (VOC) or the United Dutch East India Company, he came to reformulate reason of state in the language of jurisprudence that he learned from both Neoscholasticism and legal humanism, establishing in one fell swoop a new brand of natural law as well as one of international law.

Grotius's apology, completed in 1606, was published in its entirety in the nineteenth century under the title of *De jure praedae commentarius*. He himself, however, called it *De Indis*, in explicit reference to Vitoria's treatise on the Indian question. Yet both the political problems and their juridical solutions had changed. Whereas the vexing question for Vitoria was how to make sense of the foray of the Spanish into territories hitherto unknown to Europeans, Grotius was dealing with the competition of two European powers—the United Provinces and the Spanish Empire—over overseas trade and the colonial domination of overseas territories. Since the Portuguese and Spanish crowns were joined together in 1580, the Dutch seizure of the Portuguese ship represented an episode in the ongoing war between the United Provinces and Spain. Grappling with the unprecedented legal situation created by the Spanish conquest of the Americas, Vitoria turned from the objective order of nature towards the subject or agent of natural law and, in an attempt to mediate the rights of different subjects, brought *ius gentium* into the center of juridical attention. Concerned with the rivalry between states as he was, Grotius first looked to the key categories of reason of state—self-preservation and self-interest. In an ingenious conceptual move, he transposed these characteristics of the state onto the individual, while modulating them with the language of natural subjective right known from Neoscholastic jurisprudence.[100] Self-preservation and self-interest, then, became nothing less than human nature itself. On the basis of such a conception of the individual, he then proceeded to undertake a theoretical construction of the state as well as of the relation between states.

That every individual existence seeks to preserve itself, that self-interest is the first principle of the natural order, and that expediency gives rise to justice—all of these ideas are known, in one or the other formulation, from ancient "poets and philosophers."[101] A historian of medieval thought maintains that "it would be hard to find any medieval jurist or philosopher who disagreed with such assertions."[102] In Grotius, however, these ideas are mediated and refracted by the doctrine of reason of state. In a petition to the Estates General, which he drafted on behalf of the United Dutch East India Company, Grotius reminded the representatives of the expediency, rather than the lawfulness, of the offensive war conducted by the United Provinces against the Portuguese:

> Your Honors undoubtedly realized that it would greatly benefit the common cause not just to protect a trade against enemy violence, which is of great importance for the welfare of the common people,

but also to deny the King of Spain his revenues from the East Indies. After all, these revenues give him the wherewithal to ruin and destroy these provinces. In addition, any damage done to the enemy in the East Indies would give Your Honors occasion to undertake many more military and naval expeditions outside of these provinces, all to the detriment of the enemy.[103]

No political advisor could speak a plainer, more unabashed language of reason of state. The notions of self-preservation, self-interest, and expediency belong to the core vocabulary of this language. For Grotius, then, the individual figures as the analogue to the state, and the relation between individuals resembles that between states.[104] The Dutch seizure of the Portuguese ship *Santa Catarina* on the high seas symbolizes at once the relation between states and that between individuals outside of political society. Grotius refers to this space outside of political society as the "natural order." He recognizes, of course, that individuals, apart from some rare occasions—such as an encounter on the high seas—actually always live in a political society. So he takes the consequential step of projecting this space outside of political society on the temporal axis, so that the "natural order" becomes a condition "prior to the establishment of states."[105] Later in *De jure belli ac pacis*, he would call this condition outside of and prior to political society "the state of nature" or *statu naturae*.[106]

In the late sixteenth and early seventeenth centuries, there were a number of thinkers gesturing towards the hypothesis of a condition outside of or prior to political society. Synthesizing Ciceronian humanism and the Roman law, Fernando Vázquez de Menchaca conceived of a primeval natural liberty prior to political subjection.[107] On the basis of Jesuit theology, Francisco Suárez came to a conception of natural liberty as well. Both Vázquez and Suárez proved to be sources of inspiration for Grotius in different stages of his thought. But none of them approached natural liberty so emphatically in terms of the notions of self-interest and expediency as Grotius did. More important, Grotius recast self-interest—"the first principle of the whole natural order"—in juridical language, turning it into the "fundamental law" inherent in the natural order, the foundation of "justice and equity."[108] From this first principle he then extrapolated a number of principles that combine to establish a body of rights for the individual—the rights to life and property, and above all, the right to defend one's own rights. In the natural order, "every individual is charged with the execution of his own rights," and "the execution of one's right in itself constitutes a right."[109]

By transposing reason of state onto the individual, Grotius postulates a natural order prior to, and outside of, political society, a condition in which individuals take care of their own life, limb, and property. Such a conception of the individual leads to a new theory of political society. Although the natural order or state of nature has its laws, they could "be cast aside as invalid," and "men were scattered about with vast distances separating them and were being deprived of opportunities for mutual benefaction." With a view to "self-protection through mutual aid" and to "equal acquisition of the necessities of life," individuals formed a social unit "by a general agreement."[110] This social unit is called the state, and the individual members citizens. The state, then, is instituted to enforce the laws of nature as well as to protect and enhance the individual's interest. Once the state is instituted, individuals must obey the laws made by it—*ius civile*—and may enforce their rights only through judicial procedures.

Grotius's conceptions of human nature, law, and right make up a natural law theory radically different from the ancient tradition. According to the ancient tradition, the law of nature represents the participation of the rational creature in the universal, divinely preordained pattern of things. Grotius introduces instead the state of nature, a condition prior to, or outside of, political society. In the ancient tradition, the law of nature comes in the form of a set of precepts ingrained in the human mind. Grotius postulates one fundamental principle of human nature and then deduces various precepts from it by means of rational argumentation. In the ancient tradition, the law of nature is immediately valid in human society, and political societies that go against its commandments are tyrannies. Grotius broaches the idea that political society comes into being through voluntary agreements of individuals in the state of nature and is entrusted with the task of ensuring the validity of the laws inherent in the state of nature. These and other elements of Grotius's theory of natural law combine to make it into what can be called modern natural law theory—a theory that served as a key paradigm for political and legal thinking throughout the seventeenth and eighteenth centuries.[111]

Modern natural law theory overturns the distinction between public and private law as well as the typology of private law known from *Corpus Juris Civilis*: "Public law covers religious affairs, the priesthood, and offices of state. Private law is tripartite, being derived from principles of *jus natural, jus gentium*, or *jus civile*."[112] In the state of nature, according to Grotius, individuals abide by natural law or *ius naturale*. Once they institute a state by voluntary agreement, they submit themselves to municipal law or *ius civile*. *Ius gentium* or the law of nations, in the meantime, is assigned a new meaning—

that of the law between states. In *De Indis*, Grotius still attempts to treat the juridical issues pertaining to interstate relations in the same way as those within the state, but acknowledges the difficulty in applying any judicial procedure to interstate relations, because "there is no greater sovereign power set over the power of the state and superior to it, since the state is a self-sufficient aggregation."[113] In *De jure belli ac pacis*, he finally recognizes interstate relations as a juridical domain in its own right, and calls it *ius gentium*. As the law between states, *ius gentium* can be more appropriately called international law. It coincides mostly with the law of nature, for states exist alongside each other in the natural order or the state of nature, just as individuals do prior to the establishment of states. International law, therefore, is natural law with states as its subjects. It needs to be noted, however, that Grotius does not equate international law with the law of nature (as Hobbes and Pufendorf would do after him). In addition to the law of nature, Grotius includes in international law also those laws that states agree upon by their own volition, either tacitly or expressly.

Ius gentium in the sense of international law is no longer private law, but is rather public law, since it deals with the affairs of the state. It is what we today call public international law. A proponent of reason of state, Grotius knows that state actions are always driven by the pursuit of the state's own advantage—self-preservation and aggrandizement. Public international law "has in view the advantage, not of particular states, but of the great society of states," insofar as it provides a legal framework, within which all states could pursue their advantages.[114] In this sense, the Grotian conception is similar to that of Gentili. Yet he goes far beyond Gentili by founding public international law on an elaborate natural law theory.[115] For this reason, he can accuse Gentili of advancing arguments that are "accommodated to the special interests of clients, not to the nature of that which is equitable and upright."[116]

Without subscribing to any sharp distinction between the medieval and the modern era, this opening chapter of our long story tries to shed light on some profound transformations in the conception and figuration of world order during the sixteenth century. We see that world order had been a concern of both legal thought and poetic literature since ancient times. The reinvigoration of the ancient natural law tradition and of the classical epic answered to the needs for normative orientation in a time of wrenching changes: natural law theory postulates a set of immutable norms, while the classical epic figures a cosmic order. Yet the Neoscholastic handling of natural law and the Renaissance emulation of Homer and Virgil only served to cast doubt on the viability of ancient models of world order in a new age. The former raised the issue of the subject of natural law and moved subjective right to the center of attention, while the latter compromised the epic form and testified to the divisive forces of reason of state. The concept of subjective natural right and the doctrine of reason of state were crucial both to the theoretical construction of the sovereign state and to the conceptual elaboration of a legal code as to how sovereign states ought to relate to one another—that is, public international law. With the founding of public international law by Gentili, Grotius, and Suárez around 1600, world order became a matter of international legal order.

CHAPTER 2

The Poetics of International Legal Order

At the end of the previous chapter, we saw that the concept and the first doctrinal systems of international law as the law between sovereign states came into being around 1600. In practice, international law in this sense had begun earlier; already during the preceding century, to quote a historian of international law, "the right to make war and peace had become the monopoly of the sovereign to the exclusion of all subject powers, the exceptions being the Estates of the German Empire and the Northern Italian States, which fell under the feudal suzerainty of the emperor."[1] The recourse to legal instruments was vital to the making of the modern state system during the sixteenth century.[2] From the outset, the binding force as well as the unity of international legal norms was a matter of great concern. If princes—or the states that they embodied—insisted on their sovereignty, and if sovereignty meant, by definition, the nonrecognition of any higher authority that would make and apply laws, what could guarantee the validity of treaties or, for that matter, any other legal norms between them? And how could particular norms constitute a unified system, a normative order? Such questions turned out to be often answered by poetic means.

This chapter is concerned with the poetic operations underlying or accompanying the practice as well as the doctrinal discourse of international law in the sixteenth and seventeenth centuries. Taking various media into consideration, it examines three examples.

First, it looks at pictorial allegories of peace treaty. In the sixteenth century, as rulers resorted to treaty-making to regulate their relations, the poetic device of allegory was employed to associate legal transactions with fictive divine agents. Particular treaties were thereby invested with a universal normative force, standing *pars pro toto* for a normative order;

Second, this chapter examines narrative foundations of the doctrinal discourse. From the turn of the seventeenth century onwards, jurists—Gentili, Grotius, Suárez, and many others to follow—formulated and systematized legal doctrines for the world of states. Informed by legal learning, rational argumentation, and moral convictions, the doctrinal discourse of international law not only sets forth specific norms, but also constructs a normative whole. In doing so, it makes use of fictions—fictions of the international legal person, as well as of a community of international legal persons. The fictions are in turn substantiated by narratives. Every international legal person comes with a story about its origin and status, while the community of international legal persons—international society—rests on narratives that recount its foundation and constitution. These narratives, each with a distinctive structure, lurk behind many a model of international order still prevalent today: the Grotian narratives gesture towards a liberal internationalism, the Hobbesian narratives a grim realism, and the Leibnizian narratives a multilayered and multipolar pluralism.

Third, this chapter turns to the performance of law. While jurists laid out doctrinal systems, ceremonial rituals and mythological spectacles staged a perfect order of the international world. Most rituals and spectacles in the international world pertained to the law and could be seen as especially elaborate legal procedures. Yet at the same time they moved beyond the law, evoking invisible, transcendent powers, and thus referring the relations between sovereigns to a mythic ground.

Taken together, the allegorical elevation of fragile norms to a universal normative order, the fiction-making and narration that underpin the doctrinal visions of normative unity, and the staging of world order though ceremonies and spectacles represent some key elements of a poetics of international legal order. As a conclusion to this chapter and transition to the following two chapters, the final section interprets the poetic operations analyzed here as components of what can be called international social drama. They are the germ of the properly poetic genres that would develop in the seventeenth century—tragedy and political romance—which reflect on the structural tensions and norm conflicts of the emerging international society.

Treaty and Allegory in the Renaissance

In the political world of Renaissance Europe—a world in the grip of ruthless princes and riven by treacherous, bloody wars—peace was hard to come by and even harder to maintain. Princes signed one peace treaty after the other only to resume fighting soon afterward. Under these circumstances, a remarkable new mode of representing peace appeared. For example, in 1514, a peace treaty between England and France, "drawn up with the greatest speed," Francesco Guicciardini tells us in *Storia d'Italia* (1561), "was confirmed by a marriage contract: it was agreed that the King of England would give his sister as wife to the King of France once he had acknowledged receipt of the 400,000 scudi for her dowry."[3] A pictorial representation of Princess Mary Tudor's entry into Paris shows God high up in heaven overseeing the royal couple sitting together in the upper half of the picture. In the lower half, there are five beautiful ladies marked as personifications: France and England are united in Confederation by Friendship and Peace. The text at the bottom of the picture reads: "Le cueur du roy que dieu tient en sa main. / A incliné pour la saluation / Nourriture repos du peuple humain" (The heart of the king whom God holds in his hand is inclined towards the welfare, nourishment, and tranquility of the people) (figure 1).

Such pious wishes proved, alas, to have little effect. The enmity between England and France, like the hostile relations of almost all the states in Europe to one another, did not come to an end. After much mutual threat and belligerence, a new peace treaty between the two neighbors was drawn up in 1527.[4] The text of the ratified treaty is richly illustrated. Above the text, a young woman holds in her hands an olive branch and a banner inscribed with the words "PAX ETERNA," which leaves no doubt about her identity. She stands between the coats of arms as well as the crowns of the two contracting parties, connecting them to each other by the turn of her head. Below the text, the bucolic dancing scene suggests the peaceful life of ordinary people (figure 2).

Compared to the picture of Mary Tudor's entry into Paris and the illustration of the Franco-English treaty of 1527, the fresco usually called *Universal Peace* in the Palazzo della Cancelleria in Rome is much more complex in composition and much grander in scale. Completed by Giorgio Vasari in 1546, it is a pictorial monument to the Peace of Nice concluded in 1538. Vasari himself described the theme of the fresco as "the Universal Peace made among all Christians by means of the [. . .] Pontiff, Paul III., more particularly between the Emperor Charles V and Francis King of France, both

FIGURE 1. Pageants for the marriage of Mary Tudor, sister of Henry VIII, to Louis XII of France.
Source: Cotton Vespasian B. II, f.8v, by Pierre Gringore (Paris, 1514). Used by permission of the British Library, UK.

FIGURE 2. Ratification of the Treaty of Amiens in 1527. Used by permission of the National Archives, UK.

FIGURE 3. Giogio Vasari, *Universal Peace*. Palazzo della Cancelleria, Rome.

portraits. Here Peace is seen to burn the arms of War; the Temple of Janus is in the act of being closed; and Fury is lying in chains" (figure 3).[5]

In these three images from the early sixteenth century, the visual portrayal of a peace treaty—either in the form of a portrait of the historical personages associated with a treaty or in the form of the text of a treaty—is juxtaposed with the allegorical personification of *pax*. A legal historical transformation underlies this remarkable iconographic phenomenon: the use of the concept of *pax* to refer to a peace treaty, or the identification of *pax* with *pactum*. In the Middle Ages, as a legal historian tells us, *pax* had two dimensions: "It is, on the one hand, [. . .] *pax facta* between rulers, produced by a *pacis foedus*; on the other hand, *pax* is in content associated with *caritas, concordia, unitas* or *unanimitas* as the fundamental normative order of society [. . .] as well as the general peace in the relations of rulers to one another."[6] By the mid-sixteenth century, however, the term *pax* in the first, legal sense broke free of lexical composites such as *pax facta* or *pacis foedus* and became an independent term denoting the legal instrument (*pactum*) that makes peace—that is, the peace treaty.[7] For instance, "Peace of Lodi" actually meant the "peace treaty of Lodi." In the meantime, the term retained the second, general semantic dimension connoting the fundamental normative order of society.

This semantic development of *pax* went hand in hand with the rise of treaty law. Medieval Europe saw itself as a religious, political, and juridical unity, often referred to as the *respublica christiana*. The various political entities stood, theoretically at least, under the diarchy of the empire and papacy. Juristic theories of territorial sovereignty evolved from the late thirteenth to the mid-fifteenth century, encapsulated by the formula *superiorem non recognoscentes*. But fundamental norms—divine law, natural law, and *ius gentium*—continued to be considered binding. As a historian of medieval law points out, "The jurists besieged the fortress of absolute power by investing it with juridical norms, natural law, reason, custom, privilege, obligations, in effect, the 'constitution' of the realm."[8] In particular, the exercise of supreme power was supposed to be subject to natural reason. The great Commentator Baldus de Ubaldis (1327–1400) said, "The *princeps* is a rational creature possessing supreme power, but insofar as he is rational he should obey reason."[9] Accordingly, the fundamental norms also provided the necessary framework for the relations between rulers. In practice, contractual agreements and customs, interpreted by learned jurists, furnished the legal norms for these relations.[10] The pope was supposed to have the power to enforce such norms. Martinus Garatus's *Tractatus de confederatione, pace et conventionibus principum*, a treatise written in the mid-fifteenth century, maintained that the pope could compel princes to honor a peace treaty: "Papa potest compellere Principes ad servandam pacem inter eos contractam."[11]

In the first half of the sixteenth century, the medieval legal system of the *respublica christiana* collapsed.[12] Many factors contributed to this development, including the struggle between the Valois and the Habsburgs over hegemony in Europe, the Reformation, and the Spanish conquest of the Americas. As a consequence, princes across Europe insisted on their sovereignty in dealing with each other, disputing or at best paying lip service to what used to be considered binding fundamental norms. The pope himself became nothing more than one of the many sovereigns jockeying for political power. *Superiorem non recognoscentes*, the medieval formula that had been used to describe the *de facto* sovereignty of Italian city-republics, applied now to the sovereign princes *de jure*. Under these circumstances, treaty law emerged as part of the law between sovereigns, or international law.[13]

Treaty law was formally similar to contract law except that in contrast to a contract between private persons, a treaty was contracted by holders of sovereignty—princes or the governing councils of republics—with one another. As to the law of contract, the most important development in the early modern period was the consolidation of the doctrine of voluntary consent.[14] Numerous strands of legal thought since the twelfth century contributed to the making of this doctrine. First, drawing on the biblical injunction against untruthfulness—for instance, "But I say unto you, Swear not at all; [. . .] But let your communication be, Yea, yea; Nay, nay: for whatsoever is more than these cometh of evil" (Matthew 5:34–37)—the Canonists formulated the doctrine that all promises, in whatever form they are made, must be kept. In contrast to the emphasis of classical Roman law on formal procedure, Canonists turned consensus into the central criterion for the creation of a legal obligation. Second, Neoscholastic jurisprudence in the sixteenth century, as shown in the previous chapter, developed the ideas of the legal subject and subjective right, thereby conceiving of the contract as based on the subjective will.[15] Finally, modern natural jurisprudence inaugurated by Hugo Grotius cemented the doctrine of voluntary consent in the law of contract. The doctrine of voluntary consent was particularly applicable to the contract between sovereign persons—the peace treaty. In fact, consensus was even more important to peace treaties than to other kinds of contract, for there was no higher authority capable of enforcing a treaty, whereas a contract between private persons could be enforced by a civil magistrate. With the papacy joining the earthly princes in the competition for power, the papal jurisdiction was no longer in force.[16] Nothing else remained to ensure the validity of a treaty than the sovereign will itself.

The sovereign will that gave its consent, however, could always withdraw this consent with impunity. Consequently, a peace treaty founded on the sovereign will alone was intrinsically fragile. The personification of *pax* was a remedy against the perceived fragility of the peace treaty. By juxtaposing the portraits of real political actors or even a treaty text with personifications of peace, the images mentioned above displace *pax* in the sense of a legal instrument—a treaty or pact—by Pax as a fictive numinous agent. The Franco-English treaties of 1514 and 1527 were no more than provisional rapprochements in the unending belligerence between the two countries. Yet it was precisely the fear of the ineffectiveness of the pact that necessitated the invocation of such supernatural agents as Friendship, Peace, and Confederation. And it was precisely the awareness of the impermanence of the pact that gave birth to a transcendent agent standing for "Eternal Peace." In the case of the Peace of Nice of 1538, the hostility between Emperor Charles V and King François I was so great that they actually never met in person. Pope Paul III helped conclude the truce through separate negotiations, but he did not make peace in the capacity of a higher authority to which both monarchs deferred. Even less was he a maker of universal peace, for the papacy had forfeited the status of a universal mediator. Paul III's aggressive pursuit of his own family interests through military campaigns and other political maneuvers made him nothing more than one among many power brokers. Vasari's fresco, however, glorifies him in part by placing him in the company of the goddess Pax.[17] The personification of peace, along with other allegorical figures rubbing shoulders with historical personages, casts a divine glow on the pope, glossing over his actual modest role in the Peace of Nice and transfiguring him into a universal peacemaker.

The device of personification elevates peace from the level of legal transactions into a supralegal, supernatural realm. The iconography of personified peace was supposed to derive from Roman mythology—a female figure with attributes such as an olive branch, a cornucopia, and a scepter. During the reign of Augustus, Pax, equivalent to the Greek Eirene, was recognized as a goddess, the daughter of Jupiter and Iustitia. In reality, however, there was by no means a consensus on what peace should look like. Cesare Ripa's enormously influential emblem book and iconographic dictionary, *Iconologia* (1595), lists more than a dozen possible visual representations of peace, ranked in terms of their popularity.[18] The one on top of the list— "A young Woman, wing'd and crown'd with Olive and Ears of Corn; a Lion and Lamb together, and setting Fire to Trophies of Arms"— seems to be the most widespread (figure 4).[19] This iconographic diversity testifies to both the need for and the prevalence of peace personifications. Although visual representations of Pax already appeared in the late Middle Ages, for instance in Ambrogio Lorenzetti's *Allegory of Good Government* (1337–40) in the Palazzo Pubblico of Siena, they did not become widespread until the sixteenth century, a time when *pax* came to mean specifically a peace treaty. The allegorical personification of peace responded to and concomitantly overcame the legalization of peace.

In sum, *pax* or "peace" took on the meaning of a legal instrument between sovereign persons during the sixteenth century. At the same time, it remained a normative idea, denoting a lawful order of the world. Normative world order was thus supposed to rest on legal instruments. In the absence of a higher authority that could implement and enforce such legal instruments, allegorical figurations of peace were invented to lend them at least some semblance of normative force. Precisely at the juncture when *pax* took on a legal meaning, it was personified as a goddess—*Pax*. The personification of peace remedied the fragility of peace treaty, elevating it into a noumenal realm.

FIGURE 4. The iconography of peace in the Renaissance.
Reproduced from Cesar Ripa. *Iconologia, or Moral Emblems* (London: Motte, 1709), 54 (fig. 215).

The Founding Narratives of International Legal Personality (Grotius, Hobbes, Leibniz)

Hugo Grotius's *De iure belli ac pacis* (1625) contains perhaps the most famous definition of international law: "But just as the laws of each state have in view the advantages of that state, so by mutual consent it has become possible that certain laws should originate as between all states, or a great many states; and it is apparent that the laws thus originating had in view the advantage, not of particular states, but of the great society of states (*magna universitas*). And this is what is called the law of nations, whenever we distinguish that term from the law of nature."[20] At the heart of the definition is the powerful idea of *magna universitas*—a great international society governed by law. This idea was inspired by the medieval corporation theory, which conceived of a multitude of human beings gathered together in some form as a mystic body—that is, as a fictitious corporate entity perceptible only by the intellect. In the fourteenth century, the Commentators Bartolus and Baldus applied corporation theory to cities and kingdoms.[21] *Universitas* was the term for such a mystic body or corporate entity. Ernst Kantorowicz tells us that *universitas* is a technical term deriving from Roman law, referring to "the corporational collective at large which the early glossators defined as 'a conjunct or collection in one body of a plurality of persons.' On that basis, Bartolus could maintain that 'the whole world is some kind of *universitas*,' not to mention kingdoms and cities. Baldus could define a *populus* as 'a collection of men in one mystical body,' or call a *regnum* 'something total which both in persons and things contains its parts integrally,' or talk briefly about 'some universal person.'" As a multitude of persons treated fictitiously as one body, *universitas* is distinguished "from every natural person endowed with body and soul," and yet treated "juristically as one person."[22]

Grotius's *magna universitas* is a fictitious corporate entity. The adjective *magna*, however, gives it a unique character. It certainly suggests a grand scale. *Magna universitas* is reminiscent of the pronouncement *mundus est universitas quaedam*, "the whole world is some kind of *universitas*," which Bartolus made with regard to the universal reign of the emperor.[23] Perhaps more important, *magna* suggests complexity. *Magna universitas* is a *universitas* comprising a multitude of *universitates*. It means a plurality of states collected in one body, a fictitious corporate entity in which a multitude of fictitious corporate entities are unified. It is thus a fiction to the second power. This uniquely potentiated fiction is crucial to international law. States—fictitious corporate entities treated as juristic persons—are the subjects of international law, while the society of states—*magna universitas*—is nothing other than the community constituted by international law. Fictions are created by means of poetic operations. In the following, we discuss first the poetic operations that bring forth the state as the subject of international law, and then the poetic operations that bring forth the fiction of a law-governed society of states.

Writing in an age when the sovereign state rose as the dominant political form, Grotius applied Roman law to two kinds of legal subjects: individual persons subject to a particular state, and states themselves as corporate persons. He did the former in the so-called Dutch jurisprudence *Inleydinge tot de Hollantsche rechtsgeleertheit* (1631), and the latter in *De jure belli ac pacis*, thereby formulating a system of civil law and a system of international law respectively.[24] To install the fictitious corporate person of the state as the subject of international law involves accounting for the state's relationship to individual persons, as well as to other kinds of fictitious corporate persons either inside or outside itself. This entails two kinds of narrative: narratives of origin that explain the gathering of individual persons into the corporate person of the state, and narratives of recognition that make sense of the relationship between the state and other corporate persons.

Narratives of Origin

As discussed in the previous chapter, Grotius's conception of international law grows out of a new natural law theory. The core of this new natural theory is the postulate of a primeval condition—the state of nature—in which individual persons have to defend their natural rights to life, limb, and property on their own. With a view to "self-protection through mutual aid" and "equal acquisition of the necessities of life," they institute the state "by a general agreement."[25] Such an account of the institution of the state is at once a contractualist theory and a narrative. As a narrative, it places the origin of the state in time: at the beginning of the world, "God, who created all things in the image of His own perfection, created not a state but two human beings"; in the course of time, the number of mankind increased, so that natural power was vested in the heads of households; later on, individuals brought the state into being through a collective agreement in order to protect their rights and secure justice.[26]

In the Grotian narrative, the state turns out to be no fixed entity, but rather something unfinished, still in the making. First of all, the natural rights of the individual, including individuals' right to exercise their own natural rights, may continue to be in force after the establishment of the state. In *De Indis*, Grotius argues that "whatever there was of law at the world's beginning, prior to the establishment of states, must necessarily have continued to exist afterwards among those human beings who did not set up courts for themselves, and for whom [. . .] 'might is the measure of right.' "[27] He proceeds to suggest that this is still the case among some peoples of the present day. Even though "the license which was prevalent before the establishment of courts has been greatly restricted [. . .], there are circumstances under which such license even now holds good, that is, undoubtedly, where judicial procedure ceases to be available." Judicial procedure is suspended temporarily "when one cannot wait to refer a matter to a judge without certain danger or loss." It can also be continuously unavailable either in law or in fact: "in law, if one finds himself in places without inhabitants, as on the sea, in a wilderness, or on vacant islands, or in any other places where there is no state; in fact, if those who are subject to jurisdiction do not heed the judge, or if the judge has openly refused to take cognizance."[28] The de facto dissolution of existing jurisdiction happens in times of civil unrest, rebellion or simply general chaos.

If the natural rights of the individual persist in vestigial forms after the establishment of the state, the authority of the state may, conversely, be resisted and even actively combated by its subjects in certain circumstances. "As a general rule," Grotius stresses, "rebellion is not permitted."[29] This rule, however, tacitly leaves open the possibility of resistance in cases where the state authority fails to perform its agreed-upon function of maintaining public tranquility. Indeed, Grotius lists a wide range of circumstances in which the right of resistance may be conceded. For instance, one may resist a king who alienates the kingdom or otherwise turns against the whole people. One may also resist a king who transgresses the conditions of his exercise of power in some way. Above all, one may resist a usurper of sovereign power. In all these cases, active resistance returns the state to the moment of its founding.

In Grotius's narrative of origin, mankind has departed from its primeval natural condition and established the state but is unable to leave behind entirely the natural condition, while the state already established runs the risk of dissolving through the active resistance of its subjects. The transition from the natural condition to the state has not yet been completed and can never be so. The state as the subject of international law is thus no fixed corporate entity, but something still and always in the making.

Grotius was not merely a great jurist, but also a poet. His tragedy *Sophompaneas* (1635), published ten years after *De jure belli ac pacis*, figures the transition from the natural condition to the state by means of a dramatic plot. The play is based on the story of Joseph and his brothers told in Genesis 44–45, the only biblical story that, according to Grotius and his fellow humanists, lends itself to tragic treatment, as it contains the two elements considered crucial to a tragic plot in the Aristotelian poetics: "recognition by surprise and sudden reversal of prospects."[30] The problem of international law is inscribed in the poetic form that Grotius gives to the biblical story. The chorus is made up of Ethiopian women in Egypt, who comment on the issues concerning mankind in general. The plot climaxes at exactly the midpoint of the drama—the third act in the five-act drama—with a rebellion in the country and the sale of free men to foreign princes by the rebels. Rebellion and slavery fall within the ambit of the law of nations. Most important, the dramatic plot as a whole enacts the making of the Hebrew people as a legal person in international law. The beginning is the natural condition in which brothers, following the law of nature, care for one another. With regard to Judah's concern for his little brother Benjamin, Joseph's steward says, "This law applies everywhere and does not need to be inscribed on cedar tablets, or on brass or marble; it is written in our hearts by the hand of the Father of us all, and whoever flees this law is in fact running away from himself; even wild animals care for their kindred."[31] The end of the play predicts a time in the future when the Hebrew people will become a sovereign nation and enter into a lawful relation to Egypt. Joseph asks the pharaoh to harbor his brothers and prophesies: "Rich land of Egypt, you will not lack proper rewards for having given refuge to the Hebrews. [. . .] In future time famous kings born of our stock will maintain a league with Memphis and the heir to the throne of Israel will be born of an Egyptian mother."[32] With such a beginning and end, the plot of *Sophompaneas* recasts the events narrated in Genesis 44–45—the missing cup, Judah pleading for Benjamin, and Joseph making himself known to his brothers—as a story of the transition from the natural personhood of Joseph and his brothers towards the international legal personality of the Hebrew people.[33]

Thomas Hobbes reconceived the narrative of the origin of the sovereign state as the subject of international law. As is well known, Hobbes's speculative account of the institution of the state is premised on the fiction of the state of nature as a state of war, "and such a warre, as is of every man, against every man," a war in which all men have a natural right to all things.[34] In order to get out of this hateful state of war and to live in peace and security, men have no other choice but enter into an agreement to give up their natural right to all things, transferring it to one man or an assembly, and authorizing this man or assembly to act on behalf of them. The multitude thus united in one fictitious corporate person is a commonwealth or civil state. The civil state puts an end to wars among its subjects, quashing civil strife and enforcing domestic peace, but by no means does it end war as such. Through its institution, the right of war is merely transferred from "every particular man" to the one person who represents all: the sovereign person.[35] The sovereign henceforth finds himself in the state of nature vis-à-vis other sovereign persons. The law between sovereign persons is called the law of nations—that is, international law.[36] But since the sovereign persons coexist side by side in the state of nature, international law is nothing other than the law of nature.

Whereas in the Grotian narrative the making of the state as the subject of international law is never completed and thus unfolds in an eternal present, in the Hobbesian narrative it has been irrevocably completed and can be considered to have taken place in the mythic past. But the Hobbesian narrative is bound to the present in its own way. In the dedication of his treatise *De Cive* (1642) to William Earl of Devonshire, Hobbes writes with reference to Pontius Telesinus, the leader of the Samnites during the Social War against Rome's domination of Italy,

> As he reviewed the ranks of his army in the battle against Sulla at the Colline Gate, he cried that Rome itself must be demolished and destroyed, remarking that there would never be an end to *Wolves* preying upon the liberty of Italy, unless the forest in which they took refuge was cut down. There are two maxims which are surely both true: Man is a God to man, and Man is a wolf to Man. The former is true of the relations of citizens with each other, the latter of relations between commonwealths. In justice and charity, the virtues of peace, citizens show some likeness to God. But between commonwealths, the wickedness of bad men compels the good too to have recourse, for their own protection, to the virtues of war, which are violence and fraud, i.e. to the predatory nature of beasts.[37]

Inside the civil state there is peace, and man is truly man, the image of God. Between states, by contrast, there is war, and one man preys upon the other like a beast. The anecdote of Pontius Telesinus, along with the notorious metaphor "Man is a wolf to Man," makes it clear that Hobbes's conception of the state of nature as a state of permanent war is based on his observations about international relations. These observations were partly gained through study of ancient history. As a student of Thucydides, whose *History of the Peloponnesian War* he translated and published in 1629, Hobbes knew all too well about the "violence and fraud" that dictated the rivalry between Athens and Sparta, indeed among all Greek cities, regardless of what internal constitution they happened to have.[38] They were also gained through contemporary history, particularly through the experience of the Thirty Years' War.[39] The reality of unceasing wars among European states stands as a model for the fictitious state of nature. On the other hand, however, the fictitious state of nature provides the starting point for Hobbes's construction of the civil state as the sovereign person that ensures peace among individual persons but is embroiled in permanent war with other sovereign persons. This conception of the civil state implies a picture of international relations that corresponds uncannily to the empirical reality of seventeenth-century Europe.[40] The Hobbesian narrative of the transition from the state of nature to the civil state thus has a circular structure.

In sum, Grotius and Hobbes offer two rather different narratives of the origin of the state as the subject of international law. In Grotius's narrative, the institution of the state is an incomplete, unfolding process, always haunted by, and at the risk of dissolving into, individual persons in the state of nature. In Hobbes's narrative, by contrast, the institution of the state has been completed once and for all, but it at once presupposes and entails an international state of nature. These two narratives underpin two distinctive traditions in international law, which we can label as Grotian and Hobbesian respectively. In the Grotian tradition, individual persons may have agency and standing in international law, claiming their natural rights vis-à-vis the state as the predominant international legal person, because they have not yet been and can never been entirely incorporated into the state.[41] Associated with the idea that some rights and obligations were directly attributed to the individual in the international legal order, the Grotian tradition in international law has been often invoked to stand for the ideals of pacifism, human rights, and limited national sovereignty.[42] The Hobbesian tradition, by contrast, is that of the deniers of international law. Acknowledging only the state as an international legal person and insisting on its sovereignty, this tradition sees as little legal order in the international world as in the state of nature prior to the institution of the state.[43] International anomie serves as both the evidence and the conclusion of its arguments.

Narratives of Recognition

If international law has the sovereign state as its main subject, how does it in this capacity relate to other juristic persons? Is the sovereign state the only recognized juristic person in international law, or are there other juristic persons as well? If juristic persons share some but not all characteristics of a sovereign state, do they have standing in international law? If so, to what extent? In the seventeenth century, Grotius's doctrine of divisible sovereignty and Leibniz's doctrine of relative sovereignty contributed most to raising as well as answering such questions. Grotius and Leibniz formulated their respective doctrines in arguing for specific legal cases—the case of the capture of the Portuguese merchantman *Santa Catarina* in the Strait of Singapore by a Dutch captain in 1603, and the case of the rejection of the Duke of Braunschweig-Lüneburg's bid for sending a plenipotentiary to the Peace Congress of Nijmegen in 1676. As we know, trial advocates must not only master legal rules but also tell stories in constructing their cases. Their success depends very much on the plausibility and persuasiveness of the story that they tell before the court.[44] In arguing for their respective cases, Grotius and Leibniz also told stories. In a regular court case, it is determined in advance who the involved persons are, so storytelling usually revolves around actions—developing a consistent positions on disputed actions, harmonizing them with undisputed actions, and arranging all of the actions in a plausible plot. The stories told by Grotius and Leibniz, by contrast, turn primarily on determining who the involved persons are. They begin by constructing a large cast of juristic persons and bringing them into a complex web of relationships. Only on this basis do they proceed to select events, attribute them to actors, and arrange them in a specific order. By means of storytelling, Grotius and Leibniz came to define the concept of international legal personality.

Grotius's Defense in the Case of the Seizure of the *Santa Catarina*

In the case of the seizure of the *Santa Catarina*, Grotius's general defense strategy is to frame it as a matter for international law. By the time the incident in the Strait of Singapore took place, the Low Countries had been at war with their Spanish overlords for over thirty years, while Portugal had been joined to Spain through the union of the crowns since 1580. After setting out a series of juridical principles—including a new natural law theory and a theory of just war borrowed from the Neoscholastic jurists of the enemy country Spain—Grotius announces, "Let's turn our attention to the facts of the particular case under discussion." As befits a good lawyer beholden to the formulae of forensic rhetoric, he avows, "I will not record anything in this connexion that I myself have not found to be confirmed by the clearest testimony." Yet at the same time he allows himself considerable freedom in the narrative reconstruction of the case: "We do not feel, however, that it is necessary to give an account of every event leading up to in one way or another to the seizure in question."[45] This opening caveat captures the tendentious tenor of his narrative discourse, indeed the narrative discourse of advocates in general: it selects some events, leaves out others, lends inflection and intention to the events by arranging them in a certain sequence and presenting them from a certain perspective.[46]

Especially worth emphasizing about Grotius's narrative, however, is something else—the attribution of events to legal persons. Grotius's defense narrative is divided into two main parts: a brief chronicle of the Dutch rebellion against their Spanish overlords since 1567, and an account of the

Dutch-Portuguese trading rivalry in the East Indies. The chronicle of the Dutch rebellion reads like an abbreviated, pointedly moralizing version of his *Annales et Historiæ de Rebus Belgicis*, a history of the rebellion in the Tacitist mode (completed in 1612). As is typical of a narrative of conflict, Grotius's chronicle turns on recognition, in this case the recognition of Holland as an international legal person. Holland, the narrator asserts, is a state: "Any perfect community is (so to speak) a true state. [. . .] So, too, the domain of Holland in itself constitutes a whole state."[47] As such, it is invested with certain functions of sovereign power, although it certainly does not have all the functions of sovereign power united in itself, for it is, along with the other provinces of the Low Countries, subject to the Spanish king. For Grotius, sovereignty is divisible, liable to be distributed among several legal persons: "actus summæ potestatis divisi esse possunt penes diversos."[48] Every legal person seeks to be recognized for those functions of sovereign power due to it. If it finds itself not duly recognized, a conflict ensues. It may declare war, thus asserting its standing at international law. For example, the states of the Low Countries revolted when they saw the functions of sovereign power due to them violated by Duke Alba who, sent out as governor by King Philip II in 1567, "proceeded to alter the laws, judicial provisions, and system of taxation."[49] The crux of the matter, of course, is that there is no commonly acknowledged superior authority to decide who is entitled to what functions of sovereign power. It is up to each person to stake its claims and to fight for its recognition. War is inevitable. Furthermore, "whoever undertakes a just war in defense of a mark of sovereignty which lies within his competence also acquires the other marks."[50] The belligerent struggle for recognition leads to the redistribution of sovereign power among different parties, creating an imbalance that is bound to provoke a new struggle for recognition, and thus *ad infinitum*. The subject of international law is thus not a person on whom sovereign power is bestowed once and for all, but one constantly in quest for sovereign power. The chronicle turns out to be the most suitable narrative form for this unending quest.

Against the background of the ongoing war between the Dutch and the Spanish, Grotius proceeds to give an account of the Dutch-Portuguese commercial rivalry in the East Indies, which represents the immediate context for the capture of the *Santa Catarina*. The actors in this part of the narrative are Dutch merchants, Portuguese merchants, and local rulers of all stripes. Merchants are actually private persons. By means of an elaborate theory of legal personality, however, Grotius turns the cutthroat trading rivalry in the East Indies into a theater of war that mirrors the one unfolding in the Low Countries. First, he defines private persons—the merchants—as the agents of public persons such as the state and the magistracy. The war that a state wages to exercise its rights is a public war governed by international law. As subjects of the state, private persons are instrumental to public wars: "Public wars are justly waged by a state or a magistrate in accordance with his rank, both in conjunction with an allied state or allied magistrate, and through the agency of subjects."[51] Second, the merchants act on behalf of a private company—Verenigde Oostindische Campagnie—which, in turn, acts on behalf of the state or the magistracy. As a corporate person, a private company is the subject of the state. But when a private company operates beyond the border of a state and comes into contact with other states, magistrates, subjects or companies, it has the status of a sovereign voluntary agent: "The law of nations [. . .] places public bodies and private companies in the same categories."[52] The Dutch merchants are thus doubly agents of the States Assembly of Holland allied with the other provinces of the Low Countries. As such, they may forge alliances and sign treaties with local rulers in Asia. By the same token, the Portuguese merchants are agents of Portugal, as well as of Spain due to the union of crowns between the two countries. With legal personality thus defined, the commercial rivalry between Dutch and Portuguese merchants, triangulated by the local rulers, appears to be part of the ongoing war between the Low Countries and Spain, albeit fought in another hemisphere. Consequently, the Dutch capture of the *Santa Catarina* is a legitimate act of war. In sum, Grotius's defense of this incident implicates a large cast of voluntary agents in international law—states invested with varying functions of sovereign power, but also magistrates, subjects, and private companies. The narrative figuration of characters and events determines what act is an international legal act, and what person is an international legal person.

Leibniz's Defense in the Case of the Rejection of the Duke of Braunschweig-Lüneburg

In the case of the rejection of the duke of Braunschweig-Lüneburg's bid for sending an envoy to the Peace Congress of Nijmegen, Leibniz frames the juristic question as "whether German princes have the right to send ambassadors as their representatives, and whether the same honor should be given to them as the ambassadors of kings, Italian princes and electors."[53] It is a question about diplomatic recognition. To begin with, Leibniz develops a general theory of the legal personality of the state. For Hobbes and Pufendorf, the state is an absolute and unitary authority. Any political community that fails to conform to this conception is no more than "an Irregular Body" or "some mis-shapen Monster."[54] In Leibniz's eyes, the Hobbesian-Pufendorfian sovereign state simply does not exist in reality, "neither among the civilized peoples of Europe nor among barbarians."[55] It is a mere figment born of a speculative narrative of origin, which Hobbes constructs on the basis of the fiction of the state of nature.[56] In opposition to Hobbes and Pufendorf, Leibniz proposes to consider the personality and the actions of the state on the basis of historical records. This approach enables him to conceive of sovereignty as relative. The basic level of sovereignty, for Leibniz, is territorial hegemony, the power of a territorial lord "to obtain from his subjects, either by his dignity or, when necessary, by *force majeure*, whatever rights to remain his." The next level is supremacy, the status of holding a larger territory being recognized by "the other major powers, and by the lords of lands and peoples and the masters of human affairs, as brothers and persons of equal condition.[57] Supremacy enables a territorial lord to engage in transactions in international law—peace, war, treaties—thus making him an international legal person. In an argument that lays the foundation for a federalist theory, Leibniz states, "Several territories, moreover, can unite into one body, with the territorial hegemony of each preserved intact. We have ready examples of this in the Empire, in the Swiss body, and in the United Provinces."[58] That is to say, a territorial lord with the status of supremacy may well owe allegiance to a higher authority, as is the case with the German princes and even electors vis-à-vis the emperor.[59] Finally, sovereignty in the sense of supremacy is to be distinguished from majesty, a status accorded to kings and emperors: "Majesty is the right to command without being liable to be commanded by any other person whatsoever, whereas sovereignty is a legitimate power to constrain the subjects to obey without being liable to be constrained except by a war."[60]

Leibniz's theory of relative sovereignty postulates a continuum of corporate persons in the political world, ranging from princes with mere territorial hegemony, through princes with supremacy, to kings and emperors with majesty. The status of supremacy is defined as the threshold to recognition and inclusion in the international community. This theory leads to the concept of international legal personality: "He possesses a personality in international law (*personam juris gentium*) who represents the public liberty, such that he is not subject to the tutelage or the power of anyone else, but has in himself the power of war and of alliances; although he may perhaps be limited by the bonds of obligation towards a superior and owe him homage, fidelity and obedience."[61] For Leibniz, then, not only sovereign states that acknowledge no superior (such as France) are subjects of international law, but also states that do acknowledge a superior (such as a German principality), as well as supranational bodies such as the Holy Roman Empire.

The exposition of legal doctrines, of course, makes up only one part of a lawyerly argument. The other part is the narrative construction of the case. Leibniz's theoretical elaboration of the doctrine of relative sovereignty goes hand in hand with a historical narrative of Europe since the time of Charlemagne. It is a narrative of the origin and development of German princes that concludes with proving their right of supremacy.[62] A German prince, according to this narrative, not only has all the rights and power necessary for maintaining his authority over his subjects—territorial hegemony—but his rights also extend beyond the borders of his territory, even beyond the territories of the empire, including the rights of war and peace, alliance, military exercises, reprisal, in short, all the rights pertaining to the law of nations. German princes thus belong to the international community. At the same time, Leibniz's historical narrative is also a narrative of the law of nations in general, featuring the German princes in its vast cast of characters. Some rights pertaining to the law of nations arise from the rational principles "recognized generally in all times" or "from the custom introduced in our time among civilized peoples."[63] But "it is not necessary that this be the agreement of all peoples or for all times; for there have been many cases in which one thing was considered right in India and another in Europe, and even among us it has changed with the passage of centuries."[64] Accordingly, a historical narrative is needed to ascertain these rights. Leibniz's narrative of the law of nations turns out to be one that grants legal standing to the German princes in addition to other persons such as kings and emperors.

In Leibniz's apologia for the rights of German princes, the theoretical exposition of legal doctrine and the narrative construction of the case prove ultimately to be one and the same operation. The theory of relative sovereignty is based on putative historical records, as opposed to the ahistorical construction of the sovereign state by Hobbes and Pufendorf. These historical records also provide the evidences for the case to which the doctrine is supposed to be applied. The case is inscribed in the doctrine, while the doctrine is built for the case. As a whole, Leibniz's defense of the status of German princes as international legal persons showcases the symbolic operations accompanying the induction of a new person into an existing community: narrating this person's life with a view to proving his suitability for the community, and reconceiving the constitutive principles underlying the community to accommodate the membership of a new person. Reconceiving the principles of a community, in turn, entails narration, as the community revisits its past to construct a new identity for itself.

The issue of international legal personality has become more and more important in our own time, as various non-state actors have entered the international stage. Some jurists reserve international personality exclusively for states, some hold that non-state entities can acquire international personality if states recognize them, some see all effective actors in international relations as relevant to the international legal system, and, last but not least, there is the formal conception of international legal personality, according to which whoever is the addressee of the norms of international law is also an international person.[65] To recognize or not to recognize an entity as an international legal person is a fundamentally political gesture.[66] This is also true of the formative period of international law: Grotius granted international legal standing to whomever furthered the cause of the Dutch in their rebellion against their Spanish overlords, and Leibniz sought to promote minor German princes in European politics. Political gestures are often bolstered by stories. Behind every international legal person—a *persona* or mask—there is also a story, or rather multiple stories. In the Grotian story, international legal personality is forged in the crucible of political struggles. In principle, all persons and corporate entities may assume an international legal personality if they are engaged in political struggles beyond the border of a particular state, but they may also lose it if they are subjugated and absorbed into other entities during such struggles. Such a story advocates flexible political and legal arrangements in world affairs. The Leibnizian story sets greater store by existing political institutions than political struggles, allowing historically established political entities with varying degrees of sovereignty all to play a role in world affairs. It advocates a multilateral and multilayered pluralism.

The Founding Narratives of International Society (Grotius, Leibniz)

International legal persons—mostly fictitious corporate persons or *universitates*—gather together to form an international society or *magna universitas*. Grotius's *De jure belli ac pacis*, in which the notion of *magna universitas* is broached, develops a system of international law by applying Roman law to states as legal subjects, dealing with persons, property, and obligations in international society. The legal constitution of international society rests upon narratives of origin. Chief among them is the narrative of the emergence of property. According to this narrative, the world has departed from its primeval condition in which humankind shared the bounty of nature in common. It has been moving towards the condition of private property without, however, ever being able to reach an end. The world is caught in an endless transition. The law-governed international society thus signifies a new world order—new not only in the sense that it is different from previous models of order, but above all in the sense that it is an order that ceaselessly renews itself.

For Leibniz, the world is populated by rather heterogeneous corporate persons. Some of them are limited by bonds of obligation to a superior (for instance, German princes), some are not (for instance, the king of France). Some are states, some (like the Holy Roman Empire) are more like federations of states. Some of these corporate persons may merge into one person, for instance when a few territories are absorbed into a larger one. Some others may become extinct.[67] Leibniz does not have a system of legal doctrines to offer for the international world in the manner of *De jure belli ac pacis*, but there is never a doubt that justice, defined by him as "charity of the wise" or "universal benevolence," must also govern international persons.[68] It is on the level of metaphysics that he sets out the principles for the constitution of international society. Concerned, among other things, with the nature of the body and with how various bodies make up the universe, Leibniz's metaphysics offers what he calls a great "poem of the universe." It is also a poem of international society.

Grotius's Narrative of the Emergence of Property

Property is the crux of Grotius's natural and international law, for he deems the right to acquire, retain, and defend property to be a fundamental principle of nature, applicable to individuals and states alike. A narrative sustains this conception of property: at the beginning of the world, human beings share everything in common; the enjoyment of the universal right over things is constrained only by the condition that "whatever each had thus taken for his own needs another could not take from him except by an unjust act"; in the course of time, people become less and less satisfied with the simple and innocent life, as they gain more knowledge and pursue various kinds of arts; mutual affection gives way to rivalry and ambition; the increasing "lack of justice and kindness" militates against common ownership as well; as a result, things become subject to private ownership by means of "a kind of agreement, either expressed, as by division, or implied, as by occupation."[69]

Grotius's narrative of the emergence of property right from common ownership draws on a key doctrine of the ancient tradition of natural law. For Cicero, "nature has brought forth the common ownership of all things [. . .] for men's joint use," while "private possessions" are "designated by statutes and by civil law."[70] This doctrine is reiterated in *Decretum Gratiani* and *Summa Theologica*.[71] Grotius resorts to the ancient natural-law doctrine of common ownership, however, to draw an opposite conclusion. Whereas the ancient tradition deems common ownership to lie in the nature of things and private property to be imposed by positive laws, Grotius attempts to prove that private property is a matter of natural law as well. While concurring with the ancients that in distant days all things were at the disposal of mankind at large, he argues, "It is evident, however, that the present-day concept of distinctions in ownership was the result, not of any sudden transition, but of a gradual process whose initial steps were taken under the guidance of nature herself." Many things, he points out, are consumed by use, either in the sense that they admit of no further use after being consumed by one person or in the sense that they are less fit for additional service. Such consumption represents the first step towards private ownership. Later this basic concept is extended "by a logical process" to other movable as well as immovable things, either because the use of such things is indirectly bound up with consumption, or because these things are not sufficient for indiscriminate use by all.[72] Furthermore, things become subject to private ownership by a voluntary act of agreement, which can either take the form of division or occupation. Rooted as it is in a physical act of attachment, this process is a natural one. The forces that propel it—the human desire to lead "a more refined mode of life" as well as the ensuing erosion of "justice and kindness"—arise from the course of nature. Consequently, the law established on this matter "was patterned after nature's plan" as well.[73] It is a dictate of the law of nature that everyone should be allowed to acquire and retain property, and that no one may seize possession of that which has already been taken into the possession of another. Whoever takes away another person's property must return it or face punishment. The natural order is a lawful order of property relations.

At first glance, Grotius's narrative of the transition from common ownership to private property resembles the narrative of world ages that has been told since the very beginning of European literature. Hesiod's *Works and Days* (eighth century BCE) tells of the first race of men in the Golden Age when there was no toil, no misery, no old age, and no property. This idyllic state declines. Humankind goes through the Silver and Bronze Ages until it reaches the Iron Age in the present. Amid the general toil and misery, the present Iron Age needs to "hearken to Right"—that is, property right.[74] Ovid's retelling of the Hesiodic narrative makes this explicit. Whereas in the

Golden Age men shared the bounty of nature in common, the Iron Age witnesses the birth of property:

> And on the ground, common till then and free
> As air and sunlight, far across the fields
> By careful survey boundaries were marked.[75]

As similar to the Hesiodic and Ovidian narratives as it may seem, the Grotian narrative relates the beginning of time to the present time in such a way as to create an entirely different temporal structure. The transition from the Golden Age to the Iron Age is a steady decline, with the Silver and Bronze Ages being traversed in between. The Grotian narrative gets rid of all the intermediate stages of time, so that only the beginning and the present remain. With only two points left on its trajectory, time loses direction. Grotius makes no attempt to envision any third point—such as a possible future condition—from which to determine the direction of time. In his narrative, time seems instead to circle fitfully back and forth between a putative beginning and the present.

According to the Grotian narrative, common ownership at the beginning of time continues into the present in vestigial forms, as can be seen, for instance, in people living in "extreme simplicity," as in "certain tribes in America," and in communities based on affection as exemplified by "a goodly number who live an ascetic life."[76] More important, certain things in the world cannot become subject to private ownership. The prime example is the ocean, which resists occupation and possession, for it is so inexhaustible as to suffice for any possible use by all peoples, for instance, for drawing water, fishing, and sailing. It also resists division, as no boundaries can be drawn on it. This view, formulated initially to justify the Dutch forays into Asia and to combat the Portuguese monopoly of the Asian trade, developed later into the famous "free sea" doctrine.[77] Furthermore, certain things that are capable of being occupied or in fact have been occupied nonetheless suffice for general use by other persons without detriment to the owner. This gives rise to the right of innocent use, for example the use of running water and passage over land and river. Therefrom Grotius extrapolates the right of free travel and migration. As vestigial forms of the common, things not capable of being owned, as well as things capable of being owned but susceptible of innocent use, perform an important function for private ownership. They serve as the medium through which men can access the still unoccupied things in remote areas—the so-called *res nullius*—in order to occupy them, divide them, and turn them into private property. They also serve as the medium through which men can travel to other men in order to trade their property with one another. Without such a medium, men would be tethered to their necessarily limited possessions, leaving a great share of the vast store of nature forever unoccupied, forgoing the enjoyment of novel properties, and mired in a perpetual stasis. The vestigial forms of the common actually represent the enabling conditions for private property.

There is yet another vestigial form of the common, which has a quite different, indeed an opposite, effect on private property. It is the reversion to common ownership under extraordinary circumstances: "In direst need the primitive right of user revives, as if community of ownership had remained, since in respect to all human laws—the law of ownership included—supreme necessity seems to have been excepted."[78] Necessity suspends the right of property and resuscitates common ownership. The concept of necessity is an integral part of the discourse of reason of state. By invoking necessity, then, Grotius leaves the right of property in the international arena at the mercy of reason of state.

The vestigial forms of the common indicate that the beginning of time is by no means irretrievably lost but persists in the present, either enabling private property or suspending it. Conversely, the present time exists already in an embryonic form in the beginning. Grotius agrees with Hesiod and Ovid as well as with ancient natural law theorists that the bounty of nature is originally given to men in common, but he contends that men could not enjoy all that nature has to offer unless they traded readily available products: "Owing to the fact that the distances separating different regions prevented men from using many of the goods desirable for human life [. . .], passage to and fro was found to be a necessity."[79] Geographical proximity to things creates a primordial form of property. One man gives products in his own region to another man in the expectation that the other would give him products from his own region. Exchange, then, actually represents the precondition for common ownership. By the same token, commerce in the age of private property enables men to enjoy a share in many, if not all, things, so that "one person's lack might be remedied by means of another person's surplus."[80] For this reason, Grotius passionately defends free trade as a practice in conformity with, indeed dictated by, nature. Through free trade, private ownership paradoxically carries out the plan of nature to give all things to all men, always approximating, if never entirely restoring, common ownership.

Common ownership continues to be in force in the present time of private property, while private property strives, by means of free trade, towards common ownership that putatively existed at the beginning of time. In Grotius's narrative, the transition from common to private ownership has not yet been, and can never be, completed. Private ownership is haunted by the specter of common ownership that either serves as the enabling condition for acquiring new properties or suspends property rights in case of necessity, so that it can be said to be still in the making. At the same time, it pursues no purpose beyond itself, which would complete its making. By insisting on the capacity of commerce for making all things accessible to all people, Grotius seems to hold up common ownership as the end of private ownership, but the restoration of a golden age or abolition of private property in the future is certainly out of the question. This means that property rights are not a matter settled once and for all, but one constantly subject to challenge and contestation. It is therefore no accident that Grotius's discussion of property rights is bound up with his discussion of the right to war. War is a means of defending one's right to property in case it is challenged and contested. A settlement—peace—is always a temporary condition followed by new conflicts and hence new wars.

As a fundamental principle of the natural order, property rights apply to both the individual and the state. If the subject of rights is the state, the natural order takes the form of international order. As discussed in the previous section, Grotius conceives of the state as a liminal condition as well: Mankind has departed from its primeval natural condition and established the civil state without being able to leave behind entirely the natural condition, while the civil state already established runs the risk of reverting to natural condition through the active resistance of its subjects. Just like the transition from common ownership to private property, the transition from the natural condition to the civil state has not yet been completed, and can never be so. Both the narrative of the emergence of property and that of the emergence of the civil state portray the human world as caught up in an eternal in-between condition without offering any prospect of an end. The world depicted by Grotius is devoid of any transcendent purpose. Yet it is relentlessly dynamic in its radical immanence, as neither private property nor the state is a stable condition, but both are constantly in the making, constantly emerging.

Grotius's application of Roman law to states as legal subjects thus constructs a law-governed international society or an international legal order, and the twin narratives he deploys to explicate this legal order make it appear volatile and open-ended, with the instability of the state and the uncertainty of property rights magnifying and aggravating each other. The practical implications of the twin narratives are obvious: the one narrative performs the function of propagating global free trade as well as colonization, while the other narrative advocates flexible political arrangements and individual natural rights in the international arena.[81] Such implications hold great appeal to proponents of liberal internationalism in the twentieth and twenty-first centuries. Theoretically, Grotius's narratives raise a fundamental question regarding international legal order: is it possible at all to speak of order without postulating an end? Thomas Aquinas spoke of a twofold order: the order of creatures in relation to one another, and the order of creatures towards God. It is only through their ordered relation to a divine end that creatures can have an ordered relation to one another. Without an end, the relations of things or of persons could never stabilize into an order. There would be at most an endless process of ordering.

Leibniz's "Poem of the Universe"

Following in the footsteps of medieval jurists—references to Bartolus and Baldus are frequent—and like many political-legal theorists of his own century, Leibniz used the metaphor of the body to figure political communities, conceiving of them as fictitious corporate persons.[82] For him, there are multifarious political bodies or corporate persons, and they relate to one another in a variety of ways. Joined together, they constitute the political universe, or what we might call international society. Leibniz's account of international society is of a narrative nature: the diverse corporate persons make up a vast cast of characters; they are motivated by an internal force to interact with one another; they relate to each other and to the whole political universe from their respective perspectives, and their relations unfold in time and space, forming various sequences and patterns. In the firm belief that all the entangled relations eventually cohere into a well-ordered whole, the philosopher-narrator even pinpoints the generic identity of this narrative: it is a romance.

The principles as well as the narrative structure underlying the constitution of the political universe as imagined by Leibniz can be extrapolated from his metaphysical speculations on the nature of body. To understand the conception of body in Leibniz's metaphysics, we must begin with the more fundamental concept of substance, for a body is essentially an assemblage of substances. Substances are either simple or composite, with "simple" meaning "without parts."[83] The composite is a collection of simple substances. A simple substance is called a monad. Every monad is essentially different from every other monad. Defined as such, the monad is the individual in the strictest sense of the term. It is the soul. Because each monad is different from all others, it stands, by virtue of an internal force, in dynamic relations with others, incorporating and representing them within itself, thereby undergoing changes all the time. The differential relation of a monad to others is called perception. Perceptions differ in terms of degrees of clarity and distinctness. In fact, there is an infinite continuum from the weakest, most obscure, and most confused small perceptions (for instance, dreamless slumber) to the strongest, most lucid, most distinct consciousness. Perceptions change in time, as one perception passes into another by virtue of an internal force. Through the constantly changing perceptions that take in a multiplicity of substances, every monad represents and expresses the entire universe: "Each simple substance has relationships which express all the others, and [. . .] it is therefore a perpetual living mirror of the universe."[84] Because every monad is different, its representation of the universe is necessarily perspectival.

A body is an assemblage of substances held together through perceptions. Since perception is nothing other than a differential relation, and since there is an infinite continuum of different perceptions, a body can be measured by means of calculus. Leibniz is known to have independently invented calculus at the same time as Isaac Newton. But it is important to note that Leibniz was opposed to the mechanistic natural philosophy espoused by both Newton and Hobbes (his opposition to the Hobbesian political philosophy proves to have metaphysical roots). Since simple substances or monads are souls, a body as an assemblage of substances "has some resemblance to a soul."[85] In *Monadology* (1714), Leibniz adds a touch of poetic vivacity to this metaphysical theorem: "Every portion of matter can be thought of as a garden full of plants, or as a pond full of fish."[86]

Particularly intriguing—and particularly relevant to political philosophy—is Leibniz's conception of an organic body. An assemblage of substances makes up an organic or living body, insofar as they are informed or organized by one particular monad. The monad that provides the formative vital principle can be said to have a body, and the assemblage of substances can be said to belong to this monad. A body has many parts, or organs. These parts are not merely related to the dominant soul to which they together belong, but they are also related to one another. Each part, in turn, consists of many smaller parts that belong to one dominant monad on a lower level and are simultaneously related to one another. In fact, the infinite number of monads that make up a body are organized by and thus belong to a dominant monad on an infinite number of levels.

Leibniz's conception of an organic body offers the blueprint of a political theory. The very concept of substance has a moral-political significance, for—to quote a Leibniz scholar—"without (naturally immortal) substance or persons there can be no moral concepts, no 'subjects' of universal justice, no 'citizens' of the divine monarchy or City of God."[87] More important, perhaps, the metaphysical conception of an organic body as an assemblage of monads belonging to a dominant monad can double as a theory of the political body. Isn't the political body a collection of individual persons organized by and belonging to a dominant person? The political body can be especially likened to a human body—that is, a body that belongs to an intelligent monad or mind. The mind to which the political body belongs is the prince. Just as an organic body is organized on an infinite number of levels, with its parts on every level possessing crowds of monads, a political body is organized on many levels as well, comprising a multiplicity of constituencies—estates, consociations, and all kinds of communities. In contrast to Hobbes and Pufendorf who conceive of the political body in terms of the direct relationship of domination between the sovereign person and individual subjects, Leibniz allows for multifarious intermediate bodies between the prince and individual subjects. He even offers a classification of different societies or communities (*divisio societatum*).[88] In this sense, Leibniz advocated a more traditional way of thinking about the political body that corresponded to the reality of the Holy Roman Empire. Finally, just as every human body is different from every other human body, political bodies in Leibniz's conception differ from one another in terms of size, constitution, and power. Leibniz's theory of relative sovereignty, for instance, explains the differences in power and rank among principalities, kingdoms, as well as other political bodies.

Since monads are all connected by perception, bodies as assemblages of monads are also interlinked. They form, through infinite linkages, the universe. By the same token, political bodies are interlinked and form the political universe or what Grotius called *magna universitas*. In fact, Leibniz's metaphysics culminates in a political theory. Among all the monads, those endowed with the faculty of reason stand out. They are also called intelligent souls or minds. Already in the first systematic account of his metaphysics, Leibniz speaks of intelligent souls being "the citizens of the republic of the universe, of which God is the monarch."[89] Later on, he employs an Augustinian term: "The totality of all minds must make up the City of God—the most perfect possible state, under the most perfect of monarchs."[90] As a monad, the mind always has a body that belongs to it. Since the body belonging to a mind is, in turn, interconnected with all other bodies, the republic of the universe or the City of God can be realized only through the government of bodies in time and space. In Gilles Deleuze's words, "We are dealing with two cities, a celestial Jerusalem and an earthly one, but with the rooftops and foundation of a same city, and the two floors of a same house."[91] The celestial city is folded within the earthly one, insofar as the minds that make up the former are present in the latter in their capacity as the dominant monads to which bodies—crowds of monads—belong. The earthly city, therefore, is a conglomerate of collective bodies informed by distinctive minds. In other words, we can say that it is a conglomerate of political bodies. It is the international world.

Leibniz sees the government of bodies in time and space—the earthly city—as a romance. As will be discussed in detail in chapter 4, Leibniz was an avid reader of political romances and followed closely the romance production of his employer Duke Anton Ulrich von Braunschweig-Lüneburg. A romance creates maximum confusion in its plot in order to reach the denouement at the end. The republic of the universe or the City of God is perfectly ordered, but its realization through the government of bodies is highly confusing. To our earthly eyes, the infinite events in time and space do not fit into a coherent whole. The disposition of the world, Leibniz states in an essay on the concept of justice, "must be too great and too beautiful, for spirits of our present range to be able to appreciate it enough so soon." It is like the plot of a romance: "[To] want to see it here, is like wanting to take a romance by the tail and to pretend to decipher the plot from the first book: instead of which, the beauty of a romance is great to the degree that it finally produces more order from a greater apparent confusion. It would even be a fault in the composition, if the reader could divine the issue too soon." Whereas fictional romances imitate the creation, the realization of the divine government in time and space is a "great and true poem (that is to say, word for word, work) of the universe."[92] The true poem of the universe, of course, does not have an end. By envisioning an end—a denouement— Leibniz transforms it into a romance. In Leibniz's time, there was no dearth of projects aiming to resolve the conflicts and confusions in the world. Abbé de St Pierre's project of perpetual peace was one. Leibniz had his own project of setting up a tribunal in Rome to adjudicate the conflicts among political bodies. This project, he said dryly, "will succeed as easily as that of M. l'Abbé de St Pierre: but since it is permitted to write romances, why should we find bad the fiction which would recall the age of gold to us?"[93]

Leibniz's romance of the international world corroborates the multilateral and multilayered pluralism advocated by his narrative of international legal personality. In addition, informed by an ingenious metaphysics, it also paints a picture of the international world as multi-polar and multi-perspectival, as each political body, interlocked with and enfolded within all other political bodies, mirrors the entire political universe in itself. In contrast to Grotius and, for that matter, also to Hobbes, Pufendorf, and others of that ilk, Leibniz anchors the political universe to a divine purpose. This means that there is an underlying order, however confused and confusing the political world appears to be. Everybody that exists and everything that happens ultimately fit into the grand scheme of things. Of course, only a metaphysical optimist such as Leibniz himself can see such a grand scheme.

Spectacles of International Order

The law comes with a theatrical apparatus. It is most visible in the performance of a court trial. We all know about the solemn air and elaborate spatial arrangement of the courtroom, the ceremonial robes of the judge, the minutely choreographed procedure, the heated exchange between litigants, the rapt attention of the general public. In medieval Germanic law, the judges (*Richter*) were the ones who set up (*richten*) things for a trial. They were, in the words of Cornelia Vismann, "the directors of the performance of a thing on the stage of the law. Those summoned before the court [had to] follow them just as actors follow the instructions of a theater director." It was only with the advances of legal learning after the twelfth century "that the two functions of the court, setting up things (*Richten, Dinge einrichten*) and giving a verdict (*Urteilen*), merge[d] with each other."[94] There was no international court in early modern Europe. Precisely for this reason, other kinds of legal procedure in the international arena, for example the negotiation, signing, and invocation of treaties, were staged by all the more sophisticated and splendid theatrical means.[95] At the same time, fastidious ceremonies and dazzling spectacles were put on to prepare for, to accompany, and to commemorate legal actions. Performances were an integral part of international relations from the sixteenth to the eighteenth century. A cultural historian speaks of "mise-en-scènes of European diplomatic society."[96] Ceremonial theater and mythological spectacles exemplify the theatrical dimension of international law.

Ceremonial Theater

The rise of the modern state went hand in hand with the establishment of a ceremonial apparatus.[97] Complete with its own institutions, practices, and discourses, the ceremonial apparatus operated in conjunction with the juridical apparatus of sovereignty, as well as with the administrative apparatus of government. Its purpose was to acclaim sovereign power and to implement governmental rationality by means of ritualized performances. There were two main types of ceremonial performances: those staging internal sovereignty or dominion over subjects, and those staging external sovereignty or the relationship of one sovereign to another. The former visualized domestic order, and the latter international order. The latter type, which is our focus here, includes the entries of foreign sovereigns or their representatives, *entrevues* and audiences between sovereigns or diplomats, peace conferences and the signing of treaties, peace festivals, celebrations of victory, and the like.

In the sixteenth century, sovereigns were supposed to abide by certain customary ceremonial rules in their encounters. For Jean Bodin, "Among the absolutely sovereign princes, the most ancient republics or monarchies enjoy the prerogative of honor over against the modern and new ones, even if the latter are bigger and more powerful."[98] A chronicle of the Elizabethan reign reports that the officials charged with conducting peace negotiations between England and Spain in 1600 made the following observation: "That in the booke of *Ceremonies of the Court of Rome* [. . .] amongst Kings the first place is due to the King of *France*, the second to the King of *England*, and the third to the King of Castile."[99] Such ceremonial rules of precedence aimed to display an international order in terms of hierarchy and rank. Yet sovereignty is conceptually incompatible with precedence, for a sovereign, endowed with the absolute freedom and the highest authority, is in principle equal to every other sovereign. Not surprisingly, international encounters were often overshadowed by controversies over precedence, not only because representatives of different states fought for the most honorable place, but also because they sometimes could not agree on where the most honorable place should be—the left or the right hand side, the first or the last place in a procession.[100] In the course of the seventeenth century, precedence increasingly gave way to ceremonies of equality.[101] The space between sovereign states—the international arena—turned into an enormous ceremonial stage. An early eighteenth-century author provided, in retrospect, a concise definition of the ceremonial that sovereign states invented to manage their dealings with each other: "One could describe the ceremonial roughly in the following way: it is an orderliness [*eine Ordnung*] pertaining to sovereigns or persons on a par with them, introduced by pact, by consuetude, or by possession. They, as well as their emissaries and delegates, must follow this orderliness in their encounters, so that everyone is given his due."[102]

The ceremonial was an orderliness insofar as it employed an orderly ensemble of theatrical signs. The order of signs evoked, in turn, the order of things in the world of sovereign states. As a semiotic system, theatrical performance consists of the spatial arrangement of the stage, the actor's activities, the actor's appearance, and language, as well as nonverbal acoustic signs.[103] For ceremonial theater, the princely court, occasionally even the entire city, provided the splendidly decorated stage.[104] Visual and acoustic signs such as "colours, apparel, sounds ('sons lugubres')," as Théodore Godefroy—the author of *Le cérémonial de France* (1619)—noted, were as indispensable as the symbolic artifacts such as "scepter, orb, ring, crown, etc.," which served as props.[105] Especially crucial to ceremonial theater were, of course, the activities of ceremonial actors—movements, positions, and gestures, as well as facial and vocal expressions.[106] All of the theatrical signs utilized on the international stage were assigned fixed meanings independent of particular ceremonies. They were arbitrary signs established tacitly by consuetude or explicitly by pacts and voluntary decisions. A ceremonial performance selected, combined, and arranged these arbitrary signs in specific ways. The order of the signs made visible the order of the world through the configuration of the meanings assigned to them. For example, the meeting between the Spanish king Philipp IV and the French king Louis XIV in 1660 on the conference island in Bidassoa River illustrates the lengths to which sovereigns went in order to evoke, by ceremonial performance, an international order in accordance with the principle of equality. With spectacular pomp and circumstances, attired in opulent regalia, the two sovereigns approached each other with maximum histrionics:

> As soon as both kings entered the conference house, they went, in even and measured steps, towards each other up to the line drawn in the conference hall [. . .]; each of them knelt on one knee, and embraced one another in the most friendly manner [. . .] After the conclusion of the conference that took a good hour, both Majesties separated again with the following ceremonial: they moved backwards against the doors through which they entered, saluted each other a few times in this backward march, and looked at each other in the face all the time until they exited the doors.[107]

In this ceremonial performance, the symmetry of space and movement suggests equality, while the precise choreography signifies an inalterable order of the world.

The ceremonial staging of world order presupposed the physical presence of world political actors. But monarchs rarely came together in person, and it was almost impossible for all the monarchs to convene in one place. A figure that came into being in the Renaissance solved this problem—the resident ambassador. As the representative of one state in another state, the resident ambassador embodied the persona of the sovereign, thereby ensuring permanent physical presence on the international stage. "The civilities and ceremonies," Abraham van Wicquefort states in his classic treatise *L'Ambassadeur et ses fonctions* (1682), "are one of the most essential parts of the embassy."[108] As the main actor on the international ceremonial stage, the ambassador has to excel in histrionic skills: "He must be something of an actor, and I should add that in all the commerce of the world there is perhaps no one more theatrical than the ambassador. There is no theater more splendid than the court."[109]

Inasmuch as all interactions between states had to be carried out in accordance with ceremonial rules, the international world was nothing else than a ceremonial theater. It was a theater that featured sovereign persons and their representatives as both actors and spectators. As such, it differed from the medieval conception of world-theater, which had humans as players and God (as well as his associates) as the audience.[110] Yet the divine had not entirely disappeared. The above-mentioned ceremonial encounter between Philip IV and Louis XIV culminated in the swearing of an oath: "Both kings took the oath, simultaneously but each in his own language, and swore to keep the peace steadfastly and eternally."[111] The oath lends efficacy to a statement, assuring its truthfulness and actualization. It establishes a relationship to the divine, as it is always in the name of a transcendent agency that an oath is taken. "The oath," Giorgio Agamben argues, "represents precisely the threshold by means of which language enters into law and *religio*."[112] The ceremonial theater, of which the oath forms a part, has the character of a liturgical ritual that anchors the symbolic order of the human world to a transcendent point of reference. Ceremonies, in the words of Pierre Legendre, "give a face to Nothingness, to the opacity of origins: they speak the unspeakable by means of the ritual message at the basis of discourse. Political love is essentially religious love, it represents by theatrical means."[113] Qua ritual performance, ceremonial theater creates order in the international world by simulating a divine reference.

Mythological Spectacles

While sovereign persons and their entourage acted on the international stage, artists in their service staged extravagant spectacles to represent and to celebrate their actions. Sovereign persons themselves may or may not have participated in these spectacles directly. Usually featuring mythological figures, such spectacles lent splendid sensuality to the divine reference of the international world. Consider the machine play *La Toison d'Or*, created by France's great tragedian Pierre Corneille as part of the festivities celebrating the marriage of Louis XIV to the Spanish Infanta Maria Theresa in 1660. In the prologue—a scene peopled with allegorical *personae fictae* and the pagan divinities of war and love—the personified marriage comes forward to put an end to discord, keep war at bay, and bring the gift of peace to France and the world. The play proper tells the story of the conquest of the Golden Fleece, a story reiterated in various media in the festivities celebrating the marriage of the young king to the Spanish princess because of the association of the Spanish royal house with the Order of the Golden Fleece.[114] Besides Jason and Medea, the protagonists of this legendary story, the play boasts an enormous cast, including Olympian gods as well as a phalanx of minor deities, demigods, and heroes. In the critical preface, Corneille names a number of ancient authors and the Italian mythographer Natale Conti as his sources—without, however, making a secret of his own inventions meant to "render [the fable] more stunning and more wonderful."[115] The effect of wonderment and admiration is achieved not only by the actions, but also by spectacular set designs, wonder-working theatrical machines, and a perspectival, illusionist stage. The five acts of the play feature set designs each more opulent than the last, while ingenious theatrical machinery turns the stage into a dazzling phantasmagoria.[116] In short, *La Toison d'or* is a mythological spectacle.

From the outset, the pagan gods brought back to life by mythographers, artists, and poets in the Renaissance were closely associated with sovereign princes. Mythographies were dedicated to kings, and artworks on mythological subject matters were commissioned by princely patrons. More important, sovereign princes tried to identify themselves with pagan gods, thereby turning the mythology of the ancient Greeks and Romans into a royal mythology. The preeminent form of the mythological representation of princely persons was the spectacle. In the second half of the sixteenth century, when princely courts busied themselves with "acting out literally and in all seriousness the comedy of Olympus" through lavish festivals, pagan mythology served not only the purpose of dynastic self-representation, but increasingly also that of representing the relationship between dynasties.[117] Dealings between sovereigns were recast as fables of the gods. At the Medici court, international marriage alliances were staged in terms of the genealogy of the gods.[118] At the French court under the aegis of Catherine de'Medici, festivals with mythological themes, known as *magnificences*, were also mounted to mark other kinds of encounters between sovereigns. Famous examples include the extravaganza on the occasion of the Bayonne Interview between the French and Spanish courts in 1565, as well as the *festin* at the Tuileries Palace in 1572 in honor of the Polish ambassadors. The society of princes, embodying international society, took on the phantasmagoric form of a pantheon.

All rulers relish being likened to gods. In early modern Europe, however, every princely person eager to assert his sovereignty by comparing himself to a god had to face the reality that there were many other princely persons poised to do the same. In the dedication of *Le Ceremonial François* (1649) to the young Louis XIV, the royal historiographer Denys Godefroy conspicuously makes use of the plural form with regard to the sovereign person, speaking of the necessity of honoring "les Souverains [. . .] comme les principales images et ressemblances de la Maiesté diuine" (sovereigns [. . .] as the principal images of divine majesty).[119] For the purpose of deifying the multitude of sovereign persons, the polytheistic pagan mythology proved to be an eminently suitable symbolic resource. International relations were inscribed in every mythological representation of sovereign persons. Not only did fables about the interaction between different gods signify international relations; the portrayal of an individual sovereign person as a particular god also alluded to international relations, insofar as every pagan god acquired his or her identity only in relation to other members of the pantheon.

As a mythological spectacle in the context of a royal wedding, Corneille's *La Toison d'or* offers a scenario for international order, which is prior to, above, or simply beyond the law. The precedents for it were the Florentine *intermedi* or *intermezzi*—visually and musically sumptuous spectacles featured in the Medici wedding celebrations—as well as the opera as a theatrical form that evolved from the *intermedi* at the turn of the seventeenth century. Royal marriage was a contract supposed to help institute a legal order between states, but it lacked a higher authority mediating between the two contracting parties. In the sixteenth and seventeenth centuries, the earthly sovereign increasingly replaced God and the Church as the supreme authority overseeing marital contracts.[120] In so doing, he eviscerated his own marital contract of a reference point, for in his role as a contracting party he was not invested with the authority over another contracting party. Contracted outside of the law, royal marriage took on the form of a mythological spectacle. It was thereby projected onto a primordial space, in which the sovereign act of contracting was held, but which could not be encompassed by the law itself. The *mise-en-scène* of royal marriage opened up, to quote Pierre Legendre, "la scène non juridique du Droit," or "the non-juridical scene of the Law."[121] The international order that marriage alliances were supposed to seal proved to be something not legal in nature, but rather more fundamental or higher than the law.

The mode of signification of the mythological spectacle was allegorical. Pagan gods survived partly because fables about them were read as revealing

Christian doctrines, philosophical truths, or both.[122] The mythological figures and fables inherited from antiquity metamorphosed in the course of time into malleable, if not empty, signifiers susceptible of being continuously invested with new meanings. They became a vehicle for articulating specific ideas, doctrines, or concepts. Therefore, mythology-themed court entertainments and theatrical performances always had an allegorical character.[123] In the case of *La Toison d'or*, Corneille uses the story of Jason and Medea to link both the Bourbon and Habsburg dynasties to a heroic past as depicted in the epics of the Argonauts—he mentions particularly Valerius Flaccus's epic poem—thus lending their marriage an aura of mythic necessity. The cast of deities associated with the physical world—the Sun, the god of the sea, Tritons, and Sirens, as well as the four winds—helps to present the marriage as a cosmic event. The ethical traits displayed by Jason and Medea onstage, no less than the ethical qualities attributed to them in traditional allegorical interpretations, locate the marriage in a moral universe. Finally, the fact that mythological figures rub shoulders with allegorical persons on stage—the prologue of *La Toison d'or* features a diverse cast of allegorical *personae fictae* such as France, Victory, Peace, Marriage, Discord, and Envy—leaves no doubt about their ideational character. But it is not always easy to pin down the specific ideas conveyed by a mythological spectacle such as Corneille's. Deciphering it depends on the audience's knowledge of the mythological tradition. Aby Warburg remarked that the mythological *intermedi* at the Medici wedding of 1589 were meant for "a highly erudite audience."[124] The same can be said of *La Toison d'or*. Yet regardless of the extent of knowledge on the part of the audience, the author prompts everyone to look beyond the spectacle itself and see the higher ideas signified by it—ideas of cosmic and moral order.

The Drama of International Society

Pictorial allegories, narratives, performances: these poetic operations in various media can be understood as components of what we might call international social drama. "Social drama" is a concept used by the anthropologist Victor Turner for analyzing human societies ranging from small villages to complex nations. A social drama, according to Turner, goes through four phases: the breach of a norm in some public arena; a mounting crisis in the relation between components of a social field; the deployment of certain adjustive and redressive mechanisms, and finally either reintegration or recognition of schism.[125] The redressive mechanisms include ritual and legal procedures. Their general aim is to find solutions and to ensure social integration. Their modus operandi is usually to generate narratives from brute facts, not only narratives that serve to clarify the perceived breach and the ensuing crisis, but also foundational narratives that, in light of the crisis, either reiterate or reinvent the origin as well as the purpose of the society. At the same time, both legal and ritual procedures have a pronounced performative dimension that relates the society to an absent Other. The poetic operations scrutinized above perform the function of such redressive mechanisms in an emerging international society mired in perennial crises. The pictorial allegories of peace treaties present a fictive divine agent as the mediator between rival sovereign rulers. The narratives underlying the doctrinal discourse of international law explain what persons act in international society, how these persons come into being and come to be recognized, and how they relate to one another and to things. Finally, exemplifying the performative dimension of legal procedures and simultaneously verging on rituals, ceremonial theater and mythological spectacles refer international society to invisible powers.

Turner points out that the various modes of redress in the social drama contain "at least the germ of self-reflexivity," for they offer a public way of assessing social behavior. For this reason, they may, in keeping with the growing complexity of a society, "[move] out of the domains of law and religion into those of the various arts. [. . .] By means of such genres as theater [. . .], dance drama, and professional story-telling, performances are presented which probe a community's weaknesses, call its leaders to account, desacralize its most cherished values and beliefs, portray its characteristic conflicts and suggest remedies for them, and generally take stock of its current situation in the known 'world.' "[126] In seventeenth-century Europe, poetic literature and theater took on the task of portraying the unending conflicts of the emerging international society, suggesting imaginative remedies and solutions. International society, of course, was and still is primarily a society of states. International law has states as its primary subjects. States are fictitious corporate entities. Poetic literature, on the other hand, is all about "people doing things (*prattontōn*)," as we know from Aristotle.[127] It needs to attribute events to human or anthropomorphic agents in order to explain them in terms of a motivational structure. A political doctrine that emerged around 1600 facilitated the engagement of poetic literature with crises and conflicts in international society: the royal absolutist doctrine that identified the state with the king's person.

In reaction to the resistance theories leveled against the king's person from both the Protestant and Catholic camps, a phalanx of defenders of royal authority was formed in the years around 1600.[128] At the forefront was a monarch: James VI, king of Scotland (1567–1625), who acceded to the English throne as James I in 1603 in the union of crowns. James turned against the "infamous invectives" of Calvinists and the "superstitious rebellion" of Catholic Leaguers, as well as the papal interference in temporal affairs.[129] The king, he argued on the basis of Scripture, is God's lieutenant on earth, wielding an absolute authority over his subjects by divine right. The fundamental laws of the kingdom and the law of nature, in his view, further confirm that the lieges, as well as each and every subject, owe absolute allegiance to their king. The relationship between the people and the king, however, is not unidirectional, merely with the former subordinated to the latter. Rather the king should have no other concerns than the welfare of his subjects. This reciprocal and mutual duty entails the identity of the king's person and the commonwealth. Metaphorically, James likens the king to the head, and the people to other members of a body.[130]

As the divinely ordained overlord, the king is the source and the interpreter of all laws with which the people are governed. As such, the king is above the law. Yet "a good king will not onely delight to rule his subiects by the lawe, but euen will conforme himself in his owne actions theruvnto, alwaies keeping that ground, that the health of the common-wealth be his chiefe lawe."[131] By subjecting himself to the law that he makes to govern the subjects, the king obliterates the difference between himself and the people in the same act as he establishes it, becoming one and the same with the whole body of the people. The identity between the king's person and the state thus depends on the voluntary self-control of the king. Without this self-control, a gulf would open up between the king and the people, turning him into a tyrant. Other defenders of royal authority in the early seventeenth century were more stridently polemical. William Barclay's *De regno et regali potestate* (1600) mobilizes enormous erudition to rebut the arguments advanced by the Calvinist and Catholic resistance theorists, with the single aim of affirming the divine right and the unquestionable supreme power of the king. One conclusion that he draws, as Quentin Skinner points out, is "that the bearer of ultimate sovereignty in any kingdom or commonwealth must [. . .] be the *publica persona* of the *princeps* himself."[132] Similarly, a huge tome entitled *La Defence de la Monarchie Francoise, et avtres Monarchies* (1614), written by a French cleric by the name of Jean Baricave, provides a word-by-word refutation of the Calvinist treatise *Vindiciae Contra Tyrannos* and its putative followers. Neither William Barclay nor Jean Baricave offered substantially novel arguments going beyond those formulated by King James. In fact, royal absolutism remained remarkably static throughout the seventeenth century.[133]

CHAPTER TWO

If the state was nothing other than the king's person, the events in the life of a royal person as a human being—birth, marriage and death—necessarily took on the greatest political significance. By the same token, affairs of the state, both domestic and foreign, had to be carried out through the personal actions of the prince and his associates.[134] Given the royal absolutist doctrine, poetic literature could take on the weighty issues of the state by portraying princely characters and representing princely actions. In particular, it could engage with international law and negotiate the problem of international order by constructing plots concerning the interaction between princely persons.

According to Northrop Frye, there are two basic fictional modes: "fictions in which the hero becomes isolated from his society, and fictions in which he is incorporated into it." He calls them "tragic" and "comic" respectively.[135] Poetic literature in early modern Europe employed both fictional modes in dealing with issues of international order. The poetic plots in the tragic mode track the descent of princely persons into discord and destruction, whereas those in the comic mode track the movement of princely persons towards concord. The former take the form of tragedy, and the latter take the form of political romance—two of the principal poetic genres from the late sixteenth to the early eighteenth century. They will be the topics of analysis in the following two chapters.

Chapter 3

International Order as Tragedy

The Renaissance of Tragedy and the Problem of International Order

A principal theatrical and poetic genre of classical antiquity, tragedy came back to life in the vernacular in the sixteenth century. It assumed, from the outset, the mission of reflecting on the upheavals in the political world marked by the rise of the sovereign state. Early modern tragedy tackled all the important issues of the state, including the issues bearing on international relations and international order.

Tragedy in early modern Europe was a theatrical art.[1] But it was also an art of dramatic poetry. Beginning in the Renaissance, in the words of the theater-scholar Hans-Thies Lehmann, tragedy assumed "a specifically dramatic shape." It became dramatic theater.[2] As theater, tragedy transposed the political stage onto the stage meant for entertainment. Absolutist politics, both domestic and foreign, had a theatrical character. Queen Elizabeth I of England told the parliament in November 1586, "Princes, you know, stand upon stages so that their actions are viewed and beheld of all men."[3] Her successor King James stated, "A King is as one set on a stage, whose smallest actions and gestures, all the people gazingly doe behold."[4] Performances on the political stage, including the ceremonial theater discussed in the previous chapter, were supposed to be efficacious—for instance, to win over another state as an ally or to have a treaty signed—and thus different from performances mounted to entertain an audience. Yet efficacy and entertainment are interwoven with each other.[5] In the international arena, the ceremonial performance of a consequential political and legal action often worked in tandem with theatrical entertainments. A study of early modern diplomacy tells us that "the emergent diplomatic culture depended on a set of theatrical practices that translated seamlessly from the scene of diplomacy (the court, the summit, the negotiating room) to the stage. These practices could be grouped into three broad categories: embodied representation, performance, and spectatorship."[6] The tragic stage took over such theatrical practices from the political stage. Refined by theater artists, they fed back into the political world and might prove to be efficacious. Mounting a tragic performance for foreign diplomats or visiting sovereigns, for example, might help shape the relations to other states. Corneille's tragic theater *La Toison d'or*, discussed in the previous chapter as an exemplar of mythological spectacles, performed the function of acclaiming and consolidating the alliance between France and Spain. Above all, the transposition of the political stage onto the tragic stage thrust certain politico-legal problems of the state into the limelight and thereby helped find imaginary solutions to them.

Negotiating politico-legal problems and finding imaginary solutions to them requires the art of dramatic poetry. This chapter studies tragedy mainly as drama, while also taking into account the art of theater specific to it. As dramatic poetry, the tragedies read in the following pages create, each in its own way, a fictive world in which sovereign persons breach perceived norms, clash with one another, struggle in vain for solutions, and often meet their demise. Through ever varying fictional experiments, they exhibit the structural contradictions and norm conflicts in the international world in order to explore the possibility of a normative order through tragic experience. Tragic drama proves to be a poetic form especially suitable for representing the actions of sovereign persons: the sovereign has, by definition, a license to transgress laws, and tragic drama is designed to figure transgression.[7] Ulpian once stated: "Princeps legibus solutus est," or the prince is not bound by laws.[8] This formula of Roman law, elaborated by medieval jurists, served as the legal justification of absolute power up to the early modern period.[9] Jurists usually attached a variety of restrictions to absolute power, including the strictures of divine law, natural law, and feudal law. But in the age of absolutism these restrictions were relativized, with some of them (such as divine law) separated from the state, some others (such as feudal law) neutralized by the state, and yet others (such as natural law) subjected to recognition by the state. Tragic drama was supposed to represent actions of the prince above or outside the law. Its subject matter was usually the violence committed by the prince. Especially in their relations to each other, princes acted in a space beyond the law, and especially these relations lent themselves to tragic representation.

The Sovereign Person as Tragic Character

Beginning in the fifteenth century, the tragic poetry of classical antiquity was discovered, published, and translated. In the meantime, the rediscovery of Aristotle's *Poetics* spawned a new wave of theoretical reflections on tragedy, either in the form of Aristotle commentary or in the form of new systems of poetics.[10] In the process, there emerged the doctrine that tragedy must have royal persons as its protagonists. For Aristotle, poetic characters must be either good or bad, so "differences in characters just are differences in goodness and badness, or else they must be better than are found in the world or worse or just the same." As a poetic genre, tragedy represents "people better than are found in the world," in contrast to comedy that represents people worse than they are.[11] Aristotle's words for good and bad, *spoudaios* and *phaulos*, do not have a narrowly moralistic sense, as Northrope Frye notes, but rather "have a figurative sense of weighty and light."[12] Tragic characters are "better" than other men in the sense that they are more serious, thus superior, whereas comic characters are "worse" in the sense that they are lowly, and thus inferior. There is no requirement that tragic characters ought to be royal. Aristotle's conception of poetic characters is still retained in Francesco Robortello's *In librum Aristotelis De arte poetica explicationes*, the pioneering *Poetics* commentary published in 1548: tragedy "imitates above all men of outstanding type. By choice it unfolds the predicament of prominent people, since a greater degree of compassion is excited from their character than if the catastrophe of obscure and lowly people were passed in review." To substantiate this claim, Robortello points out that tragedies often have "disasters and miseries of a king or some hero" as their subject matter.[13] Whereas Robortello refers to the existence of princely personages in tragedies as evidence for the Aristotelian argument that tragic characters are outstanding people, in the decades after him the princely rank was soon held up as the distinctive feature of tragedy, in order finally to be declared the quintessence of the tragic form. In his grand new poetics *Poetices libri septem* of 1561, Scaliger pinpoints four distinctive features of tragedy: "In tragedy, there are kings and princes from cities, fortresses, and camps; the beginning is calmer, the end horrible; the language is solemn, refined, and far removed from vulgar speech; it is filled with anxiety: fears, threats, exiles, and death."[14]

Among these four features, the royalty of character is the most crucial one, for the solemnity of language and the anxiety-suffused atmosphere are both attributed to the princely personage. Horrible endings are preferable, but not absolutely necessary, for many tragedies have more or less happy endings.

A decade later, in Lodovico Castelvetro's *Poetica d'Aristotele vulgarizzata e sposta* of 1570, the first *Poetics* commentary in a vernacular language, the royal rank of protagonists became a self-evident requirement for tragedy: "Tragic agents are royal personages." This prescription about tragic characters comes along with a statement about tragic actions: they are actions beyond the law. Because royal persons are above laws—"princeps legibus absolutus est"—they resort to extralegal actions to solve their problems: "If they suffer or think they suffer an injury they neither seek redress from the magistrates nor possess their souls in patience, but settle their own accounts as their passions dictate, vengefully slaying persons closely or distantly related to them by blood, and sometimes in desperation even turning their hand against themselves."[15] Such actions beyond the law are tragic actions. Only sovereign princes are capable of, and are doomed to, tragic actions. Royal personage is no incidental feature of tragedy. It is constitutive of tragedy.

During the period of little more than two decades from Robortello to Castelvetro, a new doctrine was firmly anchored to poetics: tragedy represents the actions of royal persons outside of the law. This doctrine was then repeated, with minimal variations, throughout Europe for more than a century. Martin Opitz's *Buch von der Deutschen Poeterey* (1624), the fountainhead of poetics in the German language, defines tragedy as follows: "Tragedy accords with the epic in terms of majesty, but it can rarely tolerate the introduction of persons of inferior rank and of lowly things, because it deals only with the royal willfulness, killings, desperation, infanticide and patricide, conflagrations, incest, war and rebellion, lamentation, wailing, sighing, etc."[16] François Hédelin d'Aubignac's *La pratique du théâtre* (1657), a key theoretical text of French Classicism, offers a similar definition: tragedy "represents the life of princes, full of anxiety, suspicion, trials and tribulations, rebellions, wars, murders, violent passions, and great adventures."[17]

This doctrine of poetics charged tragedy with a crucial political role. In his *Defense of Poesy* (1595), Philip Sidney says of tragedy that it "openeth the greatest wounds, and showeth forth the ulcers that are covered with tissue; [it] maketh kings fear to be tyrants, and tyrants manifest their tyrannical humours."[18] Georg Philipp Harsdörffer (1607–58), an important theorist of the German Baroque, characterized tragedy as the "school of kings."[19] It was thanks to royal absolutism that tragedy could play its politico-legal role. Identifying the royal person with the state, royal absolutism considered events in the life of the prince as affairs of the state, and regarded affairs of the state, both domestic and foreign, as carried out through the personal actions of the prince. By representing the actions of royal persons, then, tragedy was able to negotiate the fundamental problems of the state and suggest solutions to them, including problems regarding the legitimacy of rule and international order.[20]

Early Modern Tragedy in the History of International Law

Tragedies dealing with relations between sovereign persons flourished in the century between the 1580s and 1680s, a century encompassing the English Renaissance, French Classicism, and the German Baroque. Dramatizing the absence, impotence, or collapse of the law, these tragedies gestured, *ex negativo*, towards an idea of international world order as something unrealized and unrealizable. The main stations in the development of the genre corresponded chronologically to three moments in the history of international law—the Gentilian, the Grotian, and the Hobbesian.

While the Oxford professor Gentili was lecturing and writing on the law of war—his lectures *De iure belli commentationes tres* were published in 1589, followed by a new version under the title *De iure belli libri tres* in 1598, and by *De armis Romanis libri duo* in 1599—the London stages were convulsed with theaters of war. As a theater historian informs us, after Marlowe's *Tamburlaine the Great* enjoyed a resounding success in 1587, "for more than ten years wars and stories of wars became the main meal on the broad platforms of the amphitheaters."[21] Gentili was notable, as discussed in chapter 1, for installing the sovereign person as the legal subject in affairs of war and legation, and for promoting the law as the most efficient means for sovereign persons in dealing with one another. The tragic stage of his time, as prominent war-themed plays such as *Tamburlaine the Great* and Shakespeare's *King John* (1596) indicate, probed questions of how the sovereign will functions and whether it is susceptible to the law.

During the first quarter of the seventeenth century, Grotius thoroughly reconceived jurisprudence in order to set forth a legal code for the international world—a monumental project that began with his legal defense of the Dutch capture of the Portuguese merchantman *Santa Catarina* in 1603 and culminated in the publication of *De jure belli ac pacis* in 1625. Grotius's jurisprudential innovation was matched by the dramatic imaginativeness of Shakespeare. In the years around 1610, towards the end of his writing career, Shakespeare produced, in rapid succession, a group of plays that experiment with various models of world order through daring plot constructions. This group of plays, including *Pericles* (1608–9), *Cymbeline* (1608–10), *The Winter's Tale* (1611), and *The Tempest* (1611), are generically hard to categorize. Shakespeareans usually refer to them as romances or tragicomedies. This chapter treats them as an intermezzo in the development of the theatrical representation of international relations, a phase in which theater, making use of its poetic license, imaginatively affirms a world order. This kind of tragicomedy of international order can be also found elsewhere, albeit in rather different forms—for example, the German poet Johan Rist's *Irenaromachia* (1630).

The tragedy of international relations came into full flower in the mid-seventeenth century, a time marked by the Hobbesian moment of international law. While Hobbes's denial of the existence of a law between states was echoed and elaborated by jurists such as Pufendorf and philosophers such as Spinoza, tragedians across Europe displayed onstage the fragility and collapse of international law, indeed the absence of all other norms. For example, the German baroque tragedian Andreas Gryphius's *Catharina von Georgien* (written 1647–48) demonstrates the futility of all kinds of legal arrangements between sovereigns. As an alternative, it gestures towards a religiously legitimated international order, but indicates that this is ultimately possible only in the imagination of the tragic audience. *Cleopatra* (1661/80) and *Sophonisbe* (1680), plays by another German baroque tragedian, Daniel Casper von Lohenstein, show that reason of state rather than law holds sway in the international world. Law is nothing more than a pawn on the chessboard of reason of state. Reason of state, however, is not conducive to a normative order. Indeed, it counteracts a normative order. If anything, the modes of behavior dictated by reason of state—simulation and dissimulation—have an inherently theatrical quality, which facilitates the poetic representation of political actions on the tragic stage. In the meantime, Pierre Corneille, the great tragedian of French Classicism, turned to the international world as well. His late plays, including *Œdipe* (1659), *La Toison d'or* (1660), *Sophonisbe* (1663), and *Attila* (1668), deal with marriage alliance as a legal arrangement constitutive of international society in the age of absolutism. Insofar as marriage alliances were instrumental to producing legitimate heirs, thus ensuring hereditary succession, they were also constitutive of the absolutist state itself. In *Œdipe*, the first of Corneille's tragedies of marriage alliance, the Oedipus-myth is retooled to illustrate the genealogical principle informing the domestic political order of the absolutist state and international order alike. The plays after *Œdipe* are more somber. They reveal, each in its own way, the lawlessness and disorder at the origin of every royal marriage. As a legal transaction that takes place beyond the reach of any juridical authority, marriage alliance turns out to separate rather than unite sovereigns.

In sum, early modern tragedy offers a bleak vision of the international world. In the works of Christopher Marlowe and William Shakespeare, the sovereign will seems to foreclose a lawful international order. The plays of the mid-seventeenth century, for their part, dramatize not only the failure of law, but also the impotence of all the other norms, techniques, and institutions in the international world. They conjure up, by means of the tragic experience that they create, a normative world order as something that is persistently unavailable.

The Sovereign Will and the Tragic Form (Marlowe's *Tamburlaine*, Shakespeare's *King John*)

With the rise of sovereignty as a juridical concept in the second half of the sixteenth century—a concept elaborated most thoroughly in Jean Bodin's *Les Six Livres de la République* (1576)—the will of the sovereign person became the crux of the law. Within his own realm, the sovereign person's will competed with, and increasingly came to displace, nature as a source of the law. Outside of his realm, a sovereign person faced the daunting task of having to reconcile his will with the will of other sovereigns. If there were to be any norms between sovereign persons, they would have to originate from the concord of their individual wills. Gentili recommended that sovereign persons agree on certain laws in dealing with one another, for such laws would provide a rational framework for pursuing their respective interests. His premise was the tacit equation of the will with reason. In contrast to the jurist, the tragic poets of the time sought to chart the vagaries of the sovereign will and to interrogate the compatibility of the willfulness of the sovereign with a lawful order of the world. One may distinguish two basic poetic models of the sovereign will: the one, exemplified by Marlowe's *Tamburlaine the Great*, portrays it as strong, relentless, and ruthless, whereas the other, exemplified by Shakespeare's *King John*, portrays it as weak, wavering, and scrupulous. As contrary to one another as they may seem, the two models reach a similar diagnosis: the sovereign will, whatever its manifestations, is incapable of either upholding or instituting a lawful world order. Indeed, it forecloses a lawful world order.

The Tragedy of the Strong Will: Marlowe's *Tamburlaine*

The prologue to *Tamburlaine the Great, Part One* introduces the eponymous protagonist to the audience thus:

> We'll lead you to the stately tent of war,
> Where you shall hear the Scythian Tamburlaine
> Threat'ning the world with high astounding terms
> And scourging kingdoms with his conquering sword.[22]

This is a brief, but sufficient plot summary, for throughout both five-act parts of the play the protagonist does little else than rant and conquer. He does encounter a variety of opponents, to be sure. But be the opponent the king of Persia, the emperor of Turkey, the sultan of Egypt, or the prince of any other exotic country, he is struck down by Tamburlaine's "astounding terms" and "conquering sword"—in ways that, for all their specificities, remain essentially the same. Tamburlaine's unremitting conquests seem to be driven by a repetition compulsion. In the pithy words of Stephen Greenblatt, "Tamburlaine no sooner annihilates one army than he sets out to annihilate another, no sooner unharnesses two kings than he hitches up two more."[23]

What propels Tamburlaine's actions is a vigorous will, a will that unrelentingly thrusts forward, verbally best captured in the future tense:

> For "will" and "shall" best fitteth Tamburlaine,
> Whose smiling stars give him assured hope
> Of martial triumph ere he meet his foes. (I.3.3.41–43)

This will is a sovereign will or a will to sovereignty, for it defies all constraints, all oppositions, all obstacles, be they human or divine. Other princes see Tamburlaine as always "thirsting with sovereignty" (I. 2.1.20) or refer to him as "that fiery thirster after sovereignty" (I. 2.6.31). It is a will that strives for nothing less than the domination of the entire world. Envisioning his future conquests "from the east unto the furthest west," and rattling off geographic names as if he were standing in front of a world map, Tamburlaine declares: "I'll win the world at last" (I. 3.3.246–260).

The sovereign will as embodied by Tamburlaine can be described in terms of Nietzsche's concept of "will to power": "My idea is that every specific body strives to become master over all space and to extend its force (- its will to power:) and to thrust back all that resists its extension. But it continually encounters similar efforts on the part of other bodies and ends by coming to an arrangement ('union') with those of them that are sufficiently related to it: thus they then conspire together for power. And the process goes on -"[24] What Nietzsche says about material bodies in this note applies eminently to Tamburlaine as a sovereign person. Tamburlaine wants to be lord of all space. He pushes back resistance and conspires together with those sufficiently related to him—consider Theridamas who is "won with [his] words and conquered with [his] looks" (I.1.2.228) in the first act. And his conquest goes on and on. As a metaphysical principle, the will to power thus underlies not only the material world but also the political world, especially the international political world as we see it in *Tamburlaine the Great*. In fact, for Tamburlaine, the sovereign will that animates his conquests is something as inexorable as what keeps the material cosmos in motion: "our souls [. . .] / always moving as the restless spheres, / Wills us to wear ourselves and never rest" (I. 2.6.61–66). Conversely, Nietzsche explicates the will to power in terms of war and conquest in the international arena: "The state organized immorality—*internally*: as police, penal law, classes, commerce, family; *externally*: as will to power, to war, to conquest, to revenge."[25]

Yet even without the help of the Nietzschean metaphysical concept, it is not hard to see that the sovereign will figures in Marlowe's play as the fundamental principle shaping and reshaping the world. It transcends all the existing as well as all the merely imaginable norms, be they legal, ethical, or religious. In particular, it runs roughshod over all those norms set forth in the discourse of international law emerging in the late sixteenth century:

First, the sovereign will ignores the legitimacy of rule. Tamburlaine does not stake his claim to rule the world on any hereditary right, proclaiming without the slightest hint of inferiority that he is "a shepherd by [his] parentage" (I. 1.2.35). From beginning to end, other potentates decry him as a "Scythian thief" (I. 1.1.36), unlawful usurper (I. 4.2.57), or "a base, usurping vagabond" (I. 4.3.21). The only response that Tamburlaine gives them is to crush them at the first opportunity;

Second, the sovereign will disdains the laws of war. Tamburlaine neither feels a need to provide a just cause for his wars nor deems it necessary to respond to his opponents' accusation that he breaks "the law of arms" (I. 2.4.20). His might is justification enough, and his victories are the only response he has to offer. The dramatic discourse seems to vindicate Tamburlaine's position. The second part of the play opens with a negotiation between Christian kings on the one side, and Muslim kings on the other, which leads to a treaty of alliance confirmed with an oath. But soon enough the Christians perjure themselves under the pretext that they need not take the oath and faith too seriously: "Assure your grace, 'tis superstition / To stand so strictly on dispensive faith" (II. 2.2.49–50). This episode has apparently no other function than to show that all the legalism in war and peace is really just hypocrisy. It lends Tamburlaine's open defiance of all the laws of war the quality of refreshing candor;

Finally, the sovereign will tramples on all of those laws in warfare that issue from moral constraints and religious piety. At the siege of Damascus, four virgins fall on their knees in supplication. Suppliants in war, Gentili emphasizes in *De jure belli*, are to be treated as members of the community of humankind rather than as enemies, hence to be spared by arms (II.20). However, in response to the virgins' plea "O, pity us," Tamburlaine tells his subordinates "Away with them, I say, and show them Death." In no time, the suppliant maidens are turned into "slaughtered carcasses" (I. 5.1.119–31). True to his self-appointed role as the scourge of God and terror to the world, he prides himself on inflicting the greatest possible cruelty on the vanquished.

In Tamburlaine's own terms, one can say that the sovereign will embodied by him is the scourge of law. Only once in the play—that is, at the end of part 1—does its law-shattering impulse seem to relent, as Tamburlaine announces a "truce with all the world" and tells his vassals to "make laws to rule your provinces" (I. 5.1.527–29). But a truce is by definition temporary. In part 2, the destructive campaign of the sovereign will resumes. The sovereign will generates violence. Indeed, it is nothing but violence—gratuitous, inexorable, fateful. It is, in brief, mythic violence. Tamburlaine's person is compared with striking frequency to the gods in Greco-Roman mythology by his opponents and supporters alike, as well as by himself. In particular, his wars of conquest are variously figured as the War of the Titans or the War of the Giants. If the War of the Giants eventually ends with the reign of the Olympians, the wars of Tamburlaine seem never to end.

Marlowe's dramatic figuration of the sovereign will as mythic violence represents an imaginary projection of the principle of sovereignty on a global, indeed cosmic scale. Approximately a decade prior to the first performance of *Tamburlaine the Great*, Jean Bodin defined sovereignty as the absolute and perpetual power of a commonwealth in his *Les six livres de la république*. In its very emphasis on absoluteness, Bodin's definition delimits the effect of sovereignty: as the power of a commonwealth over its own subjects, sovereignty is limited to a certain territorial space, as well as to a certain number of people residing in this space. The concept of sovereignty thus rests upon a distinction between inside and outside. A sovereign has absolute power inside his jurisdiction, but little or no power outside of it. He is inescapably constrained by the outside space ruled over by other sovereigns. International law, not yet a central issue for Bodin himself, but soon taken up by jurists such as Gentili, is the answer of jurisprudence to this constraint.[26] The sovereign will embodied by Tamburlaine, however, is determined to extend the boundary between inside and outside as far as possible, ceaselessly overriding it, transgressing it. Beginning as a Scythian shepherd who reigns over nothing, and progressively conquering more and more territories, he is the very symbol of transgression. His is a project of obliterating the distinction between inside and outside, absorbing international law into the sovereign will.

It is also a project of obliterating the distinction between below and above, this world and the other world, immanence and transcendence. For Bodin, a sovereign towers absolutely over his subjects, but he is beneath God, to whom he is answerable: "The laws of sovereign princes can neither alter nor change the laws of God and of nature."[27] Tamburlaine, however, has as little regard for boundaries on the vertical plane as he does for those on the horizontal plane. Theridamas, a king enchanted by his charisma, observes:

> His looks do menace heaven and dare the gods,
> His fiery eyes are fixed upon the earth,
> As if he now devised some stratagem,
> Or meant to pierce Avernus' darksome vaults
> And pull the triple-headed dog from hell. (I.1.2.157–61)

Tamburlaine's "astounding terms" and "conquering sword" collapse heaven, earth, and hell into one homogenous space, seeking to erase all traces of transcendence.

Tearing down boundaries in all dimensions, the sovereign will embodied by Tamburlaine strives to create a world of absolute homogeneity, uniformity, and immanence. Historians cannot help being reminded of imperial Rome or of the imperialist expansion of England and the entrepreneurial spirit of the Englishmen at the time.[28] Above all, Marlowe's play enacts the fantasy of a world order based on the will of one single sovereign. As we saw in chapter 1, traditional models of world order dissolved in the course of the sixteenth century. In jurisprudence, the age-old conception of the objective order of nature faltered, while the subjective will asserted itself. Legal order became a matter of the negotiation of diverging wills. Emerging as a new branch of jurisprudence, international law concerned itself with the question of how the sovereigns, driven by their own wills, may still manage to achieve a lawful, orderly coexistence. *Tamburlaine the Great* imagines a scenario in which one single sovereign will is so strong as to be able to enforce a world order on its own.

This scenario takes the form of a tragedy. Marlowe's play bears a striking resemblance to Seneca's tragedies. Tamburlaine's "astounding terms" are evidently inspired by the powerful declamations of the Roman tragedian's impassioned dramatic characters. More important, the sovereign will embodied by him is reminiscent of the Senecan characters' furious passions, their craze for power and dominion over others, their extreme violence and cruelty.[29] In his extravagant presumption to conquer the whole universe, Tamburlaine mirrors Seneca's mad Hercules.[30] In trying to commit the greatest imaginable atrocities, he seems to be Seneca's Atreus redivivus. Beside themselves with fury, Seneca's dramatic characters purposefully create and wantonly indulge in spectacles of violence and domination that lend his tragedies a metatheatrical dimension. The same applies to Tamburlaine. The most ingenious spectacles created by him include the caging of Emperor Bajazeth of Turkey and his queen, which he calls "a goodly show" (I. 4.4.61), and the use of vanquished kings as chariot-drawing horses with bits in their mouths, which he refers to as "our pageant" (II. 4.3.90).[31]

Yet Marlowe's drama of the sovereign will that presumes to ordain the course of the entire world is not merely a reenactment of the Senecan model of tragedy. Its tragic consciousness arises from the tensions and paradoxes in the sovereign will itself. As a poetic form and social institution, tragedy emerged first at a specific historical juncture—fifth-century Athens—when the archaic mythical forms of power came to be replaced by the regime of the *polis* with its politico-legal institutions. Tragic drama, in the words of the French classicist Jean-Pierre Vernant, "brings to the stage an ancient heroic legend. For the city this legendary world constitutes the past—a past sufficiently distant for the contrasts, between the mythical traditions that it embodies and the new forms of legal and political thought, to be clearly visible; yet a past still close enough for the clash of values still to be a painful one and for this clash still to be currently taking place."[32] The contrasts and the clash between old and new are played out through the actions of the tragic hero. On the one hand, the tragic hero figures as the subject of law, carrying out his actions with a sense of purpose as well as a sense of responsibility. As such, these actions instantiate the working of what is called the will in the later history of Western thought.[33] On the other hand, the tragic hero seems to be still at the mercy of mythic powers. However consciously he makes a decision, however great a will he exhibits in doing so, something greater, something divine seems to cast a spell on all that he does, defeating his purposes, upturning his actions, and usually causing his demise. In Marlowe, the tensions between higher, divine powers and the will of the agent of actions characteristic of Greek tragedy are eliminated, but only to be succeeded by new tensions and paradoxes. In *Tamburlaine the Great*, the will of the protagonist is so strong that it assumes mythic dimensions. It becomes as powerful as, indeed even more powerful than, fates and the fortune: "I hold the Fates bound fast in iron chains / And with my hand turn Fortune's wheel about" (I. 1.2. 174–75). The usurpation of divine power by the will, however, brings to the fore a new countervailing force—its mortal embodiment. The tension between the will's presumption to universal sovereignty and its embodiment by a mortal being makes Tamburlaine a character as tragic as the legendary heroes in Greek tragedy.

The only way for a human being to ordain a course for the entire world is to occupy the position of the divine. Indeed, battle cries against deities of all kinds resound throughout *Tamburlaine the Great*, reaching their shrillest pitch in the burning of the Koran towards the end of the play. Yet every vaunt about storming the heaven both presupposes and confirms a distinction between the heaven and the earth, the divine and the human. The apostrophe of Tamburlaine as "our earthly god" by his subordinates (II. 1.3.138) marks this distinction grammatically through an adjective, just as his self-designation as "the scourge of God" does so through the genitive, be it understood as subjective or objective genitive. Precisely by claiming to abolish the distinction between the human and the divine, he reproduces it. Tamburlaine's conquests, he tells us, are undertaken for the sake of fame and glory. But the pursuit of fame and glory, perhaps more than anything else, defines a human as opposed to a divine being. Fame is the recognition of the excellence of a human being by others. Homer's Achilles, to whom Tamburlaine is occasionally compared (for example, I. 2.1.24), reflects, in the midst of a personal crisis, on the reward as well as the price of fame: transmitted by the symbolic means of words and songs, fame makes it possible for a man to live on after death; but in order to achieve the highest fame, a man must risk his life in achieving the greatest excellence.[34] The pursuit of fame thus bespeaks a desire to transcend mortality and at the same time the necessity of accepting mortality. As such, it is a hallmark of the human condition. Gods have no need for fame, for they are immortal. By aspiring to fame and glory, Tamburlaine defines his identity as a human. Finally, Tamburlaine's indefatigable desire to impose his own will on the whole world follows the same logic as human desire in general: it is alive and kicking as long as its object is still tantalizingly far away, but it would cease to be operative as soon as it takes possession of its object and is thereby satisfied. As boundless as his ambition is, he can never reach divine omnipotence, for in that case his thirst for absolute sovereignty would have been quenched and his will to power would die away. The sovereign will operates paradoxically on the premise that it will never succeed in attaining what it strives for.

Two opposite forces are at work in the sovereign will. One the one side, there is the relentless striving for absolute power. On the other side, there is the constraining force of the mortal body that sustains it. The conflict of the two forces breeds a tragic consciousness. At one point, Tamburlaine compares himself to Phaeton (I. 4.2.49–52). Phaeton was allowed to steer his father's chariot—the sun—for one day. Since Phaeton was incapable of controlling the horses, the sun went off course. In order to prevent the earth from being burnt up, Zeus struck him with a thunderbolt. Tamburlaine's self-comparison with Phaeton, likewise a mortal reaching for the skies, links his boundless aspiration to inevitable death. Not surprisingly, the reference to Phaeton returns at the very end of the play, when Tamburlaine utters his final word: "For Tamburlaine, the scourge of God, must die" (II. 5.3.248). In one of the many literary references in the play, Tamburlaine also compares himself to Homer's Hector (II. 3.5.64–68). For his daring, Hector pays the ultimate price that a mortal has to pay: death. This, along with other aspects of his character, makes him the true tragic hero of Homer's poem.[35]

The invocation of such mythological and literary figures as Phaeton and Hector hints at the tragic quality of the sovereign will embodied by Tamburlaine. The dramatic discourse of *Tamburlaine the Great* makes this tragic quality explicit. In part 1, Tamburlaine sweeps from victory to victory, marching, as it seems, inexorably towards the domination of the entire world. A strand of the plot of part 1 is Tamburlaine's courtship of Zenocrate. This name, not documented historically, means the power of Zeus. Tamburlaine's courting of her, then, stands allegorically for his striving for divine omnipotence. If part 1 thus dramatizes the active force propelling the sovereign will towards absolute power, part 2 dramatizes the constraining force exerted on it by the mortal body. The prologue to part 2 announces a play "where death cuts off the progress of his [Tamburlaine's] pomp / And murd'rous Fates throws all his triumphs down." In striving to subjugate the fates, Tamburlaine ends up being overwhelmed by them instead.

At first, the pure energy of the sovereign will, however great it might be, increasingly proves to be inadequate. Under the pressure of the mortality of the human being, Tamburlaine comes to establish an institutional and disciplinary regime. It includes the "celebrated rites of marriage" (I. 5.1.534), the rational organization of the army, the building of alliances, and, above all, the training of his sons, which makes up the main part of actions in part

2.[36] Perhaps nothing testifies more clearly to the pressure of the finitude of human existence as the production and education of children, for it is often through reproduction that a human being hopes to defy death. Tamburlaine expects his sons to succeed him in conquering the world. For this purpose, he designs a disciplinary program that features, among other things, deliberate self-wounding as a method of steeling their courage, as well as the cold-blooded killing of a resistant son. Subsequently, the sovereign will succumbs to the frailty of the human body that sustains it. Upon his wife Zenocrate's death, Tamburlaine threatens, in wonted hyperboles, to storm heaven and hell to take her back. His associate Theridamas remarks poignantly: "Ah, good my lord, be patient. She is dead, / And all this raging cannot make her alive" (II. 2.4.119–20). Later on, he himself falls ill. He still wants to march against the gods, but his voice sounds hollow and pathetic: "Ah, friends, what shall I do? I cannot stand. / Come, carry me to war against the gods" (II. 5.3.51–52). In the clash between the striving for absolute power and the constraining force of the mortal body, the latter wins out. The final act of the play indicates that two sons of Tamburlaine, painstakingly trained by him, may carry on their father's project of conquering the world. Should they do so, it would be the triumph of a stringent disciplinary regime and the legal mechanism of royal succession rather than that of the sovereign will itself. But there is no clear evidence that they will indeed do so. In any case, the final word of the play, reserved for one of the sons, states unambiguously that Tamburlaine is going to have no successors: "Let earth and heaven his timeless death deplore, / For both their worths will equal him no more" (II. 5.3. 252–53).

Tamburlaine the Great dramatizes, in spite of its title, not so much the fate of a historical figure as that of a principle—that of the sovereign will. The sovereign will is a will to absolute power. As such, it seeks to impose itself on the whole world. In so doing, however, it clashes with, and is eventually undone by, the most basic, most ineluctable condition of its agent, namely mortality. A world order enforced by a single sovereign will is possible only as a project that fails.

The Tragedy of the Weak Will: Shakespeare's *King John*

That a strong sovereign will fails does not mean that a weak will has a greater chance of success. A sovereign person equipped with modest willpower is perhaps even less likely to create or enforce a normative world order. Shakespeare's *The Life and Death of King John*, written less than a decade after Marlowe's play, in the mid-1590s, portrays a sovereign person who seems to be exactly the antipode of Tamburlaine—weak-willed, uttering terms feeble and inarticulate rather than astounding, indecisive and wavering rather than forging forward with a conquering sword. Yet King John, historically the ruler of England between 1199 and 1216 and brought back to life by Shakespeare to address some pressing issues in the emerging world of sovereign states, is a character just as tragic as Tamburlaine. A weak will spawns tragedy as inevitably as a strong will does.

King John opens with the French ambassador delivering a challenge from his king to King John. With the support of his mother Eleanor, John responds forcefully at first: "Here have we war for war and blood for blood, / Controlment for controlment. So answer France."[37] He will become much less forceful as the events unfold. The play closes with the French troops landing on the English shores, John poisoned, and his son Henry instated as king. The basic situation of the dramatic plot, then, is the conflict between two states. The occasion for the conflict is a dispute over the English throne. John is the *de facto* king, but his nephew Arthur, being the son of John's elder brother Geoffrey, also stakes a claim to the throne. Since Arthur is still a minor and an orphan, his father dead, his mother a powerless woman, France takes up his cause—of course, not without self-interest. The problem of legitimacy, concerning the foundation of sovereign rule as it does, lies outside of sovereign rule itself. As such, it blends easily with the foreign affairs of a sovereign.

The encounter between John and King Philip of France before Angers, England's French possession—an encounter played out through acts 2 and 3—vividly illustrates the conditions of the international arena in the late sixteenth century. King Philip's accusation that John has usurped the right to the English throne invites a brusque rebuke from John, and a heated exchange ensues:

King John

From whom hast thou this great commission, France,
To draw my answer from thy articles?

King Philip

From that supernal judge that stirs good thoughts
In any breast of strong authority
To look into the blots and stains of right;
That judge hath made me guardian to this boy:
Under whose warrant I impeach thy wrong
And by whose help I mean to chastise it.

King John

Alack, thou dost usurp authority.

King Philip

Excuse it is to beat usurping down. (2.1.110–19)

This is a legal argument before a court that does not, or no longer, exists. King Philip invokes a "supernal judge"—God—who arbitrates in disputes between earthly rulers. Obviously, no one dares to deny the existence of God. Yet God does not speak himself, but needs someone on earth to speak on his behalf. The right to speak on behalf of God, to exercise his authority on earth, is now at stake. John denies this right to Philip. The fact is that both parties in the dispute claim to be God's spokesmen on earth. As much as Philip presumes to derive his authority from God, John considers himself "God's wrathful agent" (2.1.87). Once both assert themselves as God's agents on earth, that is, once both assert their absolute sovereignty, God is eliminated as an effective judge, a third figure that mediates between the two. This point is driven home even more pointedly with the appearance of the papal legate Cardinal Pandulph on the scene. As the head of the Church, the pope has always served as God's spokesperson. But if all kings claim to be God's agents, the pope is demoted to one of many self-appointed spokespersons. If he acts as if he had an authority higher than the kings, he must stand being accused of having usurped it. Challenged by the papal legate, King John ripostes:

> But as we, under God, are supreme head,
> So, under Him, that great supremacy
> Where we do reign, we will alone uphold
> Without th'assistance of a mortal hand,
> So tell the Pope, all reverence set apart
> To him and his usurped authority. (3.1.155–60)

Later, King Philip's son, Louis the Dauphin, rebuffs Pandulph in exactly the same manner (5.2.78–108).

If all kings insist on their sovereignty and recognize no higher authority, their relations to one another fall into a juridical vacuum. In this vacuum, there seem to be two possible courses of action. One of these is the absurd. Since France and England can reach no agreement in their dispute, they ask the citizens of Angers to decide who their king should be. But the citizens refuse to do so, declaring instead that they will obey the one who has already proved to be the king. At this point, the Bastard—the illegitimate son of John's elder brother Richard Cœur-de-Lion—proposes to destroy Angers and thereby eliminate the disagreement between the disputants. This preposterous idea proves to be the only thing that both parties can agree on. The second course of action is prudence, or what political thinkers of the time called reason of state and the Bastard in the play calls "commodity" (2.1.561–98). In the present case, it takes the form of mutually beneficial measures that, if they do not solve the problem for good, may at least alleviate the situation temporarily. Facing the imminent destruction of his city, Hubert, a citizen of Angers, suddenly comes up with the ingenious proposal that the two kings should form an alliance through the marriage of Louis the Dauphin and John's niece Blanche. This proposal wins the approval of both parties, and the two young people are promptly betrothed to one another. Yet what appears to be a way out of the quandary proves to be one more confirmation of lawlessness in international relations. At the urging of the papal legate Pandulph, King Philip revokes, albeit after much perplexity, his oath of friendship that goes along with the marriage alliance. The two kings are enemies again.[38] This episode demonstrates not merely the lack of law in the world of sovereigns, but worse still, the worthlessness of law.

There was hardly a literary text in Shakespeare's time that gave a more clear-sighted sense of the loss of lawful order ensuing from the rise of the sovereign state in the sixteenth century. There seems to be no more authority, no more binding norms left in the world.[39] While registering the collapse of the preexisting normative world order secured by the Christian belief system and institutions—in other words, the collapse of the *respublica christiana*—*King John* simultaneously paints a new picture of the ruler as an enterprising, self-aware agent of action, thus indicating the rising importance of the subjective will of rulers in their relation to one another. From the outset, King John, like his French counterparts King Philip and Louis the Dauphin, is alert to his situation, eager to take initiatives to further his interests and ready to reach some kind of accord through negotiations. The decline of a divinely preordained world order and the rise of the subjective will: these are the two basic parameters of the profound epistemic and institutional transformations with regard to the question of world order that took place in sixteenth-century Europe. They underlay the endeavors of jurists across the confessions—the Protestants Gentili and Grotius as well as the Jesuit Suárez—to formulate a legal code for the relations between sovereign rulers. In contrast to the jurists, Shakespeare created with *King John* a "dramatic laboratory" in which to assay all the ambiguities and tensions attendant upon these transformations.[40] Although the old world order has dissolved—indeed, is unapologetically rejected by all the political actors—oddly it still exercises a certain grip on them. In making decisions and taking initiatives, the subjective will ends up, despite itself, succumbing to the demands of the old regime of power. Such involuntary attachment of the will to the preexisting regime of power can be seen as a weakness. And it is a weakness that has tragic consequences: the old world order dissolves without a new one replacing it, while the sovereign person is crushed in the process.

After an initial demonstration of resolve in his wrangling with France, John holds back, unable to overcome the pressure of what he apparently perceives to be higher laws. First, he begins to doubt his own legitimacy. That he accedes to the English throne by appointment rather than primogeniture is something that he has been aware of the whole time. In the face of the challenge by France, he stands up vigorously in defense of himself. Yet curiously enough, after the confrontation with France has proved that there is no higher authority curbing the will of kings, and after he has defeated France, the legal foundation of his kingship becomes a problem for himself. There are, obviously, two options. If he does acknowledge that there is an inviolable order of things, and that primogeniture is part of it, he can abdicate in favor of his nephew Arthur. Or he can hold the sovereign will to be the highest authority, as he has already done in the argument with France, thereby disregarding primogeniture or, for that matter, any other laws not made by himself. John turns out to choose neither, or rather, both options. He tacitly accepts primogeniture as a law that he must obey without stifling his will to sovereignty. The tension between the sovereign will and what he considers a higher law leads to a fatal decision: to have Arthur eliminated. But this decision has the effect of recreating exactly the same tension. Although he wants to have Arthur killed, murder represents a problem for him. Again, there are two options. If he acknowledges that there are inviolable laws, and that the prohibition against murder is one of them, he can let Arthur go. Or if he thinks the murder is a political necessity, he can carry it out by a sovereign fiat. Again, John chooses neither, or rather both options. As a result, he gives Hubert the commission to murder Arthur without being able to say it aloud, only to be tormented by a sense of guilt afterwards.

The attachment to preexisting norms and the simultaneous insistence of the sovereign will makes every action of John's a crime. The sovereign will breaches the preexisting norms at every turn, yet because the agent of action still holds them in high esteem, this breach appears to be nothing other than criminal offense. If an action is perceived by the agent himself as a crime, he may try to cover it up. But every attempt to cover up a crime just generates more crimes. Alternatively, he can try to undo it. But the act of undoing merely highlights the crime that has been committed. Under the impression that Arthur is no more, John plans to be crowned once again in order to assert his legitimacy. Yet as one of his nobles rightly points out, the recrowning can have no other effect than exposing his very illegitimacy (4.2.30–34). Rather than covering up or undoing a crime, the agent of action may also want to return to the security afforded by preexisting norms, the comfort of the old regime of power. But this entails the abnegation of the will to sovereignty, the demise of the sovereign person. Facing the invasion of the French on English shores and the treason of his nobles, John submits himself to the pope again. He gives up his identity as a sovereign king. Before long, he also gives up his life.

Under the tension between old norms and the will to sovereignty, John flails about in the maelstrom of events, making a decision only to undo it again, abandoning the old without ever being able to find the new. Other dramatic characters behave in the same way. The only exception is the Bastard. Shakespeare portrays him as someone who shares a problem with John, but who reacts to it in an entirely different way. The problem they both share is illegitimacy. In the case of John, it concerns his rule. In the case of the Bastard, it concerns his birth. Whereas John worries about his illegitimacy, the Bastard embraces it. This attitude enables the Bastard to take an observer's stance towards the turbulent events around him, performing a role similar to that of the chorus in Greek tragedy. Without the baggage of preexisting norms, he can give free rein to the exercise of his will. For this reason, he is in the position to encourage the despondent John to "show boldness and aspiring confidence" (5.1.56). And for this reason, John entrusts him with "the ordering of this present time" (5.1.77). The agent of a new world order—whatever form this new world order may take—is someone who does not care about legitimacy, someone who can say: "I am I, howe'er I was begot" (1.1.175).[41]

At the heart of *King John* is the tension between two forces: on the one side, there are norms that have survived an old world order; on the other side, there is the willpower, and the will to power, of rulers eager to assert their sovereignty. This tension is structurally similar, though unrelated in substance, to the tension between the old and the new in Greek tragedy. As mentioned above with regard to Marlowe's *Tamburlaine the Great*, the past in Greek tragedy was the legendary world of myths with their religious beliefs and rituals, and the new age was that of the city-state with politico-legal institutions that demanded agency and responsibility of its citizens. In ways reminiscent of the legendary heroes in Greek tragedies, King John in Shakespeare's play subscribes simultaneously to the old and the new, and perishes in so doing. He is a sovereign person making calculated decisions in relation to others, yet he has difficulty leaving behind the demands and strictures of the old order. In a certain sense, *King John* can be seen as an iteration of Greek tragedy under the particular historical circumstances of early modern Europe.[42] Its ending is characterized by Sophoclean bleakness. Poisoned, John says in the throes of death:

> There is so hot a summer in my bosom
> That all my bowels crumble up to dust;
> I am a scribbled form, drawn with a pen
> Upon a parchment, and against the fire
> Do I shrink up. (5.7.30–34)

The "scribbled form" to which John compares himself may be a legal document or a map. With his death, the symbolic construction of his realm shrinks up. It is therefore even less likely for it to relate to other realms than before. The Bastard has the last word:

> Come the three corners of the world in arms
> And we shall shock them! Naught shall make us rue,
> If England to itself do rest but true. (5.7.116–18)

For all his enthusiasm in "ordering the present time," there is still no indication that the Bastard is going to bring about a new world order. Someone who does not appeal to legitimacy to assert his identity and actions is unlikely to establish a new normative order.

Marlowe's *Tamburlaine the Great* and Shakespeare's *King John* demonstrate, from two opposite angles, that the sovereign will wreaks havoc on the old world order without instituting a new one. The tragedy of international relations, which came into its own in the English Renaissance, blossomed again some half a century later, at the time around 1660. The Peace of Westphalia made the mutual recognition of sovereignty a paramount principle in international relations. The crux of the matter was accordingly no longer the unsettling, destructive potential of the sovereign will, but rather the impossibility of concord between different sovereign wills. The issues touched upon but not fully developed in *King John*—marriage alliance, the fragility of agreements and oaths, and political prudence in international affairs—moved to the center of tragic plots.

CHAPTER THREE

A Tragicomic Intermezzo: The Shapes of World Order in Shakespeare's Romances

Before the tragedy of international relations came into full flower in the mid-seventeenth century, there was another type of dramatic literature dealing with the question of international legal order—Shakespeare's last plays, including *Pericles, Cymbeline, The Winter's Tale,* and *The Tempest*.[43] Sharing much in common, these four plays are usually grouped together and referred to as tragicomedies, romances, or simply problem plays. Doubtlessly generic hybrids, they share with tragedy princely protagonists, but differ from it by their happy endings and their comedic or pastoral elements.[44] With plot elements such as wandering, a shipwreck, the mistaken identities of royal children, and the marriage of a young couple after countless adventures, they were evidently inspired by the Greek romance, a prose narrative genre that, as will be discussed in the next chapter, was rediscovered, translated, and widely imitated in the Renaissance. Written during the reign of King James I, who undertook sustained diplomatic campaigns under the motto *Beati Pacifici*, all of these plays are concerned with international relations, and the happy ending of each play encapsulates, respectively, a distinctive model of international order.[45] In this regard, they resemble the narrative genre of political romance that John Barclay, a poet close to the Jacobean court, inaugurated in 1621 with his *Argenis*. In the present context, this group of late plays by Shakespeare deserves attention for at least two reasons: first, weaving elements culled from a variety of genres into artful dramatic texts, they help bring tragedy into sharp relief as a dramatic genre of formal constraint and purity; second, with plots that move from disorder and crisis to the happy ending of reconciliation and harmony, they offer distinctively shaped models of international order, thereby putting into perspective the tragic vision of international order, which looms *ex negativo* out of death and destruction.[46]

The King's Daughter as the Medium of International Order

Pericles begins with the incest of the king of Antioch and his daughter, which looks like an open secret waiting to be punctured by the eponymous protagonist. Since this play is chronologically the first of the romances, the incest can be seen as the beginning of all of them. At the end of *Pericles*, as well as at the end of all the other romances, there is a king marrying off his daughter. The incest unleashes the plot of *Pericles*, as the king of Antioch, seeing his odious secret revealed, determines to have Pericles killed and thereby puts him to flight. This plot moves, soon enough, to an alternative to incest, as Simonides, the king of Pentapolis, marries his daughter Thaisa to Pericles. The practice of Simonides, opposed to that of the king of Antioch, proves to be the goal of the plot of *Pericles*, indeed, the goal of Shakespeare's romances in general. On the young couple's voyage back to Pericles's home country, Thaisa gives birth to a baby girl on rough seas. The mother is mistakenly believed to have died in childbirth, her body put by Pericles in a chest and thrown into the seas, while he entrusts the baby girl Marina to the care of the governor of Tarsus and his wife. Having been told that Marina is dead, Pericles finds her again many years later under most unexpected circumstances, only to give her away again, this time to the governor of Mytilene, who requests the hand of Marina in marriage. In *The Winter's Tale*, King Leontes of Sicilia believes, in a fit of jealousy, his newborn girl to be the issue of his wife's adultery and orders her to be burnt without even wanting to take a look at her. At the request of his courtier Antigonus, he agrees to commute the punishment to exposure. She is abandoned on the shores of Bohemia, where she is found and then raised by a shepherd. Leontes sees her again—or rather for the first time—sixteen years later when she, now named Perdita, returns to Sicilia in the company of her betrothed Florizel, the prince of Bohemia. As in *Pericles*, the reunion of the father and the daughter in *The Winter's Tale* also turns out to be an occasion for him to give her in marriage to a prince. Significantly, Leontes feels an incestuous desire for Perdita before she is recognized as his daughter (5.1.222–23), so that Paulina, a noble lady embodying his conscience in many ways, has to warn him:

> Sir, my liege,
> Your eye hath too much youth in't. Not a month
> Fore your queen died, she was more worth such gazes
> Than what you look on now. (5.1.223–26)

Leontes's relationship to his daughter reiterates, in condensed form, the movement from incest to exogamy that the plot of *Pericles* as a whole traces. In *The Tempest*, Prospero uses his magic to bring together his daughter Miranda and Ferdinand, the prince of Naples. They fall promptly in love and are engaged to marry at the end of the play. In *Cymbeline*, the marriage of the king's daughter Innogen has already taken place at the beginning, but the king disapproves of her husband Posthumus and banishes him from the court. At the end, the king recognizes him and blesses the marriage.

Shakespeare's romances all end in a marriage alliance sanctioned or, in the case of *The Tempest*, engineered by the bride's royal father. For social anthropologists, a marriage alliance establishes an affinal relationship between one descent group and another, thus weaving the basic fabric of society.[47] It is all of a piece with the incest taboo—that is, the prohibition against sexual relations within a descent group. "The incest prohibition," in the words of Lévi-Strauss, "expresses the transition from the natural fact of consanguinity to the cultural fact of alliance."[48] Beginning with incest and ending with marriage alliance, *Pericles*—and by extension the corpus of Shakespeare's romances as a whole—figures, by means of a romantic plot, the transition from consanguinity to a complex society transcending blood lines.[49] Since the agents of action in the romances are royal persons, and since in absolutism the royal person is identified with the state, the society constituted through marriage alliance at the end of each play is a society of states or international society. Marriage alliance was a mainstay of international relations in Shakespeare's age and beyond. For instance, in keeping with his diplomatic endeavors to make peace in Europe, James I went to great length to negotiate marriages between his children and scions of other European royal houses.[50] Every so often, the politics of marriage alliance enlisted the help of the art of theater: *The Tempest* was performed at court in celebration of Princess Elizabeth's marriage to the Elector Palatine in 1613.

As will be discussed in detail later in this chapter, marriage between royal houses made up an integral dimension of international legal order in the age of absolutism. The plots of Shakespeare's romances—the twists and turns of which, however improbable, lead invariably to marriage alliance—shed light on some basic principles that inform the ordering of international society. First of all, the romantic plots stage the legalization of international relations. In the Pentapolis scene in the early part of *Pericles*—the very first scene of royal betrothal in the romances—King Simonides, though very happy with his daughter Thaisa's choice of Pericles, decides to create some obstacles rather than announce his approval right away. He says to himself: "I must dissemble that / In show, I have determined on in heart" (Sc. 9.20–21). So he accuses Pericles of "[lying] like a traitor":

Ay, traitor,
That thus disguised art stolen into my court
With witchcraft of thy actions to bewitch
The yielding spirit of my tender child. (Sc. 9.47–50)

INTERNATIONAL ORDER AS TRAGEDY

This accusation provokes, as expected, vehement protests and indignation on the part of Pericles. Simonides then rebukes his daughter for choosing the wrong match, of course only to provoke her to protest:

> I entreat you
> To remember that I am in love,
> The power of which love cannot be confined
> By the power of your will. (Sc.9.80–83)

Now that Simonides has heightened the tension to the breaking point, he suddenly declares, to the surprise and delight of the young couple, that he actually wanted to join their hands all along:

> Therefore hear you, mistress: either frame your will to mine—
> And you, sir, hear you—either be ruled by me,
> Or I shall make you
> [*He claps their hands together*]
> man and wife. (Sc. 9. 103–05)

This little "show" put on by Simonides marks the son-in-law as a foreigner, raises the possibility that he may engage in illicit activities, and then negates this possibility. Subsequently, it raises the possibility that the daughter's love may go against the father's will, and then negates this possibility too. The message is clear: the royal marriage is a legal transaction in accordance with the sovereign will. Instead of stating this message directly, the "show" stages, by double negations as it were, the royal marriage as a transaction that is not an illicit relation to a foreign state, and that is not against the will of the sovereign. By creating tension, it also heightens the pleasure of the young couple.

Prospero, certainly even more theatrical than Simonides, uses the same trick when he accuses Ferdinand—the prince of Naples whom he himself has brought to his daughter—of being "a spy" and "a traitor" (1.2.454–61). To a certain extent, Shakespeare's romantic plots in general proceed in ways similar to Simonides's "show." They first present events that seem to disrupt relations between states or contradict the will of the sovereign, then have these events negated by their own consequences, in order finally to reach lawful international relations through royal marriage. In *The Winter's Tale*, Florizel's choice of the shepherdess Perdita as his bride provokes the harsh disapproval of his father, the king of Bohemia, but the sequence of events unleashed by this disapproval leads to the revelation of Perdita's true identity and to a royal

CHAPTER THREE

marriage that the king of Bohemia heartily approves. A plot that reaches settlement through the negation of lawlessness and conflict creates pleasure for both the dramatic characters and the audience. Significantly, the reunion of the kings and the implied ratification of the marital contract between Florizel and Perdita—events that make up the main parts, though not the entirety, of the closural settlement of *The Winter's Tale*—are not shown on stage but recounted by rapt onlookers (5.2).

The legalization of international relations through the marriage plot is perfectly illustrated by *The Tempest*. Prospero, the duke of Milan, delegates the duties of the government to his younger brother Antonio in order to devote himself to books. Antonio attempts to usurp the duchy by enlisting the help of Alonso, the king of Naples. Lured by tribute and homage, Alonso comes to Milan and drives out its rightful duke Prospero as well as his young child Miranda. In exile, as his daughter Miranda reaches the marriageable age, Prospero conjures up a tempest for the purpose of coupling her up with Ferdinand, the crown prince of Naples. The marriage between the young couple, orchestrated by Prospero, is expected to yield many benefits. The mere prospect of the marriage already elicits an apology from Prospero's inveterate enemy Alonso (5.1.110–19). In the long run, especially after Prospero's death—Prospero says that once he returns to Milan, "Every third thought shall be my grave" (5.1.311)—the marriage of Miranda and Ferdinand will lead to the union of Milan and Naples. This will prevent Antonio, the ambitious and unrepentant brother of Prospero, from ever acceding to the throne that he has tried to usurp. This will also neutralize Sebastian, the equally ambitious younger brother of Alonso, who, at the instigation of Antonio, makes an attempt on Alonso's life in order to usurp the throne of Naples. Above all, the marriage will cancel out Milan's subordination to Naples during Antonio's illegitimate regency, and ground the relationship of the two states on the legal bond that is the marital contract. Solving the problems of succession and thus safeguarding the legitimacy of the government in both Milan and Naples, and at the same time placing the relationship of the two states on a secure legal footing, the marriage alliance plotted by Prospero—the theater artist—ensures a lawful international order.

As the case of *The Tempest* indicates, the marriage of the king's daughter in Shakespeare's romances has a reconciliatory function, restoring order and harmony. In *The Winter's Tale*, the marriage of Perdita and Florizel reestablishes the bond between Sicilia and Bohemia that Leontes, in his groundless suspicion of adultery between his queen and the king of Bohemia, severs. Regarding the use of marriage alliance as a tool for international reconciliation, *Cymbeline* is a special case. Compared to his counterparts in the other three romances, King Cymbeline's son-in-law Posthumus is not a foreign prince, but the orphaned descendant of a valiant warrior in Cymbeline's own service, who had been adopted by the king and made the Gentleman of the Bedchamber. The marriage plot involving this royal son-in-law performs nonetheless the function of evoking an international legal order. Posthumus, as historically minded Shakespearean scholars have convincingly argued, stands for the Scottish *post nati*, namely those Scots born after James's accession to the English throne in 1603 in the union of the crowns of Scotland and England. His marriage to the king's daughter, then, provides an allegorical answer to the politically and legally contentious questions raised by the Anglo-Scottish union, an answer that is all the more significant because it is linked in the play to the larger international political issues associated with Britain's accommodation to Rome.[51]

However, the reconciliatory restoration of international legal order, staged by means of marriage plots, is fraught with ambiguities. As an institution that overcomes incest, marriage alliance implements not merely exogamy, coupling the king's daughter with a foreign prince and thereby connecting one state to another, but also monogamy, coupling the princess to only one prince and, consequently, connecting one state to only one other state to the exclusion of all others. The emphasis on the princess's chastity in all the plays, ranging from Marina's impassioned exhortation of Lysimachus not to deflower her in the brothel (*Pericles*, Sc. 19. 103–67) to Prospero's exaggerated warning to Ferdinand against premarital sex (*The Tempest*, 4.1.13–33), testifies to the monogamous imperative of marriage alliance. Given the exclusiveness of monogamy, while a marriage alliance makes possible a legally secured relation between one state and another state, it forecloses the possibility of the same kind of relation between this one state and any third state. By demanding sexual fidelity, monogamy also raises the specter of infidelity, hence the specter of an illicit relation between a state and a third state. In *The Winter's Tale*, an all-consuming suspicion of his wife's infidelity takes hold of Leontes, destroying his friendly relation to Bohemia. While the marriage of Perdita and Florizel restores order, it is likely that Florizel will, after the consummation of their marriage, behave in the same destructive manner as Leontes, not in spite of, but precisely because of monogamy. The scene of Miranda and Ferdinand at chess in *The Tempest* highlights the ambiguities of marriage alliance:

Miranda
Sweet lord, you play me false.

Ferdinand

No, my dearest love,
I would not for the world.

Miranda

Yes, for a score of kingdoms you should wrangle,
And I would call it fair play. (5.1.171–74)

Brief as it is, this scene rehearses the main stages of royal infidelity: accusation, denial, and willing acceptance. Marriage alliance is haunted by infidelity even before it is consummated. The international legal order based on it, then, threatens to collapse at any time. But that may be a reason why marriage alliance is always needed. For if it solved all the problems and brought about eternal peace, there would not be discord and crisis, which occasion romantic plots in the first place.

In Shakespeare's romantic plots, the king's daughter plays the crucial role of the medium of international order. In this role, she also serves as a generic marker of the plays as romances, with romance being understood in the general sense as a genre that features the integration of the hero or heroine into society—usually in the form of marriage—at the end. The king's son as a dramatic character, in contrast, tends to portend tragedy, with tragedy being understood in the general sense as a genre that features the isolation of the hero or heroine from society—usually in the form of death—at the end.[52] The main reason is that he embodies royal succession, with all its conflicts and rivalries. Hamlet is perhaps the most famous example. The king's son Mamillius in *The Winter's Tale* marks the first three acts of the play as a tragedy. He is the first victim of the king's actions, and the only victim that is not redeemed by the reconciliation at the end. Unlike his mother Hermione, he does not come back to life. Unlike Antigonus who dies after having exposed and thereby saved the king's daughter, he does not even contribute to the general reconciliation. In fact, Mamillius, the character who pronounces the title of the play—"A sad tale's best for winter" (2.1.25)—is overshadowed by death from the outset, as the winter's tale told by him begins with death: "There was a man—[. . .] dwelt by a churchyard" (2.1.29–30). His death, the ending of a tragedy, coincides with the birth of his sister, the beginning of a romance. The king's daughter is born to be a potential match for a foreign prince and to serve, through marriage, as an instrument of peace. Since the road to marriage has many detours, and since the detours lead the king's daughter far from the orbits of royal existence, to the countryside and to locales of low life, the romantic plot involves poetic genres associated with these places respectively—the pastoral (as in *The Winter's Tale* and *Cymbeline*) and comedy (as in *Pericles* and *The Tempest*). These generic elements defer the ending and, forming an integral part of the romantic plot, also add complexity to the ending.

Shapes of World Order

Whereas the tragedies discussed in this chapter invariably conclude with the impossibility of a lawful world order, the happy endings of Shakespeare's romances affirm a lawful world order and, moreover, lend concrete shape to it. The joining of two states through the marriage of the king's daughter to a foreign prince certainly makes up the core of the lawful world order. But depending on the detours that the heroine takes on her road to marriage, and depending on the circumstances under which the marriage becomes possible, the shape of world order varies from romance to romance.

Pericles's daughter's marriage interlocks with his own marriage to form a system of states. By the end of the play, Simonides, the king of Pentapolis and Pericles's father-in-law, has died. Pericles proposes to his newly rediscovered queen Thaisa that they take over Pentapolis, leaving his own kingdom of Tyre to his daughter and son-in-law (Sc. 22.101–4). Marriage alliances over two generations link three states with one another: Pericles's ancestral kingdom, the kingdom inherited by his wife, and the state governed by his son-in-law Lysimachus. All the other countries that Pericles, his daughter Marina, and his wife Thaisa have traversed on their respective wanderings are likely to join this system of states. The incestuous king of Antioch has justly met his death. In Tarsus, rebellion has overthrown the governor, because he and his wife, once upon a time saved by Pericles and entrusted with the care of his daughter Marina, have in their nefarious ingratitude tried to kill their charge. These two countries will naturally fall within Pericles's sphere of influence. Ephesus, where Thaisa was washed ashore and preserved in the temple of Diana, is sure to remain a friendly country. At the end, there looms a universal system of states, or even a naval empire, of which the historical Pericles in Thucydides is so proud.

The world order taking shape at the end of *Cymbeline*, in the form of a universal peace proclaimed by the king, is one based on the principles of Roman law. The marriage of the king's daughter in this play, as noted above, can be read as the poetic figuration of the Anglo-Scottish union. The legal principles of the union are elucidated through the subplot of British-Roman relations. When Lucius, the ambassador of Rome, comes to Cymbeline's court to extort tribute from Britain, the king rebuffs him on two grounds. First,

Britain enjoys its own ancient constitution and is therefore not beholden to Rome (3.1.57–60). Second, having subjected itself to Rome and its laws, Britain now seeks its liberties (3.1.68–75). Towards the end of the play, the first justification for resistance to Rome, going hand in hand with the jingoistic stance of the wicked queen and her moronic son Cloten, is dropped with the death of these two negative characters. The second justification is reformulated in terms of *translatio imperii* after Britain defeats Rome in a war ignited by the dispute over tribute: just as Cymbeline has served under, and learned from, Caesar, Britain is going to follow in Rome's footsteps and become an imperial power.[53] As "the Roman eagle" has flown "from south to west on wing soaring aloft," the soothsayer predicts,

> Th'imperial Caesar should again unite
> His favour with the radiant Cymbeline,
> Which shines here in the west. (5.4.475–77)

The marriage of the king's daughter and Posthumus, symbolizing the Anglo-Scottish union, will give birth to a Britain in the image of imperial Rome. Rome exercises its imperium through its laws, and these laws should also serve as the basis of its relations to Britain as the new Rome. Here war is to give way to a lawful peace (5.4.480–86).

In *The Tempest*, the marriage of Miranda and Ferdinand, meant to restore legitimacy and to set international relations on a legal footing, represents but one side of the story. While engineering this marriage to resolve his conflicts with Naples as well as with his usurping brother, Prospero proves to be curiously uninterested in resolving another problem—the legal basis of his rule over the island, on which he lives in exile after being expelled from Milan. Prior to his arrival, the island was inhabited by the sorceress Sycorax. Her son Caliban lays claim to it on the basis of inheritance: "This island's mine, by Sycorax my mother, / Which thou tak'st from me" (1.2.331–32). For Prospero, Sycorax—"this blue-eyed hag" who owned the island before (1.2.269)—is, even in her death, an enemy as "inveterate" (1.2.122) as Alonso, the king of Naples. Yet whereas he endeavors to reconcile himself with Alonso by arranging the marriage of their children, reconciliation with Sycorax seems never to have crossed his mind. Similarly, Sycorax's son Caliban resembles Alonso's son Ferdinand in that both are libidinous youths. Caliban has attempted to rape Miranda, while Prospero warns Ferdinand insistently against sex with his daughter prior to the wedding. Rebuking Miranda for her infatuation with Ferdinand, Prospero says: "Foolish wench! / To th'most of men this is a Caliban" (1.2.480–81). He burdens Ferdinand with the same physical labor as Caliban (3.1). Yet whereas he deploys all his arts to facilitate the marriage of his daughter to Ferdinand, marrying her to Caliban is apparently an utter impossibility. Sycorax is paralleled to Alonso, and Caliban to Ferdinand, only to be treated differently.

The differential treatment is particularly striking in terms of law. Prospero's overarching concern with the breach and restoration of law in the relation between his dukedom and Naples stands in stark contrast to his indifference to the legal challenge regarding his relation to the island—an indifference all the more remarkable because it is Prospero himself who has made this legal challenge possible. Prospero claims to have taught Caliban everything, including language. Teaching and learning turn out to be symbolic processes by which social relations are produced. Prospero turns into a master eager to dominate, and Caliban into a slave braced for rebellion. When Caliban tells Prospero that "this island's mine, by Sycorax my mother, / Which thou tak'st from me," he is speaking the language of law. Nowhere else could he have learned this language than from Prospero. If by teaching Caliban how to speak, Prospero just taught him "how to curse" (1.2.366), by teaching Caliban law, Prospero taught him how to litigate.[54] Prospero's failure to engage with Caliban's accusation indicates the special status of the island: it is something that he has brought into the law—not least by teaching its inhabitant the legal language—but at the same time leaves outside of the law. This status is not clarified until Prospero quells Caliban's rebellion and thus brings the island brutally under his rule. One way of making sense of this special legal status of the island is to invoke the concept of colonialism.[55] It is obvious that Prospero's occupation of the island epitomizes the relation between Europe and overseas territories, whereas his preoccupation with forging a marital alliance between Milan and Naples is a matter of the relation between European states. The model of world order that looms large at the end of *The Tempest* is thus remarkable for the asymmetry between European states and overseas territories: whereas the relations between European states such as the fictionalized Milan and Naples are to be regulated by law, the relations between Europe and overseas territories are left in a legal limbo, at once inside and outside of the law.

The model of world order developed in *The Winter's Tale* differs from those in the three other romances in that it has a pronounced spiritual dimension. The marriage alliance between Sicilia and Bohemia is intertwined with Christian notions of divine grace and providential order. Leontes's jealousy causes the death of his son, the apparent death of his wife Hermione, and the abandonment of his infant daughter, not to mention the death of his faithful courtier Antigonus in carrying out his command. Thereupon he comes to repent all that has done. Sixteen years later, at the beginning of the fifth act, one of his courtiers says to him:

> Sir, you have done enough, and have performed
> A saint-like sorrow. No fault could you make
> Which you have not redeemed, indeed, paid down
> More penitence than done trespass. At the last
> Do as the heavens have done, forget your evil.
> With them, forgive yourself. (5.1.1–6)

Penitence, as it turns out, leads indeed to the divine grace of restoration, with the abandoned daughter Perdita returning home and Hermione coming back to life in the springtime. The suggestion of miraculous resurrection is indeed hard to miss. Grace requires faith, as Paulina—an unmistakable reference to St. Paul—tells Leontes: "It is required / You do awake your faith" (5.3.94–95). Combining the Catholic sacrament of penance, the Protestant emphasis on faith, and certain pagan religious elements—the revived Hermione speaks of "gods" and "graces" in the plural (5.3.121–23)—the ending of *The Winter's Tale* affirms divine providence.[56] The relation between sovereigns, exemplified by that between the king of Sicilia and the king of Bohemia, follows a divinely preordained path.

To sum up, Shakespeare's romances proffer four distinctive models of world order, based on the ideas of states-system (*Pericles*), imperialism (*Cymbeline*), European colonialism (*The Tempest*), and spiritual salvation (*The Winter's Tale*). Each of them answers the question of the relation between states in its own way, but all of them prove to be prescient, being taken up and elaborated in later times. The model of world order based on a system of states envisioned at the end of *Pericles* gained wide currency after the Peace of Westphalia, conceptualized especially by Samuel Pufendorf in a tract entitled "De systematibus civitatem" and published in his *Dissertationes academicae selectiores* (1675). It came to renewed prominence in the twentieth century through the works of the so-called English School of International Relations.[57] The imperialist model of world order, formulated at the end of *Cymbeline*, had its heyday in the nineteenth century, although it was also at work both before and after.[58] The colonialist model developed by *The Tempest*, which places the relations among European states on a legal basis but leaves the relations between European states and overseas territories in a legal limbo, corresponds roughly to what Carl Schmitt called *ius publicum europaeum*, an international legal order that supposedly lasted from the sixteenth to the end of the nineteenth century.[59]

Finally, the spiritual model of world order, superimposed on the relation between states at the end of *The Winter's Tale*, remained part of the Christian worldview throughout the ages.

Theatrical Myths

As the endings of Shakespeare's four late plays—plays that all feature a highly improbable sequence of events traversing enormous spatial and temporal spans—these models of world order can be properly characterized as the products of the dramatic art. In the plays themselves, however, they are all attributed to the intervention of pagan gods. In *Pericles*, Diana visits the protagonist in a slumber, bidding him to go to her temple on Ephesus (Sc. 21.226–36). There, he is reunited with his wife Thaisa. In *Cymbeline*, Jupiter descends on an eagle in a dream dreamt by Posthumus at the lowest point of his life, laying upon his breast a tablet that foretells his fortune and, along with it, the final denouement of the play (5.3.187–207). In *The Winter's Tale*, the ending is prefigured by Apollo's oracle, pronounced in the climactic scene of the trial of Hermione (3.2.130–34). In *The Tempest*, Juno appears onstage along with Iris and Ceres "to celebrate / A contract of true love" (4.1.132–33), a contract to be consummated at the end of the play after all the problems will have been resolved. In each case, the dramatic plot presents itself as the design of a deity. In their role as the agent who leads the tangle of events, in spite of countless loose ends and against all odds, towards the predestined end, these deities, under whatever name they appear onstage, all stand for one figure—the figure of the dramatist adept at plot-making. They are the self-projections of the dramatist in the drama itself. The spectacular quality of their epiphanies—the descents of Diana and Jupiter belong to the most striking *coups de théâtre* in Shakespeare—draws attention to the artifice of theater making.[60] Prospero, the virtuoso theater man who mounts the masque with Juno, Iris, and Ceres in *The Tempest*, leaves no doubt as to what the deities really are—"some vanity of mine art" (4.1.41). He famously makes mention of the "globe" in that same scene, punning on the name of Shakespeare's theater.

With the dramatist inscribing himself within the drama as a deity, the dramatic plot that he constructs is implicitly supposed to be on a par with divine providence. Consequently, the world order taking shape at the end of each dramatic plot takes on the quality of a divine dispensation. This dispensation is short of the order of salvation, for the gods that it is associated with are pagan rather than Christian. In the case of *The Winter's Tale*, Apollo's oracle coexists jarringly with the soteriological implication of the ending. It was the consensus of Renaissance mythography that the pagan gods were born of the poetic imagination of the ancients. By associating the models of world order with pagan gods, Shakespeare marks them as poetic inventions. Finally, for Renaissance humanists and artists, pagan mythology was to be used primarily as allegory.[61] With the turn of events attributed to the gods, the dramatic figuration of world order in Shakespeare's romances can be considered allegorical as well. Because there was no *agora* or public assembly at which to talk about world affairs, one had to speak otherwise—*allō*—than at the *agora*, for instance on the theatrical stage.

The Tragedy of Reason of State (Lohenstein)

Happy endings became rare in the mid-seventeenth century. The tragic stage of the time exposed Shakespearean romances—and, worse still, the legal framework set up by the Peace of Westphalia for international relations—as fiction. The German baroque tragedian Andreas Gryphius's *Catharina von Georgien*, written at the time of the peace negotiations in Osnabrück and Münster, exhibits the mendacity and vulnerability of any and all legal arrangements between sovereigns. As an alternative, it develops, following the lead of the Dutch tragedian Joost van den Vondel's *Maria Stuart* (1646), a martyrological model of international order: it affirms God as the supreme arbitrator of kings and substitutes his eternal kingdom of peace for the warring kingdoms on earth by representing the conflicts between sovereigns in terms of martyrdom. This model, however, is intrinsically paradoxical, for it asserts the universal jurisdiction of God only by presupposing and then excluding the other—that is, whoever is considered the persecutor, be they pagan or heretic, Protestant or Catholic. It is also paradoxical insofar as it envisions a universal peace for the world only by renouncing the world, for martyrdom involves death and the abnegation of everything earthly. Ultimately, *Catharina von Georgien*, a prime example of martyr drama in the seventeenth century, institutes a martyrological poetics that conceives of tragedy as a poetic form capable of evoking a vision of eternal peace in the audience through the representation of violence, destruction and the resulting ruins.[62]

Cleopatra (1661) and *Sophonisbe* (performed in the 1660s and published in 1680), both by Daniel Casper von Lohenstein, Gryphius's countryman and another great tragedian of the German Baroque, deal with international law and its failings as well.[63] Whereas Gryphius's *Catharina von Geogien* turns to martyrdom as an alternative to law, Lohenstein's two plays explore the role of reason of state in the international space where law reaches its limits—

with sobering results: both demonstrate not only the impotence of law, but also the futility of reason of state with all its stratagems and subterfuges.

Ever since Giovan Giorgio Trissino's *Sofonisba* (1515) and Étienne Jodelle's *Cléopâtre captive* (1553), the colorful stories of Sophonisbe and Cleopatra known from Roman history have belonged to the materials most favored by tragedians. Recounted in Livy's history of Rome, the main events making up the story of Sophonisbe took place during the Second Punic War.[64] Sophonisbe, the daughter of a Carthaginian general, was married to Syphax, a king of Numidia allied with Carthage in its war against Rome. In the meantime, Masinissa, another king of Numidia, was allied with Rome. With his assistance, the Roman army defeated and captured Syphax. Sophonisbe faced the prospect of enslavement. Seeing her great distress, however, Masinissa fell in love with her. She instantly agreed to marry him to avoid the humiliation of being paraded in Rome's triumphal processions. But the Roman general Scipio did not give Masinissa permission to marry an enemy queen. Therefore Masinissa sent Sophonisbe a cup of poison to honor his promise of sparing her the fate of being taken to Rome. The story of the Egyptian queen Cleopatra is shrouded in legends, with Plutarch's biography of Mark Antony serving as one of the most widely cited sources. After the Battle of Actium, Antony committed suicide, allegedly after having heard the false news spread by Cleopatra about her own death. Cornered by Augustus, Cleopatra committed suicide as well, allegedly by an asp's bite, in order to avoid being paraded in Rome. In Lohenstein's handling, the stories of Rome's two famous enemy queens, separated by two centuries as they were, follow the same pattern.[65] The plots of both plays open with a crushing defeat for the heroines, proceed to show how expediency, necessity, and interest—in a word, reason of state—dictate their actions under dire circumstances, and conclude with their self-inflicted deaths as a result of the utter failure of their devious actions. As such, both plays demonstrate the inability of reason of state to bring about international order. In so doing, however, they also bring to light the theatrical principles underlying reason of state, and coopt them as the basis of a poetics of tragedy.

International Law as Dissimulation, Religion as Simulation

In the beginning, there is the fragility of law. Like Gryphius's *Catharina von Georgien*, both *Cleopatra* and *Sophonisbe* open with the complete breakdown of all legal norms in the international arena. In *Cleopatra*, no sooner is the curtain raised than Antonius, the consort of Cleopatra, concludes that law means nothing for Augustus: "No alliance, no treaty is the measure of his deeds" (I.6–7). When Augustus's emissary proclaims that he offers "treaty and peace" (I.661), Antonius replies:

> Augustus whetted the weapons on our breast /
> Before I could reach for paper and ink for the sake of our security;
> He forgot about the law of nations over against me /
> Did not proclaim war, until I felt sword and stroke
> On my skin. (I.675–79)[66]

Similarly, international law and its violation are the subject matter of the very first sentences in *Sophonisbe*:

> **Masinissa**
> Whoever breaks oath and alliance / sets up a trap for himself.
> So Sophonisbe falls and Syphax is lost /
> Because she fathered the breach of peace / And he gave birth to it. (I.2–4)

The oxymoronic phrases "she fathered" and "he gave birth to" express the unnaturalness, the perversity of breaching peace treaties, so that the factual lack of international legal order is figured as a cosmic disturbance.

In the international space outlined at the beginning of Lohenstein's plays, the problem is not so much the lack of legal norms as the willful use made of them. Augustus has contracted treaties of peace and alliance in order to bide his time. Once having gained an advantage, he has no qualms about trampling on them. Lured by the beauty of Sophonisbe, Syphax breaks a peace agreement with Rome and allies himself with Carthage. Law is merely part of a prince's carefully calibrated policies, one item in the toolkit of reason of state, one move in the calculus of interests. As the discussion of Alberico Gentili in chapter 1 indicates, international law was intertwined with reason of state from the outset, supposed to provide a legal framework for sovereign states to pursue their interests. The German historian Friedrich Meinecke described reason of state and international law as locked in an ongoing competition with one another: "International law seeks to restrain the working of reason of state and give it as much legal character as possible. Reason of state, however, resists this restriction and also very frequently uses, indeed abuses law as a means for its egoistic purposes."[67] By the mid-seventeenth century, reason of state pervaded the dealings of sovereign states to such a degree that it came to shape international law. In the words of a legal historian,

> The more the systems of natural law and international law developed and consolidated in the course of the seventeenth century, the more

they succeeded in treating arguments about the "interest of princes" (Rohan) as something legitimate and juristically relevant. "The doctrine of the interests of states" (Meinecke) conceives of these interests no longer as an incalculable factor of infringement of law, but on the contrary as an empirically verifiable topos of the formation of law, as well as of the initiation, alteration, and dissolution of treaties. It is a topos acceptable by international law. Both the territories in the Holy Roman Empire and the European states in general formulate their "interests" and act in accordance with their "reason."[68]

Reason of state was recognized by international law. Or to put it the other way around, international law came increasingly under the sway of reason of state. Treaties were initiated for the sake of interest, altered for the sake of interest, and dissolved for the sake of interest. This fact of life in the international arena stands at the beginning of both *Cleopatra* and *Sophonisbe*. In illustrating this fact, the plays shine a light on the code of behavior that guides the princes' handling of law: dissimulation. For sovereign persons such as Augustus and Syphax, legal transactions—the contracting of peace and alliance—always serve as a smokescreen for the pursuit of interests.

With treaties of peace and alliance breaking down, the international arena becomes a realm of anomie, a legal vacuum. In this space, brute force reigns supreme. In distress, the weaker party usually turns to God, the divine judge. That is what the Georgian queen Catharina does in Gryphius's *Catharina von Georgien*. That is also what the Numidian-Carthaginian queen Sophonisbe and the Egyptian queen Cleopatra in Lohenstein's plays do. Yet there is a vital difference between Gryphius and Lohenstein. Whereas Gryphius's heroine bears witness to divine justice by sacrificing her life with the greatest conviction and in accordance with a well-established martyrological procedure, the heroines in Lohenstein's two plays invoke gods at opportune moments by means of apparently arbitrary rituals. After hearing about the defeat of her country and the capture of the king by Roman forces, Sophonisbe decides to fight on. For this purpose, she considers it necessary to make a sacrifice to the gods. Remarkable, first of all, is the fact that she justifies the act of sacrifice not on the basis of faith but with reference to reports that sacrificial acts in other places and times have been efficacious (I.393–99). The sacrificial offering should be one of her sons, but there seem to be no fixed rules about which one to choose. The matter is settled by lottery. When King Syphax unexpectedly arrives on the scene and sees one of his sons is placed on the altar, he is shocked, exclaiming:

What foolish things are you going to do [. . .]?
What? Should the blood of Hierba

> Be the despicable sacrifice here? Take him away! His courage
> Should bring Numidia to freedom in time.
> [. . .] Is there no other sacrificial offering?
> The Sun and the Moon want to have the first captives
> As sacrifices on their altar surrounded by flames.
> Bring two of them here right away. They will be sweet gifts
> For the great gods. (I.436–45)

While sacrifice is deemed a necessary act to propitiate the gods, there is general confusion about what sacrificial offerings should be. It seems that offerings can be substituted freely. Consequently, it is hard to predict whether a specific offering would draw "fury or favor" from the gods (I.446). Vermina, the man entrusted with carrying out the act of sacrifice, draws the logical conclusion that humans are incapable of foreseeing divine judgment (I.447–49).

That the divine is inscrutable and unlikely to be swayed by good works is, of course, a fundamental Protestant doctrine. Yet whereas the Lutheran Gryphius still holds on to the value of the sacrifice of a martyr as a testimony to the divine, Lohenstein—a Lutheran as well, but open to other confessions, including Calvinism—offers a different assessment of sacrifice: it has no bearing on the divine itself, but is an act carried out by humans in the name of the divine to further a practical purpose.[69] Conversely, if a certain practical purpose is achieved manifestly by human means, the success can be attributed to the divine. For instance, Syphax has managed to escape captivity by bribing a prison guard, but Sophonisbe responds to this success by saying "thanks to the gods" (I.471). Because sacrifice is nothing more than the means for a certain practical end, its constitutive operations—the choice of the person ministering the sacrifice, the choice of sacrificial offerings, and the procedure of the sacrificial act—are so variable as to be arbitrary, entirely subject to expediency. Sophonisbe's son can simply be replaced by two war prisoners. The purpose of a sacrificial act may also be redefined any time. In the episode under consideration, the sacrifice is initiated by Sophonisbe for the sake of war efforts, but after Syphax's return is repurposed for celebrating his escape from captivity (I.470–75).

The sacrificial acts in Lohenstein's plays can be characterized as a simulation of the divine. Simulation represents the operation of something that does not exist, that is not accessible, or that otherwise cannot be engaged. In keeping with Protestant theology, the divine is conceived as something inaccessible and inscrutable in Lohenstein's dramatic world. Instead of resigning themselves passively to this inaccessibility, however, the sovereign persons in this world engage in acts designed to produce an appearance or an illusion of the divine at work, all with a view to achieving a certain practical effect. Accordingly, the ontological status of the divine itself becomes a matter of human decision. Different people presume the existence of different gods. If humans do not get what they want from one god, they just turn to another. Lohenstein's contemporary Blaise Pascal (1623–62), in a fragment headed *infini—rien*, posits a wager—the famous *pari de Pascal*—by which humans bet with their lives either that God exists or that God does not exist, thus making the existence of God a problem of human decision.[70] Lohenstein's plays go a step further, making the existence of God a human decision based on contingent needs and interests. With the invocation of the divine becoming a mere simulation at the behest of expediency, divine justice is implicitly dismissed as a principle in international relations, not even endued with subjective validity as is still the case in Gryphius's *Catharina von Georgien*. It becomes part of reason of state.[71] Reason of state underlies the "theological situation of the epoch," which Walter Benjamin descries in the German baroque *Trauerspiel*: "the failure of eschatology," "the renunciation of the state of grace," and "the reversion to a bare state of creation."[72]

In sum, the handling of international law and divine justice by Lohenstein's dramatic characters exemplifies, respectively, two interrelated modes of behavior dictated by reason of state: dissimulation and simulation. They determine dramatic actions throughout the plays, serving as the twin engines, as it were, of both plots. In *Cleopatra*, Augustus's stratagem of playing Antonius and Cleopatra against each other epitomizes dissimulation, just as Cleopatra's feigning of death for the purpose of getting rid of Antonius and saving herself epitomizes simulation. At a crucial moment in *Sophonisbe*, the heroine frees her husband Syphax from the dungeon, slips into his clothes, and awaits Masinissa who is expected to come to the dungeon to kill Syphax. In so doing, she pulls off an act of dissimulation, which fools two kings at once: her seemingly courageous deed of freeing Syphax, which elicits many a protestation of love and gratitude from him, actually has the purpose of meeting Masinissa in private in order to "lure him into the snare of love" (II.308)—a snare which Masinissa falls into right away.[73]

Simulation, Dissimulation, Theatricality

Simulation and dissimulation are universal human phenomena. In the sixteenth and seventeenth centuries, however, the interest in them reached an unprecedented intensity. As concepts, they took on highly nuanced meanings.[74] There is, first, an ontological dimension to them, insofar as they separate being from appearance: "Dissimulation is an attempt to make things not appear as they are. One simulates what is not there, one dissimulates what is there."[75] There is, second, an epistemological dimension, insofar as they either substitute truth for untruth or untruth for truth: "Simulation consists in pretending that what is not true is true; dissimulation consists in negating what is true."[76] There is, third, a praxeological dimension, insofar as they dissociate an action from its purpose: "the one who simulates wants to appear to do things that he does not do; the one who dissimulates does not want to appear to do the things that he does."[77] Last but not least, there is a psychological dimension, insofar as a dissembler hides his true emotions, whereas someone who simulates feigns emotions that he does not have: "There is nothing more fatal to dissimulation than the impetuosity of wrath, and the prince must so control this passion that he never betrays himself by words or other signs of anger or emotion."[78] Located at the intersection of multiple discursive fields and informed by complex meanings, simulation and dissimulation figured as a centerpiece of reason of state from the outset. Machiavelli argued that a prince "must be a great feigner and dissembler."[79] Botero stressed that "Dissimulation is a great aid."[80] Lipsius's notorious doctrine of *prudentia mixta*—the prudence involving deceit—boils down to simulation and dissimulation.[81] Indeed, there was hardly any writer on reason of state who failed to discuss simulation and dissimulation, and the general thrust of their arguments remained constant.[82]

As modes of behavior crucial to reason of state, simulation and dissimulation have a pronounced theatrical quality. According to Cesare Ripa's widely circulated *Iconologia* (1593), simulation is supposed to be personified as "a woman with a mask on her face, [wearing] iridescent dresses."[83] Pierre Charron (1541–1603), whose *De la sagesse* (1601) explicates some key tenets of reason of state on the basis of skeptical philosophy, characterizes dissimulation as an art of acting, which a public person needs to master, "not only in war, with strangers and enemies, but also in times of peace."[84] Just as a good actor practices his art in such a way that the audience does not notice his artifice, a prince "must play this part with dexterity and right to the point, neither excessively nor ineptly."[85] If princes are actors, what they do is theater. Charron concludes, "That which is done in public is but a farce, a fake, the truth is secret and in private; [. . .] *Universus mundus exercet histrioniam.*"[86]

Building on Charron's skeptical philosophy and theatrical metaphors, Gabriel Naudé (1600–1653) provided a full account of the theatricality of simulation and dissimulation. One historian refers to him as the "thinker of the theatricalization of reason of state."[87] In Naudé's view, the prince is not only an actor, but also a spectator. Elaborating on the Senecan saying

"O quam contempta res est homo nisi supra humana surrexerit" (what a contemptible thing is man, unless he rises above the human condition), he states that a prince would not be truly great "unless he has a firm and fixed eye, and as if he were placed on top of some high tower, looks down upon the whole world, which appears to him as a theater, ill regulated, and full of confusion, where some act comedies, and others tragedies." As a spectator, the prince watches out for opportunities to intervene in the events on the stage of the world, "tanquam Deus aliquis ex machina"—"like some god from a machine, as often as he pleases, or as the diverse occasions shall persuade him to do it."[88] Naudé calls these extraordinary, surprising interventions *coups d'État*: "In the *coups d'État*, the thunderbolt falls before one hears the rumbling of it in the skies, it strikes before bursting—*Ante ferit, quam flamma micet*—prayers are said before the bell is rung for them, the execution precedes the sentence; [. . .] he receives the blow, who thought himself was giving it; he dies, who believed himself to be the most secure; he suffers, who never dreamt of it; all is done at night and in the dark, in the fog and shadows."[89] Power struggle in the political world takes the form of the theatrical dynamic of acting and viewing, of histrionics and spectatorship. The prince who has been a spectator bursts on stage at opportune moments, dramatically changing the course of events, turning other actors into dumbfounded spectators in one fell swoop. The rationally calculated interests of the state are revealed and obscured at once by the clap of thunder, the flash of lightning of a *coup d'État*. Michel Foucault characterizes the *coup d'État* as "the self-manifestation of the state."[90] A *coup d'État* turns the state with all its interests into a pure appearance, a dazzling theatrical act. It is the apotheosis of dissimulation, for whatever essence, whatever truth the state may have fades away the moment it happens. It is likewise the apotheosis of simulation, for at the moment of its happening it is the only reality of the state, all that is true about the state.

Simulation and dissimulation turn the world of sovereign states into a theater, in which an unending drama unfolds—the drama of international relations. Some salient features of this drama—its poetics, as it were—are worth noting. First, it is full of intrigue and suspense. Dissimulation keeps true intentions and facts in the dark, while simulation leads others to believe in what are not true intentions and facts. They combine to create a perpetual knowledge gap, a persistent need for acquisition of information about one another among the political actors as well as spectators. This makes the gathering of intelligence a key task in international politics. As Henri de Rohan (1579–1638) points out in *De l'intérêt des princes et des Etats de la chrétienté* (1638), a prince must always pay attention to "the manner to maintain such intelligences as are necessary in all other states. He must do so by means of ambassadors [. . .]; by means of monks and preachers [. . .]; by money [. . .]. Above all, he must endeavor to win over principal ministers of other princes in order to avert dangerous designs."[91] Creating and filling knowledge gaps represent the basic dynamic of drama as a communicative process. Different levels of knowledge among the characters as well as the audience build up suspense. Characters want to find out more about each other, while the audience is eager to figure out what all the characters are up to. Not surprisingly, writers on reason of state often resort to dramatic vocabulary. Francesco Guicciardini (1483–1540) spoke of suspense, wonder, and spectatorship: "If those near you and your subjects are kept in the dark about your affairs, men will always remain in suspense and, as it were, in wonder, and your every smallest movement and action are watched."[92] "Create suspense in your affairs" is one of the maxims that Baltasar Gracián (1601–58) offered to persons in the "elevated position."[93]

Second, the drama unfolding on the international stage is informed by sophisticated poetic techniques of processing knowledge. Reason of state, by Botero's definition, is "the knowledge of the means by which [the state] may be founded, preserved and extended."[94] As such, it comprises all the knowledge about people and things in one's own state, as well as about people and things in other states, insofar as one's own state entertains various relations to other states. Knowledge from the past is equally crucial, for one learns from past examples in managing both domestic and foreign affairs in the present. Indeed, reason of state requires all the knowledge of the world. This makes the library the locus of political reason.[95] Naudé helped build Cardinal Mazarin's library, and held a passionate plea to the Parliament of Paris in 1652 to preserve it.[96] His *Avis pour dresser une bibliothèque* (1627) is one of the earliest works on librarianship. A generation later, the German polymath Gottfried Wilhelm Leibniz (1646–1716), who served as a counselor at the ducal court of Hannover after a short stint at the court of the elector of Mainz, took upon himself the task of managing the library at both places, especially in Hannover.[97] Political decision-making consists of turning book knowledge into actions on the political stage. This process has poetic and aesthetic dimensions. It is poetic, insofar as the available knowledge is mobilized to make up plots, invent stories, and project images and appearances. It is aesthetic, insofar as the political action accompanied by stories and images is carried out with such good judgment or taste as to evoke admiration, wonder, or surprise in others. For Naudé, a *coup d'État* condenses a whole library of knowledge into a spectacular act that elicits wonder and amazement: "I have not had so much practice of the world as effectually to discover the ruses and villainies that are committed in it, but I have nonetheless seen a great deal of them in histories, satires, and tragedies."[98]

From Reason of State to Tragic Play

In developing his idea of *coup d'État*, Naudé speaks repeatedly of "bloody tragedies."[99] Political action seems to be inseparable from tragic poetry. Indeed, given the theatricality of the political world, as Michel Foucault points out with regard to Naudé, literary theater functions "as the privileged site of political representation, and of representation of the *coup d'État* in particular. For after all, a part of Shakespeare's historical drama really is the drama of the *coup d'État*. Corneille, even Racine, [. . .] quite often, almost always, [. . .] are representations of *coups d'État* [. . .]. Just as in politics *raison d'État* manifests itself in a kind of theatricality, so theater is organized around the representation of this *raison d'État* in its dramatic, intense, and violent form of the *coup d'État*."[100]

The very first line of the dedicatory preface to *Sophonisbe*—"Accept this tragedy from me as a sacrifice"—indicates the continuity between political and literary theater. *Sophonisbe* features one sacrificial act after another, which, as discussed above, form part and parcel of the political theater represented by the play. By giving the play the generic characterization of tragedy and then presenting it as a sacrifice, Lohenstein seems to suggest that tragedy belongs to the political theater just as the political theater is tragic.[101] "Ich liefere nur ein Spiel"—"I proffer merely a play," says the author with seeming humility (line 19). He then proceeds to develop an elaborate theory of *homo ludens* and *mundus ludens*. Nature is a play, life is a play, the whole political world is a play, even religion is a play. The play of life is poetic in essence:

> And our short time is nothing but poetry.
> A play / in which now someone comes on stage / now someone else exits;
> It begins with tears / with weeping, it comes to naught. (lines 242–44)

As poetry, the play of life turns out to be tragic to boot. Not only does it begin and end with crying and weeping. Tears flow in the middle of life as well: "the hated house that is called the school fosters the first tragic play (*Trauerspiel*) that rouses chagrin in [the human being]" (line 91), not to mention the "bloody tragic plays" ensuing from struggles for power and domination (line 122). Not surprisingly, Lohenstein's theory of *mundus ludens* culminates in an invocation of the founding fathers of tragic poetry: Aeschylus, Sophocles, and Euripides (line 252–70). If the world and tragic play are indistinguishable from each other, *Sophonisbe* as a tragic play populated with sovereign persons must be no different from the political world. Indeed, both *Cleopatra* and *Sophonisbe* are full of intrigues and suspense in their respective plot just as political theater is. And just as calculated acts on the political stage, Lohenstein's plays draw on a library worth of book learning. In both *Cleopatra* and *Sophonisbe*, notes displaying enormous erudition make up at least a third of the text. There seems to be no speech of the dramatic characters, no elements of the plot, which is not bolstered by some profound learning.[102]

For all their homology, however, there are undeniable differences between tragic plays and the political world. There is, first of all, a radical change of spectatorship. The spectators of the political theater are other princes, as well as their subjects. The spectators of the literary theater, by contrast, are the theater-going public, a public that maintains a critical distance from the princely persons on stage. Lohenstein's tragic drama has a twofold spectatorship: choruses inside the play, and the theater audience outside the play.

While the protagonists try to outmaneuver one another on stage, they are observed by choruses. Especially worth mentioning are the choruses of Fortune and Fate in both *Cleopatra* and *Sophonisbe*. The allegorical persons of the Four Monarchies accompanying Fate serve to portray the demise of Sophonisbe as a necessary step in the inexorable march of empires from the east to the west—*translatio imperii*—thereby legitimizing the Habsburg rule as well as the extension of this rule to the New World.[103] The questions of fortune and fate, along with the related questions of the rise and fall of states, belonged to the discourse of reason of state from the outset. Machiavelli famously argued that "fortune is the arbiter of half of our actions," and he advised princes to develop *virtù* to control the fortune.[104] Lipsius regarded the "acceptance of fate" as one of the core qualities that a prince needed to have.[105] Discussions of fortune, fate, and history permeate Diego de Saavedra Fajardo's *Idea de un príncipe político cristiano* (1640), which Lohenstein draws on heavily in his plays.[106] As a kind of instrumental rationality, reason of state is concerned with the most prudent and expedient course of action under specific circumstances. Without the ground of legitimacy or any normative ideal as a point of orientation, the circumstances appear to be nothing more than fortuitous, and the outcome of actions seems to be mere fate. Lohenstein's plays reproduce the discourse of reason of state through the dramaturgical opposition between act (*Abhandlung*) and chorus (*Reyen*): while in the main acts the dramatic characters act out the maxims of reason of state, the choruses reflect on the circumstances and the outcomes of their actions with the help of the allegorical *personae fictae* of fortune and fate.

Each play, comprising both acts and choruses, is meant for an audience outside of itself. *Sophonisbe* was composed on the occasion of the wedding of Emperor Leopold I of Austria and the Spanish princess Margareta Theresia. It was later dedicated to an aristocratic diplomat and patron, while *Cleopatra* was dedicated to the Council of the City of Breslau. Both plays were originally performed within the pedagogical framework of a Protestant school in Breslau. All in all, the audience of Lohenstein's plays was either a public at a distance from the political stage, who observed the actions of sovereign persons through the medium of the tragic stage, or a courtly public in Vienna, who attended a tragic performance in order to gain a reprieve from their political business as well as an outside perspective from which to observe the political world.[107]

The changed spectatorship goes hand in hand with structural differences between political theater and literary theater. Structurally, literary theater represents what Aristotle terms a "complete action," in contrast to the open-endedness of political theater.[108] In its insistence on the state's interests and on the efficient means of realizing them, reason of state disregards questions about the origin and the ultimate purpose of the state. The calculation and pursuit of interests have neither beginning nor end. A drama enacted on the theatrical stage, however, has both a beginning and an end, which combine to bring all the actions on stage into a meaningful whole. The beginning of both *Cleopatra* and *Sophonisbe* is the defeat of the respective protagonists by the Roman forces. In the wake of this event, both parties in the international conflict take recourse to reason of state: the defeated does so in her desperate struggle for survival, while the victor does so in order to consolidate his advantages. The exercise of reason of state takes the form of a series of theatrical maneuvers. The Roman victory entails a theatrical display of power—the triumphal procession parading the conquered princes and princesses. The defeated Cleopatra and Sophonisbe want to avoid this political theater on the Roman streets at all costs, while the victorious Romans see this political theater as the crowning glory of their conquest. In order to achieve their respective goals, both parties embrace other kinds of political theater—simulation and dissimulation. The ending of both plays spotlights the blatant failure of reason of state to resolve international conflicts. After all of their ploys come to naught, cornered by the Romans, Cleopatra and Sophonisbe choose to die rather than be paraded in a Roman triumphal procession—though neither wants to go quietly. Rather, both stage their death as a martyrological spectacle. But by the fifth act, sacrificial rituals have already been revealed as simulations for the sake of expediency. The martyrological sacrifices staged by Cleopatra and Sophonisbe alike are acts that merely simulate transcendence in the wake of the failure of all other political ploys. This ultimate act of simulation, this ultimate ploy, has no effect either, for in both plays the victor has the last laugh. In sum, the beginning of both plays is the defeat of an African queen, and the ending is the confirmation of this defeat. All the ploys excogitated by reason of state turn out to be futile indeed. Bounded by such a beginning and ending, political events cease to be mere links in an endless chain, but become elements of a coherent pattern or dramatic plot. This pattern may be summarized as follows: all the norms, be they legal or religious, are subordinated to reason of state, but reason of state proves to counteract concord between sovereigns.

Related to the structural difference between political theater and literary theater is the transformation of the political actor. Tragic representation saves political actors from their physical mortality and turns them into immortal symbolic figures that we call dramatic characters. In reality, Sophonisbe and Cleopatra were mortals who perished in international power struggles. On the tragic stage, however, they always rise again after their spectacular death, thereby becoming a symbol at once of the triumph and of the impotence of reason of state—triumph over law and religion, impotence in securing international order. As symbolic figures, political actors are no longer to be judged by transient political standards, but by permanent poetic standards. In the dedicatory preface to *Cleopatra*, Lohenstein writes, "My Cleopatra harbors the desire to please you, and that Cleopatra embalmed with cedar oil does not live, whereas the reviving Cleopatra in this little book anointed with your favor will live."

Taken together, the changed spectatorship, the structuring of political events into a plot, and the figuration of political actors as dramatic characters recode international politics into tragic poetry. This kind of tragic poetry serves as a medium for observing and reflecting on the impossibility of international order in a political world under the sway of reason of state.

The Tragedy of Marriage Alliance (Corneille)

Pierre Corneille's Tragedies of Marriage Alliance

In the age of absolutism, marriage alliance was a particularly valued legal bond between states, although its practical effectiveness and symbolic prestige was rapidly declining.[109] On the surface, marriage treaty was but one of many kinds of international treaties. But it could rightfully lay claim to a special status. First, since marriage was the necessary precondition for producing a legitimate heir to the throne, royal marriage had a direct bearing on the juridical foundation—the *lex fundamentalis*—of the absolutist state. It was, accordingly, also fundamental to the legal dealings of one state with the other. Second, marriage epitomized the principles of contract and treaty law. The medieval canon law formulated the doctrine of voluntary consent as the essence of marriage. "The rules concerning consent to a marriage," a legal historian tells us, "were developed into a whole body of contract law."[110] This applied eminently to treaty law, for as a contract between sovereigns a treaty had no other basis than voluntary consent.

Poetic literature, in any case, concerned itself with royal marriage more than any other kind of legal transaction between sovereigns. As we will see in the next chapter, political romance as a major poetic genre in the seventeenth century sought to found international order entirely on the marital contract between sovereigns. This genre suffered a serious crisis at the time around 1660, although it took a great pan-European war some decades later—the War of the Spanish Succession (1701–14)—to kill it off. The year 1660 actually bore witness to a royal wedding that overshadowed all others—the wedding between France and Spain. But perhaps more than any other royal marriage, the one between the young Louis XIV and the Spanish princess Maria Theresa also exposed the inadequacy of marriage alliance for securing international peace. This was not the first union between the two royal houses. Louis XIII also married a Spanish princess (Anne of Austria), and their wedding celebrations in 1615 were equally spectacular.[111] But all this did not prevent France and Spain from going to war in 1635, a war that did not end until Philip IV offered his daughter Maria Theresa to Louis XIV in marriage at the Peace of Pyrenees in 1659. This peace, alas, was not to last either. When Philip IV died in 1665, France immediately staked a claim to the Spanish Netherlands on the basis of the right of devolution. Spain disagreed. The so-called War of Devolution broke out in 1667.

In the face of this reality, even the most optimistic romancer would be hard put to sell his rosy marriage plots. Tragedians took over. Pierre Corneille, the greatest tragic poet in France at the time, brought the tragic form to bear on the subject matter of marriage alliance in 1659, the year of the Peace of the Pyrenees. He did so by rewriting one of the most famous tragedies of the ancients, Sophocles's tragedy of the unfortunate Theban king who unknowingly killed his father and married his mother. *Œdipe* inaugurated a new phase in the writing career of Corneille.[112] More important for the present context, it marked the beginning of what can be called Corneille's tragedies of international marriage alliance. The Oedipus-myth was retooled to present dynastic marriage as the foundation of international society. One year later, as part of the festivities in celebration of Louis XIV's wedding, Corneille produced *La Toison d'or*, a machine play based on the myths of Argonauts. Other tragedies of marriage alliance followed, including *Sophonisbe* and *Attila*, the latter of which was written at the time of the War of Devolution.[113]

Concerned with marriage alliance as they all are, Corneille's tragedies from *Œdipe* to *Attila* are not homogeneous. As far as the figuration of international order is concerned, there are at least two different models. *Œdipe* affirms a normative model of international order in accordance with the fundamental law of the absolutist state, which is predicated upon hereditary succession. Hereditary succession requires a royal marriage that produces legitimate heirs. The international society constituted through marriage alliance, therefore, is inscribed in the juridical foundation of the absolutist state. Hereditary succession and marriage alliance combine to make up a genealogical principle supposed to inform domestic and international order alike.[114] *Œdipe* stages what goes against this principle as a cautionary tale, thus keeping any transgression of it at bay. The plays following *Œdipe*, by contrast, problematize the marriage between sovereigns. In the course of the seventeenth century, the earthly sovereign increasingly superseded ecclesiastical authorities as the ultimate arbitrator in marital matters. The law instituted by the sovereign person became the absolute reference for marital contracts. As a consequence, the marital contract of the sovereign person himself fell outside of the law. Corneille's tragedies from *La Toison d'or* to *Attila* dramatize, each in its own way, the transitional time, in which sovereign persons are on the verge of entering, but have not yet entered, a marriage. By representing the interplay of various forces at this liminal moment, which either facilitate or thwart the forging of a marital bond, these tragedies reveal the lawlessness and disorder at the origin of royal marriage. As a transaction beyond any juridical authority, marriage alliance turns out to separate rather unite sovereigns. There is no law capable of instituting international order. If anywhere, it is to be found in an aesthetic experience created through mythological spectacle and tragic mimesis.

The International Oedipus

By resuscitating Sophocles's mythic Theban king who commits the unspeakable crimes of killing his father and marrying his mother, Corneille's *Œdipe* seeks to dramatize, *ex negativo*, the intertwined institutions of dynastic succession and marriage alliance, through which the absolutist state and international society constitute one another. In the preface, Corneille deplores the lack of amorous elements in Sophocles's play. Because of this lack, "it is divested of the principal ornaments which usually win us the public acclaim."

As a remedy, he decides to introduce a love story in it, namely "the happy episode of the mutual love of Thésée and Dircé, whom I present as the daughter of Laïus and the sole heiress to his crown."[115] This happy episode of love, found neither in Sophocles nor in any other version of the Oedipus myth, is by no means fortuitous. Thésée is the king of Athens, and Dircé the heiress to the Theban throne. They stand, therefore, for hereditary succession and international marriage alliance. The love story of Dircé and Thésée occupies a strategically crucial position in the plot of Corneille's play. The play begins with the couple's conflict with Œdipe, who disapproves of their marriage, and it ends with the couple, as in love as ever, lamenting together the fate of Œdipe, who has just gouged out his eyes. What the dramatist himself presents as an attempt to pander to the popular taste, then, is in fact a poetic invention that radically reframes the Oedipus-myth. The royal couple who represent hereditary succession and marriage alliance appear first as the antagonists to a tyrannical king, and then as the audience of an unfolding tragedy of parricide and incest.[116]

Sophocles's tragedy focuses on the protagonist's investigation into the identity of the person ultimately responsible for the plague afflicting Thebes. This investigation ends up revealing Oedipus himself as the person who killed his father, married his mother, and thereby caused the plague. It makes Sophocles's play, in Foucault's words, "a kind of compendium of the history of Greek law."[117] In Corneille's *Œdipe*, the investigation shrinks to no more than a few brief scenes in the final two acts. The actions onstage shift to the conflict between Œdipe and the princess of Thebes as well as the king of Athens. As a result, the play sheds light on another kind of law—the fundamental law of the absolutist state, which concerns both the internal constitution of the state and its external relation to other states. Already the very first two scenes of the play offer a glimpse of the lineaments of this public law.

Towards the end of the first scene, Dircé tells her lover Thésée about her view of Œdipe, the king of Thebes:

> The King, for all the King that he is, is not my master
> And the blood of Laïus, of which I am honored to be born,
> Dispenses my heart from receiving the law
> From a throne that his death should have left to me alone.
> But since the People and the hand of my mother
> Have placed the Scepter of my father into his hands
> And because he has all the authority here,
> I can do nothing for you against his will. (I.105–12)

What is at stake is the legitimacy of sovereign power. Once upon a time, Thebes was terrorized by the Sphinx. The people promised to offer the scepter left behind by the late king Laius, and the queen promised to offer her bed to anyone who could solve the riddle of Sphinx. Œdipe came, solved the riddle, and became the king of Thebes. His power, then, is founded on his knowledge and deeds. Dircé, however, regards him as a usurper. For her, legitimacy derives solely from royal blood. Because she is born of "the blood of Laius," she lays claim to the Theban throne as her own, defying Œdipe's authority. At the beginning of the play, then, there is a competition between two different models of the legitimacy of royal rule, the one based on heroic merits, which is embodied by Œdipe, and the other based on hereditary succesion, which is embodied by Dircé.

The second scene of the first act, in which Œdipe and Thésée encounter each other, broaches another problem pertaining to sovereign persons—their relationship to one another. Fearing that a marriage between Dircé and Thésée could pose a threat to his rule, Œdipe tells the Athenian king that he has already promised Dircé's hand to Hémon, and that this promise cannot be withdrawn. Thereupon Thésée replies, "[A promise] is always sacred, always to be admired [. . .], but even the most powerful King owes something to other Kings" (I. 186–88). After a heated exchange, Thésée takes his leave of the Theban king with a warning: "If you are a King, consider other Kings" (I. 216). Whereas Œdipe seems to insist on the absolute autonomy of a king, Thésée points out that every king speaks and acts in a society of kings and therefore has certain obligations towards them. This scene not only addresses the relations between sovereigns as a problem, but as a scene of encounter between sovereigns it also stages international relations.

The first two scenes of Corneille's *Œdipe* present two fundamental legal issues pertaining to the absolutist state: the legitimacy of sovereign rule and the normativity of international relations. Two positions emerge from them: on the one side, there is the couple Dircé-Thésée, who consider hereditary succession to be the legitimate basis of sovereign power and emphasize the mutual obligations between sovereign persons; on the other side, there is Œdipe, who bases his rule on heroic deeds and holds fast to the unrestrained autonomy of the sovereign. The dramatic actions that follow elaborate the one position and demonstrate the failure of the other, in order to establish, from two opposite angles, a principle that informs sovereign rule and international relations at once. It is, as we shall see, the genealogical principle.

The dramatic elaboration of the position represented by the couple Dircé-Thésée has a number of components. One is the mystification of royal blood. Thebans go to Delphi to ask about the cause of the plague afflicting them, but gods remain silent. Instead, the ghost of the late king pronounces the oracle:

A great crime, unpunished, causes your misery;
It must be effaced by the blood of my Race. (II.605–6)

Upon learning about this oracle, Dircé is convinced that the ghost means her, declaring immediately her determination to die in order to expiate the great but unspecified crime that has caused the plague: "To die for her fatherland, is a fate full of charms" (II.625). When later on the rumor spreads that the son of the late king is still alive, Thésée believes that he must be this son. He proclaims his decision to sacrifice himself for the Theban state (III.1069–70). This episode about Laius's oracle and the reactions to it illustrates the symbolic operations that turn royal blood from a natural fluid into a supernatural, mysterious one. The idea of royal blood as an immortal, mysterious fluid emerged in the late Middle Ages for the purpose of the dynastic legitimation of kingship.[118] Corneille lends it a poetically nuanced form. First of all, the substitution of the late king's ghost for Apollo as the source of oracular pronouncements deifies the king, thus immortalizing his blood. Subsequently, both Dircé's and Thésée's eagerness to spill their blood for the sake of the state instantiates a sacrificial logic that divests royal blood of its quality as a perishable fluid of the natural body and transforms it into an eternal property of the mystic body of the state. The sacrifice of the prince is a recurring theme in the literature of the *âge classique*, meant to illustrate the transubstantiation of the natural body of the prince into the symbolic body of the state.[119] It is reinforced here by the ideological formula *pro patria mori*—in Dircé's words "to die for her fatherland"—which was often used in the late Middle Ages to promote the idea of the polity as *corpus mysticum*.[120] This formula still remained in force in the seventeenth century. Bossuet, for instance, urged everyone to be "ready to sacrifice to our country, in case of need, all that we possess, even our very lives, when there is question of war."[121] Sacrifice denaturalizes blood, turning it into a medium for affirming a higher, usually divine entity. In their willingness to offer their blood to save the state, Dircé and Thésée regard royal blood as primarily belonging to the political body. Because royal blood is seen as a property of the political body, it can function as the source of the legitimacy of sovereign power. The bloodline from the king to his descendants now stands for the continuity of the state.

The mystery of royal blood implies a specific rule of marriage: a person of royal blood can only marry another person who has equally royal but different blood. If royal blood is primarily a property of the political body, every member of the political body partakes of the same blood and is therefore disqualified as a potential spouse for the head of the political body. From this perspective, Œdipe's proposal to marry Dircé to her cousin Hémon amounts to nothing less than an incitement to incest. It also amounts to a debasement of royal blood, since for the head to marry any other members of the political body is to marry down. Dircé remarks curtly, "I have already told you, Sir, that he is not a King" (I. 404). Insisting on the royalty of her blood, Dircé would marry no one else but a foreign king—Thésée, the king of Athens. The conception of royal blood as the source of legitimate sovereign power entails marriage alliance between royal houses, hence an international society. Significantly, Dircé, who fiercely defends the royal blood of Thebes, speaks repeatedly of the importance of international society—in this case the society of Greek city-states. She pleads with her lover, "Live on for our whole Greece" (I.78); "Your arms are the firmest support for Greece,/ Live for the Public, while I die for it" (II. 729–30).[122]

The mystery of royal blood, crucial to the legitimacy of sovereign rule and to the making of international society alike, is coupled with the code of gallant love, which displaces heroic valor from the battlefield to the sphere of courtship and marriage. Corneille's play was written in the midst of the literary current of *préciosité*, which focused on the nature of love. Conducted in salons such as the Hôtel de Rambouillet as well as in the imaginary space of the political romances of Madeleine de Scudéry (1607–1701), the discourse of the *précieuses* defined an idealized code of passionate love to match the traditional aristocratic virtue of heroic valor. Published five years after Madame de Scudéry's political romance *Clélie* (which features the famous map of seduction *La carte de Tendre*), Corneille's *Œdipe* owes to the *précieuses* the character of Thésée, in whom heroic valor is married with refined passion. Thésée, as we know from Plutarch, was the heroic founding king of Athens. Trying to emulate Hercules, he rid the world of monsters and bandits, and carried out many other heroic deeds.[123] In Corneille, he becomes a hero in love:

> I'll only say that being with my Princess
> A hero is interested only in the duties of a lover,
> Even if he were the single support for the universe,
> He must do nothing else than love the object of his affection (I.93–96).

The code of gallant love as exemplified by the character of Thésée implicitly downplays the role of heroic action and military valor for ensuring peace in the world, valorizing instead love and marriage for this purpose.

This code thus joins hands with the mystery of royal blood to promote marriage alliance.

In contrast to the position represented by the couple Dircé-Thésée, the story of Œdipe demonstrates the disruption of the genealogical principle and its disastrous consequences. Œdipe, the son of the Theban king Laius, was abandoned on Mount Cithaeron as an infant, brought to Corinth, and adopted by the childless royal couple. As an adult, he left Corinth, unintentionally killed his true father Laius on the road, came to Thebes, solved the Sphinx's riddle, unknowingly married his mother Jocasta, and became the king of Thebes. The outbound journey from Thebes to Corinth exemplifies the vitiation of bloodline in every possible sense. There was first the decision of the royal parents to abandon their own infant to avoid the oracle's prophecy coming true. There was then the decision of Phorbas—the courtier charged with abandoning the infant Œdipe—to give the child to another person rather than let him die. Insofar as hereditary monarchy resembles patriarchal family, this act of disobedience, regardless of the good intention, amounts to a disregard of the royal authority as well as patriarchal authority. Phorbas would pay dearly for it. Finally, there was the decision of Iphicrate—the person who took charge of the infant Œdipe from Phorbas on Mount Cithaeron—to give the child to the heirless Corinthian king, who then raised him as the crown prince of his kingdom by subterfuge. Œdipe's return journey from Corinth to Thebes, on the other hand, exemplifies a code of behavior opposed to gallant love and marriage alliance. It is important to note at this point a significant difference between Corneille and Sophocles with regard to the adult Œdipe's motivation for leaving Corinth. In Sophocles, Œdipe flees Corinth to forestall the prophecy that he would kill his father and marry his mother. In Corneille, by contrast, he leaves his putative home country Corinth in search of glory. Taking Hercules as his role model, and roaming the world for heroic deeds (I.305–8), Corneille's Œdipe is an exact parallel to Thésée, who also strives to emulate Hercules and save the world with his courageous feats.[124] Œdipe's killing of the "bandits," one of whom proved to be his father Laius, as well as his defeat of the Sphinx by solving her riddle, belong to his heroic actions. Yet while Thésée allows his heroic valor to be tempered with gallant love, Œdipe knows nothing of amorous sentiments. Instead, he married the queen of Thebes Jocasta because the people of Thebes offered him the scepter and the queen offered him her marriage bed in exchange for his feat of having freed the country of Sphinx. It was a marriage to the state of Thebes. The metaphor of a ruler's marriage to his realm was of late medieval origin and continued to exist in France until the end of the sixteenth century. Théodore Godefroy's *Le cérémonial de France*, published in 1619, states, "On the day of coronation the King solemnly married his Kingdom."[125] Such a metaphorical marriage of the king to his kingdom, which the ambitious Œdipe implements, is distinct from a marriage alliance between royal houses, which the amorous Thésée plans to realize. It belongs to a bygone age.

Vitiating the bloodline and in pursuit of glory at all costs, Œdipe's journey from Thebes to Corinth and back results in a specific political position: he sees sovereign rule as legitimated exclusively by heroic deeds and insists on his own sovereignty without respect for other sovereigns. This position is diametrically opposed to the genealogical principle represented by the couple Dircé-Thésée. Œdipe's position is the one that fails, implicated as it is in a horrifying incest that, in turn, invites a devastating plague. This failure, once recognized, affirms the position of his opponents. The revelation of the incestuous marriage between Œdipe and his mother as the proximate cause of the plague leads to two deaths: Jocasta and Phorbas kill themselves. Jocasta's suicide cancels out the practice of a king marrying a woman within his state as well as the metaphorical marriage of a king to his state. Phorbas's suicide—an invention of Corneille's—cancels out the vitiation of the bloodline, to which he has been instrumental. Above all, Œdipe's own recognition of what has happened serves to invalidate his own position and corroborate that of Dircé and Thésée. After the truth comes to light, Œdipe laments bitterly the impotence of heroism. Herculean valor and good intentions have not prevented him from committing inadvertently the horrendous crimes of parricide and incest (V.1820–28).

Given this tension between the will of the heroic individual and the fateful course of events, one can certainly agree with a scholar's characterization of Œdipe as "the first thoroughly tragic hero of Corneille's."[126] The tragic, however, also has an affirmative function. What Œdipe's tragedy affirms is something to which he has been blind, but which he sees and imprints on his own mind by blinding himself. It has something to do with the mystery of royal blood. No sooner does the blood flowing from Œdipe's emptied eye sockets touch the earth than the plague stops and the state of Thebes is saved (V.1995–2001). The miracle happens because his blood is the royal blood inherited from Laius—this royal blood proves to have a sacramental character. It has also something to do with a norm embodied by Thésée, which consists in the conversion of heroic valor into love and marriage. Œdipe complains about the impotence of the heroic will and the tyranny of heaven. But earlier, Thésée asserts exactly the opposite in a rousing speech on the freedom of the will (III.1149–85). Blindly pursuing heroic domination, the will cannot help being thwarted. But love makes the will truly free through the interplay of domination and submission. In short, what Œdipe's tragedy affirms is the genealogical principle.

While Œdipe's story, adapted from Sophocles, is tragic, the play *Œdipe* as a whole is not. The overarching plot of the play is the conflict between the couple Dircé-Thésée on the one side, and Œdipe on the other. This conflict resolves itself when Œdipe's story comes to light and he blinds himself in despair. Dircé and Thésée play no part in the events that bring about Œdipe's tragic downfall.[127] They are rather the audience of Œdipe's tragedy. Dircé has the last word in the play:

> Let's watch this unfortunate Prince,
> Shed our tears with him over our dark destiny,
> And leave it to Gods to dispose the rest. (V.2008–10)

After having expressed horror a short while ago—"La surprenante horreur" (V.1883)—Dircé articulates in these final lines the other effects of tragic theater: pity and catharsis. Ultimately, Corneille's play is not so much an adaption of a famed tragedy of the ancients, but a dramatic enactment of tragic theater itself. In Sophocles's time, the Athenians assured themselves of their democratic constitution by watching the downfall of royal houses belonging to the mythic past on the tragic stage. *Œdipe* brings the tragic stage onto the stage. In this play, representatives of the absolutist state in Corneille's age—Dircé and Thésée—watch the tragic downfall of a king who embodies mythic disorder, in order to assure themselves of a new model of political order. This model, in sum, has two complementary elements—hereditary succession and marriage alliance. The one element ensures the legitimacy of the absolutist state, while the other ensures an orderly relationship between states. Interdependent, they constitute a genealogical principle that informs domestic political order and international order alike.

The Tragic Origin of Marriage Alliance

In *Œdipe*, royal marriage is in itself unproblematic, as the royal couple is just as much in love at the end as in the beginning, never showing even the slightest hint of disharmony. The tragic fate befalls someone who is opposed to royal marriage. In Corneille's plays following *Œdipe*, by contrast, royal marriage is endangered or compromised even before it is contracted. These works reveal the tragic origin of royal marriage.

Corneille's tragedies of royal marriage were written at a critical juncture in the history of juridical thinking about marriage. According to medieval canon law, "Marriage is contracted by consent alone. [...] From the fact that a man consents through words in the present tense to a woman with marital affection, and the woman to the man [...] there is a marriage immediately."[128] This understanding of marriage was continuous with the principle of *consensus facit nuptias* in Roman law, but at the same time radicalized it. By consent Roman jurists meant not only the consent of "those who are being united" but also the consent of "those in whose power they are," with the latter referring to the consent of family members, usually that of the *pater familias*.[129] Canon law eliminated the latter, thus making the consent of the couple the only precondition of marriage. Instead of the family father, there was now a new figure overseeing *vinculum matrimonii*—God. In canon law, marriage became the union of man and woman in the eyes of God. As such, marriage was a sacrament, because "it is a sign of a holy thing itself, that is, of the spiritual and inseparable union of Christ and the Church."[130] From the sixteenth century onwards, the law of marriage went through one momentous transformation after the other. To begin with, marriage as contract was gradually distinguished from marriage as sacrament, with Protestants and Catholics following different lines of reasoning. Accordingly, doctrines and procedures of contract law were applied to it. In juridical practice, ecclesiastical as well as temporal authorities sought to intervene in the contracting of marriage, regarding the mere consent of the couple in the eyes of God as insufficient, and eventually replacing God as the absolute reference of the marital bond. Subsequently, in the competition between the church and the state, the latter triumphed over the former also in the matter of marriage. Although weddings continued to be held in the church, and although matrimonial disputes continued to be settled by ecclesiatical courts, the ecclesiastical power was increasingly limited to the spiritual realm, entrusted with the task of administering marriage as sacrament, while the temporal power of the state took on the task of regulating marriage as contract by means of legislation. In the meantime, marriage as sacrament decreased in importance, becoming a mere annex of marriage as contract. Considered by jurists to be a civil contract entailing specific rights and duties, marriage fell more and more under the legislative and jurisdictional power of the king. In France, the juristic doctrine that affirmed the power of the king over marriage—the so-called regalist doctrine—took hold in the mid-seventeenth century, culminating in the publication of Jean Launoy's voluminous treatise *Regia in matrimonium potestas* (1674). The royal attorney Denis Talon's speech before the parlament of Paris in 1677 encapsulated this doctrine: "Since marriages, by their nature, by their object, and by their purpose, are civil contracts, they can be established only by a sovereign power. To render this contract legitimate or invalid, to render the contracting persons competent or incompetent to enter marriage—this is the effect of a sovereign power over worldly affairs."[131]

Matrimony is a main preoccupation of Corneille's dramatic *œuvre*. His early works such as *Le Cid* (1637) seek to install the king as the ultimate authority in validating a marriage. In this immensely successful piece that helped establish Corneille's lasting fame, the love story of the young couple Don Rodrigue and Chimène overcomes family rivalry and moves on to the literal destruction of parental authority—Don Rodrigue kills Chimène's father in a dispute—in order to end with the prospect of marriage under the auspices of the king. When in the mid-seventeenth century the power of the king over marriage came to be affirmed by jurisprudence, Corneille turned to a new problem—that of royal marriage. With the earthly sovereign displacing both God and the church as the absolute reference of the marital bond, the marriage of the sovereign person himself became a juridical dilemma: who has the power to render the royal marital contract legitimate or invalid, and who has the power to declare the sovereign persons who contract marriage to be able or unable to do so? In the absence of a higher authority, tragic theater stepped in as an imaginary court at which cases of royal marriage were presented, debated, and resolved. *Rodogune* (1647), *Nicomède* (1651), and to a certain extent also *Œdipe* play out the conflicts unleashed by a prospective royal marriage within the royal house, with one member of the royal family—mother, stepmother, and brother, respectively—arrogating to herself or himself the right to judge the marriage of a prince or princess. Corneille's plays after *Œdipe* address the conflicts intrinsic to a royal marriage. If the sovereign person institutes the legal framework for his subjects to contract marriage, it is outside of the law—that is, in a mythic space—that the sovereign person contracts his or her own marriage. Tragedies from *La Toison d'or* to *Attila* grapple with the primordial conflicts in such a mythic space, which either pave the way for, or foreclose the possibility of, a marriage alliance among sovereigns. In so doing, they bring to light the perils, compromises, and paradoxes inherent in a marriage alliance, and hence its inefficacy in securing international order.

The prototype of Corneille's tragedies of marriage alliance is *La Toison d'or*, produced as part of the festivities in celebration of Louis XIV's marriage in 1660. It is adapted from the myth of the Argonauts. Jason, the chief of the Argonauts, helps King Aète of Colchos push back the invasion of the neighboring kingdom. In order to safeguard his own kingdom, Aète is eager to build a permanent alliance with Jason (I.403–27). But Jason wants only one thing —the golden fleece that is in the possession of the king of Colchos. This request brings them into an irreconcilable conflict, for Aète's state depends on the golden fleece for its survival, while Jason needs the golden fleece to accede to the throne in his own kingdom back in Greece. The beginning of *La Toison d'or* thus paints a stark picture of international relations: states face each other in a fierce contest, and it is a contest that allows for only one winner. Marriage is a useful tool for the sovereign person engaged in an international contest. The golden fleece that Jason covets is jealously guarded by a phalanx of monsters. Only Médée, the princess of Colchos, can help him seize it. For this purpose, he has to court her. Yet if it were merely a matter of pursuing Médée, there would have been no drama, for Médée has already fallen in love with Jason after seeing his heroic valor in the war on behalf of her father. The dramatic tension builds up, as a queen by the name of Hypsipyle suddenly arrives in Colchos in pursuit of Jason. It turns out that he has already given his vow to this queen when he sojourned in her kingdom. Two triangular courtships ensue: Hypsipyle pursues Jason who pursues Médée, while Médée's brother Absyrte pursues Hypsipyle who pursues Jason. These two intertwined courtship plots demonstrate, if anything, that every person in a royal marriage is a placeholder, always replaceable by another person for the sake of expediency or necessity. Jason abandons Hypsipyle in favor of Médée because the latter is instrumental to his project of seizing the golden fleece. Hypsipyle gives up Jason and accepts Absyrte's hand, because she has been abandoned by Jason and has no other choice left. Corneille's other tragedies of marriage alliance share the same plot structure of intertwined triangular courtships. *Sophonisbe* invents one more queen to join the cast of one queen and two kings in Livy's story in order to create two triangles. *Attila* complicates the matter even further by making three triangles out of a cast of two princesses and three kings. This plot pattern, of course, has its basis in reality. In the matrimonial politics of European royal houses in the seventeenth century, marriageable princes and princesses usually vetted multiple potential matches before making a decision. Louis XIV was supposed to marry a princess of Savoy first, but switched to a Spanish princess for political reasons.

This status of the sovereign person as a placeholder in the institution of royal marriage has a number of far-reaching implications. First of all, as a sovereign person reviews the candidates for marriage one after the other and assesses their respective pros and cons, the marital contract is subjected to the vagaries of the sovereign will. With no higher authority, a sovereign person can just as easily withdraw his vow as give it. If the contracting of marriage is always already haunted by its undoing, the international order based on it is fragile indeed. In this regard, royal marriage functions in exactly the same way as international treaties in general.

INTERNATIONAL ORDER AS TRAGEDY 165

Second, the status of placeholder entails the division of the royal person into a public function and a private self.[132] When Médée sees that Jason is courting her because she is the custodian of the golden fleece (her function), she feels that her own self is being slighted. This distinction between function and self leads to the differentiation of love from marriage. If marriage is contracted because of the public function that a person performs, the self of the person thirsts for love. All this is evident in an indignant accusation levelled by Médée against Jason (IV.1646–56). Jason, for his part, makes use of the same distinctions in pursuing his goal. In order to secure Médée's help in getting hold of the golden fleece, he pretends that he himself loves Médée, and that he wants the golden fleece only in his public capacity as the head of the Argonauts. He urges Médée, "Separate your lover from the leader of these heroes" (II.783). Once a private self is separated from the public role, and love from marriage, the one cannot help interfering with the other. Médée's love for Jason as well as her attempt to secure his love induces her to abuse her public function as the custodian of the golden fleece, delivering to him the treasure against the interests of her father Aète and the state of Colchos. Conversely, in *Sophonisbe*, the eponymous heroine exploits the love of two kings for her—first Syphax and then Massinisse—to save her fatherland Carthage from the onslaught of the Romans, as well as to save herself from the humiliation of being paraded in Rome as a captive of war. In both cases, marriage alliances between states are infiltrated by private amorous feelings. Syphax, lamenting the woeful pass to which his love for Sophonisbe has brought him, characterizes her as "poison" (IV.1227). Consequently, any hope of instituting international order through marriage alliance is dashed. The marriage of Médée to Jason separates rather than unites Colchos and the Greeks, as she betrays her father and fatherland for the sake of her lover. In *Sophonisbe*, marriage based on amorous feelings turns out to be so feeble as to crumble immediately under political pressure—the heroine's marriage to Syphax is dissolved following his defeat by the Romans, and her marriage to Massinisse is effectively blocked by the Romans. While kings are metaphorically poisoned by Sophonisbe's feminine charm, Sophonisbe literally poisons herself for the lack of a viable marriage alliance that could save her fatherland from downfall and herself from public humiliation.[133] Marriage alliance is either of no use or is impossible. *Sophonisbe* is a true tragedy of international marriage alliance, as it negates this institution as such.

Last but not least, the status of every candidate for royal marriage as a placeholder entails a dynamic of rivalry that undermines marriage alliance. Once a person realizes that she is but one of many candidates, she cannot help comparing herself to others, trying to emphasize her worth at the cost of others, even if she may not want to be chosen. The sense of self-worth accentuated by rivalry can be best characterized in terms of *amour propre* or self-love, something that contemporaries of Corneille like Blaise Pascal and François de la Rochefoucauld (1613–80) regarded as inherent in human nature. According to la Rochefoucauld, "self-love is the love of oneself, and of all things for the sake of oneself. It makes men idolize themselves, and it would make them tyrannize other people. [. . .] Unknowingly, it breeds, nurtures, and raises a vast number of affections and hatreds. Some of them are so monstrous that, when it has given birth to them, it either fails to recognize them or cannot bring itself to acknowledge them."[134]

This portrait of self-love, penned by la Rochefoucauld probably in the early 1660s, is on full display in Corneille's tragedies of marriage alliance, which were written in exactly the same period of time.[135] In *La Toison d'or*, Médée's action of surrendering the golden fleece to Jason is at least partly motivated by the desire to prove her worth in the rivalry with Hypsipyle. In *Attila*, self-love, activated by rivalry, becomes the driving force for the plot. Attila, the king of the Huns who calls himself the scourge of God, receives two princesses through "two treaties of peace" (III.965): Honorie, the sister of the Roman emperor, and Ildione, the sister of the French king. He wavers between the two in his attempt to build an advantageous marriage alliance. In the meantime, Ardaric and Valamir, two minor kings, are secretly courting Ildione and Honorie, respectively, the one out of "un veritable amour" and the other out of "un amour politique" (I.322–24). With such a configuration of characters, *Attila* can be read as a fictional experiment designed to show how all the forces involved in the making of a marriage alliance play themselves out. One of the forces is self-love. Humiliated by the fact of being treated as merely one of two possible choices, Honorie tries hard to assert herself at the expense of her rival Ildione, although she detests Attila and dreads the prospect of being chosen. This prospect is all the more intolerable for her because it would leave Ildione to Ardaric and thus give her rival a happiness that she herself would not able to get in the arms of Attila (IV.1148–60). Thus she wants and does not want to be chosen by Attila at the same time, consumed with a vengeful fury against her rival. In Attila himself, self-love evinces the abysmal quality as described by Rochefoucauld, taking on a "monstrous" proportion, making him "idolize" himself and "tyrannize other people." With two princesses at his disposal, Attila epitomizes what Walter Benjamin calls "the tyrant's inability to make a decision."[136] Choosing one means losing the other, and that loss pains him, as it would derogate from his all-powerfulness. Even more harrowing for him is the idea that the princess not chosen by him would come into the enjoyment of another king. Unwilling to let go either of the princesses, and unwilling to let any other king marry a princess of his choice, Attila pits the one king against the other in order to have them murdered by each other. This monstrous scheme fails to materialize only because Attila is surprised by his own sudden death. While the play sends the despot to his doom to the delight of the audience, it also metes out a death sentence on marriage alliance. Not only does the project of marriage alliance come to naught because of Attila's death, but, torn apart by the horrendous self-love of all the parties involved, marriage alliance cannot help but self-destruct.

In sum, the logic by which marriage alliance operates dismantles it before it is even contracted, because a vow given can be withdrawn again, because private sentiments corrupt public functions, and because rivalry stirs up the worst of self-love. Regardless of whether at the end a wedding is in the offing or not, all of Corneille's plays under discussion uncover the lawlessness and disorder at the origin of every marriage alliance.

International Order Through Tragic Experience

In his *Ursprung des deutschen Trauerspiels,* Benjamin distinguishes the tragic drama of the German Baroque from Greek tragedy: whereas Greek tragedy stages the downfall of a mythic world and thereby gestures, through a kind of mute prophecy, towards something radically new, the representation of sovereign persons in the baroque tragic drama remains trapped in a strict historical immanence.[137] Benjamin's observation about the incapacity of German baroque drama for transcendence applies to early modern tragedy in general: the actions represented on stage are struggles of royal persons in the one or the other historical garb, and the present time of theatrical performance is shaped by struggles of royal persons as well. In light of the doctrine of the divine rights of kings, actions of royal persons can be compared to mythic violence committed by gods. Tragedy represents this kind of mythic violence without opening up a horizon for transcending it. Yet precisely in its impregnable immanence, it reflects on the political world of its time. The tragedies read in this chapter reflect on the international world of sovereigns in three important senses: first, by representing the transgression of sovereign persons, they reveal the intrinsic deficit of international law; second, tragic representation affords a distinctive aesthetic experience; and finally, by means of such aesthetic experience, they enable a recognition—anagnorisis—of international world order.

Every play discussed above constructs a fictive world of sovereigns. The violence and destruction inflicted by the sovereign persons on one another indicate not so much the lack of any rule of conduct as the lack of what H. L. A. Hart calls secondary rules: the rules of recognition determining the criteria of validity of a law; the rules of change laying out whether and how a law can be changed, modified or repealed; and the rules of adjudication specifying how to resolve legal disputes.[138] *Tamburlaine* and *King John* problematize the source and validity of laws in the international world. In Shakespeare's tragicomedies, the marriage treaty as an international legal norm proves to be a dramatic artifice and theatrical myth, while Corneille's tragedies of marriage alliance open up the abyss gaping beneath every marriage treaty. The royal characters in the works of Gryphius and Lohenstein violate international legal norms at will, embodying the absence of any rules of change and adjudication. These tragedies may thus be read as fictional experiments with the consequences of the lack of secondary rules in international law. These consequences manifest themselves, almost invariably, as violence, transgression, and disorder.

It is, of course, through the representation of violence, transgression, and disorder that tragedy achieves aesthetic effects. Corneille's theoretical treatise on tragedy *Les trois discours sur le poème dramatique* (1660) opens with the statement that "according to Aristotle the only goal of dramatic poetry is to please spectators." In order to achieve this goal, he argues, the tragedian must move beyond verisimilitude: "It is not verisimilar that Medea kills her children, that Clytemnestra murders her husband, that Orest stabs his mother: but that is how the story goes, and the representation of these great crimes is not ever disbelieved."[139] Connoting primarily the plausibility or probability of the plot, the doctrine of verisimilitude, a centerpiece of the poetics of French Classicism formulated in the 1630s and 1640s, presupposes a normative order in the human world. By challenging verisimilitude, Corneille prepares the way for his tragedies of marriage alliance, in which the world of sovereigns is depicted as a space where disorder reigns supreme. According to his reasoning, it is precisely its disorder that makes the international arena worthy of tragic representation, for disorder promises those "singular events" that would give the audience the greatest pleasure.[140] This argument of Corneille's is applicable also to the other tragedies read in this chapter.

Finally, by means of the aesthetic experience elicited by the representation of disorder and destruction, tragedy enables an understanding that would otherwise not be possible. Human beings, Aristotle argued, enjoy learning and understanding things by their very nature.[141] Our pleasure in poetry is an instance of this pleasure, for poetry, like all other kinds of mimesis, helps us understand and realize things.[142] The tragic representation of the unending bloodshed and disorder in the world of sovereigns provides a critical distance from which the audience can observe or even pass judgment on the conflicts in this world. It enables the audience to recognize a concord among sovereigns or an international order, albeit as something that inexorably comes to naught, that is stubbornly unavailable. Or, in other words, tragedy transmutes, by the magic of the art of theater and poetry, lawlessness and disorder in the international arena into the recognition of lawfulness and order. International order exists, but only in the imagination.

Chapter 4

International Order as Romance

Alongside tragedy, political romance was another generic form for the poetic figuration of international order in the seventeenth century. It also managed to negotiate affairs of the state, particularly international affairs, by constructing plots involving princely persons. The plot pattern of political romance, however, is opposed to that of tragedy. Whereas tragedy represents royal persons plunging inexorably into violence and discord, political romance represents them moving towards concord in spite of mishaps, obstacles, and adversities—indeed, in spite of themselves. The prototype of political romance is John Barclay's *Argenis*, published in 1621. Revolving around a royal love story, the convoluted plot of *Argenis* ends with a marriage alliance among a number of states. This ending stands synecdochically for an international legal order. Formally, *Argenis* is modeled on the marriage plot characteristic of the Greek romance—the plot of chaste heterosexual love consummated by marriage after many trials and tribulations. Compared to its closest Greek model, Heliodorus's *Aithiopika* (fourth century CE), Barclay's text evinces a number of formal innovations that shed light on the distinctive shape of the international legal order affirmed by its plot: it is neither an objective lawful order nor a divinely preordained order, but rather an order emerging from the free, voluntary actions of sovereign persons.

Argenis inaugurated the genre of political romance in all major European languages—called *roman héroïque* in French and *höfisch-historischer Roman* in German. The genre usually took the form of sprawling narratives running into the hundreds, even thousands of pages. It went through a serious crisis in the mid-seventeenth century, at a time when the tragic vision of international order predominated. Corneille's tragedies, as analyzed in the previous chapter, suggest that marriage alliance is poisoned even before it is contracted. In this environment, the rosy marriage plots of political romance became hard to sell. Sir Percy Herbert's *The Princess Cloria* of 1661, a political romance concerned with the English Civil War, constructs a marriage plot only to show its irrelevance for the international world. Reflecting the historical reality of marriage alliance among European royal houses, *The Princess Cloria* divests the marital contract of its normative force and reveals its true nature—royal marriage is either a matter of private passion or an item in the toolbox of international politics.

Later in the century, however, political romance received a new lease of life, entrusted with a redemptive function in the face of relentless turmoil in the international world. The champions of the genre saw in the romancer a spokesperson of God invested with the capacity for realizing, by poetic means, divine justice on earth. According to the divine-right theory of kingship, the prince is a lieutenant of God on earth, but he enforces divine justice only in his own realm. It seems that the only earthly power even higher than the prince is the romancer, as he brings about the best possible order in the entire world—by linking all the princes into a universal marriage alliance. As it happened, the most prominent romance writer in this period was also a prince—Anton Ulrich von Braunschweig-Lüneburg (also called von Braunschweig-Wolfenbüttel, 1633–1714). The fact that he was the prince of a diminutive dukedom with negligible international influence speaks volumes about what the world order envisioned by his romances actually is—a poetic fiction. Like the divine-right theory of kingship, the poetics that deifies the romance writer faces the nuisance of mortality. How can a romance writer do justice to the whole world if he dies before the world ends? How can a romance continue beyond the death of its author? If the divine-right theory of kingship came with a complex of practices, institutions and doctrines to ensure the immortality of the king, the poetics of romance were caught off guard when the aging Anton Ulrich faced death without being able to finish the political romance *Die römische Octavia* after forty years and seven thousand pages. Ultimately, the author of a romance that lives up to the expectation of realizing divine justice, as Anton Ulrich's advisor Gottfried Wilhelm Leibniz concludes in his *Theodicy* (1710), can only be God himself. Anton

Ulrich's death in 1714 marked also the death of political romance as a genre. Perhaps more than any other literary form, political romance revealed, in its short career between John Barclay and Anton Ulrich, the promises and limitations of poetic literature: it promised to institute international world order, but could never pass the test of the real.

The Romance Form and World Order (The Greek Romance, Barclay's *Argenis*)

Argenis, the Prototype of Political Romance

In 1621, the year when Hugo Grotius fled to Paris and embarked on the writing of the treatise that was to be recognized as a founding text of international law, namely *De jure belli ac pacis*, a voluminous book appeared in this city under the title *Argenis*. The title is the anagram of the Latin word *regina* (queen) with the Greek feminine ending "—is", which suggests a girl's name and the title of an epic or a romance (such as *Aeneis*). Just like Grotius's treatise published four years later, *Argenis* was dedicated to Louis XIII, the French king with the epithet *le juste*. The dedication promises a book on the same topic as Grotius's treatise—war and peace: "Now, although imbued with a kingly love of battle, you have not indulged in battle more than was right, and you allowed peace to be an enemy to the evils of war."[1] The author of the book, John Barclay (1582–1621), had all the qualifications for writing on so weighty a topic. He was the son of the Scottish jurist William Barclay (1546–1608), whose treatise *De regno et regali potestate* (1600) offered a vigorous polemical defense of royal absolutism. Barclay *fils* was close to the court of James I and familiar with all the political debates of the time. Yet *Argenis* approaches the question of war and peace in a way entirely different from Grotius's magnum opus. Although it contains at times lengthy disquisitions on politico-legal issues, and although it boasts a humanistic erudition rivaling that of Grotius, *Argenis* tells a fictional story rather than laying down a system of legal doctrines. The general setting of the story is Sicily and other Mediterranean countries in pre-Roman times, but it is, as a scholar of neo-Latin literature rightly points out, "deliberately ahistorical and humanistic-classical [. . .]. It would be vain to try to locate the adventures of Barclay's heroes anywhere in ancient history. They are acting in a non-existing but classical world born of the author's imagination."[2] In pseudohistorical garb, the text makes frequent references to the author's own time, apparently meant to be a sly intervention in contemporaneous debates.

INTERNATIONAL ORDER AS ROMANCE

It is an intervention that derives its efficacy not so much from arguments as from a romance plot. *Argenis* recounts the initially secret love between Argenis, princess of Sicily, and Poliarchus, king of France, which is consummated by marriage at the end. The road to marriage is filled with obstacles. There is first Lycogenes, the rebellious vassal of the Sicilian king Meleander, who tries to abduct Argenis and usurps sovereign power in Sicily. Then there is Radirobanes, the king of Sardinia, who comes to the aid of Meleander in suppressing Lycogenes's revolt and, in doing so, lays claim to the hand of Argenis. As Argenis does not consent to the match, Radirobanes tries to abduct her by force. Archombrotus, a foreign nobleman at Meleander's court, manages to foil this odious plot. As a reward, the king decides to bestow Argenis's hand on him.

At this point, the rivalry between Archombrotus and Poliarchus, which has been latent all along, comes to the fore. The true identities of both men are not revealed until the very end of the story. Poliarchus comes to Sicily in disguise, falls in love with Argenis, wins the favor of the king, but then loses it because of Lycogenes's machinations. He has to leave Sicily early on in the story, soon after he and Archombrotus encounter and befriend each other. He returns at the end to assert his true identity as the king of France and to claim the hand of Argenis. Archombrotus comes to Sicily in disguise as well. He falls in love with Argenis and becomes Meleander's right-hand man during Poliarchus's absence without telling anyone who he really is. After the Sicilian king decides to give him Argenis in marriage, we learn that Archombrotus is the son of Hyanisbe, the queen of Mauritania. A letter sent by Queen Hyanisbe to King Meleander reveals that Archombrotus is in fact the son of Meleander and Anna, her dead sister. Meleander lived in Africa in his youth and then left in extraordinary circumstances without knowing that his secretly wedded wife Anna was pregnant and then died in childbirth.

Once Archombrotus is revealed to be the half-brother of Argenis, the rivalry is resolved and Poliarchus can finally marry her. Archombrotus is happy to find his sister, and is made even happier by Poliarchus's offer of the hand of his own sister, the princess of France, to him. The double wedding that is in the offing at the end of the story heralds not merely a "great and powerful alliance" between France and Sicily (V.20.1). More important, it promises a stable system of states. Poliarchus's foster father Aneroestus, a religious man, predicts that Archombrotus, after joining the Mauritanian with the Sicilian crown, will annex all the smaller neighbors (V.20.6). At the same time, "[the] Rhine on the one side and the ocean on the other shall behold [Poliarchus and Argenis] as conquerors. [. . .] The neighbor nations shall admire [their] glory and power and not refuse to be conquered, to be governed by [them]" (V.20.7). As sovereigns of two consolidated world regions, Poliarchus and Archombrotus are joined together by a double marital alliance, with each one married to the other's sister. As the first token of goodwill in this alliance, Archombrotus gives Sardinia, which he has recently conquered, to his sister as dowry. An international order is established.

This skeletal plot summary does not do justice to the complex structure of *Argenis* complete with intercalated narratives, shipwrecks and pirates, wars and court masques, political speeches and gallant poetry. But it may already give an inkling of the main thrust of this sprawling text: it constructs a fictional world in which the loves and adventures of princes, bedeviled by endless contingencies and adversities as they are, eventually end in a pleasing concord based on royal marital treaties. This imaginary concord of sovereigns was particularly alluring in an age in which sovereign states scrambled to coexist peacefully without a higher authority. Not only was *Argenis* translated into all major European languages, but it also inspired a new genre in European literature: political romance.

The protagonists of *Argenis* are princely persons. Barclay operates with the assumption that the prince embodies the state, and that his actions stand for state actions. This royal absolutist doctrine served as the historical precondition for *Argenis* and the genre of political romance in general. Conversely, by constructing appealing plots for consumption by a wide audience on the basis of this doctrine, the genre of political romance contributed to cementing the cause of royal absolutism. In this sense, political romance was enmeshed with the history of political thought. *Argenis* reflects on its own condition of possibility by tracing, in its early parts, the genesis of royal absolutism. It does so on two intertwined levels—what Aristotle calls plot (*muthos*) and intellect (*dianoia*). The first two books of the romance revolve around the rebellion of the nobleman Lycogenes against the all too conciliatory king Meleander in Sicily. After many ups and downs, the rebellion is suppressed. The defeat of the rebel Lycogenes at the beginning of book 3—interestingly with the help of foreign sovereigns—reinstates the absolute authority of the king. What *Argenis* offers up to this point, then, is a plot of the defeat of aristocratic rebellion and the triumph of royal authority. This plot is framed by *dianoia*—theoretical reflections, first by observers of Meleander's court (I.2.3–6) and then by Meleander himself (III.4), on the necessity of keeping the nobility in check and cementing royal sovereignty. Other disquisitions in between—including a defense of monarchy with the help of the arguments developed by Barclay *père* in *De regno et regali potestate* (I.18) as well as a denigration of Calvin (II.5)—further corroborates the doctrine of royal absolutism.

The Greek Romance as Model

With sovereign princely persons as its main characters, *Argenis* constructs a plot that culminates in the contracting of marriage between them. Such a plot is explicitly modeled on the Greek romance. "Greek romance" is a generic term for a corpus of fictional narratives written in Greek prose from the period of the Roman Empire, which were classified as romances in early modern Europe and received their first historical-theoretical treatment in Pierre Daniel Huet's *Traitté de l'Origine des Romans* (1670).[3] It is debatable whether this corpus of texts can or should be treated as a genre at all.[4] But they certainly share many common characteristics. For instance, they all have a nostalgic tone, with the fictional actions set in a distant past. They also share a preoccupation with the learning of the classical period of Greek culture. Above all, they share the same plot pattern. A scholar of the Greek romance succinctly summarizes the general outline of these texts as follows: "A handsome youth and a beautiful girl meet by chance and fall in love, but unexpected obstacles obstruct their union; they are separated, and each is launched on a series of journeys and dangerous adventures; through all their tribulations, however, they remain faithful to each other and to the benevolent deities who at critical junctures guide their steps; and eventually they are united and live happily ever after."[5] The emphasis on chaste heterosexual love and its consummation in marriage was anything but typical of Greek society throughout the classical and Hellenistic periods. The usual plotline of the Greek romance amounted to nothing less than an "invention."[6] At the end of his *Histoire de la sexualité*, Michel Foucault concludes that the Greek romance indicates the rise of a "new erotics" in the imperial period, which "organizes itself around the symmetrical and reciprocal relationship of a man and a woman, around the high value attributed to virginity, and around the complete union in which it finds perfection."[7] Regardless of the historical accuracy of Foucault's symptomatic reading, it is obvious that the plot structure of the Greek romance valorizes marriage. As the narrative telos, the marital union between a young man and a young woman under the proper auspices of family, community, and often gods signifies a stable social order, an order that is all the more desirable because it supervenes after much wandering and many ordeals.

The rediscovery of these texts in the Renaissance led to a spate of publications, translations, adaptations, imitations, and theoretical reflections.[8] Barclay's *Argenis* refers back to the Greek romance in multiple senses: it is self-consciously draped in all things Greek; its story is set in an indeterminate past as all Greek romances are; and it places great value on learning as the Greek texts do, although the subject matters of learning have changed. Above all, of course, *Argenis* takes over the marriage plot invented by the Greek romance and puts it to an entirely different use. Given the royal absolutist doctrine of the identity between the royal person and the state, and given the ensuing entwinement between the life of the prince as a mortal human and the affairs of the state, royal marriage was a political matter of the highest significance, serving as an instrument for dynastic continuity and strategic international alliances. In *Basilicon Doron* (1598), King James counts marriage among the most important offices of the sovereign, admonishing the crown prince, among other things, to pay attention to chastity.[9] Barclay "kidnapped"—to borrow a term from Northrop Frye's critical study of romance—the standard plot structure of the Greek romance to promote the marital politics of the absolutist state, indeed to promote an ideal higher than marital politics could ever fully attain: the concord of sovereigns, or international order.[10] Kidnapping, however, cannot leave its victim unscathed. Barclay's instrumentalization of the marriage plot for the purpose of imagining international order entails transforming it in significant ways. Compared to Heliodorus's *Aithiopika*, the most complex and the most influential of Greek romances that Barclay knew well and apparently tried to emulate, the plot of *Argenis* evinces a number of significant innovations, including the privileging of the free agency of protagonists over objective laws, and the rejection of the divine control of events.[11] At the same time, diplomatic practice becomes a motor of romance plot. These new features of the plot mirror the politico-legal ideas and practices in the age of the sovereign state: the paramountcy of the sovereign will in all politico-legal matters, the subordination of religion to sovereign power, and the increasing importance of the diplomatic apparatus in the communication between sovereigns. Taken together, the formal innovations lend a distinctive shape to international order as the telos of the plot: it is a lawful order emerging from the free, voluntary and sometimes diplomatically mediated interactions between sovereign persons. Figured by means of the poetic art of plot construction as well as other fictionalizing operations, it can be called an imaginary world order.

From Providential Order to Emergent Order: *Argenis* versus *Aithiopika*

Providential Order in *Aithiopika*

Aithiopika tells the story of Charikleia and Theagenes, a girl of divine beauty and an enticingly handsome youth, who fall in love in Delphi, embark on a journey to the heroine's homeland Ethiopia, reach their destination after many adventures, and are finally united in marriage after the heroine is recognized as the long lost princess. In the climactic final book, Charikleia is restored to her birth parents, joined to Theagenes by "the laws of matrimony" (10.40), and simultaneously inducted in the priesthood.[12] The ending of *Aithiopika*—the wedding of Charikleia and Theagenes—signifies a normative model of order based on law and religion. In a narrative, the ending occupies a privileged place, as it brings closure to a series of events and thereby structures them into a coherent, meaningful whole. How does the pattern of events in *Aithiopika*—its plot structure—relate to the normative order established at the end?

Upon falling in love with Theagenes, Charikleia is dazed by pangs of desire, feeling ashamed and disoriented. Her guardian tells her, "You may rid yourself this slur of carnal desire and make your objective the lawful contract of wedlock, so transforming your malady into matrimony" (4.10). With the wedding ceremony at the end, this objective is realized. On the most basic level, then, the romantic plot of *Aithiopika*, which progresses from the initial awakening of desire towards the final wedding ceremony, enacts and enforces "the laws of matrimony." The prescriptive enforcement of lawful wedlock, however, forms merely one conspicuous layer of a general concern with law throughout the narrative. The space that the protagonists traverse on their journey from Delphi to Ethiopia is one of utter lawlessness, inhabited by people who are either outright outlaws or are otherwise outside of the law. The former category of people include pirates and bandits, while the latter includes the tyrannical wife of the Persian satrap, who covets Theagenes, and the soldiers in the warzone between Egypt and Ethiopia, who capture the young couple. Relentless wars among brigands potentiate the lawlessness. Thyamis, the bandit chieftain inflamed with desire for Charikleia, sees the world as a state of permanent warfare: "No brigand war has ever ended in a formal truce or been concluded by a treaty of peace—victory means life, and defeat inevitably death" (1.29). This assessment is echoed by the young couple's guardian Kalasiris: "an armistice" among pirates is one "with no formal guarantees, actually warfare of the cruelest imaginable kind, suspended in name only for a peace that was in truth no peace at all: the terms imposed were even more horrible than the fighting had been" (5.25). Lawlessness deprives the protagonists of all free agency, leaving them no other choice than to react to the always mercilessly dire circumstances. The protagonists' journey reaches a decisive threshold on the border between Egypt and Ethiopia. As the limit of law-governed polities, the border is the very emblem of lawlessness. As it happens, a border war is raging between Egypt and Ethiopia at the time, and our protagonists are captured when they pass the warzone. Yet this border also marks the end of lawlessness. Although the Ethiopian king has soundly defeated the Egyptians, he magnanimously promises peace and friendship. Thereupon the Persian satrap who rules Egypt voluntarily makes obeisance to him. The Ethiopian border proves to be a border between lawlessness and lawfulness. Inside Ethiopia, there is the rule of law. Charikleia regains free agency, appealing to law in her attempt to persuade the king of her identity: "In every case that comes to trial, sire, two types of evidence are recognized as most conclusive: documentary proof and corroboration by witnesses. Both types I shall adduce to demonstrate that I am your daughter" (10.12). The rule of law in Ethiopia finds its highest expression in the application of "the laws of matrimony" to its princess and her beloved.

Aithiopika can thus be read as a tale of the transition from lawlessness to lawfulness. Such a sequence of events at once shapes and is shaped by the structure of the narrative discourse. Lawlessness creates turbulence, uncertainty, and constant *peripeteia* in the life of the protagonists. They stumble from pirates' ship to bandits' dens, from bloody scuffles of brigands to battlefields of armies, captured and recaptured, always at the mercy of those who threaten their life, freedom, and chastity. The space of lawlessness is thus also a seething cauldron of narrative energy that propels, or reverses, or diverts the course of events at every turn in the most unexpected of ways. Lawfulness, by contrast, ensures stability, certainty, and security. Under the protection of law, individuals could lead a settled life within a certain circumscribed horizon. If lawlessness generates the open potentiality of the narrative, lawfulness entails resolution and closure. As the threshold between lawlessness and lawfulness, the Ethiopian border also figures as the textual border where the final book of *Aithiopika*, the book of closural settlement, begins. The enforcement of "the laws of matrimony," lawfulness *par excellence* in the world of the Greek romance, coincides with the end of the narrative.

Law as a model of normative order is accompanied, indeed trumped, by religion. Charikleia and Theagenes's wedding doubles as the ceremonial induction into the sacerdotal office and, as the final lines of the narrative indicate, as mystic initiation. The romantic plot of *Aithiopika*, which starts with the protagonists' first encounter at a ritual procession in Delphi and ends with their wedding procession in Meroe, affirms a divinely preordained order of things. The young couple's journey begins in Delphi, the site of Apollo's shrine, where Charikleia is the acolyte of Artemis. It passes through Memphis, the site of the cult of Isis and Osiris, and ends in Meroe, the site of the cult of the Sun. The heroine's three father figures—Charikles, Kalasiris, and Hydaspes—preside over these sites respectively. On this mystically-religiously coded journey, the Ethiopian border plays a crucial role, just as it performs a liminal function in terms of law.[13] The description of the events on the border in book 9 of *Aithiopika* centers around ritual actions, while the narrator gestures tantalizingly towards the "greatest mysteries" that "may not be spoken of" (9.10).[14] The journey towards Ethiopia is a progressive approximation to the divine, which reaches its end with "the more mystic parts of the wedding ritual."

The narrative discourse of *Aithiopika* is concerned with the idea of providential order from beginning to end. As discussed above, the space traversed by the protagonists' journey is one of lawlessness. Lawlessness gives rise to turbulent fluidity, uncertainty, and contingency, which translate, in turn, into infinite narrative potentiality. The work of narration consists in actualizing narrative potentiality—that is, in configuring fluid and contingent events into a goal-oriented logical sequence, an ordered whole. In a self-conscious justification of this work, the narrator attributes the sequence of events created by him to various divine agents, so that it appears as a matter of providence. He does so mostly by presenting specific events as prophesied by dreams and oracles, thus correcting the misinterpretations of these dreams and oracles by the characters concerned. The most prominent oracle in *Aithiopika* is the one pronounced by the priestess in Delphi, which all the nonplussed bystanders are "at a loss to explain" (2.35). Yet it comes true at the end. Crowned with the insignia of the priesthood, Charikleia "recalled to mind the oracle at Delphi and found the prophecy that the gods had given long ago fulfilled in fact" (10.41). The plot of the heroine's exile, itinerancy, and return is thus resignified as a vindication of providential order. The religious structure that *Aithiopika* exhibits is, as a critic puts it, "nothing more than a cypher for the control of its author."[15]

While the narrator projects the plot created by him onto a divine plane, the characters become interpreters—of both the plot and the providential order that the plot is made to signify. The lawless world robs the protagonists of free agency. They are thrown hither and thither, forced to react rather than freely acting. The actual sequence of events they experience appears to their eyes to resemble either a poetic plot or a divine plan—or both. Lamenting their life of exile and vagrancy to Theagenes, Charikleia exclaims, "To wage this campaign against us is heaven's sport, as if our lives were a drama played on stage for its pleasure. So why do we not cut short its tragic plot and give ourselves up to those whose desire it is to kill us" (5.6)? With her journey approaching its destination in spite of all the mischiefs of Fortune, however, Charikleia becomes more and more optimistic in her interpretations. After being captured by Ethiopian soldiers, Charikleia "knew now that Destiny was guiding her steps. She felt sure that their fortune was about take a turn for the better" (8.17). At the end, the romantic plot, divine providence, and the heroine's interpretation of the events all converge.

Emergent Order in *Argenis*

Argenis takes up the marriage plot perfected by *Aithiopika*. The social order enforced by the ending, however, has changed its meaning. Most notably, the marriage at the end of *Argenis*, contracted by royal persons and meant to establish international order, enters into an utterly different relationship to law and religion. Accordingly, the entire plot structure shifts in significant ways.

It is, first of all, worth noting that the law of matrimony seems no longer to be a real concern in *Argenis*. In *Aithiopika*, lawful wedlock is important because it serves to contain and channel the overwhelming and potentially destructive sexual desire. In Barclay's political romance, however, the love between Argenis and Poliarchus is so chaste that they never exchange a kiss, nor ever even touch each other. Archombrotus agrees, enthusiastically to boot, to marry Poliarchus's sister without ever having met her. With sexual desire eliminated, marriage loses its importance as the legal framework for the satisfaction of it. Wedlock assumes other functions instead. It either serves solely the practical purpose of building alliances between states, as is the case with the union of Archombrotus and Poliarchus's absent sister; or additionally it also serves to consummate some genuine affection, as is the case with the union of Poliarchus and Argenis. One way or another, what really matters now in the marital union is not the compliance with some objective law of matrimony, but the implementation of the will of sovereign persons. In fact, the sovereign will demands to be implemented even at the expense of contravening whatever laws there may be. On his journey towards Sicily to claim Argenis's hand, Poliarchus thinks to himself, "Why should Meleander now refuse him to be his son-in-law, since he now showed himself a king by his habit and the magnificence of his wealth and forces? [. . .] He hoped besides either to abrogate by the sword that law of Sicily which forbade the heir of the crown to be married to a greater kingdom, or to give it a new construction" (IV.15.4). That a marital alliance may override existing laws is reaffirmed at the end. Bestowing the hand of his daughter to Poliarchus, Meleander recalls the law of his kingdom, which forbids Sicilian princes from intermarriage with the French, but then continues, "You have deserved that we should all, with one consent, abrogate this law." It is only by accident that this law does not need to be abrogated: for the gods, Melander continues, "have restored me my son to succeed me in Sicily, and my Argenis shall not be of meaner estate, for she shall have Sardinia and Liguria and unite them to your France without breach of our laws" (V.20.1).

If the wedding ceremony at the end of *Aithiopika* enforces the laws of matrimony, the wedding at the end of *Argenis* invalidates them. This striking difference bespeaks a significant development from the Greek romance to Barclay's political romance: the general concern with laws gives way to the privileging of the free sovereign will. In *Aithiopika*, the itinerancy of the heroine and her lover is associated with lawlessness, whereas their arrival in her homeland means a return to the space of law. Lawlessness deprives the protagonists of free agency, making them the playthings of the vagaries of fortune. By contrast, the protagonists of *Argenis* peregrinate in a space beyond the law, acting freely at the urging of their will, always with a purpose in mind, even though the purpose might not be revealed initially. They do so consistently from the beginning to the end without ever descending into the space of the law, by which they may be constrained. Such a space beyond the law, it should be emphasized, is not the same as the lawless space into which the protagonists of *Aithiopika* are thrown. The latter is a space devoid of objective laws that should be in force. The former, by contrast, is a space in which no objective law is presumed and each person may exercise freely his or her will. The free exercise of the will does not mean doing whatever one pleases, as one free will may come into conflict with the other, making it necessary for one or the other to adjust himself to the given situation. For instance, at the beginning of *Argenis*, Poliarchus is forced to leave Sicily after he learns that he has lost favor at Meleander's court. In principle, he may choose to stay to confront Meleander or choose to flee from the temporary ills, as his consultations with friends also make clear. The sequence of events in the first book exhibits the struggle between individual wills without ever referring to any objective laws that may have been violated. To put it pointedly, the adventures in the Greek romance are forced upon the protagonists by the absence of objective laws, whereas in *Argenis* protagonists voluntarily embark upon adventures regardless of the existence of objective laws.

Perhaps nothing illustrates the primacy of free agency in *Argenis* better than the shipwreck-*cum*-pirates episode (II.9–10). *Aithiopika* features both a shipwreck—"the normal means of transportation" in Greek romance—and pirates, the emblem of lawlessness.[16] Both symbolize the vicissitudes of fortune, generative of turbulent uncertainty and delay as key elements of the romance plot. The inclusion of a shipwreck and pirates in the plot of *Argenis* can be seen as a conscious resumption of the generic conventions of the Greek romance. Yet the handling of these conventions in Barclay's political romance is anything but conventional. In the face of impending tempests, Poliarchus urges the unwilling pilot to put forth to sea with "many commands." When the weather situation convinces the shipmates to "bend their course towards Sicily, the nearest place offered up by fortune for [their] safety," Poliarchus "refused to go for Sicily and so drew his sword, threatening to cut off the hand of him who should first lay it on oar to row that way." In the midst of the storm, he "leapt into the lifeboat with his servant and two mariners next to him, and cutting the cable, he adventured himself to most certain shipwreck" (II.9.2). If this series of actions attests to the strong will of the hero to brave the chaos of nature, Poliarchus's subsequent encounter with pirates bears testimony to an equally strong will to cope with human conflicts. Rather than allowing himself to be victimized by the pirates, he first defends himself valiantly, killing off some of the enemies. He then devises a great strategy in the face of the overwhelming threat by freeing the captives of the pirates and requesting them to fight on his side. "Those now unbound presently set their fellows free so as now the number on both sides was almost equal" (II.10.2.). This enables him to turn around the situation completely. In the next step, he has the soundly defeated pirates chained and "reserved for due punishment," while accepting the "congratulations of the poor men who by his valour had escaped the thralldom of the robbers" (II.10.3). Finally, he harnesses the manpower now available—captivated pirates and freed captives—to sail to Africa in order to return the spoils of the pirates to their former owner, the Queen of Mauritania.

In this and other similar episodes, overpowering threats in the world of romance become tests for martial valor and moral virtue, while the helplessness of romance characters is turned to heroic triumph.[17] Such a celebration of defiant willpower and sovereign freedom in the political romance bears a distinctive historical stamp. It at once reflects and promotes a key tenet of absolutism in the seventeenth century: the sovereign recognizes no preexisting laws, but creates laws by his free will. The privileging of sovereign free agency over laws cannot help but restructure the narrative discourse as well. In the Helidorian romance, the lawlessness of the world and the concomitant helplessness of the protagonists make up the open potentiality of the narrative, while lawfulness entails narrative closure. The transition from lawlessness to lawfulness on the level of what is narrated corresponds to the movement from openness towards closure on the level of narration. The paramountcy of the free agency of protagonists in Barclay's political romance redefines narrative openness and closure. Now the freedom of the will guarantees the open potentiality of the narrative, as it produces, inexhaustibly, new actions and new situations on the basis of rational deliberation, emotional inclination, or other motivations. The freedom of the will does not cease as long as a person is alive. Since the generic conventions of romance usually do not allow its heroes to die, the narrative of the political romance is eminently open-ended, which may be one of the reasons for its extravagant length. The narrative can come to an end only if the free actions of the protagonists, alternately obstructing and propelling each other, eventually bring about a situation in which no further initiative is required. Since the protagonists of the political romance are royal persons, such a situation takes the form of the concord of sovereigns. A concord that renders all initiatives unnecessary—the ultimate closural settlement—can only be a universal, eternal peace. The form of political romance is thus, in its ideal type at least, structurally keyed to the projects of universal peace—projects such as the "grand design" of the French king Henri IV (reign 1589–1610), as well as those developed by Barclay's contemporary Eméric Crucé in *Nouveau Cynée* (1623) and by Abbé de Saint-Pierre in *Projet pour rendre la Paix perpétuelle en Europe* (1712–17).[18]

The pirates episode just discussed may again serve as an example. After having subdued the pirates, Poliarchus inspects their spoils and "finds much wealth that came out of Mauritania, most of it likely to belong to ladies" (II.10.5). His gallantry commands him to sail to Africa right away, as "not to give the queen [of Mauritania] speedy notice of the recovery of her goods were great inhumanity." He adds, "In Africa I may easily have knowledge of the affairs of Sicily and may send news of my own proceedings to Argenis" (II.10.6). His journey to the Mauritanian court is bound to have far-reaching consequences: he is going to befriend Queen Hyanisbe; her appreciation of his person will, in due time, defuse the smoldering rivalry between him and her son Archombrotus; and the spoils returned to her turn out to contain certain tokens that prove the true identity of Archombrotus as Meleander's son and Argenis's half-brother, which will then pave the way for the double wedding and general reconciliation at the end. Voluntary actions as well as situations ensuing therefrom follow one from the other, and build one upon the other, until they converge in the final settlement.

The pirates episode is paradigmatic for the narrative of *Argenis* as a whole. In the Helidorian romance, the ending, associated with lawfulness, is opposed to the preceding narrative sequences that are associated with lawlessness. The narrative sequences associated with lawlessness, on their part, succeed one another in a mostly paratactic order, with the transition from one to the other taking place mostly by happenstance. Lawlessness means contingency. Many characters who play important roles in earlier sequences simply disappear in later ones, replaced by a new cast of characters. In *Argenis*, by contrast, each narrative sequence serves as a building block for subsequent sequences, and the ending functions as the capstone. The major narrative sequences are coordinated in such a way that they build up, layer by layer, a whole edifice.[19] While each narrative sequence gives rise to a new one, the main characters are all introduced early on, with the "bad" ones—Lycogenes and Radirobanes—eliminated along the way and the "good" ones remaining in action until the last minute. The ending supervenes as the cumulative effect of all the preceding narrative sequences. For this reason, it does not restore and enforce a preexistent, objective lawful order that has been somehow held in abeyance. Rather it institutes a new order that has never existed before and that may override existing laws. This new order, symbolized by the royal marriage, can be called an emergent order.

The emergent order has no truck with divine providence. At the end of *Aithiopika*, the wedding of the protagonists, their induction into the priesthood, and their initiation into mysteries fuse into one single ceremony. The social order enforced by marriage concurs with the divinely preordained order of things to be revealed through the priestly office and mystic rites. The wedding at the end of *Argenis* stands in a rather different relation to religion. Like Charikleia, Argenis is a priestess, but the narrator suggests from the outset that religious rituals may be hoaxes at best. As it happens, Argenis must preside over a sacrificial ritual just after she learns about Poliarchus's flight from Sicily. At the altar, "whilst others sang their solemn anthems, she poured out her secret sorrows to herself" (I.20.6). As if such dereliction of duty were not enough, she feigns divine possession in order to have a pretext for absenting herself from the people's sight (I.20.17). Religion is debunked as a charade. Judgments about religious rituals later in the text are more damning still. The Mauritanian custom of sacrifice in preparation for the war with the invading Sardinians is dismissed by Poliarchus as "vile superstition" (IV.20.4), while he upbraids the Sardinian religion as "vain" (IV.22.5). At the climactic wedding ceremony, Argenis's sacerdotal role seems to be forgotten.

But there is nonetheless a religious man present at the wedding ceremony—Poliarchus's foster father Aneroestus—and the narrator gives him the last word in this enormous text. This character embodies a significant new conception of religion and of the role of religion in the political world. The reader learns from a lengthy embedded narrative (IV.8–14) that Poliarchus was captured by thieves in his infancy and carried to the court of Aneroestus, who was then a king in the Alpine region. He grew up in the king's care, but was carried off again and restored to his birth parents. Aneroestus himself was defeated by his enemies and disappeared. After Poliarchus helps the queen of Mauritania rout the invading Sardinians, her son, Archombrotus, undertakes an expedition to Sardinia and encounters there an old religious man in a temple. This old man turns out to be Aneroestus and he is reunited with his foster son, Poliarchus. He reveals that he had landed on Sardinia by accident on his peregrination after being defeated: "But there, admiring both the appearance of the place and the life of the priests, I resolved to lay aside all cares, and having been tossed with so many miseries, at last to try the gods" (V.14.1). He has led a monastic life ever since, unconcerned about earthly things and dedicating himself to contemplation instead. The reunion with his foster son, now the great king of France, does not tempt him to regain power and embrace earthly life again. Rather he resolves to maintain his austere life and safeguard the liberty of his untroubled mind "for the contemplation of heavenly things." He wishes to be in touch with this world only at one point: to "procure the gods to be favourable and successful unto you, my son, in your wars and enterprises" (V.14.14). The implication of Aneroestus's story is clear: Religion is now differentiated from politics, vaunted as an alternative way of life devoted to contemplation and the care of the self. Henceforth religion ceases to meddle in political affairs, while politics renounces religious legitimation. On the basis of their differentiation, however, religion is brought to bear on politics in a new function—that of offering ceremonial acclamation to political power. The religious Aneroestus promises to propitiate the gods for the glory and honor of the great king Poliarchus. He makes good on his promise at the close of *Argenis*. At the wedding ceremony, he serves as the encomiast, wishing "victory and triumph" as well as "a long succession of princes to the crown of Sicily" (V.20.6), and prophesying for France glory, power, and eternal fame, "which hereafter shall be spread abroad among all nations" (V.20.7). His effusive epideictic speech, it should be noted, disavows explicitly any supernatural knowledge (V.20.7). Marriage between royal persons, like political actions in general, is a purely worldly affair. The international order instituted by it has accordingly nothing to do with the providential order, if there is such a thing at all. Religion is relevant only insofar as it offers acclamation on the occasion of the contracting of royal marriage.

By redefining religion and its relation to politics, *Argenis* takes a strong position in the ongoing debates about faith and political power around 1600, debates that went hand in hand with the relentless religious wars in the wake of the Reformation. This position also has a strong impact on the narrative form of romance, which Barclay's text rewrites. In the Helidorian romance, the notion of divine providence represents an integral part of the narrative strategy, as the narrator attributes the sequence of narrated events to divine intervention. The end of the narrative coincides with the protagonists' initiation into the innermost core of divine knowledge. The decoupling of the royal wedding from the providential order at the end of *Argenis* testifies to a pervasive disbelief in divine intervention throughout the text. The narrator makes no mention of dreams, magic, oracles, or any other supernatural occurrence in presenting human events. In fact, the text even features learned discourses that ridicule the idea of supernatural foreknowledge. One disputation refutes the ability of astrologers to predict future events and the fate of individual persons (II.17). On another occasion, a priest at a temple of Fortune holds forth on the importance of making sacrifices to this goddess "so that she would teach us things to come" (IV.7.8), but the narrator shows that the priest is actually more interested in pocketing the money paid by the visitors to purchase the sacrifices, as well as in consuming the meal made of the animal sacrifices (IV.7.1–4).

If there is no divine providence, or if it is unknowable, why do things happen the way they do in the narrative? How can the sequence of events presented by the narrator be justified? The narrator answers such questions by introducing in *Argenis* a poet by the name of Nicopompus, who explains to other characters—and to the reader of *Argenis*—the poetic design of the political romance: "I will compile some stately fable in manner of a history. In it will I fold up strange events and mingle together arms, marriages, bloodshed, mirth, with many and various successes" (II.14.5). By means of the figure of the romance writer in the romance itself—a self-reflexive poetic conceit employed also by Barclay's contemporary Miguel de Cervantes in *Don Quixote* (1605 and 1615)—the narrator unabashedly admits—indeed proudly announces—that the events, as well as the order in which they are narrated, are nothing more than a fiction born of the poet's imagination. This view by Barclay, alias Nicopompus, echoes that of Philip Sidney who, in his *Defence of Poesie* (1595), famously defines the activity of the poet as "feigning notable images of virtues, vices, or what else, with that delightful teaching."[20] Fictionality now replaces divine providence as the legitimation of the narrator's control over the plot. Supernatural phenomena disappear from the narrative discourse, turning into poetic ornaments in Nicopompus's verses scattered throughout the text, which mark one or the other memorable occasion in the lives of the fictional characters.

If the events recounted in the romance are fictional, the ending is all the more so, because the narrator has to make it up in order to tie all the events into a structured whole. The international order that comes to pass at the end of Barclay's political romance is man-made, and doubly so: it is the cumulative effect of the voluntary actions of sovereign persons in a space beyond the law rather than the restoration of any objective lawful order, and it is a fictional condition conceived by the narrator rather than the realization of the providential order.

Imaginary World Order

To repeat, the concord of sovereigns reached at the end of Barclay's political romance affirms neither an objective legal order nor a providential order. It is rather an emergent legal order consequent upon the voluntary actions of sovereigns. Quite a contrast to the turmoil and discord in the real world of sovereign states, such a concord of sovereigns can be characterized as an imaginary world order. Imaginary though it is, this world order is certainly no mere figment of fantasy. The imaginary world of the romance contains many elements reminiscent of the real world. The numerous editions of *Argenis* in the seventeenth century usually provide keys that identify correspondences between people, places, and circumstances in the text and those in the real world. More importantly, the topics of the characters' conversations, their routines, their daring enterprises, the norms of their behavior, and the mechanisms of their interaction, to name just a few examples, all seem to mesh with the real political world to some degree. Why and how do such elements drawn from the real world converge towards a harmonious world order in the political romance, and why do they patently fail to do so in the real world itself? How does the political romance with its pleasing vision of concord relate to the tumultuous political world from which it is born? The key to answering such questions lies in an understanding of the operations of fictionalization. It is through fictionalization that the real political world is reconfigured into an imaginary world, that real disorder is transformed into an imaginary order.[21]

The "real political world" is in the present context not to be understood ontologically as a fixed entity prior to or independent of representation, but epistemologically as a symbolic reality constructed through a network of discourses. These discourses include:

- Norms of behavior for sovereign persons such as those laid down by King James for his son in *Basilicon Doron* (1598)
- Rights and duties of sovereign persons such as those systematically laid out by Jean Bodin's *Les Six Livres de la République* (1576), King James's *The Trew Law of Free Monarchies* (1598), or Barclay *père*'s *De regno et regali potestate* (1600)
- Chronicles of sovereign persons' actions such as William Camden's *Annals* (1615–25) or Théodore Agrippa d'Aubigné's annals of France *Histoire universelle* (1616–30)

Documents of sovereign persons' activities such as the letters and treaties pertaining to the intended marriage of Queen Elizabeth[22]

Descriptions of royal ceremonies such as Théodore Godefroy's *Le cérémonial de France* (1619)

Practical knowledge of government such as Giovanni Botero's *Della ragion di stato* (1589), Justus Lipsius's *Politica* (1589), and the flourishing literature on reason of state in their wake

Besides these and many other written materials, there was also unwritten knowledge about the world of sovereigns, which Barclay possessed due both to his proximity to the English and the papal courts and to his diplomatic missions to various European courts on behalf of King James.[23]

Argenis taps into this vast trove of knowledge about the world of sovereigns by selecting some elements of it, while excluding others. The selected elements include, first of all, those things that Barclay's contemporary Kingsmill Long—the first and probably the most successful English translator of *Argenis*—characterized as "altogether certaine."[24] They are peoples, places, and circumstances that seem to have some kind of counterpart in the real world and that require a "key to unlock." This interest in identifiable things, which Long shared with other romance readers of his time, blinded him and his contemporaries to the fact that a great part of those things characterized by him either as "altogether uncertaine" or as "of a middle sort, betweene both" are taken from the real political world as well. These things encompass words and practices, norms and attitudes, sentiments and feelings extracted from the manifold discourses constitutive of the political world. For example, the numerous dialogues and speeches about matters of state in *Argenis*—with topics ranging from fundamental issues such as royal authority (III.4) and forms of government (I.18) to concrete policies regarding litigation (III.22), army (IV.4), taxation (IV.18), and appointment of ambassadors (V.3)—could have taken place at any court in Europe. The same applies to the ceremonies and spectacles described in the text. The masque on the occasion of Argenis's birthday (III.23) resembles a Stuart court masque. Wars that make up an integral part of the plot are hardly different from those in the political reality of Europe. The behavior of the protagonists, in particular that of Poliarchus, epitomizes the norms of valor and prudence that were expected of royal persons in the sixteenth and seventeenth centuries. But however many elements *Argenis* may draw from the political world of its time, it cannot reproduce this world in its entirety. The selection of one element entails debarring an infinite number of other elements from entering the text. The obverse of selection is exclusion. The act of selection thus cuts through and breaks up the real, pitting what is included and what is excluded against one another.

Just as the text cannot reproduce everything in the real political world, not everything in the text originates from the real political world. Argenis's feint of divine possession at a sacrificial ceremony (I.20) is hardly imaginable at a seventeenth-century European court. Storms and pirates are even less so. Such things are endemic to the world of the Greek romance. Indeed, themes, conventions, and tropes of the Greek romance abound in Barclay's text. The selection of these elements from fictional texts follows the same logic as the selection of material from the real political world, with the inclusion of certain elements necessarily bound up with the exclusion of others. *Argenis* suppresses many aspects of *Aithiopika* while incorporating others. The coexistence of different sources of material cannot help conditioning the act of selection. Conventions of romance guide the engagement with the political world, while the specifics of the political world of the time determine the choice as well as the use of romance conventions.

The act of selection represents the first fictionalizing operation, as it sets in motion the interplay between the included and the excluded, as well as the interplay between different sources of material. It is followed by another fictionalizing operation, in which the selected material is combined and structured. This is the operation that poetics since Aristotle has been concerned with, involving characterization and plot construction. For instance, the character of Poliarchus synthesizes a variety of material from different sources. The Greek lexemes that the character's name comprises—*poli* or *poly* plus *archon*—suggest something like a "ruler of the city" or "ruler over many." Barclay's dedication of *Argenis* to Louis XIII relates the protagonist to a French king. The key provided in a 1627 edition associates the character with the political situation of France, regarding him as "a representation of those against whom the sacred fury of the Guise and the League raged, such as Henry IV, King of Navarre, and the Duke of Epernon."[25] He embodies valor and prudence, the two cardinal virtues expected of the prince in the political literature of the time. Of course, he also embodies the very notion of the sovereign person endowed with absolute authority, who institutes world order through both war and peaceful means. At the same time, Poliarchus is modeled on romance characters. As is the case with every romance character, he is in love and endeavors to marry his beloved at any cost. Furthermore, two embedded narratives—the story of his childhood and youth told in book 4 and the story of his initial arrival in Sicily told in book 3—place him squarely in the romance world, as both narratives follow strictly the conventions of the Greek romance, complete with disguised identities, kidnappings, and bloody fights. The character of Poliarchus emerges from the interplay between all of these symbolic layers.

Plot construction is another mode of marshaling the material that has been selected. The free agency of the romance characters independent of both laws and providence stems from the doctrine of the unconstrained freedom of the sovereign will, which underlies royal absolutism. This doctrine is grafted onto the basic plotline of the Greek romance—marriage after many adventures—so that a plot comes into being in which events succeed one another as a result of the competition or convergence of individual voluntary actions, with natural events exceeding human volition thrown in here and there for good measure. In some cases, diplomacy—another significant reference to political reality—mediates the process by which voluntary actions impact each other, at once propelling and retarding the plot. The plot thus constructed serves as the axis around which other material extracted from the political world—theoretical discussions on matters of the state, ceremonies, and wars, among other things—is organized. Through the act of combination and structuration, be it carried out by characterization, by plotting, or by other means, the selected elements are severed once and for all from the symbolic systems to which they originally belonged, semantically recoded, and configured into a new symbolic system—the fictive world of political romance.

This world makes no secret of its own fictiveness. The statement that the poet Nicopompus makes in the political romance is in fact a statement about the political romance: *Argenis* is a "stately fable in the manner of history." In such a fable, "no man's character shall be simply set down." Nicopompus continues: "I shall find many things to conceal them, which would not well agree with them if they were made known. For I, who bind not myself religiously to the writing of a true history, may take this liberty" (II.14.5). The political romance is revealed, or rather reveals itself, as fiction. History—the real world, as it were—serves as a point of reference, insofar as history furnishes material for it. Yet the romance refuses to be measured by history because it owes its existence to liberty—the "liberty" to fictionalize. The appeal to liberty shields the poet from the potential accusation of being a liar, just as Sir Philip Sidney, in whose shadow Barclay's alias Nicopompus stands, contends: "Now for the poet, he nothing affirmeth, and therefore never lieth."[26] The self-revelation of the political romance as fiction is the final fictionalizing operation that it undertakes, as this act sets it apart from the real, asserting its status as a self-contained world in its own right.

Just as this self-contained world is an imaginary world, the concord of sovereigns, which becomes possible in it, is an imaginary international order. It differs from the real political world by virtue of the fictionalizing operations that bring it into being. Obviously, the imaginary international order serves as the lodestar for the fictionalizing operations from the very beginning, but it is at the end of these operations that it takes on a concrete form. Political romance, then, can be characterized as a literary form that carries out fictionalizing operations with a view to international order, and that gives shape to it by doing so.

The Crisis of Political Romance in the Mid-Seventeenth Century (Herbert)

Political Romance, a Pan-European Genre

The imaginary international order that looms large at the end of *Argenis* cast a spell on a time that could find no resolution to the agon of sovereigns in reality. *Argenis* enjoyed great popularity throughout the seventeenth century, undergoing one new edition after the other, and being translated into all major European languages, often multiple times.[27] At the same time, it inaugurated a new genre in European literature: political romance. Usually referred to as *roman héroïque*, this genre first blossomed in France in the final years of the reign of Louis XIII and the first two decades of the reign of Louis XIV—roughly between 1640 and 1660—with Gautier de Costes de la Calprenède (1609–63) and Madeleine de Scudéry (1607–1701) as its most important representatives. In England, political romances appeared in the mid-seventeenth century as a literary means to work through the traumatic events of the English Civil War. In German-speaking countries, political romance did not flourish until the late seventeenth century, although *Argenis* was translated into German soon after its publication by Martin Opitz (1597–1639) as part of his efforts to create a firm foundation for literature in the German language.[28] Known in German literary history as the *höfisch-historischer Roman*, the genre counts among its exemplary texts Anton Ulrich von Braunschweig-Lüneburg's *Die durchleuchtige Syrerinn Aramena* (1669–73) and *Die römische Octavia* (1677–1714) as well as Daniel Casper von Lohenstein's *Großmüthiger Feldherr Arminius* (1689–90). For all the differences among the individual specimens of the genre, a number of family resemblances tie them to *Argenis*. Usually set in remote times but keyed to the present, they tell stories of princes, princesses, and their associates. The stories revolve around disguised identities and love. The revelation of identities and consummation of love are delayed, almost infinitely, by intercalated narratives of adventures and wars, by descriptions of pomp and circumstance accompanying princely actions, and by learned discourses on politics as well as other matters of interest to the princely protagonists. When after much digression the stories do come to an end, they come to a similar end—marriage. It is often the marriage not merely of one couple, but of multiple couples. A concord of sovereigns is thereby reached after many trials and tribulations.

Political romance was arguably a prestigious narrative genre in seventeenth-century Europe because of its monumental size, because of the dignity of its subject matter, because of its aristocratic readership, and above all because it satisfied imaginatively a vital need of the time—the need to create order in the world of sovereigns. But after the marriage of Louis XIV and the Restoration of the English monarchy in 1660, the genre came to an abrupt end in France and England. It received a second lease on life in Germany, and did not die its final death until Anton Ulrich died in 1714 without being able to finish his *Die römische Octavia*. The extinction of this genre deserves attention, as it sheds light on the relationship between literature and the problem of international order just as much as does the birth of the genre.

Herbert's *The Princess Cloria*: The Crisis of Political Romance

The first stage of the extinction, which occurred at the beginning of the 1660s, can be observed in the most ambitious political romance in English, Sir Percy Herbert's *The Princess CLORIA: OR, The Royal Romance [. . .] Imbellished with divers Political Notions, and singular Remarks of Modern Transactions. CONTAINING The Story of most part of EUROPE, for many Years last past*, published in 1661.[29] In this sprawling text, the marriage plot epitomized by Barclay's *Argenis* breaks down. The continuum from love to marital contract and then to the politico-legal order of sovereign states ceases to be evident, reflecting the simultaneous prevalence and political inefficacy of marital alliances among royal houses in Europe. With the marriage plot in shambles, political romance succumbed to the facticity of historical events.

Like other English romances, *The Princess Cloria* is concerned with the English Civil War, with the execution of King Charles I, alias Euarchus, taking place at the midpoint of the romance. The main axis of the plot is the courtship and marriage of the Lydian princess Cloria and the Cypriot prince Narcissus, based on the marriage between King Charles I's eldest daughter Mary, Princess Royal, and William II, Prince of Orange and Count of Nassau. As the subtitle indicates, the romance describes the political tumult in Europe during the decades preceding the publication year 1661. But in keeping with the conventions of *roman à clef*, which disguise contemporary persons, places, and circumstances in a outlandish fictional garb—conventions introduced by *Argenis* but developed by romance writers in its wake—Herbert's romance transposes Europe to a historically unspecific Asia, giving European states Asian names according to no obvious logic: England is called Lydia, France Syria, Spain Egypt, and the United Provinces of the Netherlands is Cyprus. The movers and shakers in European politics receive various Asian-sounding names. With the love, marriage, and politicking of royal persons as its main plot elements, and "[embellished] with divers Political Notions, and singular Remarks of Modern Transactions," *The Princess Cloria* has all the trappings of a political romance. Yet early on in the narrative, a seemingly subsidiary episode brings the very possibility of the genre of political romance into question.

The Princess Cloria opens with Cassianus, a prince from the war-torn Iberia (Bohemia in the midst of the Thirty Years' War), arriving in Lydia to court Cloria in order to recover his lost country with the Lydian help. He encounters a forester on his ride. In a pastoral set piece, the forester asks Cassianus to arbitrate in the rivalry between two suitors for the hand of his daughter Mantuina—a clear reference to the struggle for the Mantuan succession in the 1620s. One of the suitors, Fridius by name, is "a Shepheard by extraction, though his Predecessors left him well enough to become a Gentleman" (23). He offers "Riches and Power, the two essential properties of Greatness," and promises to have the bride "to be exalted to the highest Throne of Honour by new attempts" (24). The other, called Navarinus, is "a Nobleman born, but wanting means, hath subscribed his aims onely within the limits of a Countrey life" (23). He has a Stoic attitude to life, advocating virtues such as temperance, patience, fortitude, and magnanimity. He alleges that Mantuina "was likelier to command his affections with felicity, that sought a unity in the lowest course of life, rather then his rivals, who could be in love with none" (24). After hearing their pleas, Cassianus comes to the conclusion that "[Fridius] was endued with a Princes soul, which of necessity must put him on to dangerous and hazzardable attempts, the other more resembling a Lover was likeliest to continue the unity of affections without separation; Fridius was fitter to be a Monarch, but Navarinus to become a Husband; wherefore he judged the beauteous Mantuina to the latter for a Wife, and the Crown she carried in her hand, to the former as a Conquerour" (25). Behind the obvious contest between one suitor's worldly political ambition and another's Stoic virtues, there is a novel conception of marriage that subverts political romance as a genre.[30] Political romance assumes and affirms the continuity and ultimately the exact correspondence between affection and political ambition. What its plot does is to show how the affection between royal persons leads to a marital contract that enhances the power of both parties and thereby serves as the basis for the politico-legal order of the world. The lover is one and the same person as the monarch. The Mantuina episode, however, drives a wedge between affection and political ambition, opposing one to the other. The arbitrator of the contest defines marriage in terms of the former, while detaching it from the latter. The husband is expected to be an affectionate lover, whereas the monarch is someone who pursues political ambitions and "could be in love with none." They are two different persons, irreconcilable with one another.

The differentiation of love and politics, of the husband and the monarch, forecloses the marriage plot of political romance. If the Mantuina episode is to be read as an allegory, then it is an allegory of the death of political romance. To be sure, *The Princess Cloria*, announced as a romance in the title, still operates with the constitutive elements of political romance—love and marriage of royal persons—but it does so not to reinvigorate the marriage plot at all costs, but rather to stage its last agony. The plotline of political romance—love leading to marital contracts that found an international order—collapses into incoherent fragments.

By separating affection from political ambition, the Mantuina episode entails a distinction between two kinds of marriage: one based on love and affection, and the other contracted for political purposes. In general, the narrator valorizes the former more than the latter. In the story told by the forester to Cassianus after the Mantuina episode, the couple in love regard their bond as forged by the "sacred laws" of heaven, which defy political interference (32). In the early parts of *The Princess Cloria*, these two kinds of marriage are exemplified by Cloria's passionate relationship with Narcissus on the one hand, and Cassianus's politically motivated courtship of Cloria, on the other. Based on love only, the first kind of marriage neither wishes to be tainted by political calculation nor actually performs any political function. In the harrowing days leading up to the execution of her father King Euarchus (Charles I), Cloria's (Mary's) beloved prince Narcissus (William II) does not come to his rescue. He excuses himself thus in a letter to her: "If you blame my courage, in not being more violent in the prosecution, yet I must beseech you not to condemn my affection" (300). The consummation of their love in marriage after the death of Euarchus neither alleviates the domestic political turmoil in Lydia (England) and Cyprus (United Provinces) nor improves the relation between the two states, let alone brings about a universal peace in Asia (Europe). In fact, armed conflicts broke out between the two countries soon after the birth of their child—the first

Anglo-Dutch War. Although the marriage of Cloria and Narcissus "may be Esteem'd a blessed Unity" (59), it is merely a unity of their souls, not a unity of states.

The other kind of marriage—the one contracted for political purposes—is a tactic in political maneuvers, be they domestic or foreign. As such, it is a symbol of strife rather than concord. Cassianus courts Cloria because he needs Lydia's help in the political struggle in his home country, and the senate of Lydia (parliament of England) supports his courtship in its struggle with King Euarchus. Cloria leads him on at one point—albeit only at the instigation of her maid—in an attempt to help her father in his struggle with the senate. Although this courtship never comes to fruition, it exposes the intrigues behind every political marriage. The narrator harbors no illusion in his assessment of marital alliances. The marriage between the princess from Egypt (Spain) and the king of Syria (France) does not prevent the two states from fighting one war after the other. When Queen Andromida and Mazarius (Mazarin) propose a marital treaty between the young King Orontes (Louis XIV) and Egypt, Creses (Clarendon) remarks to Cloria, "Envy being the most predominate humour, that for the most part governs the actions of Princes, in matter of equality of power; neither at all times doth contracted marriages, hinder jealousies procured by reason of National quarrels, and seldom make friendships of a confident nature, when subjection thereby are feared; especially where the reputation of the party that undergoes the hazzard, is sure to be lessened in opinion" (507). In sum, marriage can achieve anything but a peaceful international order, be it contracted because of love or because of political expediency.[31]

The conception of marriage in *The Princess Cloria* is in fact an acknowledgement of the political reality of the time. Since the Renaissance, royal houses in Europe, both old and new, intermarried with one another for the sake of dynastic continuity as well as international alliances.[32] In the seventeenth century, the great powers of Europe used marriage as a key leverage in engineering a balance of power. The French king Louis XIII married the Habsburg princess Anne of Austria, while the English king Charles I married Louis XIII's sister Henrietta Maria. Louis XIV married the Spanish Infanta Maria Theresa. By the end of the century, all the sovereigns and half-sovereigns were connected to one another by a complex tangle of family ties.[33] But these ties had by no means the effect of averting wars. Conflicts were hardly ever resolved by means of marriage. On the contrary, marriage created new tensions that could easily escalate into war. In the face of the reality of royal marriages, to produce yet another rosy marriage plot à la *Argenis* would only prove detractors right in saying that romance does nothing other than induce illusion and delusion. Thus, what *The Princess Cloria* does is to promote love as a refuge from political reality on the one hand, and to document the gritty reality of marital politics on the other.

Without the marriage plot, *The Princess Cloria* has no other structural pattern to follow than the historical sequence of events. In the preface, Herbert tells the reader not to "look for an exact History," and invokes the privilege of a romance writer to "make use of his own invention." By "invention," however, he means mostly the liberty "to express inward passions and hidden thoughts, that of necessity accompany all Transactions of consequence." It is by means of such a "liberty for inward disputations, or supposed passions to be discovered," that "the common Occurrances of the World" could arrive at "a pitch high enough for example, or to stir up the appetite of the Reader" ("To the Reader," unpaginated). Indeed, the narrator manages to uncover the psychological motivations underlying many events; but he proves unable to organize the disparate events into a plot that transcends the vagaries, vicissitudes, and paradoxes of history. The narrative chronicles unrelenting intrigues, unrest and wars, plights of both kings and ordinary people, insoluble dilemmas, and unexpiated crimes.[34] There is, however, hardly an overarching structure that would give discrete historical events a higher meaning and redemptive direction. Herbert's rearrangement of the timeline of the marriage of Mary and William II—historically the wedding took place long before Charles I was beheaded, but in the narrative Cloria and Narcissus marry after Euarchus's death—seems to serve to bring a ray of hope into the dark night of history. Yet he hastens to resume the historical sequence of events by letting Narcissus die soon after the execution of Euarchus and the widowed Cloria fight for her infant son's status: William II died in 1650 and Mary gave birth to her son William III a few days after her husband's death. The end of the whole narrative—the wedding spectacle of Orontes and Hesperiana, and Arethusius's "glorious progress, towards the great Seat of his large Empire" (612)—records two historical events, namely the marriage of Louis XIV to the Spanish Infanta and the restoration of the English monarchy in 1660. As such, it fails to provide the closure expected in the ending of a romance plot, if only because every historical event is always followed by another one. The narrator is well aware of this fact. Because history unstoppably moves on, he has to stop the narrative by a fiat—"This now shall finish our Romance, that perhaps hath too long a season troubled the Readers patience"—while conceding the arbitrariness of such an act: "I might here enlarge my Relations" (613). Political romance is overridden—and overwritten—by history.

The Apotheosis and Extinction of Political Romance (Anton Ulrich, Leibniz)

Anton Ulrich, or the Apotheosis of Romance

Political romance, however, soon came back to life in a different place—in German principalities far from the great powers of Europe. As the prodigious literary output of Anton Ulrich von Braunschweig-Lüneburg shows, political romance, now featuring magnified and multiplied marriage plots, assumed a new, redemptive role in the face of the grim reality of discord and turmoil in the international arena. The romance writer was hailed as the representative of God on earth, and the romance plot as the poetic realization of divine justice.

As a ruler involved in both domestic and foreign politics, Anton Ulrich certainly had an even clearer view of political reality than Sir Percy Herbert. Yet instead of letting the marriage plot crumble under the weight of political reality, and instead of surrendering political romance to history, Anton Ulrich brought out, about a decade after Herbert, a political romance on a grand scale, which features multiple marriage plots: the five-volume *Die durchleuchtige Syrerinn Aramena*. It is set in the ancient Near East at the time of the biblical patriarchs, with a number of intertwined plotlines revolving around the liberation of Syria from the Assyrian rule and the marriage of the Syrian king's sister Aramena to the Celtic prince Marsius the Younger. Compared to the prototypical political romance *Argenis*, the much longer *Aramena* has a broader geographical scope, evoking an intercontinental political order spanning Mesopotamia and the Celtic-Germanic lands. By setting the actions in biblical times, it also invests the political order with a providential quality. It is therefore meant not only to continue, but also to surpass the genre of political romance that took shape in the early seventeenth century. Such an ambitious enterprise presupposed a belief in the redemptive power of fiction. In the face of the reality of discord and turmoil that Herbert described, and which everyone with eyes could see, it seemed that only the act of constructing a romance plot could keep the hope of concord and order alive. Rather than resigning himself to the facticity of historical events, Anton Ulrich sought to redeem history by means of an extravagant romance. The preface to *Aramena*, penned by Anton Ulrich's collaborator and editor Sigmund von Birken (1626–81), illuminates this conception of political romance.

Entitled "Vor-Ansprache zum edlen Leser" (Address to the noble reader), the preface to *Aramena* defines political romance as *Geschichtgedicht* or historical poem, in contrast to annals as well as to *Gedichtgeschicht* or poetic history.[35] Annals or chronicles, "the most common kind of historical writings" according to Birken, "describe histories in their original order, naming persons, time, and places." Poetic history, exemplified by Homeric and Vergilian epics, "preserves the truthful history with its main circumstances, but adds many fictive details, and does not narrate the events in the order, in which they took place." Unlike both annals and poetic histories, historical poems "either present a truthful history hidden behind the screen of fictive names, order its circumstances differently from the way in which they actually took place, and enrich it with other circumstances that could probably take place; or they are entirely fictive stories, which the author invents in order to hone his understanding as well as the language in which he writes, and in order to admonish others to turn away from vices and towards virtues by means of edifying examples." The tenor of the concept of historical poem or *Geschichtgedicht* is fictionality, as the German term *Gedicht* (poem) carries a strong connotation of invention or fiction. *Geschichtgedicht* means, therefore, a fiction crafted with elements drawn from history, whereas *Gedichtgeschichte* means histories with fictional elements. As examples of historical poems, Birken names *Tobit* and *Judith*, two fictional narratives belonging to the Apocrypha; Greek and Latin romances by Achilles Tatius, Longus, Heliodorus, and Apuleius; modern romances such as Sir Philip Sidney's *Arcadia*, Honoré d'Urfé's *Astrée*, and Barclay's *Argenis*, among others. At the end of this long list, he indicates that *Aramena*—what is being introduced to the reader by his preface—represents the culmination of this genre, as it is written by a prince and deals with and is meant for "persons of princely estate and other noble persons."

Birken's definition of the historical poem, together with the construction of a canon for it, amounts to an important theory of romance. Birken makes no secret of his privileging of this sometimes frowned-upon genre over historical writing, for romance writers, he argues, have the "freedom to tell the truth under the cover, and to introduce everything that serves the poet's good purpose and edification," while history comprises truth and falsehood, wisdom and folly, order and chaos in equal measure. The freedom lauded by Birken is the capacity of romance writers for fictionalization. It is through fictionalization that falsehood can be sifted out and truth be told. Since fictionalization involves especially the construction of plot, and since a plot marshals characters, actions, and events in a well-ordered, meaningful structure, it is also through fictionalization that the chaos of history can be transformed into order. For Birken and other associates of Anton Ulrich, the creation of order through plotting makes a political romance the model of, if not the substitute for, governance both within a state and in the world at large.

In the preface to *Aramena*, Birken likens the contruction of a romance plot to the governing of a state, as both involve the disposition and control of people, things, and actions. Plotting is a kind of knowledge of governance. Commending the aptitude of Anton Ulrich, who is a ruler and a romance writer at once, Birken states, "The one who can write wisely about the way of governing undoubtedly also knows how to govern well, or how to contribute to praiseworthy governance. Indeed, he learns [such a skill] in teaching, and inscribes into his own heart what he writes on paper." To corroborate the analogy between the writing of romance and governing, Birken surveys the putative poetic activities of great rulers in history, concluding that "so many saints, great kings and princes, in particular Salomon, the richest, wisest, and most honored among all kings, were not shamed of poetizing." By engineering the convergence of all events towards a perfect concord through the construction of a romance plot, a ruler trains himself for governing his own realm.

Along a similar line of argument, the construction of a romance plot was likened to the divine governance of the world. A eulogy printed at the beginning of the third volume of *Aramena* (1671)—"Ueber die Tugend-vollkommene unvergleichlich-schöne Aramena" (On the perfectly virtuous and incomparably beautiful Aramena)— apostrophizes the romance as a "heavenly picture," a "mirror of [God's] play," a "clear diamond-stream, in which one properly sees Heaven's dispensation."[36] The romance mirrors the divine order, because plotting is no different from God's governance of the world according to his providential plan. The romance "beautifully" manages "all the cases by coincidence," and "truly confuses the labyrinth of life," in order to show that everything fits together after all. All the confusion is deliberately created in such a way as to bring about "the most beautiful order." The reader just needs to connect all the artfully scattered dots to "see perfectly clearly the picture of providence" standing in front of him. It needs to be noted that this notion of divine providence is rather different from that in the Helidorian romance. There, providence is a preordained order, to which the narrator attributes the sequence of events in his narrative. What matters here is an external assessment of the act of plotting: the romance author arranges events in a beautiful order in the same way as God cares for and controls His creation, so that he can be seen as God's representative on earth.

The paratexts of *Aramena*—the preface by Birken and the eulogy that introduces the third volume—analogizes the romance's plot to a ruler's governance of his state on the one hand, and to God's governance of the world on the other. On the basis of this dual analogy, it is but a small step to link the romance plot to international order. Like the domestic affairs of an individual state, international affairs are of politico-legal nature. But unlike domestic political affairs, international relations defy an earthly ruler, as the sovereign ruler of a state sees himself as the highest authority on earth and has no one else but God himself to look to in dealing with other states. International order thus represents one particular dimension of divine providence. If the romance plot in general resembles divine providence, the plot of a political romance—a romance concerned with the actions of sovereigns, especially their marriage—has to be placed on an equal footing with international order. In the thought of Gottfried Wilhelm Leibniz, Anton Ulrich's librarian and political advisor, romance and international order finally became indistinguishable from one another.

Leibniz: Romance as International Order, International Order as Romance

Leibniz was an avid reader of political romance. He used Barclay's *Argenis* as an example in his early discussions of theodicy, and he reportedly reread the romance on his deathbed.[37] His abiding interest in political romance converged with his thinking about international relations at the time of the Peace of Utrecht (1713). The Peace of Utrecht, together with the ratification of the treaties of Rastatt and Baden in 1714, concluded the War of Spanish Succession (1701–14), in which all major European powers as well as some of their colonies in North America and the West Indies were embroiled. A world war to a certain degree, it figured as a real-life refutation of political romance. *Argenis* presents marriage as the basis of the concord of sovereigns; and royal houses in Europe did intermarry with each other as if they constantly wanted to reenact a romance ending. Yet marital alliances not only failed to bring about concord, but also proved to be a cause for war. When the Spanish king Charles II (1665–1700) died without producing an heir, the French Bourbons and the Austrian Habsburgs were equally entitled to the Spanish throne because of the marital and genealogical entanglements among the royal houses. A war broke out between the forces supporting the Bourbon candidate and the Grand Alliance in support of the Habsburg candidate. It was precisely at this historical juncture, when political reality seemed to have incontrovertibly proved the aims and ideals of political romance false, that romance became for Leibniz a model for thinking about international order.

In a letter to Anton Ulrich, written in Vienna on April 26, 1713, Leibniz reported on the reaction of the Imperial Court to the signing of peace treaties in Utrecht two weeks earlier. Austria was not a signatory, as hostilities between it and France were still ongoing. "I would have liked to wish that the romance of these times had had a better denouement; but perhaps it has not yet come to an end. Just as Your Excellency has not finished with your [romance] *Octavia*, so our Lord can still add a couple of tomes to his romance, which could sound better at the end."[38] Leibniz's remarkable conception of international relations as events in a romance written by God has evident philosophical underpinnings. In his *Essais de Théodicée sur la bonté de Dieu, la liberté de l'homme et l'origine du mal* (1710), romance figures as a metaphor for God's creation. He accuses his philosophical opponent of having not considered "that the romance of human life, which makes the universal history of the human race, is all invented within the divine understanding together with an infinite number of others, and that the will of God only decreed its existence because this sequence of events must have most agreed with the rest of things for the purpose of bringing about the best."[39] In this context, romance is what the philosopher Hans Blumenberg terms "absolute metaphor": "The transfer of the reflection of an object of intuition (*Anschauung*) onto an entirely different concept, to which perhaps an intuition can never directly correspond."[40] The concepts, to which no intuition can directly correspond, are usually those on "the highest level of abstraction," for instance "being," "history," and "world." Metaphors employed to make sense of them—"absolute metaphors"—"conserve the richness of their origin, which abstraction must disavow."[41] In a way similar to the metaphorical understanding of the world as a book, Leibniz invokes "romance" as a metaphor for "human life, which makes the universal history of the human race."[42] This metaphor serves to suggest that the human world may undergo seemingly endless confusion, turbulence, and deviation, but will ultimately come to a happy end. The obvious existence of evil is a temporary confusion ultimately conducive to the best possible government of the world. The letter to Anton Ulrich under consideration merely applies the same metaphor tested out in Leibniz's theodicy to international politics, with international relations conceived as a specific dimension of human life under the auspices of God. Peace treaties such as those signed in Utrecht may mark the end of one volume, but not yet the end of the whole romance.

After having tried to make sense of the political world in terms of romance, Leibniz transposes, in an ingenious move, the tenor and the vehicle of the metaphor, explaining romance as a literary form in terms of the divine governance of the world: "It is anyway one of the romance writer's best artifices to let everything fall into confusion, and then to extricate it unexpectedly. And no one imitates our Lord better than an inventor of a beautiful romance."[43] A romance plot mirrors the way of the world. The metaphorical illumination of romance and international politics in terms of each other leads logically to the equation of both: "We need nothing else than a little prince in Vienna and a grandson of the Czar in Petersburg, and then the Elector Princess on the English throne: and then Your Excellency can work on a romance of future times."[44]

Romance implies concord and order in spite of extended turmoil and perils. From the perspective of theodicy, evils in international relations—such as wars—may be just temporary deviations, if not necessary steps, in the best possible world order. It seems, then, that the equation of political romance with international politics serves not only to confirm but also to magnify an optimistic view of international order. Yet in Leibniz's international thought, optimism is mixed with irony, as illustrated by his reaction to Charles-Irénée Castel de Saint-Pierre's project of eternal peace. A participant in the negotiations leading up to the Peace of Utrecht on behalf of France, Saint-Pierre published a plan for peace in Europe under the title *Projet pour rendre la Paix perpétuelle en Europe* in 1712. Republished in different versions in the following years, and later to be hailed as a predecessor for the League of Nations, the United Nations, and the European Union, Saint-Pierre's plan made a plea for instituting a society of sovereign states and for setting up a tribunal to arbitrate international conflicts.[45] In a certain sense, it represented the continuation of both the grand design attributed to Henri IV and the peace project of Crucé a century earlier, but it was unprecedented in laying out a systematically composed and theoretically underpinned charter of international governance in Europe.[46] Leibniz greeted Saint-Pierre's project with approbation, but suggested that a reformed papacy and empire might be preferable to the French savant's proposal of a society of sovereigns.[47] Regarding the feasibility of his proposal, he remarked, "Here is a project which will succeed as easily as that of M. l'Abbé de St Pierre; but since it is permitted to write romances, why should we find bad the fiction which would recall the age of gold to us?"[48] Schemes of international governance, whatever form they might take, are thus likened by Leibniz to romances. Pointing to golden-age harmony as they do, they are fictions, just as romances are. Behind the comparison between the romance and an international politics in the care of God, and behind the optimistic vision of a harmonious world order entailed by it, there lurks the nagging sense that all this is just fictional. After all, *Pax perpetua*, or a truly peaceful world order, is the condition of the dead. Living beings, alas, have to live with all the evils, both in the real world and in the romance world prior to the ending.

The Extinction of Political Romance

The romance writer as the lieutenant of God on earth, and the romance plot as the model of divinely preordained world order: this idea placed a heavy burden on romance, so heavy that it could not help crushing the literary form. Anton Ulrich's second romance project, *Die römische Octavia*, illustrates the ways in which political romance finally collapsed under the weight of its own high expectations. With an extraordinarily convoluted plot revolving around the love story between Octavia, Nero's first consort, and the Armenian king Tyridates, *Octavia* was conceived as a political romance that would fit the bill in all respects. Anton Ulrich started working on it soon after the publication of the last volume of *Aramena* in 1673, but more than forty years and seven thousand pages later it was still unfinished by the time of his death in 1714. Many reasons can be adduced to explain the long process of gestation and the incompletion of the project, including the practical circumstances of the author as the busy ruler of a small but ambitious duchy.[49] But one main reason was certainly the structural problem entailed in the onus that the author imposes on himself to be God's perfect imitator—the problem of having to be infinitely open yet closed at the same time. To be sure, the tension between dilation and closure, between postponement and ending, is characteristic of romance in general.[50] In *Octavia*, however, it reaches a breaking point. On the one hand, the romance must come to an end, because only then will there be a complete plot to match the best possible world created by God. On the other hand, the author feels the urge to multiply confusions and delay the end, because postponement not only makes it possible to encompass more and more events into the romance so that it could mirror the entire world, but also empowers the author by giving him the opportunity to grapple with more problems. The longer the end is delayed, the more complex the confusions become, the more closely does the author approximate divine omnipotence and omniscience. Closure and the delay of closure are both necessary.

This paradox came to a head in the final year of Anton Ulrich's long life. On March 10, 1713, the duke wrote to Leibniz, punning on "Confucius" (the Chinese sage) and the "confusion" of the romance plot: "As far as Confucius is concerned, I've brought him into the *Octavia*, for he helps increase the confusion from within. With this work, I feel as if the spirit of the author of *Amadis* had entered me, so that rather than having six parts the *Octavia* should get many more. So I am still slaving away and cannot find an end."[51] On June 19 of the same year, he wrote again, "I am now working diligently on the seventh part of the *Octavia*; during the eight days since I came back, I have heard so many new things that I suppose there will be also the eighth part to the *Octavia*."[52] Almost another year elapsed, and the ducal author was adding even more parts to the romance. His health, however, was failing him. On March 6, 1714, he wrote to Leibniz, "All these lines I've written so far may give you a hint that my condition has not improved at all. What our dear Elector Princess has told you about my work on the *Octavia* is what it is; although, as the saying goes, I am on my last legs, I am also almost at the end of this romance and therefore force myself to complete it."[53] Three weeks later, on March 27, 1714, Anton Ulrich died without fulfilling his last wish of completing the *Octavia*. The romance failed because the author was a mortal being. In order for romance plot to be the model of divinely preordained world order, the author must be God himself, who could continue to add more parts to his romance without having to face death. The idea of romance, practiced by Anton Ulrich, theorized by his associates, and embedded by Leibniz in a grand metaphysical system, founders on the finitude of the human. The endlessness of *Octavia* marks the end of political romance as a genre.

In fact, at the time of Anton Ulrich's death, an entirely new form of prose fiction for imagining international order was just about to be born, namely the novel, as we will see in the final chapter.

Political romance, to sum up our brief history of this genre, showcases the major operations that poetic literature has at its disposal for imagining a normative world order. Its sprawling narratives may be condensed into three propositions: sovereign persons are free agents of action, driven by a will that is independent of all others and unfettered by any preexisting laws; in spite of their independence and unconstrained freedom, sovereign persons may reach a pact of peace and concord in the form of a marriage treaty; and, a marriage treaty binds not only two sovereigns, but leavened by love, it binds the whole world. Whereas tragedy enables the recognition of a world order through the tragic experience of transgression and lawlessness, romance creates a world order through fictionalizing operations: selecting certain elements from the real political world, combining the selected material into a coherent world through characterization, plot construction, and other poetic means, and finally revealing the self-contained world thus constructed as fictive and suspending it in the condition of as-if. The universal world order reached at the end of a political romance exists only in the subjunctive. The ups and downs of this genre in the seventeenth century reflected the changing attitudes to the subjunctive: it thrived on the willing suspension of disbelief; it withered when compared to political reality; it rose again when the subjunctive was elevated to a metaphysics; it died because its creator, alas, could not exist in the subjunctive.

Chapter 5

The Divergence between International Law and Literature around 1700

As the principal generic forms of the poetic figuration of international order in the seventeenth century, tragedy and political romance presupposed the royal absolutist doctrine of the identity of the princely person and the state. It was on the basis of this doctrine that both generic forms could negotiate legal issues between states by creating princely characters and constructing plots revolving around their interaction. With the beheading of King Charles in 1649, however, this doctrine came under pressure, for the state authority manifestly persisted even when the king was forcibly removed. The favorite trope of royal absolutism, of course, was the metaphor of the king as the head of the body politic. But now it seemed that the body politic, however gravely injured, continued to live—some would even say that it was reinvigorated—after the head had been violently detached from it. Algernon Sidney (1623–83), a member of the Long Parliament, dismantled this corporal metaphor: "The people makes or creates the figurative head, the natural is from itself, or connate with the body. The natural body cannot change or subsist without the natural head; but a people may change and subsist very well without the artificial."[1] Sidney himself was to be beheaded after the Restoration for making statements like this one. With the royal absolutist doctrine so hotly contested in the second half of the seventeenth century, poetic literature could no longer engage with affairs of the state as it had done so far, for as the mimesis of "people doing things," it needed to attribute actions to human agents (if we disregard the allegorical mode of poetic literature, which often features abstract, nonhuman agents).[2] Poetic literature and international law thus began to drift apart.

The first signs of the divergence between poetic literature and international law could be found in poetic literature itself, particularly in tragedy. This is hardly surprising, for the tragic form is designed to figure divisions. In tragedies written in the second of the seventeenth century, a number of fractures, fault lines, and divisions in the international world became visible: first, the separation of the state from the royal person embodying it, or the depersonalization of the state; second, the division between the office of representing the depersonalized state and the natural person of the representative; and third, the separation of a private self from the public persona of either the royal person or the representative of the state. The present chapter first maps these seismic changes by reading some of the most powerful tragedies of the period, including Andreas Gryphius's *Carolus Stuardus* (1657), John Milton's *Samson Agonistes* (1671), and Jean Racine's *Andromaque* (1667). All of them feature intense suffering—suffering caused by the forcible separation of the king's person from the state that it embodies, by a lack of prudence in discharging the office of representing the state, or by the insistent presence of a private self inside the public person, be this public person a representative or the royal embodiment of the state. This suffering or *pathos*—a key element of the tragic plot according to Aristotle—indexes the separating out of two spheres in the international world: the sphere of the depersonalized state to be managed by expert knowledge, and the sphere of the private individual with his or her desires, conscience, and domestic life.[3] The division between these two spheres—whether or not one calls it the division between the public and the private—led to the divergence between international law and poetic literature. The remainder of the chapter discusses the development of international law into a field of specialized knowledge about affairs of the state and the simultaneous turn of poetic literature to affairs of the private individual in the early decades of the eighteenth century.

The Depersonalization of the State (Gryphius, Milton)

Depersonalizing the State in the International World: Gryphius's *Carolus Stuardus*

The beheading of King Charles in 1649 dealt a fatal blow to the royal absolutist identification of the state with the king's person. Not only was this doctrine debunked by the proponents of republican principles—for instance by

John Milton in his eloquent tracts *The Tenure of Kings Magistrates* (1649) and *Eikonoklastes* (1649), as well as other republican writings—but the defenders of royal absolutism also had to acknowledge the fact that the state could be detached from the king's person after all. In the immediate aftermath of the regicide in England, the German tragedian Gryphius began to work on a drama dealing with the horror of the trial, conviction, and execution of King Charles: *Ermordete Majestät, Oder Carolus Stuardus*. It is a *Trauerspiel*, literally a "mourning play."[4] Yet it is precisely by mourning the regicide that *Carolus Stuardus* affirms it as a fact.

Gryphius represents the regicide in relation to international law. In the midpoint of the play—the third act of the five-act tragedy—foreign diplomats in England agonize over the impending execution of King Charles. The envoy of the Electoral Palatinate directs an anguished plea to the princes of all European countries:

> [. . .] Europe's gods, listen to
> The sighs of the prince of Stuart! Gods, learn! Learn and teach
> How easily the throne sinks! Europe's gods, recognize /
> Recognize yourselves and your duty! The great neighbor is on fire!
> Crowned heads, think about it. The blood that will flow here /
> The blood, with which Charles will sprinkle his shroud,
> Is yours, is akin to you! Crowned heads! Could you rest?
> Charles prescribes with his blood what you have to do here!
>   (III.529–36)[5]

By addressing the rulers of Europe as "gods," the envoy makes it clear that he, like all the other positive characters in the play as well as the poet himself, subscribes to the doctrine of the divine right of kings, a doctrine that goes hand in hand with the identification of the king's person with the state. Given such a doctrine, the king stands as the subject of international law. The execution of a king, then, is tantamount to the downfall of the state, depriving international law of its subject and thus imperiling international law as such. For this reason, the princes of Europe have the obligation of defending the English king. Even Thomas Fairfax, the commander-in-chief of the parliamentary forces, warns that "the law of nations forbids the killing of hereditary kings" (III. 205). In reminding the princes of Europe that the blood spilled by King Charles is akin to theirs, the envoy of the Electoral Palatinate not only alludes to the dynastic alliances among the European royal houses, but also alerts them to the prospect that the killing of one prince will lead to the death of the entire society of princes bound together by international law. The envoy of Holland pictures the gory details of this prospect:

> In my visions I already see the Channel full of ships /
> The wide port occupied / the fertile meadows of the Brits:
> Covered with camps. [. . .]
> In my visions I see the blaze,
> Which engulfed the Dutch / when the cruelty of the Spaniards
> Covered the discolored flood with their slime /
> And the blood of my fathers washed along both shores. (III.537–46)

The envoy of Holland means to second the dire warnings uttered by the envoy of the Electoral Palatinate. But something else shines through his pathos-fueled speech: it seems that the execution will neither prompt the downfall of England nor that of the international world as a whole. The seas, ports, and meadows of Britain will continue to exist; they will just be taken over by someone other than the king, although this new ruler appears to be some impersonal agent. By comparing the atrocities that this impersonal agent is likely to perpetrate with what the monarchical Spain erstwhile inflicted on Holland, the envoy even hints at the possibility that this other agent might not be so different from a king after all in terms of the effect of his actions.

The exchange between the two foreign envoys highlights a wrenching transformation of both the state and the international world: a transformation of the state from an embodiment of the king's person to an impersonal entity manipulated by an agent whose status needs to be determined anew, and a transformation of the international world from a society of princes to an assemblage of impersonal entities. Such a transformation can be characterized as depersonalization. The foreign envoys express horror at depersonalization, but in anticipating the havoc that the depersonalized England may wreak on other countries, they suggest that it is still part of the international world, albeit through the agency of some illegitimate person. After being stripped of its king, England will be impersonated by others. King Charles's own musings in the final moment of his life drive home the depersonalization of both the state and the international world in strictly legal terms:

> If someone runs rampant / without a lawful right / without a cause /
> Won't he be the same as the one / who ranges the foams of Thetis
> And, going against the law of nations, hinders the free flag /
> And who plunders the sails torn to pieces by fire and steel? (V.351–54)

Drawing on the age-old topos of the ship of state, King Charles sees the parliamentary forces as pirates who have forcibly captured England. In international law, the pirate is the very figure of the outlaw. He is an international legal person only insofar as he is excluded from the community of legal persons. Or in other words, the pirate is included in international law as the person who is excluded. Precisely in this position, however, the figure of the pirate plays a constitutive role for international law as a whole.[6] By comparing metaphorically the state of England to a ship, his political foes to pirates, and himself to a lawful captain, King Charles implicitly establishes three facts: first, the state is an entity that can be wrested from the king's person and delivered to another agent; second, the other agent who takes possession of the state does not have the legal personality of a king and exists outside of the society of princes; and finally, this agent is nonetheless included in international law—precisely as someone who is excluded from the society of princes.

Representing the State in the International World: Milton's *Samson Agonistes*

Gryphius's *Carolus Stuardus* dramatizes the dissociation of the state from the king's person and the state's subsequent impersonation by an agent who lays claim to sovereign power without the legitimizing trappings of kingship. Hobbes's *Leviathan* (1651) accomplishes the same by theoretical means. Contrary to the royal absolutist identification of the state with the king's person, Hobbes conceives of the state as an artificial person created by the multitude through an original covenant for the purpose of ensuring "Peace at home, and mutuall Ayd against their enemies abroad" (XVII).[7] But in and of itself this artificial person "is no Person, nor has capacity to doe any thing" (XXVI). It "is but a word, without substance, and cannot stand" (XXXI). The state can act only through a representative invested with sovereign power. The sovereign is the representative of the state, not the proprietor of the state. Rather than identical to the state, the sovereign is a person who "carryeth" the artificial person of the state (XVIII), or in other words, a person whom the multitude authorizes to impersonate the state. Defined as such, sovereigns are, to quote Quentin Skinner's explication of the Hobbesian theory, "holders of offices with duties attached, their fundamental duty being to procure the safety and contentment of the people. Although they are granted the right to exercise complete sovereign power, this power is merely 'placed' and 'resideth' in them by virtue of the office they are asked to discharge."[8]

Once the state is dissociated from the king's person endowed with divine right, it becomes an impersonal entity that can act only through a representative. John Milton, the most compelling voice against royal absolutism in the English Civil War, offered his own theory of why the state should be dissociated from the king's person and entrusted to a representative most capable of ensuring the welfare of the people. In his republican writings and his writings on regicide, Milton invoked on many occasions the biblical Samson to illustrate the issues involved in representing the state.[9] His interest in Samson culminated in the tragic poem *Samson Agonistes*. Milton's single venture into the genre of tragedy, this poem retains and amplifies two quintessential structural features of the biblical story of Samson: first, the ongoing struggle between the Israelites and the Philistines, and second, the role of Samson as the champion for Israel's deliverance. The Philistines are portrayed as the archenemies of the Israelites in the Deuteronomistic history. In the Septuagint, they are often simply referred to as "other nations." From the perspective of the seventeenth century, the struggle between the Israelites and the Philistines is emblematic of international conflicts.[10] Given his work as secretary of foreign tongues after the parliamentary victory, Milton was familiar with international relations. Against this background, the role of Samson as the champion for Israel's deliverance serves to illustrate the complex problem of political representation in the international world.

Notable, to begin with, is the chorus, a poetic device that Milton adds to the biblical narrative. Made up of Samson's kinsmen, the chorus serves as the sounding board for Samson's anguished lament about his failure in performing the role as the champion of Israel, and as the empathetic observer to Samson's woeful state. The choral function in Milton's tragedy thus expresses what it means for a people to have someone as their representative and what it means for an individual person to represent his people. The dialogue between the chorus and Samson addresses some typical issues pertaining to political representation. For instance, Samson complains to the chorus that "Israel's governors" and "heads of tribes" have failed to acknowledge his deeds (241–49).[11] But the choral function is merely one poetic device of tragedy. Prefaced by a short yet incisive tract on "that sort of dramatic poem which is called tragedy," *Samson Agonistes* is not only a tragedy of Samson as the representative of Israelites in their struggle against the Philistines, but it stages the tragic form itself. The problem of representing a people or state in the international world is inextricably linked to that of the tragic form.

Samson Agonistes opens with the protagonist lamenting his sorry condition:

> Promise was that I
> Should Israel from Philistian yoke deliver;
> As for this great deliverer now, and find him
> Eyeless in Gaza at the mill with slaves,
> Himself in bonds under Philistian yoke; (38–42)

Born under the sign of the divine and endowed with prodigious strength, Samson is supposed to deliver Israel from the Philistines. But he has, in a moment of weakness, revealed the secret of his strength—his hair—to his wife Dalila. Dalila subsequently passed the secret on to the Philistine lords who then had Samson shorn, blinded, and enslaved. This sequence of events that have already taken place before the curtain lifts, together with the ensuing suffering shown on stage, constitute a plot that testifies to Samson's failure to perform his role as the representative of Israel. It is a tragic plot. In his opening soliloquy, Samson imagines himself as the unfortunate protagonist in a tragic spectacle:

> [. . .] if I must die
> Betrayed, captivated, and both my eyes put out,
> Made of my enemies the scorn and gaze. (32–34)

The three main episodes following Samson's soliloquy—the encounters with his father Manoa, with his wife Dalila, and with the giant Harapha of Gath—stage tragic spectatorship, with the three interlocutors acting as the audience of the tragedy in which Samson figures as the hero. A salient feature of the tragic spectatorship staged here, as a scholar of Milton points out, is that the aesthetic response to tragic theater prompts action.[12] Manoa, Dalila, and Harapha are not merely spectators, but also agents of action. Manoa seeks to ransom his son and Dalila offers reconciliation to her husband, while Harapha poses a challenge. Their actions result from their respective responses to the tragedy of Samson. The staging of tragic spectatorship enables Samson himself to gain a certain aesthetic distance from his own tragedy as well, which, in turn, goads him towards further actions. *Samson Agonistes* is thus a two-layered tragedy. One layer is the tragic plot that has already taken place before the drama onstage begins—Samson's revelation of his secret to Dalila and his subsequent capture and blinding by the Philistines. Another layer is the tragic plot unfolding onstage—Manoa's attempt to ransom his son, Dalila's offer of reconciliation with her husband, Harapha's challenge, Samson's repudiation of all three, his agreement to entertain the Philistine lords at their great feast, and finally his pulling down of the temple of the Philistines. The dramatic persons in the tragic plot unfolding on stage (the second layer) are spectators of the tragic plot that has already occurred (the first layer), and their actions are occasioned by the passions stirred up by what they see. Both of these layers turn on the question of political representation.

The crux of the first layer of Samson's tragedy is *hamartia*—Samson's succumbing to his wife's importunate questioning about the source of his strength. This tragic flaw or error alludes to what matters most to the representative of the state:

> But what is strength without a double share
> Of wisdom, vast, unwieldy, burdensome,
> Proudly secure, yet liable to fall
> By weakest subtleties, not made to rule,
> But to subserve where wisdom bears command. (53–57)

Samson possesses extraordinary strength, but renders it useless by betraying the secret of its source. This indicates what the office of the representative of the state actually consists of—knowledge. In order to serve the people, the representative of the state certainly needs to have material resources at his disposal, as Samson does with his God-given strength. But material resources are "not made to rule." What "bears command" is wisdom, to be understood generally as the knowledge of how to make use of the available resources, as well as other kinds of knowledge necessary for government. For the representative of the state, the knowledge of how to rule is just as important as the right to rule. Samson's *hamartia* thus brings to light a main concern of modern statecraft from the late seventeenth seventh century onwards—handling governmental knowledge. Samuel Pufendorf's *Einleitung zu der Historie der Vornehmsten Reichen und Staaten* (1682) was one of the first systematic treatments of this kind of governmental knowledge, designed for the training of state officials. It includes, Pufendorf tells the reader in the preface, "observations [. . .] concerning good and bad qualities of each nation," as well as "what concerns the nature, strength, and weakness of each country, and its form of government."[13]

The importance of knowledge for the welfare of the state is brought to the fore, *ex negativo*, by Samson's tragic flaw. It is also illustrated positively by the use that his antagonists make of his secret. Once the Philistines learn from Dalila that the source of Samson's strength lies in his hair, they manage to neutralize him completely by having him shorn, thereby gaining the upper hand over Israel. Dalila, having elicited Samson's secret, can therefore pride herself on being the honored representative of the Philistines (982–87).

The Birth of the Private Individual (Milton, Racine)

The Separation of the Private and the Public in *Samson Agonistes*

Samson's *hamartia* in the first layer of the tragedy not only draws attention to the importance of knowledge for the welfare of the state, but also shines a light on a hitherto invisible figure embedded in political space: the private person. Samson names, retrospectively, two interrelated reasons for his dereliction of duty: first, he succumbs to a burning desire for Dalila, which prompts him to divulge the secret; second, he places too great a trust in the matrimonial bond. To Dalila, who is a Philistine, Samson says:

> Being once a wife, for me thou wast to leave
> Parents and country; nor was I their subject,
> Nor under their protection but my own,
> Thou mine, not theirs: if aught against my life
> Thy country sought of thee, it sought unjustly,
> Against the law of nature, law of nations. (885–90)

For Samson, the matrimonial bond is separate from the public enmities between the two nations, constituting an autonomous sphere—that of private domestic life. It is within this private sphere, in a communication between husband and wife, that Samson entrusts the secret to Dalila. Dalila, however, puts the secret to public use by turning it over to the Philistine lords, arguing that "private respects" must yield to "public good" (867–68).

With hindsight, as a spectator of his own tragedy, Samson realizes that he has allowed his private interests—sexual desire and domestic life—to compromise his role as the champion of the public good of the Israelites. This belated realization takes place in the second layer of the tragedy. It is this layer that marks the explicit separation of the private from the public or, in the words of a literary historian, "an 'explicitation' of what tacitly had always been there but now, in becoming explicit, also takes on a new life."[14] In the face of Samson's suffering, his father Manoa responds first as a typical spectator of tragedy does—by expressing pity: "O miserable change!" (340). He then proposes domestic life as the way out of the misery. Dalila, Samson's wife, responds also as a spectator of tragedy commonly does—by shedding "tears" (735). The alternative to misery, which she proposes to Samson, is conjugal bliss:

> Life yet hath many solaces, enjoyed
> Where other senses want not their delights
> At home in leisure and domestic ease. (915–17).

The giant Harapha of Gath looks on Samson's suffering with scorn and mockery rather than pity and fear, but his purpose is remarkably similar to those of Manoa and Dalila—to reduce Samson to a private person: "a man condemned, a slave enrolled, / Due by the law to capital punishment" (1224–25).

Through the three encounters, as well as through his own reflection, Samson comes to see himself as a private person. Yet he rejects all the proposals made by his interlocutors to lead an exclusively private life. He is not willing to relinquish his role as the public representative of his people. Countering the proposals of his kin to return him to hearth and home, he insists on his determination to "serve / My nation" (564–65). Samson confronts head-on the paradox of being a private person and performing a public function at the same time:

> But I a private person, whom my country
> As a league-breaker gave up bound, presumed
> Single Rebellion and did Hostile Acts.
> I was no private but a person raised
> With strength sufficient and command from heaven
> To free my country; (1208–13)

Samson's solution to the paradox is at once simple and radical: he believes that God has appointed him as the champion of his country. Incapacitated, blinded, languishing in captivity, Samson retreats in faith: "My trust is in the living God who gave me / At my nativity this strength" (1140–41). The painful experience enables him to cultivate his "conscience and internal peace" (1334). Faith and an interior religious conscience belong to the private sphere.[15] But it is precisely out of this private sphere, by virtue of his deeply personal faith, that Samson carries out the public mission of saving his country: he pulls down the temple of the Philistines, bringing death to all the Philistine lords to whom Israel has been subjected, while sacrificing his own life in doing so.[16] Samson's act of saving his country by means of faith-inspired violence implies a novel conception of the state: it is not merely a multitude to be managed by means of governmental knowledge, but rather a community with a spiritual mission. The work of commemoration that Samson's father vows to dedicate to his son's violent act and death—building "a monument" and collecting "acts enrolled in copious legend, or sweet lyric song" (1733; 1737)—further corroborates this protonationalist conception of the state.[17]

To sum up, Milton's tragic poem lays bare a number of momentous political processes. First, the king as the personal embodiment of the state is replaced by the representative of the state, someone entrusted with the office of procuring the safety of the people. Samson's tragic *hamartia*—divulging the secret of his strength—cuts to the quick of the office of the representative, indicating that what matters most to this office is knowledge; second, the proximate causes of Samson's *hamartia*—sexual desire and conjugal trust—indicate the separation of a private sphere from the public office of the representative of the state. Once differentiated, the private and the public sphere cannot help contaminating each other; third, in a turn that at once reinforces and bridges the separation between the private and the public, the deeply inward religious experience of the private person—faith and conscience—becomes the motive force of the public action of the representative of the state, giving rise to a conception of the state as a spiritual nation.

The Tragic Birth of the Private Self in Racine

Samson Agonistes was written after the Restoration of the Stuart monarchy, under political circumstances that predisposed the republican Milton towards inwardness and private virtue. The tragedies by Jean Racine, by contrast, were written at a time when royal absolutism reached its pinnacle in France under the reign of Louis XIV, the king known for the pronouncement "L'état, c'est moi." Yet they nonetheless dramatize, in even starker terms to boot, the separation between the private and the public. His main works all turn on the star-crossed love between royal persons, resembling on the surface Pierre Corneille's tragedies of marriage alliance from *Œdipe* (1659) to *Attila* (1668), which we discussed in chapter 3. However, the source of tragic conflict is no longer located between royal persons, but rather within each individual royal person. In plays from *Andromaque* to *Bérénice* (1670) and *Phèdre* (1677), secret and uncontainable desires of the royal protagonists erupt, with savage force, into the public ceremonious space that these protagonists inhabit, creating an abysmal rift between a private self and a public persona.

CHAPTER FIVE

What is remarkable about Racinian tragedy is, first of all, the design of the choral function: the chorus as a dramaturgical device is replaced by the figure of the confidant(e). The chorus places individual protagonists under public scrutiny, thereby making them into public figures. The confidant, by contrast, is a figure that allows protagonists to confess what is hidden from public view. The Racinian confidant, usually "linked to the hero by a kind of feudal tie," as Roland Barthes points out, is designed to perform the function of "opening up the secret, defining the exact status of the hero's dilemma," and producing a solution "by naively representing to him a hypothesis contrary to his impulse."[18] Precisely by proposing alternatives and solutions, the confidant abets the protagonist's confession of his secret passions, serving as an instrument for "the incitement to discourse."[19] Royal persons are public persons. Incited by their confidants to talk, again and again, about the stirrings of their heart, they counter their public roles with hidden desire, irrepressible passion, and inexplicable impulses of the flesh—in one word, with love.

The Racinian conception of love comes into sharp relief particularly in *Andromaque*. The drama opens with the arrival of Orestes at the court of Pyrrhus in his capacity as the envoy of the alliance of Greek cities. After the fall of Troy, Pyrrhus holds Hector's widow and son captive. Orestes's mission is to ask Pyrrhus to deliver Hector's son, so that the Trojan blood could be exterminated once and for all. This official mission, however, also makes it possible for him to see his beloved Hermione once again, who has been sent by her father Menelaus to marry Pyrrhus. In the meantime, Hermione's duty to marry Pyrrhus has transformed into a passionate love for him, but Pyrrhus has fallen in love with Andromache who still spends all her time mourning her dead husband Hector. In short, the dramatic plot is constructed according to the following formula: Orestes loves Hermione, who loves Pyrrhus, who loves Andromache, who loves Hector, who is dead. The love that connects the protagonists—who are, in turn, accompanied by their respective confidants—has a number of salient characteristics. First, love is all-powerful, knows no compromise, and overrides all other concerns. For the sake of love, Pyrrhus is willing to betray his Greek allies, Orestes is willing to commit regicide, Hermione is willing to swallow shame and humiliation, and Andromache is willing to sacrifice her own life. Second, love is indivisible. It only has a single object and can under no circumstances be shared with another person. Even though Pyrrhus, rejected by Andromache, considers marrying Hermione in order to fulfill his duty, and even though Hermione, rejected by Pyrrhus, considers giving in to Orestes's pursuit, both of them rush back to their true object of love at the first opportunity. Not to be shared among different persons, love allows for no variation in degree or strength either. Everyone loves equally, with the highest intensity. Third, love is absolute, not dependent on, or explicable by, any particular qualities of the individuals involved. Pyrrhus loves Andromache in spite of her captive status, and Hermione does not love Orestes in spite of his "great virtues."[20] Love is an autonomous force unconstrained by any other considerations. Fourth, love is perpetual. Once it comes into being, it never changes and never ceases, not even after the death of the beloved. Andromache loves Hector as deeply after he is dead as when he was still alive. Hermione's love for Pyrrhus even intensifies after he is murdered, as his death robs her love of any possibility of satisfaction.

All-powerful, indivisible, unconditional, perpetual—these characteristics of love as dramatically conceived by Racine mirror the hallmarks of sovereignty as theorized by Jean Bodin a century earlier. In *Six livres de la République* (1576), Bodin defines sovereignty as "the absolute and perpetual power of a commonwealth"—that is, as a power that is "not limited either in power, or in function, or in length of time."[21] The prince, in whom sovereign power is vested, recognizes nothing, after God, that is greater than himself. He neither shares his power with anyone else on earth nor allows anyone else to encroach on it. He exercises his power by making, altering, and enforcing laws without himself being bound by them. Once acquired, the power of the sovereign prince can neither be delegated nor transferred, not during his lifetime, nor even after his death. In short, sovereignty means a supreme power that is indivisible, unconditional, and perpetual. Bodin's theory of sovereignty laid the groundwork for royal absolutism. Yet precisely at the moment when royal absolutism found its consummate realization in Louis XIV's personal reign, the absolute and perpetual power that was sovereignty encountered an uncanny double, a formidable competing power—that which Racine called love. If the rights of sovereignty are public and appertain to the prince as a public person, love is a passion lurking behind and beneath the public persona, reigning over a realm secluded from the public. This realm is that of the heart, the private interior of the self. Racinian tragedy, then, opens up a secret dimension in the royal person and, at the same time, pits this secret dimension against the royal person's public rights and offices. The royal person is now split violently apart by two countervailing powers—the public rights of sovereignty on the one hand, and the secret demands of the heart on the other. Since love is just as absolute, as indivisible, and as perpetual as sovereignty, the conflict between these two powers cannot find a solution without the royal person being annihilated.

This conflict and its necessary outcome—death—are perhaps nowhere more poignantly articulated than in Pyrrhus's admonition to Andromache: "I tell you, you must die or reign."[22] Either public rights and private desires converge, in which case Andromache is crowned queen, or they do not converge, in which case Andromache dies. In Racine's tragedies, the public and private never converge. His dramatic plots are all constructed in such a way as to demonstrate the inevitability with which royal persons meet their doom. In one play, *Bérénice*, death does not actually take place, but the departure of the eponymous heroine for her home country in the Orient at the end is tantamount to death. By positing love as the secret double of public sovereign power, always at cross-purposes with the latter, Racine uncovers a new source of the tragic: it is the conflict between the political and the sexual, between public persona and private desire. Whereas in many of Corneille's tragedies the dramatic conflict usually lies in the dilemma between sexual desire and political imperatives that are external to and go against this desire, the conflict in Racine is, to borrow the words of a Racine scholar, "an internal division that can never be sutured."[23]

Racinian tragedy made visible secret passions as the obverse of public sovereign power. Soon they were recognized as a fact of life. Towards the end of the seventeenth century, still within Racine's lifetime, the prince came to be regarded as both a public and a private person, as a person driven by public rights and private passions alike. Pufendorf pointed out in 1862, "Some of the most exquisite parts of Modern History consists [sic] in this: that one knows the Person who is the Sovereign, or the Ministers, which rule a State, their Capacity, Inclinations, Caprices, private Interests, manner of proceeding, and the like: Since on this depends, in good measure, the good or ill management of a State."[24] Leibniz distinguished, in the preface to his *Codex juris gentium diplomaticus* published in 1693, between a public and a secret history.[25]

International Law as a Field of Expert Knowledge

Taken together, Gryphius's *Carolus Stuardus*, Milton's *Samson Agonistes*, and Racine's tragedies uncover two intertwined genealogies: that of the depersonalized state governed by a representative, and that of the private individual with his or her innermost passions and feelings. From the late seventeenth century onwards, literature came increasingly to occupy itself with affairs of the private individual, shedding affairs of the state as its subject matter. At the same time, the knowledge needed by the representatives of the depersonalized state—for instance, knowledge of government and of public law—took on new forms.[26] This was particularly true of international law—the knowledge of the legal relations between states. Up to the final quarter of the seventeenth century, the study of international law was still quite rare. But in the period of a little more than half a century between roughly 1690 and 1750, the discourse of international law flourished, expanding into a vast, independent field of expert knowledge. First, legal instruments as well as other material in international affairs, previously considered part of *arcana imperii* and kept under lock and key, were collected and published; second, the collecting and scrutiny of legal instruments led to the making of *Le droit public de l'Europe* or the public law of Europe, something like an international legal code; finally, international law became a professional field of study, a discipline within jurisprudence.

Publicizing *arcana imperii*

The Peace of Westphalia marked a watershed in international legal history in many senses. Among other things, it inaugurated the practice of publicizing international treaties. Treaties had always belonged to the jealously guarded mysteries of the state. With the exception of Melchior Goldast's collections of the constitutional documents of the Holy Roman Empire *Constitutiones imperiales* (1607–13) and *Monarchia sacri romani imperii* (1612–14), hardly any international legal instruments had ever been published. At the time of the Westphalian peace congress, however, details of diplomatic negotiations were published in pamphlets and newspapers. The treaties reached at the end of the congress were printed in many languages across Europe.[27] In the following decades, there were some sporadic attempts to publicize treaties that had been contracted in the past. Sometime around 1660, a book entitled *Recueil des traittez de paix, treves et neutralité entre des couronnes d'Espagne et de France* was published anonymously, possibly in the liberal Netherlands. It contains the major treaties between France and Spain from the Treaty of Madrid of 1526 to the Treaty of the Pyrenees of 1659. In the preface, the anonymous publisher presents the book as a kind of celebration of the general peace established by the recent Treaty of the Pyrenees. However, the lack of a place and time of publication, no less than the anonymity of the publisher, indicates that publicizing peace treaties did not really belong to the officially endorsed celebrations that took place in France during the year following the signing of the Peace of Pyrenees. The publisher justifies this transgression by pointing to the potential of the printed word to contribute to peace. In the meantime, the irenic power of the printed word was already taken for granted in other parts of Europe. In 1663, a publisher in Nuremberg printed a collection of international treaties on a much larger scale: *Theatrum Pacis, hoc est: tractatuum atqve instrumentorum præcipuorum, ab anno inde MDCXLVII. ad MDCLX. vsqve, in Europa initorum et conclusorum collectio*. Nuremberg was known for its spectacular peace festivals after the signing of the Treaties of Westphalia in 1648. With this compilation of principal legal instruments from 1648 to 1660, the city continued its peace celebrations, as it were, by means of printed pages. In 1685, the publisher of the book brought out an additional volume under the same title, which contains treaties contracted after 1660.

In the years around 1700, the number of treaty collections mushroomed in all major European countries. The most prominent among them include *Codex ius gentium diplomaticus* (1693–1700) edited by the German Gottfried Wilhelm Leibniz, *Recueil des traitéz de paix, de trêves, de neutralité, de suspension d'armes, de confédération, d'alliance, de commerce, de garantie et d'autres actes publics* (1700) by the Frenchman Jacques Bernard, and *Foedera, conventiones, literae, et cujuscumque generis acta publica inter reges Angliae, et alios quosvis imperatores, reges, pontifices, principes, vel communitates* (1704–35) by the Englishman Thomas Rymer. In the prefaces, the editors unanimously emphasize the importance of the knowledge of legal instruments from the past for the sovereigns and their ministers. Bernard, for instance, proclaims: "Nothing is more useful to politicians, and to all those who are supposed to draw up acts and treaties than a book, in which one will find an infinite number of different formulas that have all been drawn up, and in which one can choose those that one likes most, and those that best accommodate the circumstances."[28] In the same breath, the editors also point out the value of such knowledge for the general reading public. For Jean Yves de Saint-Prest (1640–1721), the director of the *dépôt des archives* in the French ministry of foreign affairs, the study of treaties serves the "public good." Because treaties are so often violated, he observes at the beginning of *Histoire des traités de paix, et autres negotiations du dix-septième siècle* (1725), certain people regard treaties as mere tricks that are no different from "nuts [used to] amuse children," while others "have likened them to spider webs that catch only flies." But once treaties are compiled and published, readers can compare what different sovereigns have agreed upon and what they have actually done, thereby forming their own judgments on international affairs. For instance, by perusing treaties, "the public has the liberty to examine whether the causes [of war] are genuine and legitimate, and whether through the multiplicity of reasons for taking to the arms, as so often is the case, one discovers nothing else but the fact that the ambition of the aggressor is the only motive of war."[29]

The explicitly stated rationales for compiling and publishing international treaties imply a new conception of the validity or effectiveness of the treaty.

As an agreement entered into by sovereigns with one another, the treaty is an expression of the sovereign will. Since the sovereign will allows for no curbs, a treaty is in principle not enforceable, vulnerable to violation by one or both parties if doing so seems to be more advantageous. The publishing of collected treaties embedded the voluntary act of treaty-making in the textual corpus of existing legal instruments on the one hand, and in the general reading public on the other. A public sphere constituted through the book market was superimposed on the sovereign will as the main source of the validity of the treaty. This public sphere was sometimes considered so important that certain states used it as a forum for furthering their causes in international negotiations. For example, a collection of treaties published in London in the midst of the War of the Spanish Succession—*A General Collection of Treatys, Declarations of War, Manifestos, and Other Publick Papers* (1710)—is prefaced with a propagandistic tract entitled "A brief HISTORY of the French King's Perfidiousness in the Breach of solemn Treatys, by way of INTRODUCTION."

Along with treaties, many other documents of what traditionally fell under *arcana imperii* were compiled and published. They included speeches and correspondences by potentates and their representatives, for example *Das durchlauchtige Archiv Worinnen enthalten Vieler Käyser/Päbste/Könige [. . .] nachdenkliche und curiose Reden [. . .]* (1691) or the twelve-volume book series *Grosser Herren, vornehmer Ministren und anderer berühmten Männer gehaltene Reden* (1707–22). They also included accounts of disputes between sovereigns, for example *Theatrum Historicum Praetensionum et Controversiarum Illustrium* (1712–27). Ceremonials in the international arena, which had become standardized in the course of the sixteenth and seventeenth centuries, began to see the light of the day. Early publications such as the anonymous *Ceremoniale Brandenburgicum* (1699) describe ceremonial practices at particular courts, but soon enough compilers brought together ceremonial customs all across Europe. Notable collections include Gottfried Stieve's *Europäisches Hoff-Ceremoniel* (1715) and Johann Christian Lünig's massive *Theatrum ceremoniale historico-politicum* (1719–20). The study of the ceremonial became a scholarly pursuit, referred to in German as *Zeremonialwissenschaft* or the "science of the ceremonial."[30]

The publicizing of words and actions in the international arena culminated in Jean Dumont's monumental project *Corps universel diplomatique du Droit des Gens*, which began to appear in 1726. In the preface, Dumont makes no secret of his ambition: *Corps universel diplomatique* "could be put to the same use in the law of nations as Justinian's corpus of laws in the civil law." It is supposed to serve as a "portable archive" for "kings, princes, republics, their ministers, counselors, ambassadors, and others, [. . .] perhaps no less useful than the archive kept in the vaults of their chancelleries as well as other public or individual cabinets."[31]

Making *Le droit public de l'Europe*

Conceived as a code of international law on a par with Justinian's code of civil law, Dumont's *Corps universel diplomatique du Droit des Gens* represented an attempt to establish international legal order on the basis of the textual corpus of legal instruments. In "The Confirmation of the *Digest*," Justinian admits that neither the enactments of emperors nor the doctrines of jurists could stop the flow of time.[32] No sooner was the codification project completed than Justinian began to make new laws—the *novellae*. Similarly, international affairs did not stop with *Corps universel diplomatique du Droit des Gens*. Treaties continued to be sealed—and broken—day in and day out. Dumont's mammoth publishing project was accompanied and succeeded by the publication of new legal documents, for example Guillaume de Lamberty's fourteen-volume *Mémoires pour servir à l'histoire du XVIII siècle: Contenant les negociations, traitez, resolutions, et autres documens authentiques concernant les affaires d'état* (1724–40) and Jean Rousset de Missy's twenty-volume *Recueil historique d'actes, négociations, mémoires et traitez* (1728–55). The code of international law as envisioned by Dumont was open-ended.

However, the code of international law found in the reading public a point of reference—and thus also a certain degree of coherence. The numerous and massive publication projects that sought to bring international legal instruments to political decision-makers and general readers alike illustrated a profound transformation of the conception of the public in the early eighteenth century. So far "the public" had meant that which pertained to the state or *res publica*. Since a treaty pertained to affairs of the state, it belonged to public law. In the decades around 1700, "the public" acquired the additional meaning of that which pertained to the sphere constituted through the book market and reading.[33] The publication of collected treaties made treaty law also a matter of the reading public. In the preface to his *Recueil historique d'actes, négociations, mémoires et traitez*, Rousset de Missy states, "Here I am not going to lay out the benefits of collections in general, and of this collection in particular. I have no right to demand of the public that it believes in my words: it is up to the public itself to examine and to make its own judgment on this issue."[34] The public was supposed to make its own judgment, of course, not only on the quality of the collection of treaties, but also on what treaties were meant to institute, namely international legal order. The reading public became the arbitrator in an international arena riven with disputes.

In the meantime, the vast number of treaties from the past to the present was systematized into a coherent whole through historical narration. Jacques Bernard's *Recueil des traitéz de paix* of 1700 includes a detailed narrative account of the treaties contracted in Europe during the past two and a half centuries: "Observations historiques et politiques sur les traitez des princes," penned by Abraham Nicholas Amelot de la Houssaie (1634–1706).[35] Dumont's *Corps universel diplomatique du Droit des Gens* features, in the form of two supplemental volumes, a history of ancient treaties by the noted jurist Jean Barbeyrac (1674–1744). Both Lamberty's and Rousset de Missy's compilations connect disparate treaties together by means of historical narration. Narrative plots are constructed by the choice that the narrator makes as to which treaties to include and which to exclude, as well as by the causal connections that the narrator establishes between the treaties. The title of Amelot de la Houssaie's history of treaties draws attention to the interventions of the narrator—"historical and political observations"—which make out of the events of treaty-making a narrative plot. Rousset de Missy even informs his reader of the specific operations that he undertakes in his narrative: "I have joined all the items together by means of a historical narrative. It explains in a few words the circumstances that gave rise to these items. Often such an explanation sheds as much light as the documents themselves." The historical narrative, he adds, aims at as much precision and as much impartiality as possible, but his "conscience" as well as "a legitimate and indispensable submission" to his own sovereign rulers often tips the balance in his account of the treaties and the events.[36]

Alongside the numerous projects of collecting, publishing, systematizing, and narrativizing treaties, there were also projects of securing peace by institutional means. The most famous of these was associated with the name of the French savant Charles Irénée Castel de Saint-Pierre (1658–1743). His *Projet pour rendre la Paix perpétuelle en Europe* (1713–17) opens with the observation that "the present constitution of Europe can produce nothing else but almost continuous wars because it is unable to procure a sufficient guarantee for the execution of treaties."[37] To remedy this problem, Saint-Pierre put forward the scheme of a confederation of European states held together by institutions invested with sufficient power to arbitrate disputes and to make laws. He also advocated the establishment of a "police durable"—a permanent governmental apparatus—to regulate the relations between the sovereigns.[38] His project of perpetual peace, then, was in fact a project of international governance. Like other contemporaneous proposals for perpetual peace, Saint-Pierre's project was not implemented in his time.[39] There was, however, one institution concerned with international order that came of age in Saint-Pierre's time—diplomacy. The institution of resident diplomacy came into being in the Renaissance.[40] In the late seventeenth and early eighteenth centuries, it acquired an administrative framework and developed a set of practices, which are still in use today, including foreign ministries, hierarchically organized embassies, standardized modes of communication, and above all permanent negotiations.[41] In his *De la Manière de Negocier avec les Souverains* (1716), published around the same time as Saint-Pierre's book on perpetual peace and destined to become a classic in the theory of diplomacy, François de Callières (1645–1717) describes Europe as a kind of commonwealth: "All the states of Europe have necessary ties and commerce one with another, so that we can regard them as members of the same commonwealth."[42] The most important, indeed the only institution that holds this commonwealth together is diplomacy. Diplomatic negotiation, Callières points out, "gives the form, good or bad, to general affairs, and to a great number of particular ones, and it has a greater power over the conduct of men than all the laws that have been invented." It mediates between sovereigns, resolving disputes by treaties and agreements and thereby "procuring peace to them."[43]

The reading public, historical narration, and nascent institutions in the international arena—these were some of the main factors that contributed to the making of the concept of *le droit public de l'Europe*, the public law of Europe. The term was coined by Gabriel Bonnot de Mably (1709–85), serving as the title of his book *Le droit public de l'Europe, fondé sur les traités* (1746). In the "Avertissement de l'Auteur," Mably commends the many compilers of his age for making treaties available to the reading public, but contends that it is more important to "extract from the immense mass of treaties concluded by princes those articles that [. . .] form an essential part of the public law of Europe."[44] By "the public law of Europe," Mably meant a code of law governing the relations among European states. Whereas for Jean Dumont a collection of treaty texts already amounted to a code of international law, for Mably such a code had to be "extracted" from all the treaties. The "extraction" takes the form of narration. In Mably's narrative, the agents of action are the sovereign territorial states that came to be clearly defined through the Treaties of Westphalia. As narrator, he analyzes the motivations of each state in terms of its interests vis-à-vis other states, thereby linking actions of states causally one with another. Every treaty is presented as the result of a causal chain of actions. At the same time, it serves also as the starting point for a new chain of actions, which leads to yet another treaty. Moving thus from one treaty to another, Mably's narrative weaves a complex web of legal relations among sovereign states in Europe during the century from the Peace of Westphalia to his own day. It is this web of legal relations that he calls "le droit public de l'Europe." The narrative, he points out, is not constructed for its own sake, but for "le public"—that is, the reading public. It is up to the reading public to accept or reject the plot of the narrative—"the order, in which I have distributed the materials that I had to deal with"— and "it is also up to the reading public to judge whether by the reflections and remarks spread throughout my extracts I have reached the goal set by myself." The "public law of Europe" is public not only because the web of legal relations makes Europe resemble a commonwealth, but also because it concerns a pan-European reading public. That the ever-maturing institution of diplomacy had contributed to the web of legal relations in Europe was emphasized throughout Mably's narrative. He considered this institution so important that he wrote a separate book on its principles: *Des principes des négociations pour servir d'introduction au droit public d'Europe* (1757).

With its connotation of a code of positive legal norms for the regulation of the relations between European states, Mably's concept of "le droit public de l'Europe" was one answer of the eighteenth century to the question of international order. It found great resonance in its own time. With reference to Mably, the German jurist Johann Jakob Moser (1701–85) laid out, in a systematic manner, the positive legal norms currently in use among European states on the basis of the conception of Europe as a unique "Staats-Cörper" or commonwealth.[45] In our time, historians of international law sometimes apply this concept to the period between the Peace of Westphalia and the Congress of Vienna.[46] In his *Nomos der Erde*, Carl Schmitt even universalizes this concept, under the Latinized name *ius publicum Europaeum*, into an overarching principle of international legal order for the entire modern age, from the discovery of the New World to the turn of the twentieth century.

The Rise of International Law as a Discipline

The publication of treaties and the making of the concept of "le droit public de l'Europe" took place at a time when European states increasingly interacted with one another on a legal basis, whether in peace or in war. To deal with one another on a legal basis required a secure knowledge of law. Legal professionals for international affairs became indispensable to every state. The task of training legal professionals fell to universities. Under these circumstances, international law established itself as a discipline.

In the introduction to his *Codex juris gentium diplomaticus*, Leibniz mentions international law as a "discipline," praising Samuel Pufendorf as a deserving contributor to it.[47] Indeed, Pufendorf can be seen as the embodiment of the discipline of international law, which took shape during the decades around 1700. In 1661, Karl Ludwig, the Elector Palatine, created for Pufendorf a new chair in *ius naturae et gentium* at the University of Heidelberg, the first of its kind in the history of European universities. In 1668, he followed the call of the king of Sweden to a chair in the law of nations at the newly founded University of Lund. Later, he served the royal houses of Sweden and Brandenburg as royal historiographer and advisor. Pufendorf's dual role as law professor and politico-legal counselor for sovereigns indicates that from the outset international law was an academic discipline in the service of the state. With few exceptions, all of the major figures in the doctrinal history of international law from Pufendorf to the mid-eighteenth century—most of whom, as it happened, were German—held both the position of university professor and that of court counselor.[48]

While Pufendorf's professional career gives a glimpse of the institutional framework of the discipline of international law, his writings address the key issues and formulated the main concepts and methods of this discipline. Pufendorf was both a jurist and a historian. His juristic magnum opus *De jure naturae et gentium* (1672) elaborates on the modern natural law theory inaugurated by Hugo Grotius and further developed by Thomas Hobbes, seeking to deduce all of the laws of nature from one fundamental principle—the principle of sociability. Following Hobbes, Pufendorf considers *ius gentium* or international law to be nothing more than the application of the laws of nature to sovereign states. There is, he argues, no voluntary or positive international law. Whatever voluntary agreements between states there may be, they have no "force of law," for there is no "superior" to enforce them.[49] Neither do customs have the force of law, and this for exactly the same reason. For Pufendorf, express as well as tacit agreements—treaties and customs—belong to the province of history rather than law. In his *Einleitung zu der Historie der vornehmsten Reiche und Staaten*, Pufendorf the historian documents, analyzes, and narrates the political agency of European states in international relations as exhibited in treaty-making, alliance-building, diplomacy, and warfare.

Natural law, voluntary or positive law of nations, history—these were the signposts in the rise of this field of study as a discipline. First, the decades around 1700 witnessed a spate of publications on natural jurisprudence, often bearing titles similar to Pufendorf's *De iure naturae et gentium* and regurgitating similar material.[50] This theoretical discourse was accompanied by historical accounts of the development of natural law.[51] With Jean Barbeyrac's foreword to his French translation of Pufendorf's *Le droit de la nature et des gens* (1706) and Christian Thomasius's foreword to the first German translation of Grotius's *Drey Bücher vom Rechte des Krieges und des Friedens* (1707) as its representative texts, the historiography of natural law theory performed, among other things, the function of canonization in the face of the ever proliferating publications. It was at this time that Grotius and Pufendorf were canonized as the most important authors of natural jurisprudence. Insofar as both of them conceived of natural law as the basis of international law, they also became the core authors for the study of international law at universities.

Second, the voluntary or positive law of nations emerged as a rival, or at least a complement to the natural law of nations. Grotius conceived of international law as grounded in natural law, but also acknowledged the significance of voluntary agreements between states, be they expressly stated or merely tacitly accepted. Pufendorf's verdict that voluntary agreements between states lack the force of law provoked a great deal of controversy. His contemporary Samuel Rachel (1628–91) asserted the opposite in his *De jure naturae et gentium dissertationes* (1676). This controversy as to whether the law of nations flows merely from nature or also from voluntary agreements between states—a controversy often depicted by historians as the quarrel between naturalists and positivists—shaped the vibrant theoretical debates about the sources of international legal norms in the early eighteenth century.

Finally, the historical interest in the relations between states intensified, taking the form of painstaking compilations as well as narrative accounts of treaties and other international legal instruments throughout the ages, as discussed above. The historical study of treaties belonged to the academic curriculum in international law, as evidenced by course books such as *Corpus Juris Gentium Academicum, enthaltend die vornehmsten Grund-Gesetze, Friedens- und Commercien-Tractate, Bündnüsse und andere Pacta der Königreiche, Republiquen und Staaten von Europa* (1730).

Taken together, natural law theory, historiography of natural law, theoretical debates about the sources of international law, and finally the history of treaties made up an eclectic curriculum for the study of international law in the early eighteenth century. The state of the arts can be glimpsed from the full—still baroque—title of a voluminous book published in 1723 by Adam Friedrich Glafey: *The Law of Reason and of Nations, wherein the teachings of this science are laid out on demonstrative grounds, and thereafter the disputes that hitherto have taken place among sovereign nations as well as among learned men are discussed, in addition to a history of the law of reason, wherein not only the teachings of every writer in* jure naturae *are presented and examined, but there is also a complete* bibliotheca juris naturae et gentium, *which lists all the books, dissertations, deductions, and* pièces volantes *hitherto published in this discipline according to subject matters and in the alphabetical order.*[52] In addition to testifying to the eclecticism of the study of international law, the title also gives an intimation of this study as a pedagogical project that combined dogmatic and historical material.[53]

A breakthrough came with the publication of Christian Wolff's *Jus gentium methodo scientifica pertractatum* in 1749, which turned the multifarious material in the field of international law into a coherent system. A few years later, Emer de Vattel's *Droit des gens*, published in 1758, presented Wolff's system in a more accessible manner. Wolff and Vattel solved two important theoretical problems: mediating the natural and the positive laws of nations, and mediating juristic doctrines and history. As to the first problem, they agreed with the by now canonized authors of modern natural law theory—Grotius, Hobbes, and Pufendorf—who conceived of international law as the application of the law of nature to sovereign states. They went beyond their predecessors, however, by distinguishing various modes of application. The law of nature directly applied to states is called the necessary law of nations.[54] Yet the law of nature inevitably undergoes modifications if it is applied to states, because states are corporate persons and, as such, are different from individual persons. The law pertaining to the entirety of sovereign states in the world—a fictive collective body that Wolff terms "the supreme state" (*civitas maxima*) and that Vattel simply terms the natural society of states—is called the voluntary law of nations, because it can be considered "to have proceeded from the will of nations."[55] This voluntary law of nations is derived from natural law in the same sense as the law of a particular state is, for it is an imperative of nature that the society of men, be it the society of individuals in a state or the society of states in the world at large, should be governed by laws. In addition, there are the conventional and the customary law of nations, which are based respectively on express agreements (treaties) and tacit agreements. Both are derived from the law of nature, insofar as the law of nature commands that agreements must be kept. By distinguishing the different modes of applying the law of nature to the corporate persons of states, Wolff and Vattel effectively settled the controversy between naturalists and positivists, creating a system of international legal norms that encompasses everything from principles deduced by reason to those distilled from treaties and customs. In doing so, they also harmonized the congeries of doctrinal and historical material in the field of international law. So far juristic doctrines in international law had mostly been associated with natural law, putatively deduced by reason from an overarching principle, while the historical material, particularly histories of treaties, formed the bulk of the so-called positive law of nations. The system of international legal norms constructed by Wolff and Vattel represented a selection and synthesis of natural-law doctrines as well as historical treaties and customs. The criterion of selection and synthesis was an idea that bore the stamp of the age in which they wrote—the age of the Enlightenment. For Wolff, it was the approbation of the "more civilized nations," *quod gentibus moratioribus placuit*.[56] For Vattel, it was the liberty and the welfare of the nations.[57]

With Wolff and Vattel, international law reached its "classical" form.[58] The sovereign state as a corporate person figured as the subject of this law, invested with a set of rights and obligations, while the system of norms, arranged properly as a set of concisely formulated articles, laid down an objective international legal order. Their books, or at least the more readable book by Vattel, were to become the manual for generations of students and practitioners of international law.

Literature and the Private Individual

The practitioners of international law as a field of expert knowledge about affairs of the state wanted no truck with poetic literature. In the preface to his *Le droit public de l'Europe*, Mably declares that a contribution to the study of international law is not meant to entertain readers "as novels do."[59] Poetic literature, in the meantime, wanted no truck with international law either, for it was moving away from the issues of public rights and turning towards matters of private life. The gruesome death of royal persons in Racine heralded their gradual disappearance from the theatrical stage. They came to be replaced by private persons. In the mid eighteenth century, Diderot called upon dramatic poets to "get close to real life."[60] By "real life," he meant bourgeois family life, which the bourgeois audience could relate itself to and identify itself with. The kind of tragic stage that depicted "real life" was bourgeois domestic tragedy. This kind of tragedy is "closer to ourselves. It represents the misfortunes which are all around us." In his characteristically effusive style, Diderot exclaimed, "What! can you not imagine the effect upon you of a real background, authentic dress, speeches adapted to actions, simple actions, dangers which you cannot fail to have feared for your relations, your friends, yourself?"[61] Feelings, emotions, and sentiments—around which domestic tragedy revolved—came to define what it meant to be human, whereas public power came to be seen as opposed to human nature. In *Hamburgische Dramaturgie* (1767), Gotthold Ephraim Lessing famously argues that theater is not interested in kings and states, but only in private individuals: "Our sympathy requires an individual object, and a state is far too abstract a conception for our feelings."[62] Diderot and Lessing sought, as it were, to ban public persons from the tragic stage. They declared war against the *opera seria* that continued to populate its stage with princes and heroes throughout the eighteenth century.

Just like the tragic stage, prose fiction abandoned princely persons as well. Political romance gave way to a new kind of prose fiction that sought to represent the lives of private individuals—the novel. In turning to the affairs of the private person, literature seemed to abjure its engagement with problems pertaining to the state.

❧ Chapter 6

The Novel and International Order in the Eighteenth Century

The literary figuration of international world order reached a significant turning point at the beginning of the eighteenth century. With the affairs of the state taken over by professional scholars in government and law, international law became an autonomous field of expert knowledge. Tragedy and political romance as the principal literary genres concerned with international order had gone into decline. The new generic forms rising from their ashes, domestic tragedy and the novel, seemed to have nothing on their agenda but the concerns of private persons. This, however, did not mean that literature had ceased to concern itself with the problem of international order altogether. Rather, the relationship between international law and literature was being reconfigured. In particular, precisely by representing the affairs of private individuals, the novel became a key player in the literary figuration of international order.

"The novel" emerged as a dominant and standard term for a new kind of prose fiction in mid-eighteenth-century England—prose fiction dealing with the ordinary life and manners of the private individual. The term was often used polemically in contradistinction to romance.[1] In French and German, there was no such terminological breakthrough, as the name for romance—*le roman* and *der Roman* respectively—continued to be used for this new kind of prose fiction. The nature of the novel is a matter of much controversy, if for no other reason than that the eighteenth century witnessed a spate of innovations and experimentations in prose fiction.[2] By canvassing the poetics of fiction and sampling some key fictional texts, this chapter argues that the eighteenth-century novel was closely associated with the fictional construction of human society as conceived by modern natural jurisprudence. Initiated by Hugo Grotius, elaborated by Thomas Hobbes, and reaching its mature form in Samuel Pufendorf's *De jure naturae et gentium* (1672), modern natural jurisprudence is predicated on the fiction of the state of nature—a hypothetical condition, in which individuals coexist without any social institutions, especially without the authorities of a political society. This fiction makes it possible for jurists to construct human society as resulting from the contractual relations between discrete, presocial individuals. Crucial to the fiction of the state of nature is the analogy between the individual and the sovereign state. Sovereign states relate to one another in exactly the same way as individuals do in the state of nature, for they share no social institutions, certainly no supreme authority of a political society. The world of sovereign states—the international world—is the state of nature. Consequently, the theoretical as well as the narrative construction of human society on the basis of the fiction of the state of nature is always also a construction of international society. The novel was conceived by its early theorists, some of whom were jurists themselves, as a kind of fictional construction of society. Using the analogy between the individual and the sovereign state, the novel could explore, explicitly or implicitly, the possibility of a normative order of international society by narrating the formation of social bonds between private individuals.

The eighteenth-century novel developed three distinctive models of international order. First, Daniel Defoe, a jack of all trades and an eclectic polymath, occupied himself with natural jurisprudence and published on international relations, especially during the first two decades of the eighteenth century. His main novels, from *Robinson Crusoe* of 1719 to *Roxana* of 1724, are set mostly in spaces embodying the state of nature in the sense of natural jurisprudence and tell stories of enterprising individuals engaging in commerce of all kinds. For Pufendorf and his eighteenth-century followers, individuals in the state of nature are predisposed to commerce. The natural human society, before and beyond the state, is a commercial society. Reading at times like vivid enactments of the tenets of the Pufendorfian school of natural jurisprudence, Defoe's novels are stories of the making of commercial society beyond the state. With characters implementing the values of commercial society across political borders and beyond the reach of any sovereign state, they evoke a transnational commercial world order;

Second, the sentimental novel of the mid-eighteenth century envisions a universal community constituted through sympathy—the sentimental community. Perhaps no other text of the period better illustrates this function of the novel than Christian Fürchtegott Gellert's *Das Leben der schwedischen Gräfin von G**** (1747/48). Against the backdrop of unending bellicosity among European states, this novel narrates the making of a community enabled by emotional bonding across political boundaries and beyond the law. The conception of the sentimental community as a normative ideal for the international world even left its traces in theoretical treatises such as Emer de Vattel's enormously influential *Le droit des gens* (1758). But it became clear very soon that this normative ideal might be nothing more than a wishful fantasy. Sentimental world order falls victim to a self-indulgent cult of feeling in Laurence Sterne's iconic *A Sentimental Journey Through France and Italy* (1768).

Third, the novel of education or development—a type of novel that took shape in the late eighteenth century and was later to be called the *Bildungsroman*—narrates the making of an individual person who qualifies as a citizen of the human world as a whole, thus underwriting a cosmopolitan world order. Cosmopolitanism is an ancient philosophical idea. The Stoics regarded man as a citizen of the cosmic city in addition to being a citizen of a particular political community, insofar as man partakes of the common rationality informing the entire cosmos. Martin Christoph Wieland's *Geschichte des Agathon* (first version published in 1766/67; final version in 1794) and Johann Wolfgang Goethe's *Wilhelm Meisters Lehrjahre* (1795/96), the first exemplars of the *Bildungsroman*, represent world citizenship as a subjective disposition and a normative personality, which an individual has to achieve after many experiences and reflections on these experiences. They offer a narrative of the genesis of the cosmopolitan subject. In so doing, they effect a subjective turn of cosmopolitanism. From the Kantian *ius cosmopoliticum* to the contemporary discourse of international human rights, modern cosmopolitanism has been associated with advocating for the fundamental rights that appertain to the individual person as a member of human society at large. The cosmopolitan world order is a world order in which the individual person is invested with fundamental rights both inside and outside the state, hence is recognized as a legal subject alongside and over against the state.

The Fictional Construction of Society: *Ius Naturae et Gentium*

Fictio figura veritatis, a dictum that played an important role in medieval political thought, seemed to come true again in the age of reason, albeit within rather different parameters.[3] Hobbesian political theory, Pufendorfian jurisprudence, and much of what Enlightenment thinkers had to say about society in general and about political society in particular were all informed by a powerful fiction: the fiction of the state of nature. Intimated by Grotius, and put forward as a basis of theoretical reasoning by Hobbes in *Leviathan*, the fiction of the state of nature is thoroughly conceptualized by Pufendorf in his *De jure naturae et gentium*:

> By the natural state of man we do not understand that condition which nature intended should be most perfect and for his greatest good, but that condition for which man is understood to be constituted, by the mere fact of his birth, all inventions and institutions, either of man or suggested to him from above, being disregarded, since they give a very different aspect to the life of man. By them we understand not only the different forms and general culture of the life of man, but especially civil societies, at the formation of which a suitable order was introduced into mankind's existence.[4]

The state of nature, by this account, is a condition of human life that has neither social and political institutions nor material and cultural improvements, a condition in which men exist as individual persons free of political membership, social belonging, and cultural properties, hence free by themselves and equal to one another. Since in reality human life always takes place within the framework of some kind of institution and is rarely ever destitute of cultural achievements altogether, this privative condition is a pure fiction. It is a fiction deliberately made up to perform an important function—the function of spotlighting the inventions and institutions of humankind, so that they can be observed and understood in new ways. By disregarding all the inventions and institutions in the first step, the fiction of the state of nature makes it possible, in the second step, to reconsider them, to reconceive them, to reconstruct why and how they come into being and take the form as they do. It paves the way for tracing the formation of civil society, for finding out how "a suitable order was introduced into mankind's existence." In short, it serves to enable, or at least to facilitate, the discovery of the truth about human society.

The project of discovering the truth about human society by means of the fiction of the state of nature is part and parcel of modern natural jurisprudence. The ancient tradition of natural law theory postulates a set of norms that are supposed to be immediately valid in all kinds of society. Challenged by Spanish Neoscholasticism in the sixteenth century, this ancient tradition gave way to a modern natural law theory in the seventeenth century, associated with the names of Grotius, Hobbes, and Pufendorf. Instead of postulating a set of norms, modern natural jurisprudence first posits a fundamental principle of human nature without regard to the institutions and norms of society—a principle underlying the state of nature. It then seeks to deduce, by power of reason, all the norms of human society from this principle. The norms deduced by reason (the laws of nature) are not immediately valid in society, but achieve validity through the recognition by a civil authority.[5] One key concern of modern natural jurisprudence is to explain how society comes into being on the basis of the principle of human nature, or in other words, to explain the transition from the presocial state of nature to social life with all of its institutions. Insofar as the state of nature is a fiction, this concern of natural jurisprudence can be characterized as the fictional construction of society.

There are two different approaches to the fictional construction of society, represented respectively by Thomas Hobbes and Samuel Pufendorf. Hobbes is concerned primarily with constructing political society—that is, the state or *civitas*. Pufendorf shares this Hobbesian concern, but in contrast to Hobbes, he seeks at the same time to carve out a social sphere beyond or at least differentiated from the state, a nonpolitical society that can exist both inside and alongside the state. This nonpolitical society or *societas* comprises commerce, family, the arts and sciences, and the like.[6] For Pufendorf, man in the state of nature shares with all beings the desire for self-preservation. But compared to animals, men are weak and needy, not equipped with the physical properties and the instincts necessary for survival.[7] They need to cultivate the arts that minister to the necessities and conveniences of life. Such arts are all the more important, as the desire of men is boundless. Whereas the needs of animals are satisfied by their instincts, in men one need is satisfied only to give rise to another need. For this reason, men have no other choice but to cooperate with each other—to be sociable. "It is altogether due to the aid of other men," he writes in *De officio hominis* (1673), "that out of such feebleness we have been able to grow up, that we now enjoy untold comforts, and that we improve mind and body for own advantage and that of others."[8] Sociability is thus the fundamental law of nature: for man "to live and enjoy the good things that in his world attend his condition, it is necessary that he be sociable, that is, be willing to join himself with others like him, and conduct himself towards them in such a way that, far from having any cause to do him harm, they may feel that there is reason to preserve and increase his good fortune."[9] An individual person has to cooperate with others for his own sake, out of self-love and the need for self-preservation. This utility-based sociability—Immanuel Kant was later to characterize it as "unsocial sociability"—gives rise to obligations, commerce, and matrimony, as well as other kinds of associations of private persons.[10] On the basis of sociability as the fundamental law of nature, Pufendorf manages to construct an entire system of private law. It is a system of norms sustaining a society of private persons, a nonpolitical society.

Having constructed a nonpolitical society or *societas* on the basis of the law of nature, Pufendorf attends to the origin of the state or *civitas*. In this regard, he follows in Hobbes's footsteps. For Hobbes, a state, once founded, relates to other states in exactly the same way as individuals relate to one another in the state of nature. In the relations between states, there is no political authority. If the state of nature exists at all, it does so in the international world of states. Or rather, the international world of states stands as a model for the fictional state of nature. Consequently, the laws of the international world are none other than the laws of nature.[11] Yet in light of the construction of *societas*, this Hobbesian equation between international law and the law of nature acquires a new valence. If the fundamental law of nature is sociability, and if individuals in the state of nature constitute a society based on the law of person, property, and obligation, then this equation implies that international law is also informed by sociability, and that the international world of states also makes up a lawful society. Conversely, in light of the construction of *civitas*, the Pufendorfian conception of sociability gains a new valence as well. If states, with respect to their relation to one another, exist in the state of nature, then sociability, this principle beyond the state, must also apply to them. The law of person, property, and obligation must be the ligament of the international world as well. Joined together, Pufendorf's simultaneous construction of *societas* and *civitas* implies a significant reconceptualization of international order: although there is no acknowledged common superior, no politico-judicial institution in the international world, there is nonetheless a normative international order beyond the state, one founded on sociability. Pufendorf thus raises the possibility of an international world order skirting state sovereignty, exemplified by today's global economy and global civil society.

Pufendorf's natural jurisprudence, doubling as a theory of international law, inaugurated a jurisprudential paradigm that held sway for more than a century. Following Pufendorf, there were scores of books bearing the title *De jure naturae et gentium* or some kind of variation on it.[12] Many others carried on his thought without bearing this title. In legal history, the period between Pufendorf and the turn of the nineteenth century is usually referred to as the age of natural law. His construction of a human society made up of private individual persons—a civil society beyond the state—lay at the heart of eighteenth-century moral and political thought. On the basis of the analogy between the state and the individual person in the state of nature, such a society was regarded as the model of international society. In particular, commerce was mapped onto the international world. For Adam Smith (1723–90) and other theorists of commercial society, states trade with one another just as individuals do, thereby constituting an international commercial society. Accordingly, norms of commerce apply to individual persons and to states alike. In *A Treatise of Human Nature* (1739–40), David Hume (1711–76) summarizes the key tenets of the theory of international world order based on commercial sociability, concluding that "the advantages [. . .] of peace, commerce, and mutual succor, make us extend to different kingdoms the same notions of justice, which take place among individuals."[13] Similarly, Emer de Vattel states in *Le Droit des Gens* (1758), "Men are [. . .] bound to carry on such commerce if they would not depart from the views of nature, and the obligation extends to entire Nations or States as well."[14]

Yet this is not the full story. No sooner does Hume affirm this theory of international order, which seems to transcend state sovereignty, than he relativizes it again: "Tho' the morality of princes has the same *extent*, yet has not the same *force* as that of private persons, and may lawfully be transgress'd from a more trivial motive." The reason for the fragility of international norms lies, in part, in the relative self-sufficiency of the state.[15] That the state compromises the norms of natural human society and thereby forecloses the possibility of international order was stressed in especially dramatic terms by Jean-Jacques Rousseau (1712–78). Deeply indebted to Pufendorf's natural jurisprudence,[16] Rousseau conceived of the state as founded by a contract by free and equal individuals in the state of nature, and regarded states, once founded, as coexisting in the state of nature. But the state of nature, in which states exist side by side—the international state of nature—is no longer the same as the state of nature prior to the founding of the state. It is haunted by the state that has been founded. Whereas the relationship among naturally free and equal men "is not sufficiently stable to constitute either a state of peace or a state of war," states as free and equal artificial persons are caught up in a permanent state of war, because the state, "being an artificial body, has no determinate measure, it is without definite proper size, it can always increase it, it feels weak so long as some are stronger than it."[17] Unequal in power, yet laying claim to their natural rights nonetheless, states cannot help colliding with each other head-on. "As for what is commonly called the right of nations," Rousseau concludes, "it is certain that, for want of sanction, its laws are nothing but chimeras even weaker than the law of nature. This latter at least speaks to the heart of individuals, whereas the right of nations, having no other guarantee than its utility to the one who submits to it, its decisions are respected only as long as self-interest confirms them."[18]

In sum, the Pufendorfian natural jurisprudence—*ius naturae et gentium*—constructs, on the basis of the fiction of the state of nature, a twofold human society—the state or *civitas*, and a nonpolitical society or *societas*. It then applies the norms of the nonpolitical society to the space between states, turning it into the foundation of international world order. As attractive as this theoretical model is, its blind spots soon become apparent, as Hume and Rousseau demonstrated. Applied to the society of states, the norms of the society of individuals cannot help being distorted, corrupted, and invalidated—by the states themselves.

The Fictional Construction of Society: Poetics of the Novel

Pufendorf's fiction of the state of nature consists of a thought experiment: what would human beings do if they were left outside of society and bereft of all material comfort? One version of this thought experiment looks like this: "If [. . .] we imagine many such men left entirely to their own resources on this still virgin earth, what a miserable and animal-like existence would they lead, until by their own experience and ingenuity, or, as the opportunity arose, by observing the cunning of some animals they slowly advanced to a kind of ordered life."[19] Almost a century later, the Pufendorfian thought experiment was alive and well. In a lecture delivered at the University of Glasgow in 1762, Adam Smith mused about what would happen "if we should suppose 10 or 12 persons of different sexes settled in an uninhabited island [. . .]."[20] But the imagination is certainly no privilege of jurists. The thought experiment of leaving a human being on the "virgin earth" or "uninhabited island" is fleshed out, with mesmerizing vividness, in a book published in London in 1719, which is anything but a juristic treatise: *The Life and Strange Surprising Adventures of Robinson Crusoe, of York, Mariner: Who lived Eight and Twenty Years, all alone in an un-inhabited Island on the Coast of America [. . .]*. It is a fictional story. In the wake of its great success, similar fictional stories of one or more individuals stranded on a desert island were all the rage throughout Europe.[21] Soon enough, the story of Robinson Crusoe was coopted by jurisprudence. In a book bearing a title that proclaims its Pufendorfian lineage—*Ausführlicher Discours über das Natur- und Völcker-Recht* (1734)—the jurist Nicolaus Hieronymus Gundling recommends that all jurists should read *Robinson Crusoe* in order better to understand the state of nature: "Nowadays *homines privati* very rarely live in *statu libertatis*, and it happens only *par harzard*, that if you and I were stranded on an island together, no one would be subject to the other. In this regard, one can read the first part of the Robinson Crusoe, from which we may learn to understand this *statum naturalem*."[22]

Robinson Crusoe was one of the first exemplars of a new kind of prose fiction, which by the mid-eighteenth century was to be designated as "the novel." Its striking affinity with the Pufendorfian thought experiment about the state of nature is an indication of the structural parallel between the novel and natural jurisprudence. Both can be understood in terms of the fictional construction of human society. Two rhetorical moves are crucial to natural jurisprudence: first, disregarding all the "inventions and institutions" of human society and postulating a fictional state of nature in which individual human beings are left with nothing other than their intrinsic faculties; and second, reconstructing how individuals in the state of nature, sociable by necessity, engage in social intercourse with one another. The norms of the society thus constituted make up the so-called law of nature and of nations. The selfsame moves are constitutive of the novel as well.

The first thing that the novel does is to dislodge its protagonists from a defined social position. Protagonists are either already cut off from all social bonds at birth—Defoe's Moll Flanders and Colonel Jack are both orphans, as is Fielding's Tom Jones—or they leave behind an existing social status due to restlessness, ambition, or eroticism; or they are ejected from the wonted social world for reasons beyond their control. In a second move, the novel then sends this individual, unmoored from all kinds of social belonging, out into the wide world. Forced to fend for themselves, protagonists of novels forge and dissolve contractual relations with others, acquire and lose property. At the end, they attain a certain position adequate to their worth. Whether associated with success or with failure, the position attained at the end encapsulates the prevailing values and norms of society: the novel "tends [. . .] to validate the perspective of the newly conceptualized modern individual, whose particularized and personalized view of the world is explored as if it were somehow prior to a communal or social world."[23] The hypothetical condition "prior to a communal or social world" is nothing other than what is called the state of nature in natural jurisprudence. The novel vivifies the fiction of the state of nature by naming individual persons and detailing the temporal and spatial particulars of their actions. In so doing, it turns the natural law construction of society into engrossing narratives of individual lives. But framed by the rhetorical moves of dislodging individuals from the social world in order then to reconstitute the social world through their sociability, novelistic narratives perform the fictional construction of human society just as natural jurisprudence does.[24]

Since by the logic of natural jurisprudence states relate to each other as individuals do in the state of nature, the social values and norms validated by novelistic narratives apply, in principle, to the international world of states. Indeed, the eighteenth-century novel offered a number of distinctive models of international order. These were models that remedied the intrinsic problems of international law—problems as diagnosed by Hume and Rousseau, among others.

It was perhaps no accident that the pioneering theorist of the novel was a jurist in the Pufendorfian school—Christian Thomasius (1655–1728). At around the same time that he published *Institutiones iurisprudentiae divinae* (1688)—a treatise on natural law, which aimed to demonstrate and corroborate Pufendorf—Thomasius began to review prose fiction. His arguments foreshadowed the key tenets of the poetics of the novel in the eighteenth century. Reviewing Eberhard Werner Happel's *Der afrikanische Tarnolast* (1689)—a sprawling text still very much in the mold of political romance and bearing little resemblance to the novel—Thomasius maintains that prose fiction should portray their protagonists as humans rather than idealizing them as if they were "angels, even half gods": "Humans would always be humans, and even the greatest heroes would always be subject to human weaknesses. They would eat, drink, sleep, love, hate, be angry and so on just as other people do. Accordingly, it would not be quite right, should one represent the heroes in the romances/novels (*Romanen*) as if they had almost nothing human about them."[25]

Thomasius's call for the humanness of fictional characters bespeaks the belief in the existence of a human nature independent of whatever elevated status a person might happen to have. This is also the belief underlying the fiction of the state of nature, for to postulate a state of nature is to believe that a substrate of human nature remains even if we disregard everything that society confers upon and contributes to individuals. Of course, natural law theorists do not always agree precisely on the characteristics of man in the state of human nature—Pufendorf, stressing the neediness of human existence, would certainly include "eat, drink, sleep" in human nature; "love, hate, be angry" belong to those qualities that Thomasius would emphasize in his new theory of natural law developed in *Fundamenta Juris Naturae et gentium ex sensu communi deducta* (1705), a theory that conceives of human nature in terms of the affects of pleasure, ambition, and avarice. In any case, human nature is an abstraction, since it is what remains of man after he has been abstracted from all the inventions and institutions of society. As an abstraction, it is universal, for it is what all human beings share regardless of their differing social status.

The humanness that Thomasius expects of fictional characters means nothing more and nothing less than this abstract, universal human nature. With such an expectation, one would have to leave behind political romance, the protagonists of which, as discussed in chapter 4, are embodiments of political societies. The kind of prose fiction whose protagonists exemplify universal human nature was the novel of the eighteenth century. The humanness of fictional characters as demanded by Thomasius was emphasized, again and again, in the poetics of the novel. According to Friedrich von Blanckenburg's *Versuch über den Roman* (1774), for instance, what is at stake in the novel is "naked humanness" (*die nackte Menschheit*), humanness denuded of "all that morals, status, and coincidence can add to it."[26] It is this concern with naked humanness that makes the novel the poetic form of modern times, in contrast to the epic as the distinctive poetic form of antiquity: whereas "the epic sings public deeds and events, that is, the actions of the citizen [. . .], the novel concerns itself with the actions and sentiments of man."[27]

Assuming an abstract, universal human nature, natural jurisprudence lays out a normative order of human society by rational argumentation. The novel is supposed to accomplish the same by poetic means. In the early eighteenth century, moral didactic literature sought to clad natural law doctrines in a pleasing poetic form.[28] Although many novelists and critics of the time tended to legitimize the new genre by invoking the Horatian dictum of *prodesse et delectare*, emphasizing its capacity for providing moral instruction through entertaining stories, the novel differs from moral didactic literature in that it is no mere illustration of ready-made precepts. Rather, it shows how norms of human society come about in the first place. For Thomasius, the novel narrates "the different inclinations and modes of human nature" in order to guide the reader in figuring out what the norms of human life should be.[29] That is to say, the novel performs the transformation of human nature from the nonnormative sense of what man *is* by nature into the normative sense of what man *should be* by nature—a transformation from facticity to normativity.

The novel employs a variety of poetic devices to effect the transformation from facticity to normativity, including the use of ordinary names for protagonists, circumstantial description of times, places, and mental conditions, and above all plot construction in accordance with the principle of probability. These poetic devices all serve to mediate between the particular and the general. They lend an aura of uniqueness to the experience of the protagonist and simultaneously make it exemplary of human experience in general. In contrast to the outlandish names of the protagonists of the political romance, the protagonists of novels bear the most ordinary of names, such as Pamela Andrews or Tom Jones. Such names identify the protagonists as particular individuals. At the same time, however, the ordinariness of the names suggests that the protagonists can be really anyone in the world—in other words, they stand for individuals in general. Also characteristic of the novel are richly detailed descriptions of the spatio-temporal circumstances in which actions take place, as well as of the appearance and mental states of the agents of action. In his effusive "Éloge de Richardson" (1762), Denis Diderot sings the praises of the sheer endless details in the novels of Samuel Richardson (1689–1761): "I know the Harlowes' house as I know my own; my father's home is no more familiar to me than Grandison's." With regard to *Clarissa*, he exclaims, "What an immense variety of different shades!," adding, "In this immortal book, as in nature in springtime, you cannot find two leaves which are exactly the same green." The details mark out the particularity of the world of the protagonists. Yet at the same time, the multitude of details give rise to an illusion of truth, turning the particular world of the protagonists into a symbol of human life in general. It is precisely due to the details that the novel elevates the particular individual to "the human race," particular words and deeds to general "truth," the particular "portion of time" and the particular "point on the surface of the globe" to "all times and all places."[30]

Perhaps the most important poetic device that the novel employs to elevate the particular to the general is the probable plot. Of course, Aristotle long ago underscored the crucial significance of probability, considering it the principle that governs the structure of plot and guarantees the universality of poetry.[31] For neoclassical poetics in the seventeenth century, probability or verisimilitude meant the concordance between poetic representation and the natural course of things, between invention and the general norms dictated by reason. In the eighteenth-century discussion of the novel, however, probability was fundamentally reconceived. It was no longer gauged with reference to any naturalized, universally accepted norms, but with reference to the subjective judgment of the reader or the author. The breakthrough came with the Swiss critic Johann Jacob Bodmer's (1698–1783) analysis of Cervantes's masterpiece, *Don Quixote*, often considered a forerunner of the novel. Observing Don Quixote as a reader of chivalric romances, Bodmer comes to the conclusion that "in the romances the probable refers directly to the reader, the subject matters must appear to the reader in such a way as they are described, and he must find order and connection in them." Extrapolating from such an observation, Bodmer argues that "even historical truth is nothing else than probability resting upon the consistent and combined testimonies of those writers whom we consider faithful and honest."[32] In other words, probability is what the reader finds probable. Verisimilitude is what seems to be true to the reader. Bodmer published his critical observations in 1741, at a time when the novel was taking off in England. Soon afterwards, the author was also brought to bear on probability. For instance, Henry Fielding's *History of Tom Jones* (1749) and Christoph Martin Wieland's *Geschichte des Agathon* (1766–67)—both titles bespeak a claim to historical truth—feature various frames for the main narrative, in which the author or the fictive editor or the narrator self-consciously comment on the plot and its probability.[33] In the very first sentence of the prefatory frame of *Geschichte des Agathon*, the fictive editor states that the probability of the novelistic plot is not to be sought in something outside of itself. It is rather the effect of the author's thought experiment, of a scheme of modeling human affairs: if the author chooses a set of characters, considers carefully "the nature of every passion, with all the particular colors and shadings that it receives through the individual character and the circumstances of every person," and in addition pays attention to "the peculiar character of the country, the place, and the time in which the story is set," then events cannot help taking place in accordance with a certain causal pattern.[34] The plot that evinces this pattern is probable, seems to be true. By relating probability to the reader and the author, the eighteenth-century theory of the novel conceives of the rational, normative pattern of things associated with it—the truth—no longer as something that is already objectively established, demonstrated with certainty, and universally valid, but rather as something that is subjectively constructed. It now means the semblance of the true in the eyes of the observer.[35] The probable plot is a device that elicits the semblance of the true from particular, contingent events.

By means of such poetic devices as the use of ordinary proper names, circumstantial descriptions, and probable plots, the novel transforms human nature as it is exemplified by particular individuals under particular circumstances into general norms or what man should be by nature. The novel bridges and, precisely in so doing, constantly produces the difference between the particular and the general, between the facticity of human nature denoted by particulars and the general norms that go by the name of human nature as well. It is in this difference that the defining feature of the novel resides—its fictionality. The novelistic characters who are particular individuals designated by proper names and who at the same time cover all the cases in the human species are nobodies.[36] The events that happen to these purely imaginary individuals and that somehow cohere into a plot revealing a general pattern of human affairs are to be found nowhere outside the novel itself. The truth evoked by the rich details and the probable plot is an illusion of the reader. The local referentiality of political romance, with characters referring to certain real persons and with events referring to certain real events in accordance with the conventions of *roman à clef*, gives way to the complete nonreferentiality of the novel.[37] But it is a nonreferentiality that could be seen as a greater referentiality because the novel aims to offer a plausible story about human nature in general. The novel thus reveals and conceals fictionality all at once.[38]

Many novels of the eighteenth century held up the fictionally constructed norms of human nature as models of international order. Just as there were different approaches and positions in natural jurisprudence, the novelistic construction of human nature was far from uniform. The norms of human nature that were constructed, as well as the modes of construction, evolved steadily throughout the century. Accordingly, the novelistic models of international order varied as well. One can distinguish, chronologically, three main models: transnational commercial world order early in the eighteenth century, sentimental world order in the mid-century, and cosmopolitan world order later in the century.

Transnational Commercial World Order (Defoe)

Daniel Defoe was a man of many careers. Prior to his meteoric rise as the writer of enthralling fictions, he was also a journalist and pamphleteer with a strong interest in international affairs. During the two decades leading up to the publication of *Robinson Crusoe* in 1719, especially during the War of the Spanish Succession (1701–14), Defoe wrote scores of essays and pamphlets on some key issues of international relations, including the balance of power, war, and treaty-making. In the words of a historian of diplomacy, "His observations taken as a whole form a corpus that is as understandable and worth studying as the more formal works of such well-known authors on diplomatic thought as Hugo Grotius and Samuel Pufendorf."[39] Occasionally, Defoe speculated about the possibility of some kind of international institution, for instance "a Court of Appeals for all the injur'd and oppressed, whether they are Princes or People, that are or ever shall be in *Europe* to the End of the World."[40] In those moments, he sounded like his contemporary Charles Irénée Castel de Saint-Pierre with his project of perpetual peace. But by and large, Defoe's assumptions and ideas foreshadowed what is called realism in international relations theory. For realists, states are actors bent on pursuing their interests by means of rational calculation, thereby securing their survival and dominance in a cutthroat competition with one another.

Defoe was a realist *avant la lettre* in his clear-eyed observations on the ruthless, rationally calculated power politics, in his emphasis on pragmatism and prudence, and in his nonmoral view on international legal matters. Beginning with *Robinson Crusoe*, Defoe took to a new type of writing—the novel. In a string of novels written in rapid succession between 1719 and 1724, all of which are animated by a new narrative style to be christened realism by literary historians, Defoe devises a radically new way of addressing the question of world order.

One of Defoe's great narrative innovations is the choice of settings: his novels are mostly set in spaces where individuals hailing from different nations encounter each other. The typical settings include battlefields and military camps (*Memoirs of a Cavalier* and *Col. Jacque*), wilderness and the high seas (*Robinson Crusoe* and *Captain Singleton*), and various places of commerce inside Europe and around the globe (as can be seen in almost all of his novels). They are all spaces outside of a state or between states. As such, they can be properly characterized as physical embodiments of the state of nature in the sense of modern natural law theory. Defoe's new art of prose fiction makes the state of nature come to life by describing, in abundant and vivid details, the physical spaces embodying it, while providing a full circumstantial first-person report of the events taking placing in these spaces. This innovation became possible, of course, under specific historical conditions. The pan-European wars of the seventeenth and eighteenth centuries—*Memoirs of a Cavalier*, for instance, is set during the Thirty Years' War—drew attention to the battlefield as a focal point of human actions, while colonial commerce opened up wildernesses and high seas, populating them with traders, explorers, and adventurers. But this innovation was also theoretically motivated. Defoe's thinking about human nature, social institutions, and political authority was molded by modern natural law theory. As a political writer, he cited and synthesized all the major theorists, including Grotius, Hobbes, and Pufendorf.[41] By setting the actions of his novels in the spaces that embody the state of nature, he could illustrate or problematize, by narrative means, certain propositions or arguments of natural law theory.[42]

Since the state of nature, according to modern natural law theory, corresponds to the condition between states, the human events unfolding in the spaces embodying the state of nature, which Defoe's novels narrate, can be mapped onto the international world. Accordingly, the narrative plots constructed and the values validated by the novels stand as a model for international order. However, it would be misguided to correlate the individual characters simply with states and their interactions with international relations. Defoe's fictional worlds are far more than mere allegories of the world of sovereign states. In fact, the much-vaunted realism of the novel pits it against the allegorical mode. The characters in his novels hail from various nations—warring, trading, or seafaring nations both in Europe and on other continents, as well as "savage" nations living in the wilderness. Engaging with one another in spaces that embody the state of nature, they represent their respective native countries without forfeiting their unique quality as natural individual persons. The human society constituted in these spaces can be best described as a transnational society. It is a society that refers to the international world with an interstate as well as a colonial dimension, as its members come from the one or the other state or colony, but it is constituted and operates outside of any particular state or colony. Or in other words, it is a society cutting across the boundary—and, as it were, haunted by the shadow—of the state or colonial empire.[43] Through the fictional construction of such a society, Defoe's novels provide a distinctive model of world order—a transnational world order. *Robinson Crusoe* and *Roxana*, the first and the last of Defoe's novels, stand as the best examples.

Robinson Crusoe

The plot of *Robinson Crusoe* is organized into three distinctive episodes: first, Robinson's escape from his family in England, his early adventures, and his operation of a thriving plantation and trading business in Brazil; second, the central episode of his twenty-eight years on a desolate island; and finally, his return to Europe and his business trip from England to Portugal. Following one upon another in a chronological sequence as they do, the three episodes represent three logically connected components of an overarching vision of transnational world order.

Triggered by the implacable restlessness of the protagonist, the plot of *Robinson Crusoe* opens with Robinson escaping from his father's house and going to sea. Belonging to the "middle Station of life" (6), the father's house is an emblem of the established structures and institutions of society.[44] The seafaring life that Robinson escapes into is, by contrast, one beyond existing institutions of society. As the inaugural plot element, Robinson's escape performs the key argumentative operation or thought experiment of modern natural law theory—the operation of disregarding the existing institutions of society and imagining a state of nature. The life that Robinson embarks on away from the father's house, with all its terrors, uncertainties, and excitements, visualizes the state of nature in multiple ways. There are, first of all, the raging elements of nature—Robinson is caught continually in sea storms. There are then piratical attacks on the high seas and the ensuing enslavement of Robinson. Robinson's own behavior on his escape from North African enslavement encapsulates the lawlessness of the Hobbesian state of nature. For the sake of self-preservation, he has no qualms about victimizing others by stealth: "I stept forward to where the Moor was, and making as if I stoopt for something behind him, I took him by Surprize with my Arm under his Twist, and tost him clear over-board into the Sea" (21). With the help of only a little bit of casuistry, he even blithely sells Xury, the good-natured boy devoted to him with all his heart, into slavery. But the high seas prove to be a place of benevolence, generosity, and charity as well, for Robinson owes his deliverance ultimately to a Portuguese captain who evinces all of these qualities. Here it corresponds more to the state of nature as conceived by early eighteenth-century moral philosophers intent on refuting Hobbes, such as Lord Shaftesbury (1671–1713) and Francis Hutcheson (1694–1746). Last but not least, there are the cultivation of the soil (for example, Robinson's plantation business in Brazil) and commerce, both of which Pufendorf and John Locke (1632–1704) emphasize in their conceptions of the state of nature. With the business in Brazil prospering, however, Robinson reproduces what his father's house symbolizes and what he forsook—the "Middle Station" of life: "I was coming into the very Middle Station, or Upper Degree of low Life, which my Father advised me to before" (30–31). At the end of the first episode of the novel, Robinson's life seems to come to full circle. The "middle Station" stands for an established and structured society. Beginning with the "middle Station" and then moving into spaces outside of society—the state of nature—in order to retrace how the "middle Station" comes about, the first episode of the novel offers a narrative of the origin of society. It is a society that has a predominantly commercial character.

By returning to the starting point of the plot—the "middle Station" of life—the endpoint of the first episode of the novel is strategically positioned to propel the plot, for it is the protagonist's dissatisfaction with the "middle Station" that set the plot in motion in the first place. The "middle Station" achieved in Brazil at the end of the first episode foments the same dissatisfaction, thereby restarting the plot with the same propulsive force. Robinson goes to sea and thus plunges yet again into the state of nature. What follows is the central episode of the novel—Robinson's sojourn on his island. This episode also provides a narrative of origin—one of the origin of political rule or the state. Robinson's ingenuity in containing the unruliness, and harnessing the resources, of physical nature has earned him the reputation as the prototype of *homo economicus*. The human domination over raw nature for economic purposes, however, entails political domination. No sooner does Robinson manage to make a living than he speaks of the island as "my little kingdom" (116), of "my Reign" over the island (117). With regard to his livestock, he says: "there was my Majesty the Prince and Lord of the whole Island; I had the Lives of all my Subjects at my absolute Command. I could hang, draw, give Liberty, and take it away, and no Rebels among my Subjects" (125). The rule over territory sets the stage for the rule over men. Friday, the good-natured savage rescued by Robinson, becomes the first human subject of his island kingdom. Chance brings still more subjects to it. Towards the end of the island-episode of the novel, the narrator Robinson concludes with a sense of satisfaction: "My Island was now peopled, and I thought my self very rich in Subjects; and it was a merry Reflection which I frequently made, How like a King I look'd" (203).

As a narrative of the founding of a political society, the island episode resonates with a discordant chorus of political theories. Robinson bases his reign over the island on the fact that he has cultivated it, and the political reign is unambiguously meant to protect, legitimize, and enforce his property rights. For this reason, the narrative seems to illustrate Lockean political theory.[45] But the narrative smacks of Hobbesian theory in its depiction of human interactions on the island. Yearning for human company as he does, Robinson is thunderstruck when he happens to see a human footprint on the shore. Fear reigns in the state of nature. Or as Robinson himself puts it, "What is one Man's Safety, is another Man's Destruction" (157). Only the sovereign authority to which Robinson lays claim grants safety to everyone—of course under the condition that everyone surrenders his natural liberty.[46] Robinson's political language, in the meantime, is borrowed from the absolutist divine-right theory of kingship.[47] But his claim to absolute dominion and indefeasible right over the island rings archly parodic. Robinson first preens himself on being the absolute lord over goats and kids. The chronological correspondence between Robinson's reign on his island—he is stranded on September 30, 1659 and returns to England on June 11, 1687—and the reign of the restored Stuarts on the British Isles is a poignant reminder of the political predicaments and plights of England.[48] Finally, the colonial discourse is inscribed in the narrative of Robinson's cultivation of the island and dominion over its native inhabitants.[49] Modern natural law theorists, including Hobbes and Pufendorf, saw America as the instantiation of the state of nature, so that their construction of the civil state as something that supersedes the state of nature by means of a contract of subjection also served as a theoretical model for the colonial appropriation of the New World by European states.[50] If anything, Robinson's island-state is a colonial state.

Given the conflation of these hardly reconcilable strains of thought, it is perhaps safe to say that *Robinson Crusoe* does not subscribe to any specific political theory. Yet precisely by drawing upon various political theories without subscribing to any of them—a privilege of the poetic imagination—this novel crafts a mythic narrative of the origin of political rule. After twenty-eight years, the desert island where Robinson was shipwrecked and stranded becomes a body politic. Not only does it exercise internal sovereignty through the personal rule of Robinson. It also demonstrates external sovereignty by sending envoys and treating with other peoples in the area: Robinson dispatches the Spaniard—a subject of his—on a diplomatic mission to the mainland, giving him "a strict Charge in Writing," which contains terms of peaceful coexistence (209). He even proves to be a skillful practitioner of "Reasons of State" (225).

Towards the end of the mythic narrative that makes up the island episode of *Robinson Crusoe*, a body politic is founded. Robinson, erstwhile the castaway, asserts himself as its absolute sovereign. In this capacity, he leaves one island kingdom—his own—for another island kingdom: England. The final episode of *Robinson Crusoe*, following upon the central island episode, tells a less gripping story of Robinson settling his business affairs in Europe, after his plantation business in Brazil has continued to prosper during his absence, making him a wealthy man. It picks up the thread of the first episode of the novel again and spins it further, reconnecting the protagonist with his social network forged prior to his sojourn on the island, while reporting the outcome of events during the intervening years. It is a narrative of the ordinary operations of commercial society. This narrative, however, is haunted by the state—that which is established at the end of the second episode. Robinson is now not merely a private businessperson; crowned with the nimbus of an absolute sovereign, he figures also as a political body. Every action that he carries out is in a certain sense also an action of the state. The persons whom he deals with are subjects of different states and are identified as such—the *English* captain's widow, the *Portuguese* captain, and the like. Significantly, the events are set in locales across a number of European states, with the protagonist traveling from England to Portugal and then back again. His decision to "travel all the Way by Land," of course "except from Calais to Dover" (243), helps visualize the existence of individual states, as well as the divisions and connections among them. Perhaps nowhere is the presence of the state more effectively evoked than in the episode of Friday fighting the bear in the mountainous border region between Spain and France on Robinson's return journey from Portugal to England. Apart from its obvious function of amusing the reader at a point where the wonders and excitements animating the story so far are petering out, this entertaining cameo recapitulates the founding of the state by reintroducing a key character in the narrative of foundation—the savage islander Friday—as well as by rehearsing the key action in the narrative of foundation, the human domination of raw nature. Its setting—the border region—highlights the territorial extent of the state. The state thus asserts its presence in commercial society in multiple senses: as a spectral agent of action, as the authority over individual agents of action, and as the territorial space in and across which actions take place. Insofar as this society is haunted by more than one state, it is transnational.

To put it schematically, the first episode of *Robinson Crusoe* provides a founding narrative of commercial society. The second episode provides a founding narrative of political society or the state. The third episode folds what emerges from these two narratives—commercial society and the state—within each other. Taken together, the three episodes combine to constitute yet another founding narrative—that of a transnational commercial society that integrates persons, things, and actions across the territorial spaces of different states, "savage" nations, and uninhabited wildernesses and high seas. Traversing different states as it does, transnational commercial society eludes the coercive legal order of any one state, thus exhibiting a more flexible, more open-ended, and more volatile normative structure. As *Robinson Crusoe* draws to a close, it becomes clear that Robinson's business partners, properties, and obligations spread over England, Portugal, the Portuguese colony Brazil, Spain, his own island kingdom—and potentially many other countries, as he is poised to embark on further adventures. At the same time, however, the agents of action in transnational commercial society are subject to the jurisdiction of the state where they reside or hail from, the properties are subject to the jurisdiction of the state where they are located, and the obligations to the jurisdiction of the state where they are contracted. Its normative structure is therefore less volatile than, or at least different from, that of the international society of states, which has no acknowledged superior authority at all. This normative structure can be called transnational world order.

Roxana

Defoe's novels turn on the figuration of transnational world order in varying ways. His last novel *Roxana* is particularly noteworthy as it throws transnational world order in sharp relief by distinguishing it from a coercive legal order on the one hand, and from international order on the other. The first-person narrator, with the pseudonym Roxana, inhabits a number of transnational spaces. Born in France to a Protestant family and brought to England as her parents "fled for their religion about the Year 1683" (5), she belongs, to begin with, to a transnational religious community—the Huguenots, who were scattered across many European countries.[51] With her father selling "French Brandy, Paper, and other Goods [. . .] very much to Advantage" in England (5), she grows up with transnational commerce. She stumbles into one transnational space after the other, after her husband makes away one day, leaving her with five children and no means with which to care for them. Having disposed of her children in one way or another, she falls in with an English jeweler who brings her along on his business to Paris. After the jeweler is murdered under mysterious circumstances, she becomes the mistress of a foreign prince (who is later identified as German) at the French court and then accompanies him on extended diplomatic missions through Italian cities and principalities on what she calls a "Grand Tour" (102). The prince eventually dissolves the liaison, and she then becomes involved with a Dutch merchant doing business in Paris. Roxana is thus the very figure of transnational sociability, unmoored from the settled courses of life in particular localities and engaged instead in social intercourse across boundaries of nations as well as those of ranks. Transnational sociability can take a number of forms—religious (in the case of her Huguenot parents), commercial (in the case of the English jeweler and the Dutch merchant), diplomatic (in the case of the prince), and military (in the case of her disappeared husband sighted as a soldier in Paris).

Entangled in all of these different types of transnational sociability as she is, Roxana embodies the type that overshadows all the others—the commercial. She is, in her own words, "a Woman of Business, and of great Business too" (131). With canniness and good fortune, she carves out a highly lucrative niche market—companionship for wealthy men—while growing the wealth made on this market by means of smart investment strategies.[52] Roxana's business with her body and charm involves persons from many countries—the English jeweler, the German prince, the Dutch merchant—who, in turn, have their respective business dealings across Europe. The transnational commercial society in which Roxana operates and which her operations help produce functions through written or unwritten contracts between accountable persons. For instance, the jeweler initiates a relationship with Roxana with a contract: "He shew'd me a Contract in Writing, wherein he engag'd himself to me; to cohabit constantly with me; to provide for me in all Respects as a Wife; and repeating in the Preamble, a long Account of the Nature and Reason of our living together, and an Obligation in the Penalty of 7000 l. never to abandon me; and at last, shew'd me a Bond for 500 l. to be paid to me, or to my Assigns, within three Months after his Death" (42). In such contractual relationships, the national origins of the contracting parties are irrelevant. Even the name, the signifier for the identity of the person concerned, seems to matter little. None of the main characters in *Roxana* are named. Not even the real name of the protagonist is ever told, for Roxana is a mere pseudonym. It is with pseudonyms—exchangeable masks—that she can move from one powerful man to another, from one country to another, thereby achieving enormous success. Her daughter, desperate for a connection with the human being behind the masks, says: "I know my Lady's Name and Family very well; *Roxana* was not her Name, that's true indeed" (289).

Constituted as it is through contractual relationships across borders, transnational commercial society exceeds the coercive jurisdictions of particular states. Perhaps nothing illustrates this better than Roxana's escape from France. After her relationship with the prince comes to an end, she decides to settle her business in Paris. The jewelry she owns is recognized by a Jew as the property of the murdered English jeweler. A legal case looms large. The contract offered to her by the English jeweler has certainly served her purpose very well. Yet it is anything but a marital contract. Noticing the murkiness of her relationship to the English jeweler, the Jew threatens to report her to the French authority. However, she succeeds in fleeing France and thereby eschewing a coercive domestic legal order with the help of a series of complex cross-border commercial transactions—transactions carefully coordinated by the Dutch merchant, her man after the prince (121).

In evading or undercutting the domestic legal order, transnational commercial society resembles the international society of states. Having shown the working of transnational commercial society by tracing the protagonist's dealings with a slew of wealthy men, *Roxana* proceeds to address a number of issues pertaining to its normative structure, above all the issues of contract and personhood. These issues indicate the linkages as well as the differences between the transnational and the international world order.

As the Dutch merchant sues her for marriage, the protagonist of *Roxana* contrasts the specific kind of contractual relationship between a courtesan and her keeper to the laws of matrimony and opts for the former: "I knew that while I was a Mistress, it is customary for the Person kept, to receive from them that keep; but if I shou'd be a Wife, all I had then, was given up to the husband, and I was thenceforth to be under his Authority only; and as I had Money enough, and needed not fear being what they call a *cast-off Mistress*, so I had no need to give him twenty Thousand Pound to marry me, which had been buying my Lodging too dear a great deal" (144).

The first-person narrator defends a contractual relationship that has a number of distinctive features. First, it concerns the two contracting parties only, neither involving a higher authority watching over the performance of the contract such as the church or the magistracy in the case of a marriage contract, nor implying a potential third party such as "the legal Posterity" established by a marriage (151). Serving exclusively to satisfy the respective interests of the contracting parties, it can be canceled with impunity whenever one party no longer needs it. It is a nonenforceable contract between seller and buyer. In the narrator's unsentimental words with regard to her relationship to the Dutch merchant, "So I granted him the Favour, as he call'd it, to balance the Account of Favours receiv'd from him, and keep the thousand Pistoles with a good Grace" (144). Insofar as such a contractual relationship is not enforceable by law, it is tantamount to "unlawful Freedoms" (145). Second, the two contracting parties in this relationship are equal to each other, as opposed to the subordination of the wife to the husband in a marriage. The narrator observes repeatedly that "a Woman gave herself entirely away from herself, in Marriage, and capitulated only to be, at best, but an *Upper-Servant*" (147–48). Third, the parties enter into this contractual relationship by voluntary consent, and they retain their freedom once it is established. "I thought," says the narrator, "a Woman was a free Agent, as well as a Man, and was born free, and cou'd she manage herself suitably, might enjoy that Liberty to as much Purpose as the Men do" (147). A marriage may be entered into by voluntary consent, but after it is sealed, the wife must give up her liberty to the man. Finally, the contracting parties are independent in their decision-making: "While a Woman was single, she was a Masculine in her politick Capacity; that she had then the full Command of what she had, and the full Direction of what she did; that she was a Man in her separated Capacity, to all Intents and Purposes that a Man cou'd be so to himself" (148). Taken together, the first-person narrator's characterization of courtesanship—an unenforceable contractual relationship between equal, free, and independent persons, in contrast to the enforceable marriage contract that entails inequality, subordination, and dependency—amounts to an outline of the normative structure of transnational commercial society. Such a contractual relationship seems to be hardly distinguishable from a treaty between sovereign states, for sovereign states insist on nothing more than their equality, freedom, and independence, and treaties between them are not enforceable for lack of a universally acknowledged superior authority. Courtesanship practiced and validated by the narrator's successful career seems to offer a model for international order.

CHAPTER SIX

The mode in which courtesanship—a contractual relationship characteristic of transnational commercial society at large—bears on international order becomes clear in the masquerade episode in the middle of the novel. After she escapes the threat of legal troubles in Paris, the first-person narrator settles in London, having become extraordinarily wealthy by her dealings with wealthy men, and becoming all the wealthier through clever investment. Her ambition soars under these circumstances, aiming to become nothing less than the mistress of the king. At the lavish masked balls mounted at her city lodging, she appears "in the Habit of *a Turkish Princess*" (173)—a habit acquired on her "Grand Tour" in the company of the prince some years back. She acquires the nickname Roxana (176). "Roxana" is a generic name for oriental queens in dramas of the late seventeenth and eighteenth centuries. At the height of her career, the first-person narrator assumes the persona of the queen. In the meantime, the real king is supposed to be present at the masquerades and may have danced with Roxana, although this cannot be confirmed definitely, since everyone is masked (288). An oriental queen meets the king of England—the masquerade at Roxana's lodging produces an illusion of the international stage. This episode highlights the vital issue of personhood. As a courtesan—the epitome of the businessperson—the protagonist is a private person engaging in commercial contracts. As such, she remains anonymous, a placeholder in the web of contractual relationships making up transnational commercial society. The masquerade turns her into the oriental queen Roxana. The queen is a public person, embodying the state. Named Roxana, however, this public person is a fictional and theatrical mask hiding a private person. The king—identified as Charles II of England by the full title of the novel—is a public person embodying the state. By attending the balls of a courtesan and even dancing with her, the king of England merges into the society of private persons, turning into a private person himself. But such a private person is a mere mask hiding a public person. Roxana's masquerade thus stages a metamorphosis of the private into the public person and vice versa.

Masquerade was a favorite entertainment at the English court in the early seventeenth century. Staged annually to celebrate the Stuart dynasty before it was brought to an end by the Civil War, court masques were spectacles of state, displaying and legitimating absolutist kingship.[53] In such spectacles, the state usually appeared as an allegorical person. By representing interactions between allegorical persons, masques can perform the important function of visualizing international order.[54] Held at a wealthy courtesan's city lodging and resembling more the popular masquerades in eighteenth-century London, which were attended by people from all ranks of society and associated with the carnivalesque transgression of various social boundaries, than the court masques, the masquerades in *Roxana* can be seen as a travesty of spectacles of state, crossing the boundary between public and private.[55] Or perhaps they can be more appropriately characterized as games of deception. As a courtesan, the anonymous protagonist is a private person belonging to and embodying transnational commercial society. As the oriental queen Roxana, however, she assumes the appearance of a public person, supposedly dancing with another public person—the king of England—and thereby simulating an international society. It is an international society suffused with the character of dramatic theater, which the generic name Roxana carries. Conversely, the king of England is a public person invested with external sovereignty and representing a member of international society. Dancing with a courtesan, however, he assumes the appearance of a private person and merges into the transnational commercial society that she embodies—a transnational commercial society haunted by the putative presence of the sovereign state that the king himself stands for. The game of deception between being and appearance, set to work by the mask or theatrical persona, refers the private person and the public person to each another, and precisely in so doing, distinguishes them from each other. Accordingly, the normative structure of transnational commercial society (the web of contractual relationships among private persons) points to international world order (the web of contractual relationships among sovereign public persons called states) without ever converging with it.

Sentimental World Order (Gellert, Sterne)

The life stories of dauntlessly enterprising individuals told by Defoe's novels validate the values and norms of a nascent transnational commercial society. Interestingly enough, as commercial society progressed in the course of the eighteenth century, it receded into the background in the novel. In novels of the mid-century, commerce in the sense of exchange of goods and services was gradually overshadowed by what the narrator of Laurence Sterne's *A Sentimental Journey* refers to as "sentimental commerce."[56] The term "sentimental" emerged in the 1740s to articulate the dynamic interrelation between internal impulses of passion and externally held opinions, between emotions and principles, between feelings and norms. Along with the noun "sentiment" and other cognate terms, it came to designate a new ethical disposition that located the foundation of moral norms in the affective nature of man.[57] In close association with this ethical disposition, the "sentimental" emerged as a literary mode that aimed to represent the social bond and normative order as the outcome of internal, affective impulses. The sentimental mode can be found across forms and genres, but it was especially through the novel that it came to fruition.[58] The sentimental novel that flourished in the mid-eighteenth century was concerned with normative order, and this concern had a direct bearing on the question of international world order.

Moral Sentimentalism

Crucial to the sentimental mode in literature was the moral sense theory. Taking issue with the conception of human nature in Hobbes and others of his ilk, moral sense theorists saw sociability and benevolence instead of the individual struggle for existence in the state of nature. Above all, they believed it was possible to detect in human nature an affective capacity for social bonding and normative order. For Shaftesbury, the founder of moral sense theory, every motive to action involves affection or passion, for reason alone cannot motivate. We humans are conscious of, and reflect on, our affections, liking some of them and disliking others. The capacity for feeling like or dislike towards our affections—a second-order affection, as it were—is called by Shaftesbury the sense of right or wrong, or moral sense. While arguing that moral judgments and human virtue involve affections, Shaftesbury also insists that there is an objective, immutable normative order determining what is right and what is wrong: what promotes the well-being of humanity is right, and what harms the well-being of humanity is wrong. Right and wrong are "eternal Measures," independent of the human mind.[59]

The happy marriage established by Shaftesbury between affections and norms, between subjective disposition and objective world order dissolved soon after him. In *A Treatise of Human Nature*, Hume declares war against "the system, which establishes eternal rational measures of right and wrong," maintaining that " morality is more properly felt than judg'd of."[60] The keyword in Hume's moral theory is sympathy—a psychological mechanism that enables one person to receive by communication the feelings or sentiments of another person. Observation of another person's condition and its outward expression in words, countenance, or body conveys an idea of that person's passion into the spectator's mind. Because of the resemblance and contiguity between the observed person and the spectator, the idea of an observed person's passion becomes an impression in the mind of the spectator, so that the spectator actually experiences this passion. Observing that a certain trait or action tends to produce happiness in people, the spectator takes sympathetic pleasure in this happiness, which finds expression in approval. The trait that elicits the spectator's approval is called virtue. Conversely, observing that a certain trait or action tends to cause pain in people, the spectator shares this pain sympathetically, which finds expression in disapproval. The trait that elicits disapproval is vice.

The sympathetic transmission of sentiments, of course, concerns only the actual sentiments of an observed person. Our moral judgments, in contrast, are meant to be universal. For this reason, Hume argues that we make our moral judgments not from our individual points of view, but from a common point of view.[61] In order to reach a common perspective, we need to acquaint ourselves with the individual perspectives of all the people who interact directly with the person being evaluated. This entails sympathizing imaginatively with each and every one of these people in their dealings with the subject of our evaluation. Furthermore, since vicissitudes of fortune may render a trait more or less effectual or even hinder a trait from being effectual at all, we must acquaint ourselves with all possible circumstances and imagine how people would feel if a trait were able to operate under ordinary circumstances. The praise or blame that we feel towards our subject of evaluation is ultimately the result of such imaginative exercises. In sum, Hume's moral sentimentalism implies a conception of human society as an affective community bound together by sympathy. With sympathy extending imaginatively to all individuals and all circumstances, the emotional bond forged by it assumes a universal valence and normative character.

In a decisive theoretical step that moves far beyond Hume, Adam Smith conceives of sympathy no longer in terms of the one-directional transmission of passions from one person to another, but as mutual approach, indeed as a recursive loop. While sympathy leads the spectator to look at the situation of the observed person with the eyes of the observed person, sympathy likewise leads the observed person to examine his or her own situation with the eyes of the spectator. By imagining themselves in the situation of the observed person, the spectators move beyond the immediate situation, thus shedding their partiality. At the same time, by imagining how he or she would be affected as the spectator, the observed person also moves beyond the immediate situation, "lowering his passion to that pitch, in which the spectators are capable of going along with him."[62] If both the spectator and the observed person thus transcend their own positions and try to look at things from an imaginary—or rather virtual—third position, both strip their respective passion of its natural tone and thereby reach harmony and concord. This virtual third position is that of "the impartial spectator": "The precise and distinct measure [of moral judgment] can be found nowhere but in the sympathetic feelings of the impartial and well-informed spectator."[63]

Like Hume's moral sentimentalism, Smith's theory of moral sentiments also implies a conception of human society as an affective community bound together through sympathy. But with sympathy now reconceived as an infinite approach to the virtual position of the impartial spectator, the emotional bond—or rather, the emotional "flow"—forged by it can never be something established, only something always in the making, bringing about a self-regulating, emergent normative order.

The sentimental novel emerged in the age of Hume and Smith. Conceiving moral life in terms of observation and spectatorship, the moral sentimentalists could not help taking a great interest in literature. For Hume, "a very play or romance may afford us instances of this pleasure, which virtue conveys to us; and pain, which arises from vice."[64] Speaking of sympathy, Smith states, "Our joy for the deliverance of those heroes of tragedy or romance who interest us, is as sincere as our grief for their distress, and our fellow-being with their misery is not more real than that with their happiness."[65] The literary form most suitable for playing out the working of moral sentiments turned out to be the novel. Beginning with Samuel Richardson's *Pamela*, published in 1740, the same year as Hume's *A Treatise of Human Nature*, the novel turned to the questions addressed by moral sense theorists, including especially those of emotion, moral judgment, and sympathy.[66] Novelistic texts dealing with such questions—the sentimental novel—add flesh and blood, proper names and circumstantial details, and above all infinite variations and complexities to the theoretical propositions of Hume or Smith. They feature fictional characters deeply engaged in the affective lives of one another. Narrators, usually doubling as protagonists, observe, sympathize with, and evaluate the characters and their behavior, while readers observe, sympathize with, and evaluate the narrators as well as the other characters.

By staging the multilayered observation, sympathy, and evaluation among characters, narrators, and readers, the sentimental novel evokes a community that is at once affective and moral—affective insofar as it is constituted through the sympathetic transmission and circulation of feelings, and moral insofar as feelings serve as the basis of moral evaluation. It can thus be characterized as a sentimental community. The sentimental community claims to be the universal community of humankind. It is the overarching assumption of literary as well as philosophical sentimentalism that the affective faculty is common to all humans, that feeling is a universal language, and that sympathy is the defining feature of humanity. "Sympathy with distress," in the words of an eighteenth-century writer, "is thought so essential to human nature, that the want of it has been called inhumanity."[67] As such, sympathy transcends all the differences in the human world, be they differences in language, nationality, political and legal status, social rank, or kinship relations.

The universal character of the sentimental community has much to do with the medium of writing. The eighteenth century witnessed the spread of literacy and the expansion of the book market. The sentimental novel was fashioned by this media-historical situation to a great extent.[68] It usually features a letter-writing first-person narrator, who describes in painstaking details all the intricacies, all the twists and turns of feelings; and it always takes the form of a book offered to the reading public. In contrast to physical presence in face-to-face communication, the medium of writing gives free rein to the imagination, thus enabling individuals to sympathize with persons anywhere in time and space, persons either real or fictional. The community of sympathy mediated by writing, then, knows neither bounds nor boundaries.

In its universality, the sentimental community performs a number of political functions. A scholar speaks of the "politics of tears"—the fluid that serves as the glue of such a community.[69] Cutting across national boundaries, the sentimental community is transnational in scope.[70] Insofar as sympathy on the global level often involves the people in the metropole as subjects and those in the colonies as objects, the sentimental community constituted by it at once reveals and conceals the power structure of empire.[71] Among its many political functions, the sentimental community also serves as a model of international order. Christian Fürchtegott Gellert's novel *Leben der Schwedischen Gräfinn von G**** (1747–48) stands as a good example in this regard.

Gellert's *Leben der Schwedischen Gräfinn von G****

Gellert (1715–69) was a key representative of sentimentalism in the German Enlightenment.[72] Published at around the same time as Richardson's massive *Clarissa*, Gellert's *Leben der Schwedischen Gräfinn von G**** is a relatively short novel with a convoluted plot about the marriage, separation, and reunion of the eponymous first-person narrator and her husband.[73] The orphaned daughter of a Livonian nobleman, the first-person narrator moves to Sweden to marry the Count von G***. Their marital bliss, however, proves to be short-lived. The count is an officer in the Swedish army. After having lost a battle in the war between Sweden and Poland, he is sentenced to death by martial law. The real reason for the sentence, as the first-person narrator tells us, lies somewhere else: the countess has angrily rebuffed the amorous advances by the powerful Prince von S** during her husband's absence, and now the prince finds a pretext for taking revenge. Heartbroken at the news of her husband's death, and afraid of being pestered further by the prince, the countess flees Sweden together with her husband's best friend Herr R**, bound for Holland. There she marries Herr R** and is later joined by her husband's former mistress Caroline. The countess had met Caroline back in Sweden and took a great liking to her, despite the fact that the latter had previously borne two children to the count out of wedlock. Joined together by fate, the countess, her husband's best friend, and her husband's former mistress, as well as their children, relatives, and friends, form a large, loving family.

Their contented life, however, is upset by an extraordinary event: one day the countess's husband shows up again. As it turns out, the count did not die. Three days prior to the date of execution, he was captured by the Russian army and, under a pseudonym, taken to Russia. The second part of *Leben der Schwedischen Gräfinn von G**** tells the story of the count's captivity in Siberia, which revolves around friendships with an English inmate by the name of Steeley, a Polish Jew doing business in the area where the prison is located, and Amalia, the wife of the provincial governor in charge of the prison. In due time, all of these friends who sympathized with the count when he was in distress come to visit him in Holland, joining the expanding sentimental community. Towards the end of the novel, the count and countess, whose marriage is now renewed, go to England to visit Steeley's father. There they encounter, by coincidence, their erstwhile enemy Prince von S**, who is on a diplomatic mission in London. Partly due to the agitation caused by this encounter, the count dies soon afterwards, followed by the death of his best friend Herr R**.

This cursory plot summary indicates the vast span of the space in which the actions of the novel take place—a space ranging from Siberia to London, from the Baltic countries of Livonia, Sweden, and Poland to the maritime commercial centers in Holland. The characters acting in this vast space hail from European countries big and small, with some (like Caroline's brother Andreas) having gathered experiences in the overseas colonies. The novelistic narrative centers upon the working of sympathy across political borders and social ranks. The community constituted through sympathy—the sentimental community—is thus transnational in nature. This transnational, emotionally bonded community provides an alternative to, as well as a normative ideal for, the international world of states.

The plot of Gellert's novel unfolds against the background of a tumultuous international world of states. Diplomacy, the key institutional framework for orderly international relations, is apparently not working. The count's father was, once upon a time, the Swedish king's envoy to Russia, but he certainly did not prevent the war between Sweden and Russia from continuing and his son from being captured by Russians and humiliated on a street of the Russian capital. The count laments, "In precisely the city, in which my father enjoyed in his youth the honor of a royal envoy, I was a worthless Swede, and perhaps on the same square where his ceremonial entry took place, his son was exposed to the rage of a woman" (48). The English ambassador in Stockholm, mentioned numerous times, seems to accomplish just as little. The international world is locked in endless wars. War, however, proves to be crucial to the narrative. To a certain extent, the turbulent uncertainty created by the war fuels and propels the plot. More importantly, war mobilizes sympathy. It provides the occasion for the sympathetic bonding between the countess and the count's best friend Herr R**, which eventually leads to the making of a sentimental community. The capture of the count by the Russian army and the ensuing captivity in Siberia, in the meantime, trigger the operation of sympathy in another setting and the making of another sentimental community. It is thanks to this sentimental community that the count could endure the pain of captivity and eventually escape this captivity. Although "the war with the Russians and Swedes was still going on," the sympathy of the governor's wife Amalia towards the count secures his release (65). In due time, the sentimental community in Siberia merges with the one in Holland. In short, the death and distress caused by war sets sympathy to work and generates a universal sentimental community that offers solace and relief, while implicitly also leveling an indictment against war. Provoked into being in times of war, yet suggesting the possibility of overcoming it, the sentimental community represents a normative ideal for the international world—something that can be characterized as a sentimental world order.

Something so important deserves a closer look. To begin with, it is worth noting that the sentimental community transcends the law. The treatment of the law of matrimony is exemplary in this regard. In the early stage of Gellert's novel, the protagonist and first-person narrator discovers, to her surprise, that her husband used to have a mistress by the name of Caroline and even fathered a son with her. But after learning that the count was in fact in love with Caroline and that he could not marry her because of her status, the countess takes pity on her rival and befriends her. Later on, in the belief that her husband has died, the countess marries his best friend Herr R**. After her husband unexpectedly comes back alive, she leaves Herr R** and renews her previous marriage, but the reunited couple bonds even more strongly with Herr R**, rather than excluding him. In the meantime,

Carlson, the illegitimate son of Caroline and the count, falls in love and marries a girl by the name of Mariane—who turns out to be his sister. The discovery of the incest causes horror and distress. Yet precisely for this reason, it brings the sentimental community even more closely together. Clearly, the making of the sentimental community defies the law of matrimony. Indeed, it is made possible partly by the violation of the law of matrimony, for the emotional turmoil and distress incited by the violation of the law stirs up sympathy. A much more pernicious breach of law proves to have the same effect: Dormund, Carlson's comrade in the army, covets Mariane, and kills Carlson in order to possess her. Even such a craven murder activates sympathy and fortifies the sentimental community: "We had to hate him [Dormund] as a murderer," says the narrator, "yet the general love of mankind joined us also in sympathy" (35).

Second, the making of the sentimental community presupposes and displaces the commercial economy. Sympathizing with one another requires leisure. After arriving in Holland, the countess turns her jewelry into capital investment. "Our small investments," the narrator informs us, "almost doubled in value within six years in trade" (22). As a result of the financial security achieved through capital investment, the narrator continues, "we lived without either commanding or obeying others. We were not accountable to anyone else than ourselves. We had more than we desired, and hence enough to do good to others. We kept company with people according to our inclinations" (23). The sentimental community is possible only if a functioning commercial economy frees certain people from the necessity of work and allows them to indulge in the luxury of trading feelings with one another. It is the affective spin-off from the commercial economy. Once brought into being by the commercial economy, the sentimental community deliberately suspends the logic of commercial exchange by doling out wealth to others without expecting material gain in turn. For instance, with his wealth growing day by day on the capital market, the count "inquired about miserable and unfortunate persons, in a word, the poor, the sick, and prisoners [. . .]" (70). Instead of commercial advantages, philanthropy generates feelings and quickens sympathy, thereby strengthening the sentimental community. The sentimental community is thus a product of and an alternative to commercial society at the same time.[74]

Defying the law and constituted by the transgression of the law, the sentimental community is a normative order that is nonjuridical in nature, or that relates to the juridical only insofar as the juridical is suspended. Enabled by the commercial economy yet ostentatiously going beyond it at the same time, the sentimental community is not commercial either. As a normative ideal for the international world, it challenges both the juridical and the economic approach to world order as represented by international law and economics respectively. It derives its normativity and universality from a conception of the human condition that is more fundamental than both law and commerce. The most fundamental human condition is mortality. In Gellert's novel, death occurs with frightening frequency, carrying off the large cast of characters one after the other, with the narrator seeming to be the only surviving person at the end. Every so often, one gets the impression that the narrator introduces new characters only to deliver them to their deaths a couple of pages later. This morbid impulse in the plot construction has something to do with the emotional capital that can be made out of death. The death of a family member or a friend causes so much distress that it is sure to elicit sympathy and enable emotional bonding. The sentimental community in *Das Leben der Schwedischen Gräfin* is built on the dead bodies of those dearest to its members.[75]

Gellert's novel ends on the death of the two male protagonists equally dear to the first-person narrator: the Count von G*** and Herr von R***. The two deaths, occurring in rapid succession, prompt the reader to sympathize with the narrator, thus creating a sentimental community made up of readers. This sentimental community of readers is also transnational in scope, just as the one portrayed in the novel is. Although the novel was written in German, it was soon translated into other languages—into French as *La comtesse suédoise, ou Mémoires* (1754), into Polish as *Przypadki Szwedzkiey Hrabiny G*** (1755), into English as *The History of the Swedish Countess of G** (1755) and again as *The History of the Swedish Countess of Guildenstern* (1757), and into Dutch as *Charlotta of de gevallen eener Zweedsche Gravinne* (1760). The translation into multiple languages was by no means unique to Gellert's novel. In fact, crucial to the emergence of the novel was its circulation across languages in translation, and this was particularly true of the sentimental novel.[76] Translation brought the sentimental novel to readers across linguistic and political borders, lending a transnational scope to the sentimental community constituted through the readers' sympathy with the characters and narrators.

As a community based on the mutual recognition of one another's humanity, the sentimental community was also acknowledged by international lawyers as a normative ideal. In his *Droit des Gens*, published in 1758, Emer de Vattel postulates an original sympathy in the state of nature. Men are meant by nature "to live together (*converser ensemble*) and mutually to aid and assist one another." This original sympathy constitutes a universal community, which he calls the natural society of mankind.[77] Since by the logic of natural jurisprudence sovereign states are to be considered free persons living together in the state of nature, they are bound to sympathize with one another as well. The sympathy between states gives rise to a great international society. "The end of the great society established by nature among all nations is likewise that of mutual assistance in order to perfect themselves and their condition."[78]

Sentimentalism and Diplomacy

As a normative ideal for the international world, the sentimental community configured by the novel proved to be rather short-lived. Two decades after *Das Leben der Schwedischen Gräfin*, Laurence Sterne (1713–68) published an idiosyncratic text that was to go down in literary history as the consummate expression of the sentimental novel: *A Sentimental Journey Through France and Italy by Mr. Yorick*. It is precisely in this text, however, that the sentimental world order unravels. The actions of Sterne's novel take place in a transnational space, as already indicated by the title.[79] And the plot, just like that of Gellert's novel, unfolds against the background of war. Midway in the novel, the first-person narrator mentions that he needs to get a passport because his country, England, is at war with France. Yet unlike in Gellert's novel, the sympathy that the first-person narrator, Mr. Yorick, has been cultivating all along fails to offer a normative ideal beyond the war. It offers, at best, a self-indulgent escape from the violence convulsing the international world: "I had left London with so much precipitation, that it never enter'd my mind that we were at war with France" (67–68). One needs to look no further than the beginning and the end of the novel to find out why this is so: sentimental sympathy is similar to—hence just as ineffective as—the art of diplomacy in creating a normative order.

At the beginning of *A Sentimental Journey*, the narrator compares himself, in a tone wavering between mockery and affection, to a sovereign monarch—a comparison culminating in the hypothetical identification, "Now, was I a King of France, cried I" (4). The sentimental sympathy that he indulges in—entering sympathetically into the situations of others, as well as reflecting on his own actions from the point of view not his own—seems to be little different from treaty-making as the main mode of interaction between sovereigns: "I was at peace with the world before, and this finish'd the treaty with myself" (4). The final episode of the novel, in which the narrator finds himself in the delicate situation of having to share a room for the night with a foreign lady, plays out the metaphorical equation between sentimental sympathy and diplomatic negotiation of a treaty: "We turn'd it every way, and debated and considered it in all kind of lights in the course of a two hours negociation; at the end of which the articles were settled finally betwixt us, and stipulated for in form and manner of a treaty of peace—and I believe with as much religion and good faith on both sides, as in any treaty which as yet had the honour of being handed down to posterity" (123). There follows a facetious enumeration of the various articles, provisos, and the like.

That Sterne's narrative of sentimental sympathy culminates in the extended metaphor of diplomatic negotiation and treaty-making is not mere whimsical humor. Eighteenth-century manuals on diplomacy describe negotiation as an exercise in observation that very much resembles the operation of sympathy as conceived by moral sentimentalists. In his *De la manière de négocier avec les souverains* (1716), a classic text of diplomatic theory, François de Callières stresses the importance for a negotiator to find out, through observation, "the sentiments and designs of those with whom he treats": the negotiator "governs his discourses and his conduct according to what he discovers, partly by the responses that are made him, and partly by the motions of their countenance; by the tone and air with which they speak, and by all the other circumstances which may contribute to enable him to penetrate into the thoughts and designs of whose with whom he treats. And after having made a discovery of the disposition of their minds, of their capacity, of the state of the affairs, their passions, and their interests, he makes use of this knowledge to lead him by degree to the goal that he aims at."[80] Antoine Pecquet's *Discours sur l'art de négocier* (1737), another important treatise on diplomatic theory, opens with the remark that human society in general works through "continuous negotiation." Just as sovereign states interact with one another through diplomatic negotiations, the interaction between private persons is "a daily commerce in objects, views and wishes."[81] In interacting with a man, "my first step is to get to know him and to acquaint myself with his innermost thoughts, in order to learn the way to please him and to inspire in him the same inclination toward me that I believe I feel toward him. Everything is thus, so to speak, commerce or negotiation in life."[82] Diplomatic theorists see negotiation in a similar way as moral sentimentalists see sympathy. Both diplomatic negotiation and sentimental sympathy involve observing the other and observing one's own actions imaginatively from the point of view of another. This structural similarity underlies the sentimental traveler Mr. Yorick's account of his interaction with the foreign lady in the final episode of *A Sentimental Journey* in terms of international treaty-making.

Sterne's metaphorical equation between sentimental sympathy and diplomatic negotiation highlights the potential of the sentimental novel for engaging with the problem of international order. But it suggests that sympathy may achieve just as little as diplomatic negotiation does in reality. Just as international treaties are intrinsically fragile for lack of a mutually acknowledged superior to enforce them, the foreign lady soon warns Mr. Yorick against "an infraction of the treaty" (124). There is a constant fear that "hostilities would ensue" (125). As the iconic text of the sentimentalist vogue, *A Sentimental Journey* exhibits, as a literary historian points out, "the failure of feeling": "Sterne was offering his audience a text in which sentimental tastes were at one level amply catered for, but at another level mocked as shallow and self-deluding, and subjected to implicit critique."[83] It certainly marks the failure of feeling to serve as the principle of world order.

Cosmopolitan World Order (Wieland, Goethe, Kant)

A year before the publication of Sterne's *A Sentimental Journey* unleashed a sentimental vogue across Europe, Christoph Martin Wieland (1733–1813) published, in two installments, a lengthy novel under the title of *Geschichte des Agathon*—a novel that was to be considered one of the foundational texts of the *Bildungsroman*. The concept of the *Bildungsroman* was an invention of the nineteenth century, used by Wilhelm Dilthey (1833–1911) to refer to the novels concerned with "the human development in various stages, shapes, and life phases," which "make up the school of *Wilhelm Meister*."[84] Since Dilthey, literary historians have often regarded Wieland's *Geschichte des Agathon* as a precursor of Goethe's (1749–1832) *Wilhelm Meisters Lehrjahre*. By means of their characteristic plot structure as well as other formal devices, both novels depict the making of an individual person who is qualified to serve as the rightful subject of the great society of humanity as a whole. In so doing, they underwrite a world order that holds the greatest appeal for our time—the cosmopolitan world order. If one had to pinpoint the birth hour of modern cosmopolitanism, it must have been sometime around 1795. It was in that year that Immanuel Kant published his treatise *Zum ewigen Frieden*, in which the modern idea of a cosmopolitan world order finds its most powerful expression. A year earlier, Wieland issued the definitive version of *Geschichte des Agathon*, which significantly expanded on the first version of 1766/67 as well as the second version of 1773. In the same year, Goethe published *Wilhelm Meisters Lehrjahre*. Kantian cosmopolitanism postulates a rights-bearing human subject who acts as both the citizen of a particular state and the citizen of the world at large. The two novels by Wieland and Goethe offer, for their part, a narrative of the genesis of this new cosmopolitan subject.

The Birth of the Cosmopolitan Subject in Wieland's Agathon Project

The narrative of *Geschichte des Agathon* is set in classical Greece. Apart from the apparent Philhellenism, this historical setting provides a convenient vehicle for representing the international world. The ancient world of Greek city-states resembles the modern world of sovereign states in that neither has a commonly acknowledged superior. Thucydides's *History of the Peloponnesian War*, which recounts the wars and shifting alliances in the world of Greek city-states in the fifth century BCE, has always served as a reference book for the theorists and practitioners of international relations in modern times. It was no accident that Thomas Hobbes translated Thucydides in the early seventeenth century and used his book as a manual for understanding the sovereign state and the relation between sovereign states.[85] The main episodes of the *Geschichte des Agathon* are associated with a number of independent polities scattered across the entire ancient Greek world: Athens, Smyrna (in Asia Minor), Syracuse (on Sicily), and Tarentum (in southern Italy). Together with the cultic site Delphi where the eponymous hero is educated in his early youth, these far-flung locales combine to evoke a large world not so different from the international world of the eighteenth century. The narrator's constant references to the present time—for instance the comparison between the slave market in Smyrna with that on Barbados—further illustrate the correspondence between the historical setting and the modern international world of European states and their overseas colonies.[86]

If the setting of *Geschichte des Agathon* evokes an international world, then the novel's plot manages to configure a normative order of this world. With a similarly international setting and a cast of characters hailing from many countries, Gellert's *Das Leben der Schwedischen Gräfin von G**** depicts sympathy as the universal bond of humanity. *Geschichte des Agathon* develops a rather different model. Sympathy, embodied by the protagonist in his youthful days, appears to be something that is commendable but ultimately alien to the ways of the world. Wieland's novel depicts rather how the protagonist learns the ways of the world in different polities. Each polity featured in the novel represents one station in the learning process: in Athens Agathon learns how democratic politics works; in Smyrna he learns how love works; in Syracuse he learns how monarchical politics works. Agathon's journey through life is a journey through the international world. Accordingly, the person that the protagonist becomes at the end stands for a general idea of the international world. In Tarentum, the final station on Agathon's journey, we see that the individual who has learned the ways of the world, gathered life experiences and fully developed his personality is a person who qualifies as the subject of universal laws. In this capacity, he stands for a normative world order that applies to individual persons as well as polities, a world order that can be characterized as cosmopolitan. The cosmopolitan idea is hinted at in the 1767 version of *Geschichte des Agathon*, and then elaborated systematically in the 1794 version. More important, in this final version of the novel, the cosmopolitan idea and the narrative of the development of the individual person are keyed in with each other, with the narrative of the development of the individual person now serving as the founding narrative of the cosmopolitan idea, and with the cosmopolitan idea serving as the goal of the narrative.

The three decades separating the first and the third versions of *Geschichte des Agathon*—the last third of the eighteenth century—was a period in which the ancient philosophical idea of cosmopolitanism or world citizenship was revived and reconceived.[87] The term "cosmopolitan" can be dated back to the fourth century BCE, ascribed to the Cynic philosopher Diogenes of Sinope. When asked about his origin, he answered: "I am a citizen of the world."[88] With this answer he seemed to mean that he did not belong to any particular polis. Such a rejection of any allegiance to a particular city represented a negative conception of world citizenship. In ancient cosmopolitan traditions, however, there was also a positive conception of world citizenship, mostly associated with the Stoics.[89] The positive conception presupposed a commitment to human society beyond the confines of the city-state, affirming moral obligations to humans anywhere in the world on the ground that all human beings participate in reason and hence share law and justice. Zeno of Citium (c. 334–262 BCE), the founder of Stoicism, was reputed to argue that "our household arrangements should not be based on cities or parishes, each one marked out by its own legal system, but we should regard all men as our fellow-citizens and local residents, and there should be one way of life and order, like that of a herd grazing together and nurtured by a common law."[90] Later Stoics advocated a kind of dual citizenship, maintaining that an individual human being could be a member of the cosmos and a member of a particular political community at the same time. Seneca (c. 4 BCE–65 CE), for instance, said, "Let us grasp the idea that there are two commonwealths—the one, a vast and truly common state, which embraces alike gods and men, in which we look neither to this corner of earth nor to that, but measure the bounds of our citizenship by the path of the sun; the other, the one to which we have been assigned by the accident of birth. This will be the commonwealth of the Athenians or of the Carthaginians, or of any other city that belongs, not to all, but some particular race of men."[91]

Wieland was a key figure in reviving ancient cosmopolitanism and developing it into a modern idea in the late eighteenth century. His novels *Sokrates Mainomenos oder die Dialogen des Diogenes von Sinope* (1770) and *Die Abderiten* (1774), both set in ancient Greece, illustrate the main tenets of cosmopolitanism. His extensive journalistic writings bring these tenets to bear on the intense political debates of the time.[92] In the 1794 version of *Geschichte des Agathon*, completed in the wake of the French Revolution, the tenets of cosmopolitanism are elaborated yet again, this time in the form of the "life wisdom" of a fictional character, namely the Tarentine sage Archytas.[93] The core of Archytas's discourse is the idea of world citizenship. In a vocabulary that sounds Stoic—although he is supposed to belong to the Pythagorean school—Archytas emphasizes the rational nature of man. Because reason is the principle of the whole world, man is a member of the whole world (or cosmos) in partnership with God. As a creature endowed with reason, Archytas says, "[I have] the dignity of a citizen of the city of God, which makes me the fellow member of a higher order of things." As a consequence, "I belong neither exclusively to myself, nor to a family, nor to a particular civil society, nor to a single species, not to the place on earth, which I call my fatherland: I belong with all my powers to the larger whole" (404). What Archytas calls the city of God reminds us of Cicero's notion of the whole universe "as a single community shared by gods and men" or Seneca's notion of "vast and truly common state, which embraces alike gods and men."[94] In a move reminiscent of the Stoic argument about man's dual citizenship in the cosmic city and the particular city in which one happens to be born, Archytas then contends that an individual, precisely in his capacity as the citizen of the world, also has obligations towards his fatherland and the people around him, for his fatherland is the place to which he is assigned in the world, and the people around him are his immediate companions in the larger world.

Archytas's presentation of cosmopolitanism, however, is not meant to be a mere reformulation of Stoic doctrines. Rather it is strategically aligned with narration, embedded within the novelistic narrative on the one hand and lending overall coherence and a distinctive structure to the novelistic narrative on the other. Thanks to the strategic positioning of Archytas's presentation, the cosmopolitan idea and the novelistic narrative become formative principles of each other. This positioning has three dimensions.

First, the presentation of cosmopolitanism comes in the wake of the writing, reading, and interpreting of the protagonist's life story (book 16, chaps. 1–2). Reflecting on his past experience, Agathon is gripped by a desire to "commit to paper the *history of his soul* in the various epochs of his life" (361, italics in the original). Archytas reads Agathon's account of his own life story with interest and empathy. Thereupon the two men engage in a conversation about what Agathon has written down. Archytas proves to be a perceptive reader, offering insightful comments on every episode of Agathon's life, which in turn helps Agathon gain a better understanding of himself. Writing down one's life experience is an act of reflection, lending a structure and direction to the past; reading is an act of interpretation, creating a meaningful structure out of the events and characters represented in writing. The dialogue between the author and the reader is an interplay between writing and reading, enacting the final transmutation of the raw material of life into a narrative. The narrative of Agathon's life, of course, is already known to the reader of the novel at this point. The acts of writing, reading, and interpretation as undertaken by the protagonist and his interlocutor perform the function of validating the novelistic narrative. The subjective validation of the novelistic narrative resolves the problem of the probability of the events as presented by the authorial narrator—the problem bedeviling the first version of the novel—for the protagonist and his interlocutor now take the events to be given and seek to make sense of them. The subjective validation also helps lend a direction to the novelistic narrative, ordering the past events into successive stages leading up to their present condition. It is at this point, when Agathon's life has been turned into a subjectively validated narrative of development, that Archytas lays out the tenets of cosmopolitanism. Only the individual person capable of reflecting on and thereby subjectively validating his life can accede to cosmopolitanism.

Second, the presentation of cosmopolitanism follows from Archytas's telling of his own life story, an act that parallels the Agathon's writing of his life story (book 16, chap. 3). Archytas begins by saying that he has arrived at his theory not through book knowledge, but rather through life experience. Archytas's life experience bears a remarkable resemblance to that of Agathon's, shaped likewise by a journey through the international world. Archytas took part in a war between Tarentum and a neighboring country in his youth: "When peace was re-established in my fatherland, I undertook a journey to Greece, Asia and Egypt. I let myself be initiated into the mysteries of Eleusis and Samothrace, and into the secret orders of Isis and Osiris in Sais. And accidentally I made the acquaintance of many philosophers and sophists by profession" (389). By reflecting on his practical experiences as well as the theoretical ideas that he has been exposed to, Archytas becomes a sovereign individual: "I feel myself free, independent, autonomous, and I am not only a legislator and king of a world in myself, but am also capable of making myself the master of my body and of everything else that lies within the borders of my sphere of activities" (393). Such a sovereign individual is not only a citizen of his own country, but also a citizen of the world. The recognition of this sovereignty leads naturally to the cosmopolitan idea. Cosmopolitanism as presented by Archytas is thus no abstract theory, but a "narrated philosophy," or more precisely a philosophy that suggests itself after the individual person has transmuted his life experience into a narrative of development.[95] Archytas's life story is also meant to be a mirror for Agathon. Just as the old sage of Tarentum comes to formulate the main tenets of cosmopolitanism by reflecting on his life experience, Agathon's life journey, once reflected upon and turned into a subjectively validated narrative, should lead to a cosmopolitan philosophy as well. Cosmopolitanism is the *telos* of the novelistic narrative.

Third, the presentation of cosmopolitanism is followed by the protagonist's reenactment and renewed validation of his life journey (book 16, chap. 4). Archytas's philosophy helps Agathon calm down somewhat, but not entirely. He decides to absent himself from Tarentum for a while in order to "[travel] through all the provinces of the known world of that time." Agathon's travel reenacts his life journey. But he is no longer personally attached to what he experiences, remaining instead "a mere spectator of the spectacle of the world" (418). By observing the world, he also gains a sense of perspective about his own life. As a result, cosmopolitanism ceases to be merely an idea for him. He begins to practice it. Agathon returns to Tarentum as a true cosmopolitan—a citizen of the world and at the same time a good citizen of the country in which he lives: he "devoted himself, with pleasure and enthusiasm, to the public affairs of this republic" (424). As this very long novel draws to a close, the reader sees that the life story of Agathon—*Geschichte des Agathon*—is not a linear, but rather a spiraling narrative: there is first the life journey with its many stations, there is then the reflection on and the subjective validation of the life journey, then the intensification of this reflection through the telling of a parallel life story, and finally the reenactment of the life journey and renewed reflection. The spiral culminates in the realization of cosmopolitanism.

In sum, Wieland's novel offers a narrative of the development of the individual person into a cosmopolitan subject. Cosmopolitanism, originally a Stoic idea, triggers an innovation of the novel form: *Geschichte des Agathon* is the first novel featuring a protagonist who goes through many stages in life, constantly reflects on them, and thereby develops an ever more complex personality—a personality that eventually qualifies him to be a citizen of the world. In the *Bildungsroman*, however, cosmopolitanism ceases to be merely an idea of the ancient Stoics. For the Stoics, there is a universally valid world order—the cosmopolis—that encompasses both gods and humans. Man is by nature a citizen of the world because man shares in the common rationality that informs the cosmopolis. In Wieland's novel, the cosmospolis and the rationality informing it are not longer universally acknowledged, but become a matter of subjective disposition—something that an individual person comes to realize after many life experiences and ongoing reflections on these experiences. Man is far from a citizen of the world by nature; he has to become one. Cosmopolitanism, then, turns into a normative ideal. The novel represents an imaginative realization of this ideal.

Making the Cosmopolitan Subject, Making the *Bildungsroman*

In narrating the development of an individual person into a cosmopolitan subject, *Geschichte des Agathon* has recourse to many generic forms of narrative fiction available in the eighteenth century. In fact, every station on the protagonist's life journey is associated with one or more generic forms, so that the development of the individual person into a cosmopolitan subject corresponds to the development of narrative fiction into the novel form meant to represent it—the *Bildungsroman*.

Geschichte des Agathon opens *in medias res* with the protagonist stranded on a foreign coast at the time of sunset. Without knowing where to spend the night, indeed without knowing how his physical survival might be possible, he is surprised by a group of dancing maenads who mistake him—a youth with divinely handsome looks—for the god Bacchus. But the frenzied festival of the bacchantes is interrupted unexpectedly by a horde of pirates who drag Agathon to their ship and sail away. In the pirates' ship, he is surprised to see his beloved Psyche who, overjoyed, recounts what has happened to her. At this point, every reader can see what generic conventions the author is working with—the Greek romance. The beginning of *Geschichte des Agathon* is explicitly modeled on the beginning of Heliodorus's *Aithiopika*, the most influential of Greek romances. Heliodorus's romantic tale opens also *in medias res* with the heroine and the hero stranded on Egyptian shores and in despair about their physical survival, after which they are unexpectedly separated and abducted by bandits. The chaste love between Agathon and Psyche, which germinated in the sacred groves of Delphi, as well as the setting of the story in the classical period of Greece, are both reminiscent of *Aithiopika*.

Agathon is unexpectedly separated from Psyche again—another plot element borrowed from the Greek romance—and then sold on the slave market of Smyrna to a Sophist named Hippias. From here on, *Geschichte des Agathon* leaves behind the generic mold of the Greek romance. The initially fast-paced plot is slowed down by philosophical dialogues between Agathon, advocate of a part theosophical, part Platonic idealism, and Hippias, representative of French materialism in the garb of an ancient Sophist. This part of the novel stands in the tradition of the eighteenth-century philosophical fiction exemplified by Voltaire's *Candide* (1759) and Denis Diderot's *Le Neveu de Rameau* (written in 1762 but not published until much later).

In order to cure Agathon of his idealistic enthusiasm, Hippias sets him up with an ex-hetaera by the name of Danae. What follows, however, moves beyond the generic mold of philosophical fiction. Agathon and Danae fall in love with each other. Their love story, told by the narrator with great psychological finesse, is cast in the mold of the mid-eighteenth-century English novel. The Danae episode evinces the kind of pointed psychological and moral assessment of characters that Henry Fielding's novels are known for. It is mostly for this reason that Friedrich Blanckenburg, a contemporary critic, placed *Geschichte des Agathon* on par with Fielding's 1749 novel *The History of Tom Jones* and extolled it as the first true novel in the German language.[96] What Ian Watt calls the "realism of assessment" in Fielding—"a wise assessment of life" related to the "the whole tradition of civilized values"— applies eminently to the Danae episode in Wieland's novel.[97]

Yet *Geschichte des Agathon* outgrows the kind of realist fiction exemplified by Fielding as quickly as it outgrew the philosophical fiction some chapters earlier. As his relationship to Danae evolves, Agathon feels the urge to tell her all about his previous life. The ensuing narrative of Agathon's early life on the hallowed ground of Delphi and his involvement in the democratic politics of Athens is an autobiography. The eighteenth century witnessed the proliferation of autobiographical writings. They ranged from the religious autobiographies in the Pietist tradition early in the century to the diverse autobiographies of scholars and artists later in the century. The best known, of course, was Rousseau's *Confessions* (completed 1769, published 1782). Wieland belonged to the major theorists of autobiography, regarding the psychological and moral coherence of the individual self as the main criterion of this genre of writing. In a letter written in 1759, for instance, he spoke of the "analogy" and "connection" that an individual could find "in the developments, excesses, leaps, flights and metamorphoses of his spirit" in writing up his life experiences.[98] Agathon's autobiography is exemplary in this regard.

Shocked by the revelation of Danae's past as a hetaera, Agathon escapes Smyrna and moves on to become a councilor at the court of Syracuse. With its description of court intrigues and the ills of monarchical politics, the Syracuse episode plays with the generic conventions of *Staatsroman*—a kind of political fiction concerned with the governance of the monarchical state and the education of the prince, as exemplified by Wieland's own 1772 novel *Der Goldne Spiegel*. The Syracuse episode in *Geschichte des Agathon* can be characterized as a negative *Staatsroman*, as it demonstrates the dysfunction of a monarchical government and the futility of the education of the prince.[99]

Agathon maneuvers himself into grave danger in Syracuse and moves on to Tarentum, where he again meets Danae. In the second and the third version of *Geschichte des Agathon*, the Tarentum episode features a lengthy "Secret History of Danae" (third version, books 14–15). A history of Danae's life told by herself, it is a female autobiography, a counterpoint to Agathon's autobiography back in Smyrna. But as its title already indicates, the "Secret History of Danae" taps into the generic resources of secret history as a specific kind of narrative current since the late seventeenth century. Initially, the generic category of secret history referred to stories revealing the personal secrets of rulers. In the course of the eighteenth century, it designated the narratives of private life with varying degrees of fictiveness, which could take many forms, including autobiography and the novel.[100]

In short, *Geschichte des Agathon* deploys a great variety of narrative genres— romance, philosophical fiction, the realist psychological novel, autobiography, *Staatsroman*, and secret history. Each of them is tailored to represent a specific kind of individual experience—erratic turns of life events, formation of beliefs and values, intricacies of feeling and moral judgment, the sense of the self, engagement in public affairs, and negotiation of privacy and public attention. Insofar as an individual is not a citizen of the world by nature but has to become one through all kinds of life experience, the novel supposed to portray a citizen of the world does not merely contain a philosophical doctrine but is a literary form that marshals all the genres tailored to represent many different kinds of life experience. The making of the cosmopolitan subject, then, is one and the same process as the making of the literary form that tracks it—the *Bildungsroman*.

Cosmopolitanism and the Novel Form in Goethe's *Wilhelm Meisters Lehrjahre*

The classic exemplar of what literary historians call the *Bildungsroman*, of course, is Goethe's *Wilhelm Meisters Lehrjahre*. The notion of *Bildung* in the sense of the free and full development of individual personality pervades the novel as its leitmotif, and the plot of the novel instantiates this notion. In telling the story of the development of its eponymous hero, who is born to a bourgeois family, tries to pursue a theater career, and quits it after many ups and downs, the novel corroborates the finding that we have reached on the basis of Wieland's *Geschichte des Agathon*—the necessary connection between the genesis of the cosmopolitan subject and the form of *Bildungsroman*. In Goethe's novel, however, cosmopolitanism is presented not as the wisdom of a sage, but as associated with a secret society. What constitutes cosmopolitanism has also assumed a new dimension: it becomes, first and foremost, a matter of economic rationality.

The discourse of cosmopolitanism that flourished in the age of the Enlightenment was closely associated with secret societies. Wieland's essay "Das Geheimniss des Kosmopolitenordens" ("The Secret of the Order of Cosmopolitans"), published in 1788, highlighted this fact by exploring the possibility of a cosmopolitanism without secrecy. To become a citizen of the world was a rallying call for the Freemasons and the Illuminati.[101] Stoic philosophers with their cosmopolitan ideas belonged to the required readings for the Freemasons in the eighteenth century.[102] According to the Stoics, the rational nature of man made him a citizen of the cosmopolis, although he physically lived in a particular political community. Stoic sages scattered in conventional political communities around the world were fellow members of the cosmic city, united by their shared way of life and the universal law of nature. Freemasonry can be understood as an attempt to realize cosmopolitanism by providing a place where citizens of the cosmic city could gather—the lodge. In the form of a delimited physical space, the lodge referred to the world as a whole. Located within the earthly city, it stood for the cosmic city. Rituals of initiation and secrecy served to secure this symbolic function of the lodge. Cosmopolitanism took the form of an Arcanum. The Masonic emplacement of the cosmos implied drawing a distinction between an inside and an outside, between the ones who are initiated into the Arcanum of cosmopolitanism and the ones who are not. The cosmos, however, can by definition not be delimited and separated. The emplacement of the cosmos, therefore, is counterbalanced by the Masonic endeavor to transcend these distinctions, to draw the entire world into the lodge, to turn the uninitiated into the initiated. In the words of Karl Philip Moritz (1756–93), a friend of Goethe's and a practicing Mason, "The scattered mankind should assemble in our lodge, here should be the seat of mutual communication, as well as of harmony and peace."[103] Confining the cosmos to the lodge only to assert its unboundedness, casting a veil of secrecy over cosmopolitanism only to initiate people into it, eighteenth-century Freemasonry did not simply regard world citizenship as consisting in the rational nature of man, but took upon itself the practical task of converting individual persons into world citizens.[104]

In Goethe's *Wilhelm Meisters Lehrjahre*, the Masonic conversion of individual persons into world citizens takes the form of a novelistic narrative. Wilhelm's life journey culminates in his induction in the secret Society of the Tower. At the time of the initiation, Wilhelm realizes that the most important people on his life's journey seem to have been the members of the Society of the Tower, and that the seemingly contingent events have actually been orchestrated by the society. "How curious! He said to himself, maybe the accidental events are connected? And maybe what we call fate is merely coincidence?" (872).[105] The plot of the novel turns out to be the secret plot designed by the Society of the Tower to recruit Wilhelm. The recruiting strategy of the Society of the Tower follows a pedagogical plan, albeit a flexible one. The society intervenes in Wilhelm's life at critical junctures to steer him in a certain direction. But in general the interventions are few and far between so that Wilhelm may do many things of his free volition and errs often. Wilhelm wonders, "If so many people were concerned about you, knew about the journey of your life, and know what to do on this journey, why didn't they lead you more strictly? Why not more seriously? Why did they favor your games rather than lead you away from them?" (873). He soon finds the answer to these questions himself: "Because nature forms (*bildet*) us in her pleasant manner into all that we should be. Oh, the strange requirements of the bourgeois society that first confuses and misguides us and then demands more of us than nature itself. Woe betides any kind of education (*Bildung*), which destroys the most effective means of true education and directs us to the end rather than makes us happy on the journey itself" (881). Allowed to act as they please, individuals may make many mistakes along the way, but they also gather more experiences and develop more complex and fuller personalities in doing so. The true and natural education, or *Bildung*, means the free and full development of an individual person.

Free and natural as it is, *Bildung* has an end—a normative personality, "all that we should be." Wilhelm is steered towards this end by the Society of the Tower. With his initiation into this secret society, he is told that "[his] apprenticeship is over" and that "nature has released [him]" (876). The actions undertaken by the protagonist of his free volition, which entail erring and confusion, postpone the ending. Precisely in so doing, they make up the plot of the novel. For if he were led straight to the goal, if there were no ups and downs, no back and forth, there would have been no plot either. The Society of the Tower that steers Wilhelm's development towards a normative end also marks the endpoint of the plot of *Wilhelm Meisters Lehrjahre*. In short, *Bildung* takes the form of the novel—the *Bildungsroman*. Insofar as the secret Society of the Tower stands for cosmopolitanism, Goethe's *Bildungsroman* is a novel of the education of an individual person into a cosmopolitan subject.

The Society of the Tower does stand for cosmopolitanism, but it is cosmopolitanism of a new stripe. Whereas the eighteenth-century discourse of cosmopolitanism draws heavily on the Stoic vocabulary of nature and reason (as Archytas in Wieland's *Geschichte des Agathon* does), the secret society in Goethe's novel embodies a new kind of nature and a new kind of reason—the economic one. The young romantic poet Novalis was right when he complained that in *Wilhelm Meisters Lehrjahre* "the economic nature is the true—that which remains."[106] This economic reason is universal insofar it is global in scope. Jarno, a member of the Society of the Tower, tells Wilhelm after his initiation:

> At the present moment there is nothing less advisable than to have one's property only in one locality, to invest one's money in only one place, but on the other hand it is difficult to manage them if they are in different localities. For this reason we have worked out a new plan: from our old Tower a new society shall emerge, which will extend into all corners of the world, and people from all over the world will be able to join it. We will cooperate in insuring our means of existence, in case a political revolution should displace one or the other from all the property he owns. I shall now go over to America in order to take advantage of the favorable conditions that our friend created during his stay there. The Abbé will go to Russia, and you shall have the choice [. . .] either to stay with Lothario in Germany or go with me. (945).

The cosmopolis now takes the form of a global commercial empire. The cosmopolitan subject, then, is a globally mobile businessman.[107]

From the *Bildungsroman* to Kantian Cosmopolitanism

Wieland's *Geschichte des Agathon* and Goethe's *Wilhelm Meisters Lehrjahre*, the first exemplars of the so-called *Bildungsroman*, effected a subjective turn of cosmopolitanism. By narrating the development of an individual person into a cosmopolitan, they represent world citizenship as a subjective disposition and normative personality. Immanuel Kant's *Zum ewigen Frieden*, a treatise on international law published around the same time as *Geschichte des Agathon* (in its third and final version) and *Wilhelm Meisters Lehrjahre*, treats cosmopolitanism, for the first time, in terms of a type of subjective right: "But any legal constitution, as far as the persons who live under it are concerned, will conform to one of the three following types: (1), a constitution based on the *civil right* of individuals within a nation (*ius civitatis*), (2), a constitution based on the *international right* of states in their relationships with one another (*ius gentium*), (3), a constitution based on *cosmopolitan right*, in so far as individuals and states, coexisting in an external relationship of mutual influences, may be regarded as citizens of a universal state of mankind (*ius cosmopoliticum*)."[108] Kant was an active participant in the debates on cosmopolitanism in the late eighteenth century.[109] With "reason" as the keyword in his philosophical vocabulary, Kant's discussion of cosmopolitanism may remind one of the Stoics in many ways.[110] But his approach is radically different. Whereas the Stoics believed in an objective world order based on the right reason and deduced man's world citizenship from his participation in the right reason, Kant conceived of normative order entirely in subjective terms, regarding world citizenship as a right of the subject. The cosmopolitan right, for Kant, "means the right of a stranger not to be treated with hostility when he arrives on someone else's territory. [. . .] The stranger cannot claim the *right of a guest* to be entertained, for this would require a special friendly agreement whereby he might become a member of the native household for a certain time. He may only claim a *right of resort*, for all men are entitled to present themselves in the society of others by virtue of their right to communal possession of the earth's surface."[111]

The Kantian conception of world citizenship as a subjective right entails granting the individual the status of a legal subject in public international law. The cosmopolitan right is a right of the individual in the world of states—that is, a right pertaining to individuals in relation to states other than the ones of which they are citizens. Once individuals are recognized as legal persons in the world of states, their right in relation to the states of which they are citizens (their civil right) becomes an issue in public international law as well. For Kant, civil right, international right (the right of states in relation to one another), and cosmopolitan right represent the three pillars of international legal order. By installing the individual person as a legal subject in the international world, Kant inaugurated a cosmopolitan tradition in international legal thought.[112] The fundamental premise of this tradition is that individual persons are rights-bearing subjects all over the world, both inside and outside of the particular states of which they are citizens. The *Bildungsroman* tells the story of the genesis of this subject.

In the eighteenth century, natural jurisprudence and the novel represented two interconnected modes of constructing human society based on the hypothesis of a "natural" existence of individual persons prior to or outside of civil institutions. In particular, they laid out, by argumentative and narrative means respectively, some models of international world order that remain compelling today. Defoe's novels figure a transnational world order that integrates persons, things, and obligations according to the logic of global commerce and refers them at the same time to the jurisdiction of states. Such a model foreshadows, remotely at least, today's international world shaped by the collaboration and coordination of the agents of the global economy and those of states (as well as intergovernmental organizations). The sentimental world order prefigures certain aspects of international human rights law as well as international criminal law. The historian Lynn Hunt points out that today's idea of human rights began with the sentimental literature in the eighteenth century. Sentimental novels, she argues, generated imagined empathy "by inducing new sensations about the inner self," and thereby "reinforced the notion of a community who could relate beyond their immediate families, religious affiliations, or even nations to greater universal values."[113] The international lawyer Gerry Simpson stresses the use and abuse of sympathy in international law today, particularly in war crime cases.[114] Finally, the cosmopolitan world order proves to be as appealing in our time as ever. As a novelistic subgenre concerned with the development of the individual person into a rights-bearing subject, the *Bildungsroman* continues to play a key role in the human rights discourse.[115] In sum, the eighteenth-century novel illustrates some concrete ways in which imaginative literature engages with international law, transcends it by developing nonlegal models of international world order, and ultimately performs a lawmaking function.

Epilogue

Traversing three turbulent centuries, our long story comes to an end without, however, reaching closure. In *Zum ewigen Frieden*, the 1795 legal philosophical treatise on which our story ends, Immanuel Kant sardonically characterizes all notable international lawyers—"Hugo Grotius, Pufendorf, Vattel, and the rest"—as "sorry comforters," remarking that "their philosophically or diplomatically formulated codes do not and cannot have the slightest legal force, since states are not subject to a common external constraint."[1] The same fate, alas, befalls Kant himself. If anything, the public use of reason so insistently advocated by him just heightens our awareness of the unending crises in the international world, as well as of the limitations of international law. The problems and responses addressed by this book—the imperative to establish a normative world order, the inefficacy of international law as a response to this imperative, literary interventions, and the ensuing development of literary forms—continued undiminished after this treatise of Kant's, the chronological ending point of our story.[2]

The time around 1800 witnessed the end of *ius naturae et gentium* (as discussed in the last chapter) and the rise of historical jurisprudence. A new paradigm of international law came into being that would dominate the century from the Congress of Vienna to the First World War: the so-called international law of civilized nations. It postulated a legal community of European nations (later also the United States) based on shared history and "civilization," while dismissing peoples in other parts of the world as barbarous and denying them the status of international legal subject. This paradigm, which leaves its traces even in the Statute of the International Court of Justice (Article 38 speaks of "the general principles of law recognized by civilized nations"), worked in tandem with European imperialism. Beginning with the establishment of the Permanent Court of Arbitration in The Hague in 1900 and culminating in the founding of the United Nations after the Second World War, international law in the twentieth century was shaped by institution-building. In the meantime, a great variety of doctrines thrived.[3] As a problem-solving mechanism aimed at international social integration, international law after 1800 operated in fundamentally different ways than it had done during the centuries discussed in this book. Accordingly, literary interventions could not help functioning differently as well, not only because the problems raised by international law changed, but also because what was called literature was being constantly redefined.

Notes

Introduction

1. A good recent example is Kissinger 2014.
2. We are often reminded of this fact, most recently by a universal history of the subject (Neff 2014, 5–136). The articles under the heading "Regions" in Fassbender and Peters 2012 show a cross section of the various traditions of international law. Today certain non-Western traditions, especially the Chinese, may again play a role in shaping global order, as for example Yan (2013) implies.
3. A number of articles in Fassbender and Peters 2012 discuss this process. Underlying this process was the shift from the multicentered law of early empires to the state-centered law of the colonial and postcolonial world as traced by Benton (2002). Liu analyzes the process in terms of translation (2009, "Translating International Law," 108–39). This process was all of a piece with the Westernization of political order as analyzed by Badie (2000).
4. Schmitt 1997.
5. Bentham 1970, 6.
6. Justinian 1985, 1.1.1.3–4.
7. On these areas in the Roman *ius gentium*, see Kaser 1993, 23–39.
8. On the conceptual transformation of *ius gentium* into international law, see especially Schröder 2000; also, "Völkerrecht," in Brunner et al. 2004, 7:108–12.
9. On the much-studied emergence of the modern state, see for instance Joseph Strayer's 1970 book, *On the Medieval Origins of the Modern State,* which focuses on England and France. "Partly in response to Strayer's contribution," the political historian Charles Tilly tells us in his foreword to the Princeton Classic edition, "several waves of scholars have written comparative-historical analyses of state formation" in Western and Southern Europe (xiii).
10. Weber 1978, 56. For a classic account of the making of this concept, see Skinner 1978.
11 "Staat und Souveränität," in Brunner et al. 2004, 6:1.
12. Bodin 1986, book 1, chap. 10.
13. Bodin 1986, book 1, chap. 8.
14. Cf. Mohnhaupt 1972.
15. See Bartelson 2009, chap. 4.
16. Ellickson 1994.
17. Jens Bartelson (1995) points out that the domestic order and the international are, historically speaking, two sides of the same coin: "A history of sovereignty cannot begin by separating the sovereign state from its international outside, for it must be capable of accounting for the formation of the domestic and the international

as imposed interpretations which organize modern political reality as well as our understanding of that reality as empirically given and analytically evident. Thus, a history of sovereignty must be a history of how and by what means this kind of differentiation into inside and outside, into sameness and otherness, is carried out" (53–54).

18. Hobbes 1996, 191 (chap. 26).
19. See Simon 2005.
20. Hobbes 1998, 161–62.
21. Hobbes 1996, 96 (chap. 14).
22. These different positions on the legality of international law are laid out by Mégret (2012, 72–81).
23. Kelsen 1967, 31 (§ 6a).
24. Kelsen 1967, 286 (§ 41).
25. Kelsen 1967, 323 (§ 42b).
26. Hart 1994, 104.
27. Hart 1994, 214.
28. Hart 1994, 227.
29. Möllers 2015, 373.
30. Lauterpacht 1932, 318.
31. Lévi-Strauss 1966, 234.
32. Kant 1991b, 126
33. Posner 2009. See also Binder and Weisberg 2000.
34. Quintilian 2001, book 8, vi.
35. On this point, see Carty 2007, 1–25.
36. Peter Goodrich concludes his review of Carty 2007 with a daring, albeit cursory proposal to complement doctrinal intervention with an "artistic intervention" on the basis of Nicolas Bourriaud's concept of relational aesthetics. Goodrich 2008, 340. I argue that the doctrinal intervention itself makes use of poetic operations.
37. Tans 2014.
38. See Conklin 2001.
39. Derrida 1990; Legendre 1985, 240.
40. On such narratives aiming to legitimize and protect institutions, see Koschorke 2012, 324–28.
41. On the last point, see Fögen 2002.
42. Cover 1983–84, 4.
43. Cf. Warren 2010.
44. Grotius 1925, prolegomena § 17; Wolff 1934, prolegomena § 10.
45. Quoted from Olivier 1975, 15.
46. Quoted from MacLean 1999, 4.
47. On the Commentators' conception of the purposes of legal fiction, see MacLean 1999, 5–6.
48. Quoted from MacLean 1999, 6.
49. Walton 1993.
50. Neff 2014, 143.

51. On the discussions of the relationship between legal fiction and poetic fiction in Renaissance jurisprudence, see MacLean 1999, 8–9.
52. Aristotle 1972, 1451b.
53. Sidney 1890, 36.
54. Kermode 2000, 39.
55. Plutarch 1914, I:214–15; 410–11.
56. See Kantorowicz 1961. Jacob Burckhardt famously speaks of "the state as work of art" in his 1860 book *Die Kultur der Renaissance in Italien* (1989, 11–136).
57. Kant 1977, § 46.
58. See André Chénier's ode "Le Jeu de Paume. A Louis David, Peintre," in Chénier 1958, 167. As Wisner (1997) puts it, "Chénier's 'coupe d'ambroisie' symbolically replaces the holy ampulla of the *sacre du roi*, and thus endows the poet, and by extension the painter, with a new authority as lawgiver in the highest degree" (122).
59. Shelley 2003, 677, 701.
60. Aristotle 1972, 1448a.
61. Hart 1994, 104.
62. Bruner 1986, 26.
63. Alexander Hamilton writes in *Federalist Papers* (Nr. 22), "Laws are a dead letter without courts to expound and define their true meaning and operation. The treaties of the United States, to have any force at all, must be considered part of the law of the land. Their true import, as far as respects individuals, must, like all other laws, be ascertained by judicial determinations. To produce uniformity in these determinations, they ought to be submitted, in the last resort, to one SUPREME TRIBUNAL. And this tribunal ought to be instituted under the same authority which forms the treaties themselves." Hamilton, Madison, Jay 1999, 118.
64. Bentham 1843, 547.
65. Eden 1986, chap. 1.
66. See Brooks and Gewirtz 1996; Brooks 2005; Bruner 2002, 37–62.
67. Aristotle 1972, 1448a.
68. Dworkin 1986, 228.
69. Dworkin 1986, 231.
70. Bruner 2002, 39.
71. Schiller 1988, 190.
72. See Cover 1985–86.
73. Such is the key finding of Eden 1986, which studies the question of poetic jurisdiction from ancient Greece to the Renaissance.
74. This was the case in the formative phase of common law according to Cormack 2008.
75. See Gurr 2004; Auerbach 1933; Merlin 1994.
76. Dworkin 1986, 245.
77. See Tang 2010.
78. Cover 1985–86, 1601.
79. The twenty-two-volume "Classics of International Law," published from 1911 to 1950 under the general editorship of James Brown Scott, dated mostly from

this period. Standard histories of international law such as Grewe 2000 and Neff 2014 treat the time around 1800—or more precisely the Congress of Vienna in 1815—as a historical threshold.

80. This is the professed aim of Fassbender et al. 2012. See the editors' "Introduction: Towards a Global History of International Law," 1–24.

81. This book differs from Warren 2015, the only book-length study on the relationship between literature and international law, in terms of scope, intent, and argument. Warren's book is concerned with English literature in the century named in its title (1580–1680), while the present book deals with literature in major European languages (English, German, and French, as well as other romance languages) during the three centuries from the Renaissance to the end of the eighteenth century. Warren's book seeks to demonstrate "how the genres of epic, comedy, tragicomedy, history, and biblical tragedy organized persons, actions, events, and evidence into recognizably modern legal categories like the laws of war, private international law, and human rights" (2). The present book, by contrast, studies how literature engaged with public international law, imagined a normative world order that public international law was incapable of realizing, and in the process contributed to the formation of a set of genres such as romance, tragedy, and the novel.

82. On the normativity of the genre in the general sense, see Möllers 2015, 217–21.

1. The Old World Order Dissolving

1. Schmitt 1997, 54–69. For a critical revision of Schmitt's notion of "global linear thinking," see Duve 2017.

2. Grewe 2000, 13.

3. Muldoon 2013, 203. For the general resistance to all too clear distinctions between the medieval and the modern, see Aers 1992.

4. Cicero 1998, *De legibus*, I.23. References to Cicero indicate book and section number.

5. Cicero 1998, *De re publica* III.33.

6. Cicero 1998, *De re publica* III.33.

7. Augustine 1988–95, book 49, section 12.

8. Justinian 1985, 1.1.1.3. References to the *Digest of Justinian* indicate book, chapter, section, and paragraph.

9. Aquinas 1981, IaIIae q. 90, a. 1. I follow the conventional method of citing *Summa Theologia*, indicating the place of the quotation in the system.

10. Cf. Lisska 1996; Krings 1982.

11. Agamben 2011a, 87.

12. Soto 1995, 176. Soto refers to Ps.35,7.

13. Brett 2011, 37–48; Scattola 1999, 161–78.

14. Vitoria 1992, 248. This point made by Vitoria in *De Indis* is fully elaborated by Domingo de Soto in his 1556 treatise *De iustitia et iure*, lib. IV, q. 1, a. 2 (Soto 1967). For a detailed analysis of this point, see Seelmann 2007.

15. Vitoria 1992, 6–7.

16. Vitoria 1992, 10.

17. Vitoria 1995–97, 2:114.
18. Vitoria, 1995–97, 2:116.
19. Vitoria, 1995–97, 2:146.
20. Vitoria, 1995–97, 2:176,
21. For a broad discussion of the question of human agency in sixteenth-century natural law thought, see Brett 2011, 37–61.
22. On Sepúlveda's humanism and his stance on the Amerindians, see Fernández-Santamaria 1977, 196–236. Tierney points out the influence of the late medieval notion of subjective right on Las Casas's defense of the Amerindians. See Tierney 1997, 272–87. Whereas the notion of right certainly played an important role in Las Casas's approach, my argument here focuses on the fact that he appealed to natural law from the perspective of its subject.
23. "Summary of Sepúlveda's Position," in Las Casas 1974, 11.
24. Las Casas 1974, 48.
25. See Brett 1997, 123–37; Tierney 1997, 256–65.
26. Vitoria 1992, 247–48.
27. Vitoria's international legal thought in connection with his justification of the Spanish conquest has been often studied. For a most recent study with references to existing scholarship, see Bunge 2017.
28. Vitoria 1992, 315–25.
29. See Anghie 2005, 13–31; Pagden 1987, 79–98.
30. On *ius gentium* in Roman law, see Kaser 1993.
31. Justinian 1985, 1.1.1.4.
32. Justinian 1985, 1.1.5.
33. Vitoria 1992, 40.
34. Vitoria 1992, 278. Gaius's definition quoted by Vitoria is at *Institutiones* 1.2.1 (Justinian 1987, 37).
35. Vitoria 1934–35, I,14. The passage in question is Aquinas 1981, IIaIIae, q. 57, a. 3.
36. On Vitoria's inconsistency on this matter, see Tierney 2007, 110–14.
37. Vitoria 1992, 281.
38. Bartolus 1538, 13. On this distinction in the Commentators, see Seelmann 1979, 126–31.
39. Vázquez de Menchaca 1572, 235.
40. For a detailed account of the multifaceted treatment of *ius gentium* in the second half of the sixteenth century, see Brett 2011, 77–89.
41. Soto 1967, lib.I, q. 5, a. 4 (1:45).
42. Johann Wolfgang Goethe and Friedrich Schiller, "Über epische und dramatische Dichtung," in Goethe 1985–99, 18:445.
43. Bakhtin 1981, 16.
44. Homer 1996, book 6, 1–14.
45. Grotius 1925, 1.4.1; Rousseau 1997, 1.4.3.
46. Bederman 2001, 135–36.
47. Jhering 1887, 359, 358.
48. Segal 1994, 113–41.
49. Virgil 2010, I. 874–75.

50. Zetzel points out that the "Virgilian world-order is not so one-sided" and that "all three great prophecies of Rome's future are, in one way or another, equivocal" (1996, 311–12).

51. See Hardie 1986.

52. See O'Hara 1990, 132–63.

53. Quint 1993, 21.

54. The seminal works in this critical tradition include Parry 1963, Clausen 1964, and Putnam 1965. For a review of the critical controversy about whether Aeneas's slaying of Turnus at the end confirms or undercuts the idea of cosmic justice, see Braund 1997, 214–16.

55. In-text references indicate the canto and stanza numbers. The Portuguese edition used: Camões 1973. The English translation used: Camões 1997.

56. See Subrahmanyam 1998, 76–163.

57. "The Renaissance failed to produce a Virgil, in the sense of a great poet whose work resembles the *Aeneid*. Perhaps the Renaissance even failed to produce poetry which can properly be described as epic at all in many important senses of the word. [. . .] The important poems it did produce in the Virgilian tradition are not at harmony with themselves to the degree of the *Aeneid*, to say nothing of the truly homogeneous Homeric poems. The Renaissance poems [. . .] are most of them imperfectly coherent, uncertainly unified, divided by powerful forces not altogether controlled and understood." Greene 1963, 4.

58. See Livermore 1973. Significantly, the historical character of the poem is emphasized in a seventeenth-century English translation (see Camões 1655).

59. Raman argues that Camões's epic world "wrestles instead with a radical separation between the divine and human realms" (2001, 44).

60. Gil and Macedo demonstrate that in *Os Lusíadas* the narrative of voyage counteracts the founding of a "new kingdom" (2009, 33–85).

61. Skinner 1978, 1:113–38.

62. In the mid-sixteenth century, as "the old republics withered, with Florence being merely the most spectacular example, the genre of advice books for princes became dominant, and with it its by now traditional content." Tuck 1993, 33. See also Bireley 1990 and Truman 1999.

63. Virgil 2010. VI. 914–16.

64. Foucault 2007, 259, 260.

65. Machiavelli 1988, preface.

66. Machiavelli 2003, I, preface, 98.

67. Lipsius's Tacitus editions and commentaries include: *C. Cornelii Taciti Historiarum et Annalium qui exstant Justi Lipsii studio emendati et illustrate* (1574); *Ad Annales Corn. Taciti liber commentarius sive notae* (1581).

68. See Schnelhase 1977; Tuck 1993, 39–45; Gajda 2009.

69. Tacitus 2008, 3.

70. Guicciardini 1994, 159.

71. Botero 1956b, 3.

72. See Viroli 1992.

73. Descendre 2009, 109.

74. Botero 1956b, 66.

75. Botero 1956b, 41.
76. For a history of the idea of reason of state, see the classic Meinecke 1963. For Foucault, the idea of reason of state lies at the root of governmentality (2007, 227–32).
77. Pocock 1975, 165.
78. Frigo 2000, 32.
79. Machiavelli 1988, chap. 18.
80. Machiavelli 2003, book 2.13.
81. Guicciardini 1991, 104 and 105.
82. In the words of a Camões scholar, the "Isle of Love is an emphatically pastoral allegory, combining all the Arcadian images with all the mythical associations of the Golden Age. [. . .] The idyllic erotic pleasures [. . .] result in the reconciliation of all opposites in a new universal harmony." Gil and Macedo 2009, 25. On the pastoral vision of the isle of love, see also Macedo 1983, 11–15.
83. The applicability of this conclusion to other epic poems in the Renaissance requires detailed analysis. On the disruption of cosmic order and reason of state in Torquato Tasso's great epic poem *Gerusalemma Liberata* (1581), see for example Zatti 2006, 135–215.
84. Suárez 1944. In-text references indicate the book, chapter, and paragraph number.
85. On Suárez's constitutionalist theory of the state, see Skinner 1978, 2:148–66; Tierney 1997, 301–315; Höpfl 2004, 248–61; Fernández-Santamaría 2005–6, 1:175–225; Brett 2011, 125–28.
86. The Jesuit theologian Luis de Molina developed this idea in his 1588 book *Libri Arbitri cum Gratiae Donis, Divina Praescientia, Providentia, Praedestinatione et Reprobatione Concordia*.
87. On Gentili and epic poetry, see Warren 2015, 31–61.
88. Gentili 2011, 153.
89. Gentili 2011, 151.
90. See Koskenniemi 2010.
91. Gentili 1924, 7.
92. Gentili 1933, 15.
93. Gentili 1924, 90; Gentili 1933, 56.
94. On the "overarching ethical direction" that Tasso accords to diplomacy, see Hampton 2009, 59. Gentili 1924, 17
95. Gentili 1933, 31.
96. Gentili 1924, 198, 174. Gentili's distinction between the public and private personality of the ambassador represents a major conceptual innovation in sixteenth-century discussions. See Hampton 2009, 62.
97. Gentili 1933, 12; 250.
98. On "war in due form," see Neff 2005, 83–130. Carl Schmitt regards the war in due form as a major achievement of international law in modern times: Schmitt 1997, 123–43.
99. Tuck 1993, 160.
100. Straumann 2015 shows that Grotius's concept of natural rights also has classical roots.

101. Grotius 2006, 21.
102. Tierney 1997, 322.
103 "Petition of the United Dutch East India Company. Drafted by Hugo Grotius. Submitted to the Estates General on March 4, 1606," in Grotius 2006, appendix 2, 548. On this point, see Ittersum 2006, 177–86.
104. Tuck notes the analogy between the individual and the state in Grotius particularly with regard to the right to punish, but does not explain how this analogy comes about (2001, 82).
105. Grotius 2006, 133.
106. Grotius 1925, 2.5.15.2; 3.7.1.1.
107. See Brett 1997, 165–204.
108. Grotius 2006, 21. For Brett, Grotius "took the key step in translating natural liberty into natural right, and he did so ultimately by importing the scholastic concept of rights into a legal framework that he derived [. . .] from a different tradition of thought" (2011, 103).
109. Grotius 2006, 92; 106.
110. Grotius 2006, 35–36.
111. On the distinctions between the ancient and the modern theories of natural law, see Scattola 2001. On Grotius as the threshold between an ancient and a modern natural law theory, see also Haakonssen 1996; Tuck 1979; Tuck 1987.
112. Justinian 1985, 1.1.1.2.
113. Grotius 2006, 47.
114. Grotius 1925, prolegomena 17.
115. In connection with the law of embassy, Gentili does argue that "international law is based on natural principles which have been implanted in all by nature, and which are so well known that they need neither argument nor art to establish them" (1924, 111). But he does not offer a natural law theory. Cf. Waldron 2010.
116. Grotius 1925, prolegomena 38.

2. The Poetics of International Legal Order

1. Lesaffer 2012, 81.
2. Cf. Anderson 1998.
3. Guicciardini 1984, 282.
4. Guicciardini 1984, 392–94.
5. Vasari 1852, 5:530.
6. Steiger 2010, 616.
7. Ziegler 2004, 147.
8. Pennington 1993, 76
9. Quoted in Canning 1988, 455.
10. See Grewe 2000, part 1; Kitzinger 2012.
11. Garatus 2004, Quaestio 19.
12. Lesaffer 2000, 195.
13. See Lesaffer 2004.
14. Decock 2013, 105–214; Zimmermann 1996, 537–45; 559–76.
15. See Gordley 1991.

16. On the role of the pope among princes, see Russell 1986, 21–66.

17. That Vasari's fresco as well as other contemporary pictorial representations of the Truce of Nice glorifies Pope Paul III has been widely noted. See Kaulbach 1998, 593–94; Jong 2013, 108–10.

18. Ripa 1709, 375–78.

19. Ripa 1709, 54 (fig. 215).

20. Grotius 1925, prolegomena 17.

21. See Canning 1987, chap. 5; Canning 1988.

22. Kantorowicz 1957, 304 and 306.

23. Kantorowicz 1957, 304n70.

24. This is noted, for instance, in Coing 1973–88, II.1, IX–X.

25. Grotius 2006, 36.

26. Grotius 2006, 137.

27. Grotius 2006, 138.

28. Grotius 1925, 1.3.2.1.

29. Grotius 1925, 1.4.2.

30. Grotius's dedication of *Sophompaneas* to Gerard Vossius, in Grotius 1992, 129.

31. Grotius 1992, act 2, 334–43.

32. Grotius 1992, act 5. 1210–19.

33. Warren interprets Joseph as "the model *persona juris gentium*" (2015, 191). This is not plausible, as Joseph is neither a corporate person standing for the Hebrews or the Egyptians nor an individual person in the state of nature.

34. Hobbes 1996, 88.

35. Hobbes 1996, 120.

36. Hobbes 1994, 182.

37. Hobbes 1998, 3–4.

38. On Hobbes's translation of Thucydides and the history of international law, see Warren 2015, 127–59.

39. See Malcolm 2007.

40. See Armitage, 2006; Hüning 2000.

41. The term "Grotian tradition" appears first in Lauterpacht 1946. For a critical perspective, see Parry 2014. On the historical background for the invention of "the Grotian tradition," see Ittersum 2016. The recognition of the international legal personality of individuals became widespread after the Second World War. See for example Lauterpacht 1947; Korowicz 1956.

42. Lesaffer 2002, 109.

43. Malcolm makes a case that Hobbes's state of nature is much more substantively regulated on the level of international relations than on the interpersonal level (2002, 432–56). May 2013 argues that Hobbes allows for certain rules in international relations.

44. See Brooks and Gewirtz 1996.

45. Grotius 2006, 244; 260–61; 244.

46. See the tendentious tenor of Grotius's narrative, see Ittersum 2006, chap. 2.

47. Grotius 2006, 392.

48. Grotius 1994, § 4.

49. Grotius 2006, 245.

50. Grotius 1994, § 8.
51. Grotius 2006, 100.
52. Grotius 2006, 158. On the VOC as corporate sovereign, see Wilson 2008, chap. 4.
53. Leibniz 1963a, Cap. 6. On Leibniz's defense of German princes in this case, see Nijman 2004, chap. 2; Toyoda 2011, chap. 4.
54. Pufendorf 2007, 176.
55. Leibniz 1963a, Cap. 11.
56. Leibniz 1988, 61.
57. Leibniz 1963a, Cap. 10.
58. Leibniz 1963a, Cap. 11. English translation from Leibniz 1988, 117.
59. On this issue, see Schröder 2001. On Leibniz's federalist theory, see for example Riley 1976.
60. Leibniz 1963b, 308.
61. Leibniz 2004, 200. The English translation quoted from Leibniz 1988, 175.
62. Leibniz 1963a, Cap. XIV–XVIII.
63. Leibniz 1963b, 306.
64. Leibniz 2004, 172. English translation from Leibniz 1988, 174.
65. See Portmann 2010; Parfitt 2016.
66. Such is the conclusion of Klabbers 2005.
67. Leibniz 2004, 202.
68. Leibniz 2004, 166. See Riley 1996. On justice applied to international persons, see Nijman 2004, 68–76.
69. Grotius 1925, 2.2.2.1; 2.2.2.4–5.
70. Cicero 2000, I.51–52.
71. Gratian 1993, D. 8, pars. 1; Aquinas 1981, IaIIae 66, a. 2.
72. Grotius 2006, 317.
73. Grotius 2006, 318.
74. Hesiod 1988, 40–43.
75. Ovid 1987, book 1, 137–39.
76. Grotius 1925, 2.2.2.1.
77. See Grotius 2004.
78. Grotius 1925, 2.2.6.
79. Grotius 2006, 354.
80. Grotius 2006, 354.
81. See Grotius 2005, 1:xxvii–xxxi; Porras 2006.
82. For example Leibniz 1963a, Cap. 10, 13, 32, 51.
83. Leibniz 1998b, 1.
84. Leibniz 1998b, 56.
85. Leibniz 1998a, 12.
86. Leibniz 1998b, 67. On Leibniz's conception of body as a collection of substances held together by perceptions, see Deleuze 1993, chap. 7.
87. Riley 1996, 51.
88. See his short piece "On Natural Law," in Leibniz 1988, 77–80.
89. Leibniz 1998a, 12.
90. Leibniz 1998b, 85.

91. Deleuze 1993, 119.

92. Leibniz 1988, 52. The translator of this passage renders the original French term *roman* as *novel*. I have corrected it to "romance," as "the novel" refers to a new kind of prose fiction emerging in the eighteenth century. The difference between "novel" and "romance" will be discussed in chapter 6.

93. Leibniz 1988, 184.

94. Vismann 2011, 20–21.

95. For detailed descriptions of ceremonial performances pertaining to peace treaties in early modern Europe, see Lünig 1719–20, 1:786–1009.

96. Welch 2017, 4.

97. Duindam 2003, 181–219.

98. Bodin 1986, 1:287.

99. Camden 1635, 519.

100. Camden 1635, 487–88.

101. Debates about precedence among European sovereigns petered out after the Peace of Westphalia. By the early eighteenth century, the question of precedence commanded no more than antiquarian interest, as evidenced by Zwantzig 1709. International ceremonials described in Lünig 1719–20 mostly concern equality between sovereign persons. For a historical analysis, see Roosen 1980.

102. Stieve 1715, 2.

103. See Fischer-Lichte 1992, 13–141.

104. On the theatrical character of the princely court, see Alewyn 1959, 51–59.

105. Theodore Godefroy's unpublished remarks about the nature of ceremonial, quoted from Duindam 2003, 183.

106. Godefroy 1649, 2:771.

107. Lünig 1719–20, 1:200–201.

108. Wicquefort 1682, 1:287. On the specific ceremonies expected of the ambassador, 1:287–454.

109. Wicquefort 1682, 2:1.

110. See, for instance, Salisbury 1595, III.9.

111. Lünig 1719–20, 1:200.

112. Agamben 2011b, 28.

113. Legendre 1997, 161.

114. See Zanger 1997, 98–130.

115. Corneille 1980–87, 3:209.

116. See the editor's introduction to Corneille 1998, 46–76.

117. Seznec 1972, 33.

118. The climax of the celebration of the 1565 Medici wedding was the "Masque of the Genealogy of the Gods," described in detailed in Baldini 1565. On mythology-themed royal weddings, see Seznec 1972, 280–83; Strong 1984, 126–52; Bull 2005, 43–47.

119. Godefroy 1619, n.p.

120. This historical development will be discussed in more detail in connection with Corneille's tragedies of marriage alliance in the next chapter.

121. Legendre 1988, 153.

122. See Seznec 1972, 84–121 and 269–78.

123. On allegories in court entertainments, see Hoxby 2010, 195–203. On mythological figures as allegories on the seventeenth-century stage, see Brown 2007, 128–31.
124. Warburg 2010, 151–52.
125. Turner 1982, 68–71.
126. Turner 1982, 11.
127. Aristotle 1972, 1448a.
128. See Skinner 1978, vol. 2, part 3: "Calvinism and the Theory of Revolution."
129. James I 1994, 46, 82, 85–131.
130. James I 1994, 76–77.
131. James I 1994, 75.
132. Skinner 2002, 2:398.
133. See Sommerville 1991.
134. See Bély 1999.
135. Frye 1957, 35.

3. International Order as Tragedy

1. This is emphasized most recently by Hoxby 2015, 47–48.
2. See Lehmann 2013. Quotation at 255.
3. Elizabeth I 2000, 189.
4. James I 1994, 49.
5. See Schechner 1988, chap. 4.
6. Welch 2017, 3. On the intimate relationship between diplomacy and theater meant for entertainment, see also Rivère de Carles 2016.
7. On transgression as the hallmark of the tragic, see Lehmann 2013, 84–131.
8. Justinian 1985, 1.3.31.
9. Cf. Tierney 1963; Wyduckel 1979.
10. See Weinberg 1961.
11. Aristotle 1972, 1448a; 1454b.
12. Frye 1957, 33.
13. Robortello 1548, 23. Translation quoted from Sidnell 1991, 1:87.
14. Scaliger 1994–2011, lib. 1, cap. 6.
15. Castelvetro 1984, 151.
16. Opitz 1970, 30.
17. Aubignac 2001, 210. Benjamin distinguishes *Trauerspiel*—the German term for tragic drama in the seventeenth century—from tragedy partly with reference to the fact that the former features royal personage and historical subject matter (1974, 242–45). Since royal personage became a requirement for the tragic form in the Renaissance, we can say that tragedy in early modern Europe was in general *Trauerspiel*. A strict terminological distinction between *Trauerspiel* and tragedy may not be necessary.
18. Sidney 1890, 28.
19. Harsdörffer 1648–1653, 2:80.
20. It goes without saying that the royal rank of characters makes up only a small part of the poetics of tragedy in early modern Europe. For a complete account, see Hoxby 2015, chap. 2.

21. Gurr 2004, 161.

22. Marlowe 2003. In-text references in the following indicate part, act, scene, and line.

23. Greenblatt 1980, 200.

24. Nietzsche 1967, 340.

25. Nietzsche 1967, 382.

26. Bodin's theory does, however, have implications for international law. See Scattola 2017.

27. Bodin 1986, 1:215.

28. Cf. Hopkins 2008, chap. 3; Bartels 1993, chap. 3; Greenblatt 1980, chap. 5.

29. On *Tamburlaine the Great* and Seneca, see Braden 1985, 182–97; Boyle 1997, 160–70.

30. Seneca, *Hercules*, act 4. See Waith 1962, 60–87.

31. On the metatheatrical dimension of Senecan tragedy, see Boyle 1997, 112–37; Littlewood 2004, chap. 4; Schiesaro 2003, 235–43. On metatheatricality in *Tamburlaine the Great*, see Cheney 2004, 135–41.

32. Vernant and Vidal-Naquet 1990, 33.

33. Vernant and Vidal-Naquet 1990, 49–84.

34. Homer 2011, book 9.

35. See Redfield 1994.

36. See Cahill 2008, 24–70.

37. Shakespeare 1989, 1.1.19–20. References for this and subsequent Shakespeare works discussed indicate act, scene, and line.

38. Watkins argues that *King John* "register(s) the perceived inadequacy of interdynastic marriage as a diplomatic practice" (2017, 152).

39. For Peter Lake, *King John* shows that "relations between princes become an endless struggle for 'vantage.' This is a war of all against all, a struggle for self-interest and self-preservations, which, when played out between kings, kills thousands" (2016, 204). While certainly paying attention to international politics, Lake does not discuss the play in terms of international law. Nor do previous readers of the play. In his influential essay "The Ordering of this Present Time," Sigurd Burckhardt notes the pervasive sense of the loss of order in *King John*, arguing that "in writing it, Shakespeare was or became 'modern'" (1968, 117). Burckhardt's reading aims to show Shakespeare's representation of a "world picture," touching upon neither the question of law in general nor the question of international law in particular. It inspired a distinctive critical tradition that sees in the play the collapse of order in almost every possible sense: see Curren-Aquino 1989. Zurcher discusses legal questions raised by *King John* without paying much attention to international relations (2010, 187–201).

40. Womersley 2010, 273.

41. Lake speaks of "the apotheosis of the bastard" (2016, 221–25). The Bastard has always fascinated critics, since he seems to represent an alternative to John. Anderson argues that in his disregard for legitimacy the Bastard exemplifies "the powerful claims of an emerging bureaucratic network of authority" (2004, 36). Along this line of argument, we can draw the following conclusion: if the Bastard is the agent of a new world order, then it is an order based on bureaucratic procedures. This accords

with Gentili's conception of a world legal order based on procedural rationality as discussed in chapter 1. See also Gieskes 1998.

42. *King John* was listed as one of Shakespeare's tragedies in Francis Meres's *Palladis Tamia* (1598). That the play appears under the heading of histories in the First Folio was, of course, the result of the editor's decision to create a generic category for the plays about English kings.

43. The Oxford Shakespeare edition will be used: Shakespeare 1987; Shakespeare 1996; Shakespeare 1998; Shakespeare 2003.

44. Happy endings, however, were not unheard of in early modern tragedy. Hoxby discusses a subgenre of tragedy, which he calls "the complex tragedy with a happy ending" (2015, 162–99).

45. See Patterson 1997.

46. Cormack discusses the issue of international relations in *Cymbeline* and *Pericles* (2008, 227–90). Warren relates *Pericles* and *Tempest* to private international law and *A Winter's Tale* to the union (2015, 62–95, 96–126). Forman 2008 and Lesser 2007 address the issue of international relations in these plays in economic, not legal and political terms.

47. See Dumont 2006, part 3, "The Theory of Marriage Alliance."

48. Lévi-Strauss 1969, 30.

49. McCabe argues that Shakespeare's romances resolve the problem of incest "through a sublimation of forbidden desire, an assumption of the temporal and profane into the eternal and the sacred frequently symbolized by the intervention of some *deus ex machina*" (1993, 179). In contrast to McCabe, I offer a politico-legal reading of the problem of incest in the romances.

50. Stephen Orgel draws attention to the relationship between James I's marriage negotiations on behalf of his children and the romances. See his introduction to Shakespeare 1987, at 30–31, and to Shakespeare 1996, at 47–50. Also Bergeron 1985.

51. See Marcus 1988, 125–36; Cormack 2008, 242–53; Marie O'Connor, "A British People: *Cymbeline* and the Anglo-Scottish Union Issue," in Cormack, Nussbaum, and Strier 2013, 231–55.

52. My discussion of romance and tragedy at this juncture follows Northrope Frye's distinction between the comic and the tragic mode of fiction. Frye 1957, 35.

53. On the implicit embrace of Roman law and Roman imperialism in *Cymbeline*, see Lockey 2006, 160–86. On the figuration of *translatio imperii* in this play, see James 1997, 151–88.

54. Cf. Greenblatt 1990, 16–39.

55. The question of colonialism has been a major concern in the scholarship on *The Tempest*. See, for example, Hulme and Sherman 2000; Fuchs 1997; Lupton 2000. For a survey on this line of research, see Graff and Phelan 2009.

56. On the Catholic dimension, see Beauregard 2008, 109–23. On the question of providence, see Shell 2010, 175–222.

57. See Wight 1977.

58. See for instance Anghie 2005.

59. Schmitt 1997.

60. On the deities and theatricality, see Kiefer 2003, chap. 6.

61. See Seznec 1972, 84–121 and 269–78.

62. See Tang 2014.
63. Lohenstein 1970; Lohenstein 2008. In the following, in-text references indicate act and line.
64. Livy 2006 (*Ab urbe condita*), XXX.12–15.
65. On historical sources and literary precedents for the dramatization of stories of Sophonisbe and Cleopatra, see Béhar 1988, 119–39 and 154–80.
66. On the theme of international law in *Cleopatra*, see Wichert 1991, 126–35.
67. Meinecke 1963, 246.
68. Stolleis 1988–2012, 1:212.
69. See Wichert 1991, 188–99.
70. Pascale 1995, nr. 680. Cf. Hacking 2006, chap. 8.
71. Cf. Schings 1983.
72. Benjamin 1974, 259–60.
73. On reason of state in Lohenstein, see for example Mulagk 1973.
74. See Cavaillé 2002, 11–31.
75. Acceto 1943, § VIII.
76. The author of this definition was Franceso da Buti (1324–1406). Quoted from Cavaillé 2002, 14.
77. Isidore of Serville, *De differentiis verborum*, n. 541. Quoted from Cavaillé 2002, 19.
78. Botero 1956b, 48–49.
79. Machiavelli 1988, XVIII.
80. Botero 1956b, 47–48.
81. Lipsius 2004, IV.14.
82. See Snyder 2009, chap. 4. Bireley 1990 also deals with the conceptions of simulation and dissimulation in its discussion of the main theorists of reason of state from Botero to Saavedra Fajardo.
83. Ripa 1603, 455.
84. Tuck 1993, 82–94.
85. Charron 1656, 400 (III.2.7).
86. Charron 1656, 208 (I.49).
87. Sfez 2000, 78. See also Koschorke et al. 2007, 184–91.
88. Naudé 2004, 78.
89. Naudé 2004, 104–5.
90. Foucault 2007, 262.
91. Rohan 1995, 167.
92. Guicciardini 1991, nr. 88.
93. Gracían 2011, nr. 3.
94. Botero 1956b, 3.
95. See Damien 1995.
96. Naudé 1907.
97. See Hartbecke 2008.
98. Naudé 2004, 79.
99. Naudé 2004, 132; 146.
100. Foucault 2007, 265.
101. On the theme of sacrificial ritual in *Sophonisbe* and its significance, see Barner 1989. Also Borgstedt 2010; Niefanger 2010.

102. See Newman 2000.
103. On this point, see Béhar 1988, 284–344; Niefanger 2005, 193–213.
104. Machiavelli 1988, XXV.
105. Lipsius 2004, I.4.
106. Bireley 1990, 212–15.
107. Béhar 1988, 245–47 ("Le public de Lohenstein").
108. Aristotle 1972, 1449b.
109. Such is the overarching argument of Watkins 2017.
110. Berman 1983, 227–28.
111. See McGowan 2013.
112. *Œdipe* is usually considered to be the beginning of the "old Corneille." See Couton 2003; Prigent 1986, 365–550.
113. These plays will be quoted from the Pléiade-edition: Corneille 1980–87. In-text references indicate act and verse number. Watkins's literary history of premodern marriage diplomacy does not mention these plays, discussing instead an early Corneille play *Horace* (1640) and Corneille's final work *Tite et Bérénice* (1670) in order to demonstrate "marriage diplomacy's declining prestige" and the emergence of an international system "that operated by its own competitive and defensive logic, often without regard to dynastic *gloire*." Watkins 2017, 175.
114. I borrow the concept of "genealogical principle" from Legendre 1985.
115. Corneille 1980–87, 3:19.
116. Biet labels the couple programmatically as "héros modernes," but does not pay attention to their political as well as dramaturgical significance highlighted here. Biet 1994, 204.
117. Foucault 1994, 33 ("Truth and Juridical Forms").
118. Kantorowicz 1957, 331.
119. See Apostelidès 1985.
120. See Kantorowicz 1957, 232–72.
121. Bossuet 1990, 27.
122. Bilis 2010 reads Dircé as the representative of hereditary succession without, however, paying attention to the question of marriage alliance.
123. Plutarch 1914, 1:1–87.
124. The parallel between Œdipe and Thésée in Corneille is discussed in detail by Delmas 1985, 157–79.
125. Godefroy 1619, 661. Kantorowicz discusses the metaphor of the king's marriage to his kingdom (1957, 212–23). See also Descimon 1992.
126. Prigent 1986, 382. See also Biet 1994, 213–19.
127. For this reason, some critics say that Corneille's play lacks the unity of action, having instead two disjointed plots. See Louvat and Escola 1998.
128. Raymond of Penyafort 2005, 19–20.
129. Justinian 1985, 23.2.2.
130. Raymond of Penyafort 2005, 25.
131. Maultrot 1788, 12–13. On the historical development presented here, see Bethery de la Brosse 2011; Schwab 1967; Stone 1990, 49–120.
132. We see here one particular manifestation of the distinction between the king's two bodies. On this distinction in French thought and literature of the seventeenth century, see Merlin-Kajman 2000.

133. With regard to the poison by which Sophonisbe kills herself, there is a significant difference between Livy and Corneille. In Livy, she uses the poison sent to her by Massinisse (*Ab urbe condita*, XXX.15), while in Corneille she uses her own poison, repudiating Massinisse's gift as unworthy of her (*Sophonisbe*, V. 1770–1802).

134. La Rochefoucauld 2007, 148–49.

135. This portrait of self-love was withdrawn after the first edition of *Maximes* published in 1664.

136. Benjamin 1974, 250.

137. Benjamin 1974, 259.

138. Hart 1994, chap. 5.

139. Corneille 1980–87, 3:117–18 (*Les trois discours sur le poème dramatique*).

140. Corneille 1980–87, 3:168.

141. Aristotle 1984, 1371a.

142. Aristotle 1972, 1448b.

4. International Order as Romance

1. Barclay 2004, 97. In-text references indicate book, chapter, and paragraph number.

2. Ijsewijn 1983, 9.

3. In recent scholarship, this corpus of texts is also referred to as the Greek novel. See Whitmarsh 2008. The standard English translation of these texts is entitled *Collected Ancient Greek Novels* (Reardon 1989). "Novel" was a term coined in the eighteenth century for a new kind of prose fiction that came into being at that time, as will be discussed in chapter 6. Because the generic difference between romance and the novel is important to this book, I use the term "Greek romance."

4. See Simon Goldhill, "Genre," in Whitmarsh 2008, 185–200.

5. Reardon 1991, 5.

6. See John J. Winkler, "The Invention of Romance," in Tatum 1994, 23–38.

7. Foucault 1990, 3:232.

8. On the reception of the Greek romance in early modern Europe, see Plazenet 1997. Also Michael Reave, "The Re-emergence of Ancient Novels in Western Europe, 1300–1810" and Gerald Sandy, "Novels Ancient and Modern," in Whitmarsh 2008, 282–98 and 299–320.

9. James I 1994, 38–39.

10. Frye 1976, 29.

11. On Barclay's knowledge of Heliodorus and various parallels between *Argenis* and *Aithiopika*, see the editor's introduction to Barclay 2004, 26–28.

12. Heliodorus 1989. In-text references indicate the book and paragraph number.

13. The Greek romance, particularly *Aithiopika*, has often been read as an allegorical representation of mystery religions. See Kerényi 1973; Merkelbach 1962.

14. On the crucial significance of book 9 in this sense, see Whitmarsh 2011, 129–35.

15. Morgan 1989, 319. In an important study, John Winkler concludes that "the religious re-signification of the plot is not religiously meant, but is rather part of Heliodorus' playful exploration of popular narrative and its audience." Winkler 1999, 347. Whitmarsh speaks of "godlike narrators and predictive texting" (2011, 191).

16. Frye 1976, 4.

17. On this episode, see Jowitt 2011, 164.

18. See Sully 1767 and 1921; Crucé 1972; Saint-Pierre 1981.

19. This contradicts Mikhail Bakhtin's view that the seventeenth-century political romance shares the same narrative structure as the Greek romance. See Bakhtin 1981, 94.

20. Sidney 1890, 11.

21. The concepts of the fictive, fictionalization, and the imaginary are borrowed from Iser 1991, 18–51, 377–411.

22. These documents were published after the writing of *Argenis*: Digges 1655. But Barclay might have known about these as well as other documents because of his connections with the English court.

23. In 1609, John Barclay undertook a diplomatic mission to the courts of Europe to promote King James's *Premonition of his Maiesties*. On Barclay's life, see the editor's introduction to Barclay 2004, 8–11.

24. See the translator's introduction to Barclay 1636: "A discourse upon the historie of John Barclay, called Argenis, for the more easie understanding of some things contained in the same" (unpaginated). The following quotations are all from the same text.

25. Barclay 2004, appendix 1, 47–48.

26. Sidney 1890, 35.

27. See Siegl-Mocavini 1999, 1–11.

28. Barclay 1626.

29. Herbert 1661. In-text references indicate the page number.

30. See Zurcher 2007, 154–55.

31. Victoria Kahn reaches a similar conclusion from a different perspective: "The marriages in this text are either really based on love or purely political, but not a symbol of the unity of the two. Marriage is no longer an emblem of peace and harmony; at most, it is one instrument among others in the politician's arsenal." Kahn 2004, 229.

32. See Bély 1999, 165–382.

33. For a historical overview of this tangle, see Lossky 1970, 168.

34. See Salzman 1985, 157–76.

35. Birken's "Vor-Ansprache zum edlen Leser" is printed at the beginning of Anton Ulrich 1669–73.

36. This poem, signed off by "the unknown female friend," is attributed to Catharina Regina von Greiffenberg (1633–94), a noble lady in Anton Ulrich's orbit and a main participant in the pastoral play that *Aramena* partly stages. See Spahr 1966, 131–54. The poem is unpaginated. I quote from the original 1671 edition.

37. "The *Argenis* of Barclay is possible, i.e. is clearly and distinctly imaginable, even if it is quite certain that she never lived, nor do I believe that she will ever live." Leibniz 2005, 57–59. These lines were written probably in 1672. On the anecdote about reading *Argenis* on his deathbed, see the editor's note to Leibniz 2005, 156n8.

38. Leibniz and Anton Ulrich 1888, 233.

39. Leibniz 1996, 460–62. On the relationship between Leibniz' metaphysics and his poetics of romance, see Vogl 2004, 148–50.

40. Blumenberg 1999, 12.
41. Blumenberg 2001, 196.
42. Cf. Blumenberg 1981.
43. Leibniz and Anton Ulrich 1888, 233–34.
44. Leibniz and Anton Ulrich 1888, 234.
45. See the editor's afterword to Saint-Pierre 1981, 582–604.
46. The title of the 1717 edition indicates clearly Saint-Pierre's indebtedness to Henri IV's grand design: *Project de traité pour rendre la paix perpétuelle entre les souverains chrétiens, [. . .] Proposé autre fois par Henry le Grand, Roy de France.*
47. Leibniz, "Observations on the Abbé de St Pierre's 'Project for Perpetual Peace' (1715)," in Leibniz 1988, 178–83.
48. Leibniz's letter to Grimarest in June 1712, in Leibniz 1988, 183–84.
49. See Kraft 2004, 137–55.
50. This point is made by Fuchs 2004.
51. Leibniz and Anton Ulrich 1888, 232.
52. Leibniz and Anton Ulrich 1888, 234.
53. Leibniz and Anton Ulrich 1888, 238.

5. The Divergence between International Law and Literature around 1700

1. Sidney 1763, 428.
2. Aristotle 1972, 1448a.
3. Aristotle 1972, 1452b.
4. Walter Benjamin stresses the work of mourning that *Trauerspiel* performs. See Benjamin 1974, 317–35.
5. Gryphius 1991. In-text references in the following indicate act and verse number.
6. See Heller-Roazen 2009; Kempe 2010.
7. Hobbes 1996. In-text references indicate the chapter number.
8. Skinner 2002, 2:200.
9. On the figure of Samson in Milton's prose writings, see Warren 2015, 170–72.
10. The question of international law in *Samson Agonistes* has been widely noted. See Kahn 2008; Sauer 2014, 136–58; Gregerson 2014, 675; Warren 2015, 174–81.
11. Milton 1991, 671–715. In-text references indicate the verse number.
12. Kahn 2004, 270–76.
13. Pufendorf 2013, 7.
14. McKeon 2005, ix–xx. On the establishment of the intimate domain of the conjugal family in the modern separation of the public and the private, 110–61.
15. On the cultivation of an interior religious conscience as a key moment in the rise of a separate private sphere, see McKeon 2005, 33–43.
16. Samson's faith-inspired violence at the end of Milton's tragic poem has caused much controversy. For a survey on this issue, see Serjeantson 2009. Recently, Samson has been seen as the literary predecessor of suicide bombers active at the turn of the twenty-first century, and *Samson Agonistes* has been read as the literary prefiguration of the intervention of religious faith in the secular political world; see, for instance, Mohamed 2011, chap. 4.

17. On Milton's nationalism, see Loewenstein and Stevens 2008.
18. Barthes 1983, 53–54.
19. Foucault 1990, 1:17–35. For a Foucauldian analysis of the confessional discourse in Racinian tragedy, particularly in *Phédre*, see Balke 2009, 357–89.
20. Racine 1999, line 535.
21. Bodin 1992, 1, 3.
22. Racine 1999, line 972.
23. Greenberg 2010, 14.
24. Pufendorf 2013, 9.
25. Leibniz 1988, 168.
26. Regarding the discourse of government, the period under consideration was characterized by the rise of economic knowledge. See Vogl 2004, 54–82. Regarding the discourse of public law, the developments in the late seventeenth century varied from country to country. In France, the period under question was shaped by the initiatives of Louis XIV. See Sueur 2001. In the German speaking countries, it was shaped by the professional study of the imperial constitution. See Stolleis 1988–2012, 1:225–67.
27. Cf. Repgen 2015, 231–58 ("Über die Publikation ACTA PACIS WESTPHALICAE") and 967–1010 ("Der Westfälische Friede und die zeitgenössische Öffentlichkeit").
28. Bernard 1700, 1:iii.
29. Saint-Prest 1725, i, iii.
30. See Vec 1998.
31. Dumont 1726–39, 1:vi, xi.
32. "Now things divine are entirely perfect, but the character of human law is always to hasten onward, and there is nothing in it which can abide forever, since nature is eager to produce new forms. We therefore do not cease to expect that matters will henceforth arise that are not secured in legal bonds." Justinian 1985, vol. 1, "The Confirmation of the *Digest*" (unpaginated).
33. See Habermas 1990, 54–121.
34. Rousset de Missy 1728–55, 1:ix.
35. Amelot de la Houssaie 1700.
36. Rousset de Missy 1728–55, 1:viii–ix.
37. Saint-Pierre 1981, 135.
38. Saint-Pierre 1981, 407.
39. On other projects of perpetual peace in Saint-Pierre's time, see Aksu 2008.
40. See Mattingly 1962.
41. See Hamilton and Langhorne 2011, chap. 3; Roosen 1976.
42. Callières 1716, 8.
43. Callières 1716, 16–17; 18.
44. Mably 1748, "Avertissement de l'Auteur," unpaginated.
45. See Moser 1750. This volume on positive legal norms in times of peace was followed by a volume on those in times of war: Moser 1752.
46. For example, Grewe 2000, part 3, "Droit Public de l'Europe: The International Legal Order during the French Age 1648–1815."
47. Here Leibniz refers to the pseudonym Monzambano, under which Pufendorf published *De statu imperii Germanici* in 1667. See Leibniz 2004, 200–202.

48. See Toyoda 2011.
49. Pufendorf 1934, book 2, chap. 3, section 23.
50. The hundreds of listings on natural law from the period under consideration in the catalogues of major research libraries in Europe attest to this fact. See for example the subject call numbers FI 4200—FI 7085 in the catalogue of the State Library in Berlin (Staatsbibliothek zu Berlin, Preußischer Kulturbesitz).
51. See Hochstrasser 2000.
52. Original in German. On Glafey's contributions to the discipline of international law, see Schmidt 2007.
53. This was also the state of the arts of legal studies in general in the period under consideration. See Hammerstein 1972; Stolleis 1988–2012, vol. 1, chaps. 6 and 7.
54. Wolff 1934, § 4.
55. Vattel 1916, Preliminaires, § 12; Wolff 1934, § 22.
56. Wolff 1934, § 20.
57. Jouannet 2012 argues that the Vattelian idea of the liberty and welfare of the nations represents the tenor of modern international law in general.
58. See Jouannet 1998.
59. Mably 1748, "Avertissement de l'Auteur," unpaginated.
60. Diderot 1994, 56.
61. Diderot 1994, 57.
62. Lessing 1985, 251.

6. The Novel and International Order in the Eighteenth Century

1. See McKeon 1987, chap. 1.
2. The scholarly debates about Ian Watt's literary historical narrative of the "rise of the novel" as a kind of prose fiction characterized by "formal realism" are a measure of this controversy. For a polemical rejection, see Doody 1996; for an attempt to resist, see Aravamudan 2012. On innovations and experimentations, see Spacks 2006, also Nandrea 2015.
3. Wilks 1963, 24n5; Kantorowicz 1957, 291–313.
4. Pufendorf 1934, 2.2.1. References indicate book, chapter, and section number.
5. See Scattola 2001.
6. On Pufendorf's construction of *societas* as opposed to *civitas*, see Hont 2005, 37–51 and 159–84.
7. Pufendorf 1934, 2.3.14.
8. Pufendorf 1927, 2.1.4.
9. Pufendorf 1934, 2.3.15.
10. Kant 1991a, 44.
11. Hobbes 1994, 182.
12. See Schröder 2000, 56n52.
13. Hume 2007, 363.
14. Vattel 1916, 2.2.21. References indicate book, chapter, and section number.
15. Hume 2007, 363.
16. See Wokler 2012, 88–112; Silvestrini 2010.
17. Rousseau 1997, 46, 169 ("The State of War").

18. Rousseau 1997, 163.
19. Pufendorf 1934, 2.2.2.
20. Smith 1978, 1:27.
21. See Mann 1916; Stach 1991.
22. Gundling 1734, 82.
23. Richetti 1996, 5.

24. Kay 1988 relates the eighteenth-century novel to natural law theory, speaking of both in terms of fictional constructions. However, using Hobbes as her main point of reference, Kay focuses on the construction of political society, neglecting the construction of *societas* in the Pufendorfian tradition. It is the latter, I argue, that is truly relevant to our understanding of the novel.

25. Thomasius 1688–90, 4:731.
26. Blanckenburg 1774, XV.
27. Blanckenburg 1774, 17.
28. See Vollhardt 2001, 211–60.
29. Thomasius 2006, 160.
30. Diderot 1994, 89–90.
31. Aristotle 1972, 1451a–b.
32. Bodmer 1741, 531, 539.
33. See Campe 2002, 309–43.
34. Wieland 2008, 3.
35. See Campe 2002, part 2, "Der Schein des Wahren."
36. Cf. Gallagher 1994.

37. The translations of Barclay's *Argenis* in the eighteenth century illustrate this transition from local referentiality of political romance to the complete nonreferentiality or fictionality of the novel. See Rösch 2004, 71–78.

38. See Gallagher 2006.
39. Roosen 1986, 9–10.
40. Defoe 2000, 11.
41. See Novak 1963, chap. 1; Dickey 2006.
42. See Novak 1963, chap. 2 and 3; Schmidgen 2002, chap. 2.

43. DeGabriele 2015 points out the presence of sovereign power in the social sphere of private persons as represented in eighteenth-century literature. This applies also to Defoe's novels.

44. Defoe 2007.
45. See Bell 1988.
46. On Hobbesian thought in Defoe, see Kay 1988, 66–92.
47. On the anti-Lockean, conservative, and royalist strain, see Schonhorn 1991.
48. See Seidel 1981.

49. At the latest since Hulme 1986, colonialism has been a recurring topic in the scholarship on *Robinson Crusoe*. For a critical review on this line of research, see Carey 2009. Carey points out that Robinson and Friday do not merely illustrate colonial domination, but also appear "in a series of structurally related ways as father and son, master and servant, teacher and pupil, monarch and subject" (128).

50. See Aravamudan 2009; Tang 2011c.
51. Defoe 1996.

52. Cf. Kibbie 1995; Healy 2006.
53. Butler 2009, 8.
54. See Peter Holbrook, "Jacobean Masques and the Jacobean Peace," in Bevington and Holbrook 1998, 67–87.
55. See Castle 1986.
56. Sterne 1968, 9.
57. On the rise of "sentiment" as the keyword in British ethical thought in the eighteenth century, see Rivers 2005.
58. On the sentimental mode, see Chandler 2013.
59. Shaftesbury 1999, 1:206.
60. Hume 2007, 303, 302.
61. See Hume 2007, book 3, part 3, section 1.
62. Smith 1976, 22.
63. Smith 1976, 294.
64. Hume 2007, 302–3.
65. Smith 1976, 10.
66. On the intimate relationship between Richardson's novels and Hume's moral sentimentalism, see Kay 1988, chap. 3.
67. Beattie 1790–93, 1:180.
68. See Koschorke 1999.
69. Denby 1994, 1.
70. See Alliston 2002.
71. See Festa 2006.
72. See Engbers 2001; Schönborn and Viehöver 2009.
73. Gellert 1989.
74. The intricate relationship between the sentimental novel and commercial economy has been widely noted. See Bellamy 1998; Skinner 1999. On this issue in Gellert's novel specifically, see also Vogl 2004, 182–85.
75. Cf. Richards 2006. Cohen 2002 distinguishes two kinds of sentimentality: the tragic and the melodramatic. While the violation of laws generates tragic sentimentality, death scenes are crucial to melodramatic sentimentality.
76. See McMurran 2009.
77. Vattel 1916, Prelim. § 10.
78. Vattel 1916, Prelim. § 12.
79. See Polloczek 1999, chap. 2.
80. Callières 1716, 161–62.
81. Pecquet 1737, vii.
82. Pecquet 1737, ix–x.
83. Keymer 2009, 92.
84. Dilthey 1870, 282.
85. Hobbes's translation of *The History of the Peloponnesian War* was first published in 1629. On Thucydides and Hobbes in the history of international law, see Warren 2015, 127–59.
86. Wieland 2008, 30.
87. See Albrecht 2005.
88. Diogenes Laertius 1925, 6:63.

89. See Konstan 2009.

90. Plutarch, *On the Fortune of Alexander* 329A-B. Quoted from Long and Sedley 1987, 429.

91. Seneca 1932, IV.1. On Stoic cosmopolitanism, see Schofield 1991, 57–92; also Brown 2009.

92. See Sahmland 1991, 217–72; Manger 1996; Albrecht 2005, 82–94 and 97–105; Kleingeld 2012, 13–39.

93. Wieland 1794, volume 3, book 16, chap. 3. All quotations are from volume 3.

94. Cicero 1998, *De Legibus* I.23.

95. On this point, see Erhart 1991, 382–89.

96. Blanckenburg 1774, Vorbericht, unpaginated.

97. Watt 1957, 288.

98. See Niggl 1977, quotation from Wieland at 46.

99. See Jordheim 2007.

100. See McKeon 2005, part 3: "Secret Histories," 467–717.

101. On the cosmopolitanism of the Illuminati, see Albrecht 2005, 140–68.

102. See Voges 1987, 102. On the relationship between Stoic philosophy and Freemasonry, see Preiß 2006, 15–56.

103. Moritz 1793, 230.

104. On the political function of secret societies in the Enlightenment, see Koselleck 1973, 49–103.

105. Johann Wolfgang Goethe, *Wilhelm Meisters Lehrjahre*, in Goethe 1985–99, 9:355–992.

106. Novalis 1968, 3:646. The note is dated to 1800.

107. On *Bildung* and cosmopolitanism, see Noyes 2006.

108. Kant 1991b, 98–99n.

109. See Kleingeld 2012.

110. See Nussbaum 1997.

111. Kant 1991b, 105–6.

112. See Werner and Gordon 2016.

113. Hunt 2007, 32.

114. Simpson 2015.

115. On the *Bildungsroman* and international human rights law, see Slaughter 2007.

Epilogue

1. Kant 1991b, 103.

2. See my studies of international law and literary forms at the time around 1800 and in the nineteenth century: Tang 2012, 2010, 2011a, 2011b.

3. See Koskenniemi 2001.

References

Accetto, Torquato. 1943. *Della dissimulazione onesta*. Florence: Felice le Monnier.
Aers, David. 1992. "A Whisper in the Ear of Early Modernists; or Reflections on Literary Critics Writing the 'History of the Subject.'" In *Culture and History 1350–1600*, edited by David Aers, 177–202. New York: Harvester Wheatsheaf.
Aeschylus. 2013. *Oresteia*. Translated by David Greene and Richmond Lattimore. 3rd ed. Chicago: University of Chicago Press.
Agamben, Giorgio. 2011a. *The Kingdom and the Glory*. Translated by Lorenzo Chiesa. Stanford: Stanford University Press.
———. 2011b. *The Sacrament of Language*. Translated by Adam Kotsko. Stanford: Stanford University Press.
Aksu, Eşref, ed. 2008. *Early Notions of Global Governance: Selected Eighteenth-Century Proposals for "Perpetual Peace."* Cardiff: University of Wales Press.
Albrecht, Andrea. 2005. *Kosmopolitismus. Weltbürgerdiskurse in Literatur, Philosophie und Publizistik um 1800*. Berlin: Walter de Gruyter.
Alewyn, Richard. 1959. *Das große Welttheater*. Munich: Beck.
Alliston, April. 2002. "Transnational Sympathies, Imaginary Communities." In *The Literary Channel*, edited by Margaret Cohen, 133–48. Princeton, NJ: Princeton University Press.
Amelot de la Houssaie, Abraham Nicolas. 1700. "Observations historiques et politiques sur les traitez des princes." In *Recueil des traitéz de paix, de trêves, de neutralité [. . .]*, edited by Jacques Bernard, vol. 2, i–lx. Amsterdam: Boom.
Anderson, M. S. 1998. *The Origins of the Modern European State System, 1491–1618*. London: Longman.
Anderson, Thomas. 2004. "'Legitimation, Name, All is Gone': Bastardy and Bureaucracy in Shakespeare's *King John*." *Journal for Early Modern Cultural Studies* 4: 35–61.
Anghie, Antony. 2005. *Imperialism, Sovereignty and the Making of International Law*. Cambridge: Cambridge University Press.
Anton Ulrich, Herzog von Braunschweig-Lüneburg [also Herzog von Brauschweig-Wolfenbüttel]. 1669–73. *Die durchlauchtige Syrerinn Aramena*. Nürnberg: Hoffmann.
———. 1993–2007. *Die römische Octavia. Werke: historisch-kritische Ausgabe*, vol. 3–9. Edited by Rolf Tarot. Stuttgart: Anton Hiersemann.
Apostelidès, Jean-Marie. 1985. *Le prince sacrifié*. Paris: Minuit.
Aquinas, Thomas. 1981. *Summa Theologica*. Translated by Fathers of the English Dominican Province. Notre Dame, IN: Christian Classics.

Aravamudan, Srinivas. 2009. "Hobbes and America." In *The Postcolonial Enlightenment: Eighteenth-Century Colonialism and Postcolonial Theory*, edited by Daniel Carey and Lynn Festa, 37–70. Oxford: Oxford University Press.

———. 2012. *Enlightenment Orientalism: Resisting the Rise of the Novel*. Chicago: University of Chicago Press.

Aristotle. 1972. *Poetics*. In *Ancient Literary Criticism*. Edited by D. A. Russell and M. Winterbottom, 85–132. Oxford: Oxford University Press.

———. 1984. *Rhetoric*. In *The Complete Works of Aristotle*, edited by Jonathan Barnes, vol. 2 2152–2269. Princeton, NJ: Princeton University Press.

Armitage, David. 2006. "Hobbes and the Foundations of Modern International Thought." In *Rethinking Foundations of Modern Political Thought*, edited by Annabel Brett, 219–35. Cambridge: Cambridge University Press.

———. 2013. *Foundations of Modern International Thought*. Cambridge: Cambridge University Press.

Aubignac, François Hédelin d'. 2001. *La pratique du théâtre*. Edited by Hélène Baby. Paris: Champion.

Aubigné, Théodore Agrippa d'. 1616–30. *Histoire universelle*. Maillé: Jean Moussat.

Auerbach, Erich. 1933. *Das französische Publikum des 17. Jahrhunderts*. Munich: Hueber.

Augustine. 1988–95. *Tractates on the Gospel of John*. Translated by John Rettig. Washington DC: Catholic University of America Press.

Badie, Bertrand. 2000. *The Imported State: The Westernization of Political Order*. Translated by Claudia Royal. Stanford: Stanford University Press, 2000.

Bakhtin, Mikhail. 1981. *The Dialogic Imagination*. Edited by Michael Holquist. Austin: University of Texas Press.

Baldini, Baccio. 1565. *Discorso sopra la Mascherata della genealogia degl'iddei de'gentili*. Florence: Appresso I Giunti.

Balke, Friedrich. 2009. *Figuren der Souveränität*. Munich: Fink.

Barclay, John. 1626. *Johann Barclaijens Argenis, Deutsch gemacht durch Martin Opitzen*. Breslau: David Müller.

———. 1636. *Argenis*. Translated by Kingsmill Long. 2nd ed. London: Henry Seile.

———. 2004. *Argenis*. Edited and translated by Mark Riley and Dorothy Pritchard Huber. Assen: Royal Van Gorcum.

Barclay, William. 1954. *The Kingdom and the Regal Power*. Translated by George Albert Moore. Chevy Chase, MD: Country Dollar Press.

Baricave, Jean. 1614. *La Defence de la Monarchie Francoise, et avtres Monarchies [. . .]*. Toulouse: Dominique Bosc.

Barner, Wilfried. 1989. "Disponible Festlichkeit—Zu Lohensteins *Sophonisbe*." In *Das Fest*, edited by Walter Haug and Rainer Warning, 247–75. Munich: Fink.

Bartolus de Saxoferrato. 1538. *Commentaria in primam ff. (digesti) Veteris partem*. Lugdunum: s.n.

Barbeyrac, Jean. 1706. "Préface du Traducteur." In *Le Droit de la nature et des gens*, by Samuel Pufendorf, translated by Jean Barbeyrac. Amsterdam: Schelte.

———. 1739. *Supplement au Corps Universel Diplomatique du Droit des Gens. Tome Premier: Histoire des anciens traitez [. . .]*. Amsterdam: Janssons.

Bartels, Emily. 1993. *Spectacles of Strangeness*. Philadelphia: University of Pennsylvania Press.

Bartelson, Jens. 1995. *A Genealogy of Sovereignty*. Cambridge: Cambridge University Press.
———. 2009. *Visions of World Community*. Cambridge: Cambridge University Press.
Barthes, Roland. 1983. *On Racine*. Translated by Richard Howard. New York: Performing Arts Journal Publications.
Beattie, James. 1790–93. *Elements of Moral Science*. Edinburgh: Cadell.
Beauregard, David. 2008. *Catholic Theology in Shakespeare's Plays*. Newark: Delaware University Press.
Bederman, David. 2001. *International Law in Antiquity*. Cambridge: Cambridge University Press.
Béhar, Pierre. 1988. *Silesia Tragica: épanouissement et fin de l'école dramatique silésienne dans l'œuvre tragique de Daniel Casper von Lohenstein (1635–1683)*. Wiesbaden: Harrassowitz.
Bell, Ian. 1988. "King Crusoe: Locke's Political Theory in *Robinson Crusoe*." *English Studies* 69: 27–36.
Bellamy, Liz. 1998. *Commerce, Morality and the Eighteenth-Century Novel*. Cambridge: Cambridge University Press.
Bély, Lucien. 1999. *La société des princes: XVIe–XVIIIe siècle*. Paris: Fayard.
Benjamin, Walter. 1974. *Ursprung des deutschen Trauerspiels*. In *Gesammelte Schriften*, edited by Rolf Tiedemann and Hermann Schweppenhäuser, vol. I.1, 203–430. Frankfurt am Main: Suhrkamp.
Bentham, Jeremy. 1843. "Principles of International Law." In *The Works of Jeremy Bentham*, edited by John Bowring, vol. 2, 537–60. Edinburgh: Tait.
———. 1970. *An Introduction to the Principles of Morals and Legislation*. Edited by J. H. Burns and H. L. A. Hart. Oxford: Oxford University Press.
Benton, Lauren. 2002. *Law and Colonial Cultures: Legal Regimes in World History, 1400–1900*. Cambridge: Cambridge University Press.
Bergeron, David. 1985. *Shakespeare's Romances and the Royal Family*. Lawrence: University Press of Kansas.
Berman, Harold. 1983. *Law and Revolution*. Cambridge, MA: Harvard University Press.
Bernard, Jacques, ed. 1700. *Recueil des traitéz de paix, de trêves, de neutralité [. . .]*. Amsterdam: Boom.
Besson, Samantha, and John Tasioulas, eds. 2010. *The Philosophy of International Law*. Cambridge: Cambridge University Press.
Bethery de la Brosse, Arnould. 2011. *Entre amour et droit: le lien conjugal dans la pensée juridique moderne (XVIe–XXIe siècles)*. Paris: LGDJ.
Bevington, David, and Peter Holbrook, eds. 1998. *The Politics of Stuart Court Masque*. Cambridge: Cambridge University Press.
Biet, Christian. 1994. *Œdipe en monarchie. Tragédie et théorie juridique à l'âge classique*. Paris: Klincksieck.
Bilis, Hélène. 2010. "Corneille's *Œdipe* and the Politics of Seventeenth-Century Royal Succession." *MLN* 125: 873–894.
Binder, Guyora, and Robert Weisberg. 2000. *Literary Criticisms of Law*. Princeton, NJ: Princeton University Press.
Bireley, Robert. 1990. *The Counter-Reformation Prince*. Chapel Hill: University of North Carolina Press.

Birken, Sigmund von. 1669. "Vor-Ansprache zum Edlen Leser." In *Die durchleuchtige Syrerinn Aramena*, by Anton Ulrich von Braunschweig-Lüneburg, vol. 1, unpaginated. Nürnberg: Hoffmann.

Blanckenburg, Friedrich von. 1774. *Versuch über den Roman*. Leipzig: David Siegerts Witwe.

Blumenberg, Hans. 1981. *Die Lesbarkeit der Welt*. Frankfurt am Main: Suhrkamp.

———. 1999. *Paradigmen zu einer Metaphorologie*. 2nd ed. Frankfurt am Main: Suhrkamp.

———. 2001. *Ästhetische und metaphorologische Schriften*. Frankfurt am Main: Suhrkamp.

Bodin, Jean. 1986. *Les six livres de la république*. Paris: Fayard.

———. 1992. *On Sovereignty*. Edited and translated by Julian Franklin. Cambridge: Cambridge University Press.

Bodmer, Johann Jacob. 1741. *Critische Betrachtungen über die poetischen Gemählde der Dichter*. Zurich: Conrad Orell.

Borgstedt, Thomas. 2010. "Die Erfindung der Tragödie als panegyrisches Opferspiel in Lohensteins Sophonisbe." *Wolfenbütteler Barock-Nachrichten* 37: 47–63.

Bossuet, Jacques-Benigne. 1990. *Politics Drawn from the Very Words of Holy Scripture*. Translated by Patrick Riley. Cambridge: Cambridge University Press.

Botero, Giovanni. 1956a. *The Greatness of Cities*. Translated by Robert Peterson. New Haven, CT: Yale University Press.

———. 1956b. *The Reason of State*. Translated by P. J. and D. P. Waley. New Haven, CT: Yale University Press.

Boyle, Anthony James. 1997. *Tragic Seneca*. London and New York: Routledge.

Braden, Gordon. 1985. *Renaissance Tragedy and the Senecan Tradition*. New Haven, CT: Yale University Press.

Braund, Susanna. 1997. "Virgil and the Cosmos: Religious and Philosophical Ideas." In *The Cambridge Companion to Virgil*, edited by Charles Martindale, 204–21. Cambridge: Cambridge University Press.

Brett, Annabel. 1997. *Liberty, Right and Nature: Individual Rights in Later Scholastic Thought*. Cambridge: Cambridge University Press.

———. 2011. *Changes of State: Nature and the Limits of the City in Early Modern Natural Law*. Princeton, NJ: Princeton University Press.

Brooks, Peter. 2005. "Narrative in and of the Law." In *A Companion to Narrative Theory*, edited by James Phelan and Peter Rabinowitz, 415–26. Malden, MA: Blackwell.

Brooks, Peter, and Paul Gewirtz, eds. 1996. *Law's Stories: Narrative and Rhetoric in the Law*. New Haven, CT: Yale University Press.

Brown, Eric. 2009. "The Emergence of Natural Law and the Cosmopolis." In *The Cambridge Companion to Greek Political Thought*, edited by Stephen Salkevar, 331–63. Cambridge: Cambridge University Press.

Brown, Jane. 2007. *The Persistence of Allegory*. Philadelphia: University of Pennsylvania Press.

Bruner, Jerome. 1986. *Actual Minds, Possible Worlds*. Cambridge, MA: Harvard University Press.

———. 2002. *Making Stories: Law, Literature, Life*. Cambridge, MA: Harvard University Press.

Brunner, Otto, Werner Conze, and Reinhardt Koselleck, eds. 2004. *Geschichtliche Grundbegriffe: Historisches Lexikon zur politisch-sozialen Sprache in Deutschland*. Stuttgart: Klett-Cotta.

Bull, Hedley. 1977. *The Anarchical Society*. New York: Columbia University Press.
Bull, Malcolm. 2005. *The Mirror of the Gods*. Oxford: Oxford University Press.
Bunge, Kirstin. 2017. "Francisco de Vitoria: A Redesign of Global Order on the Threshold of the Middle Ages to Modern Times." In *System, Order and International Law: The Early History of International Legal Thought from Machiavelli to Hegel*, edited by Stefan Kadelbach, Thomas Kleinlein, and David Roth-Isigkeit, 38–55. Oxford: Oxford University Press.
Burckhardt, Jakob. 1989. *Die Kultur der Renaissance in Italien*. Edited by Horst Günther. Frankfurt am Main: Deutscher Klassiker Verlag.
Burckhardt, Sigurd. 1968. *Shakespearean Meanings*. Princeton, NJ: Princeton University Press.
Butler, Martin. 2009. *The Stuart Court Masque and Political Culture*. Cambridge: Cambridge University Press.
Cahill, Patricia. 2008. *Unto the Breach: Martial Formations, Historical Trauma, and the Early Modern Stage*. Oxford: Oxford University Press.
Callières, François de. 1716. *De la Manière de Negocier avec les Souverains*. Amsterdam: Pour la Compagnie.
Camden, William. 1635. *Annals, Or the History of the Most Renowned and Victorious Princess Elizabeth, Late Queen of England*. 3rd ed. London: Benjamin Fisher.
Camões, Luís Vaz de. 1655. *The Lusiad, or Portugals Historicall Poem: WRITTEN in the Portingall Language by Louis de Camoens; and Now newly put into English by Richard Fanshaw*. London: Humphrey Moseley.
———. 1973. *Os Lusíadas*. Edited by Frank Pierce. Oxford: Clarendon Press.
———. 1997. *The Lusiads*. Translated by Landeg White. Oxford: Oxford University Press.
Campe, Rüdiger. 2002. *Spiel der Wahrscheinlichkeit: Literatur und Berechnung zwischen Pascale und Kleist*. Göttingen: Wallstein.
Canning, J. P. 1987. *The Political Thought of Baldus de Ubaldis*. Cambridge: Cambridge University Press.
———. 1988. "Law, Sovereignty and Corporation Theory, 1300–1450." In *The Cambridge History of Medieval Political Thought, c. 350—c.1450*, edited by J. H. Burns, 454–76. Cambridge: Cambridge University Press.
Carey, Daniel. 2009. "Reading Contrapuntally: Robinson Crusoe, Slavery, and Postcolonial Theory." In *The Postcolonial Enlightenment: Eighteenth-Century Colonialism and Postcolonial Theory*, edited by Daniel Carey and Lynn Festa, 105–36. Oxford: Oxford University Press.
Carty, Anthony. 2007. *Philosophy of International Law*. Edinburgh: Edinburgh University Press.
Castelvetro, Lodovico. 1984. *On the Art of Poetry: An Abridged Translation of Lodovico Castelvetro's Poetica d'Aristotele vulgarizzata e sposta*. Translated by Andrew Bongiorno. Binghamton: Medieval and Renaissance Texts and Studies.
Castle, Terry. 1986. *Masquerade and Civilization: The Carnivalesque in Eighteenth-Century English Culture and Fiction*. Stanford: Stanford University Press.
Cavaillé, Jean-Pierre. 2002. *Dis/simulations*. Paris: Champion, 2002.
Ceremoniale Brandenbvrgicvm. 1699. Tremoniae: s.n.
Chandler, James. 2013. *An Archaeology of Sympathy: The Sentimental Mode in Literature and Cinema*. Chicago: University of Chicago Press.

Charron, Pierre. 1656. *De la sagesse*. Leide: Jean Elsevier.
Cheney, Patrick, ed. 2004. *The Cambridge Companion to Christopher Marlowe*. Cambridge: Cambridge University Press.
Chénier, André. 1958. *Œuvres Complètes*. Paris: Gallimard.
Chronologie des allgemeinen Staats-Archivs, Worin die Friedens-Schlüsse [. . .]. 1704. Hamburg: Benjamin Schiller.
Cicero, Marcus Tullius. 1998. *The Republic and The Laws*. Translated by Niall Rudd. Oxford: Oxford University Press.
———. 2000. *On Obligations*. Translated by P. G. Walsh. Oxford: Oxford University Press.
Clausen, Wendell. 1964. "An Interpretation of the *Aeneid*." *Harvard Studies in Classical Philology* 68: 139–47.
Cohen, Margaret. 2002. "Sentimental Communities." In *The Literary Channel*, edited by Margaret Cohen, 106–32. Princeton, NJ: Princeton University Press.
Coing, Helmut, ed. 1973–88. *Handbuch der Quellen und Literatur der neueren europäischen Privatrechtsgeschichte*. Munich: Beck.
Conklin, William. 2001. *The Invisible Origins of Legal Positivism*. Dordrecht: Kluwer.
Conti, Natale. 2006. *Mythologiae*. Translated by John Mulryan and Steven Brown. Tempe, AZ: Arizona Center for Medieval and Renaissance Studies.
Cormack, Bradin. 2008. *A Power to Do Justice: Jurisdiction, English Literature, and the Rise of Common Law*. Chicago: University of Chicago Press.
Cormack, Bradin, Martha Nussbaum, and Richard Strier, eds. 2013. *Shakespeare and the Law: A Conversation Among Disciplines and Professions*. Chicago: University of Chicago Press.
Corneille, Pierre. 1980–87. *Œuvres complètes*. Edited by Georges Couton (Bibliothèque de la Pléiade). Paris: Gallimard.
———. 1998. *La conquête de la Toison d'or*. Edited by Marie-France Wagner. Paris: Champion.
Couton, Georges. 2003. *La vieillesse de Corneille*. Paris: Eurédit.
Cover, Robert. 1983–84. "The Supreme Court 1982 Term. Foreword: Nomos and Narrative." *Harvard Law Review* 97: 4–68.
———. 1985–86. "Violence and the Word." *Yale Law Journal* 95: 1601–29.
Crucé, Eméric. 1972. *The New Cineas*. Translated by C. Frederick Farrell Jr. and Edith R. Farrell. New York: Garland.
Curren-Aquino, Deborah, ed. 1989. *King John: New Perspectives*. Newark: University of Delaware Press.
Curtis, Ernst Robert. *European Literature and the Latin Middle Ages*. Princeton, NJ: Princeton University Press.
Damien, Robert. 1995. *Bibliothèque et État: Naissance d'une raison politique dans la France du XVIIe siècle*. Paris: Presses Universitaires de France.
Dante Alighieri. 1996. *Monarchy*. Translated by Prue Shaw. Cambridge: Cambridge University Press.
Decock, Wim. 2013. *Theologians and Contract Law: The Moral Transformation of the Ius Commune (ca. 1500–1650)*. Leiden: Nijhoff.
Defoe, Daniel. 1996. *Roxana: The Fortunate Mistress*. Edited by John Mullan. Oxford: Oxford University Press.

———. 2000. *International Relations*. Vol. 5 of *Political and Economic Writings of Daniel Defoe*, edited by P. N. Furbank. London: Pickering & Chatto.

———. 2007. *Robinson Crusoe*. Edited by Thomas Keymer. Oxford: Oxford University Press.

———. 2008a. *The Life, Adventures, and Pyracies, of the Famous Captain Singleton*. Vol. 5 of *The Novels of Daniel Defoe*, edited by P. N. Furbank. London: Pickering & Chatto.

———. 2008b. *Memoirs of a Cavalier*. Vol. 4 of *The Novels of Daniel Defoe*, edited by N. H. Keeble. London: Pickering & Chatto.

DeGabriele, Peter. 2015. *Sovereign Power and the Enlightenment: Eighteenth-Century Literature and the Problem of the Political*. Lewisburg, MD: Bucknell University Press.

Deleuze, Gilles. 1993. *The Fold: Leibniz and the Baroque*. Minneapolis: University of Minnesota Press.

Delmas, Christian. 1985. *Mythologie et mythe dans le théâtre français (1650–1676)*. Geneva: Droz.

Denby, David. 1994. *Sentimental Narrative and the Social Order in France, 1760–1820*. Cambridge: Cambridge University Press.

Derrida, Jacques. 1990. "Force of Law: The 'Mythical Foundation of Authority.'" *Cardozo Law Review* 11: 919–1045.

Descendre, Romain. 2009. *L'État du Monde*. Geneva: Droz.

Descimon, Robert. 1992. "Les fonctions le la métaphore du mariage politique du roi et de la république en France, XVe–XVIIIe siècles." *Annales. Économies, Sociétés, Civilisations* 47, no. 6: 1127–47.

Dickey, Laurence. 2006. "Power, Commerce, and Natural Law in Daniel Defoe's Political Writings 1698–1707." In *A Union for Empire: Political Thought and the British Union of 1707*, edited by John Robertson, 63–96. Cambridge: Cambridge University Press.

Diderot, Denis. 1994. *Selected Writings on Art and Literature*. Translated by Geoffrey Bremner. London: Penguin Books.

Digges, Dudley. 1655. *The Compleat Ambassador: Or Two Treaties of Intended Marriage of Queen Elizabeth of Glorious Memory*. London: Gabriel Bedall and Thomas Collins.

Dilthey, Wilhelm. 1870. *Das Leben Schleiermachers*. Berlin: Reimer.

Diogenes Laertius. 1925. *Lives of Eminent Philosophers*. Edited and translated by Robert Drew. Cambridge, MA: Harvard University Press.

Doody, Margaret Anne. 1996. *The True History of the Novel*. New Brunswick: Rutgers University Press.

Duindam, Jeroen. 2003. *Vienna and Versailles: The Courts of Europe's Dynastic Rivals*. Cambridge: Cambridge University Press.

Dumont, Jean, ed. 1726–39. *Corps universel diplomatique du Droit des Gens [. . .]*. Amsterdam: Brunel.

Dumont, Louis. 2006. *Introduction to Two Theories of Social Anthropology*. Translated by Robert Parkin. New York: Berghahn Books.

Duve, Thomas. 2017. "Spatial Perceptions, Juridical Practices, and Early International Legal Thought around 1500: From Tordesillas to Saragossa." In *System,*

Order and International Law: The Early History of International Legal Thought from Machiavelli to Hegel, edited by Stefan Kadelbach, Thomas Kleinlein, and David Roth-Isigkeit, 418–42. Oxford: Oxford University Press.

Dworkin, Ronald. 1986. *Law's Empire*. Cambridge, MA: Harvard University Press.

Eden, Kathy. 1986. *Poetic and Legal Fiction in the Aristotelian Tradition*. Princeton, NJ: Princeton University Press.

Ellickson, Robert. 1994. *Order Without Law: How Neighbors Settle Disputes*. Cambridge, MA: Harvard University Press.

Engbers, Jan. 2001. *Der "Moral-Sense" bei Gellert, Lessing und Wieland*. Heidelberg: Winter.

Elizabeth I, Queen of England. 2000. *Collected Works*. Edited by Leah Marcus, Janel Mueller, and Mary Beth Rose. Chicago: University of Chicago Press.

Erhart, Walter. 1991. *Entzweiung und Selbstaufklärung: Christoph Martin Wielands "Agathon"-Projekt*. Tübingen: Niemeyer.

Fassbender, Bardo, and Anne Peters, eds. 2012. *The Oxford Handbook of the History of International Law*. Oxford: Oxford University Press.

Fernández-Santamaria, J. A. 1977. *The State, War and Peace*. Cambridge: Cambridge University Press.

———. 2005–6. *Natural Law, Constitutionalism, Reason of State, and War*. New York: Peter Lang.

Festa, Lynn. 2006. *Sentimental Figures of Empire in Eighteenth-Century Britain and France*. Baltimore: Johns Hopkins University Press.

Fielding, Henry. 1967. *Joseph Andrews*. Oxford: Clarendon Press, 1967.

———. 1974. *The History of Tom Jones*. Oxford: Oxford University Press.

Filmer, Robert. 1991. *Patriacha and Other Writings*. Edited by Johann Sommerville. Cambridge: Cambridge University Press.

Fischer-Lichte, Erika. 1992. *The Semiotics of Theater*. Translated by Jeremey Gaines. Bloomington: Indiana University Press.

Fögen, Marie Therese. 2002. *Römische Rechtsgeschichten*. Göttingen: Vandenhoek und Ruprecht.

Forman, Valerie. 2008. *Tragicomic Redemptions: Global Economics and the Early Modern English Stage*. Philadelphia: University of Pennsylvania Press.

Foucault, Michel. 1990. *The History of Sexuality*. Translated by Robert Hurley. New York: Vintage Books.

———. 1994. *Power*. Edited by James Faubion. New York: The New Press.

———. 2007. *Security, Territory, Population: Lectures at the Collège de France 1977–1978*. Translated by Graham Burchell. New York: Palgrave Macmillan.

Frigo, Daniella, ed. 2000. *Politics and Diplomacy in Early Modern Italy*. Translated by Adrian Belton. Cambridge: Cambridge University Press.

Frye, Northrop. 1957. *Anatomy of Criticism*. Princeton, NJ: Princeton University Press.

———. 1976. *The Secular Scripture*. Cambridge, MA: Harvard University Press.

Fuchs, Barbara. 1997. "Conquering Islands: Contextualizing *The Tempest*." *Shakespeare Quarterly* 48: 45–62.

———. 2004. *Romance*. London: Routledge.

Gajda, Alexandra. 2009. "Tacitus and Political Thought in Early Modern Europe, c.1530–1640." In *The Cambridge Companion to Tacitus*, edited by A. J. Woodman, 253–68. Cambridge: Cambridge University Press.

Gallagher, Catherine. 1994. *Nobody's Story: The Vanishing Acts of Women Writers in the Marketplace, 1670–1920*. Berkeley: University of California Press.
———. 2006. "The Rise of Fictionality." In *The Novel*, edited by Franco Moretti, vol. 1, 336–63. Princeton, NJ: Princeton University Press.
Garatus, Martinus 2004. *Tractatus de confederatione, pace et conventionibus principum*. Edited by Alain Wijffels. In *Peace Treaties and International Law in European History*, edited by Randall Lesaffer, 412–47. Cambridge: Cambridge University Press.
Gellert, Christian Fürchtegott. 1989. *Leben der Schwedischen Gräfinn von G****. In *Gesammelte Schriften*, edited by Bernd Witte, vol. 4, 1–96. Berlin: Walter de Gruyter.
A General Collection of Treatys, Declarations of War, [. . .] From 1648 to the Present Time. 1710–32. London: Darby.
Gentili, Alberico. 1924. *De legationibus libri tres*. Translated by Gordon Laing. New York: Oxford University Press.
———. 1933. *De iure belli libri tres*. Translated by John C. Rolfe. Oxford: Clarendon Press.
———. 2011. *The Wars of the Romans*. Translated by David Lupher. Oxford: Oxford University Press.
Gieskes, Edward. 1998. "'He Is but a Bastard to the Time': Status and Service in *The Troublesome Reign of King John* and Shakespeare's *King John*." *ELH* 65: 779–98.
Gil, Fernando, and Helder Macedo. 2009. *The Traveling Eye: Retrospection, Vision, and Prophecy in the Portuguese Renaissance*. Dartmouth: University of Massachusetts-Dartmouth Press.
Glafey, Adam Friedrich. 1723. *Vernünfft- und Völcker-Recht [. . .]*. Frankfurt: Riegel.
Godefroy, Denys. 1649. *Le Ceremonial François*. Paris: Cramoisy.
Godefroy, Théodore. 1619. *Le cérémonial de France*. Paris: Pacard.
Goethe, Johann Wolfgang. 1985–99. *Sämtliche Werke, Briefe, Tagebücher und Gespräche*. Edited by Friedmar Apel et al. Frankfurt am Main: Deutscher Klassiker Verlag.
Goodrich, Peter. 2008. "On the Relational Aesthetics of International Law: *Philosophy of International Law*, Anthony Carty." *Journal of the History of International Law* 10: 321–41.
Gordley, James. 1991. *The Philosophical Origins of Modern Contract Doctrine*. Oxford: Oxford University Press.
Gottsched, Johann Christoph. 1973. *Versuch einer critischen Dichtkunst*. Vol. 6, no. 1, of *Ausgewählte Werke*, edited by Joachim Birke and Brigitte Birke. Berlin: Walter de Gruyter.
Gracián, Baltasar. 2011. *The Pocket Oracle and Art of Prudence*. Translated by Jeremy Robbins. London: Penguin Books.
Graff, Gerald, and James Phelan, eds. 2009. *William Shakespeare, The Tempest: A Case Study in Critical Controversy*, 2nd ed. Boston: Bedford.
Gratian. 1993. *The Treatise on Laws (Decretum DD. 1–20)*. Translated by Augustine Thompson. Washington, DC: Catholic University of America Press.
Greenberg, Mitchel. 2010. *Racine: From Ancient Myth to Tragic Modernity*. Minneapolis: University of Minnesota Press.
Greenblatt, Stephen. 1980. *Renaissance Self-Fashioning: From More to Shakespeare*. Chicago: University of Chicago Press.
———. 1990. *Learning to Curse: Essays in Early Modern Culture*. New York: Routledge.

Greene, Thomas. 1963. *The Descent from Heaven*. New Haven, CT: Yale University Press.
Gregerson, Linda. 2014. "Milton and the Tragedy of Nations." *PMLA* 129, no. 4: 672–87.
Grewe, Wilhelm, ed. 1988–1995. *Fontes Historiae Iuris Gentium*. Berlin and New York: Walter de Gruyter.
———. 2000. *Epochs of International Law*. Translated by Michael Byers. Berlin: Walter de Gruyter.
Grotius, Hugo. 1658. *Annales et Historiae de Rebus Belgicis*. Amsterdam: Blaeu.
———. 1845. *The Introduction to Dutch Jurisprudence*. Translated by Charles Herbert. London: John van Voorst.
———. 1925. *De jure belli ac pacis libri tres*. Translated by Francis Kelsey. Oxford: Clarendon.
———. 1992. *The Poetry of Hugo Grotius: Sophompaneas, 1635*. Edited by Arthur Eyffinger. Assen: Van Gorcum.
———. 1994. "Commentarius in Theses XI." In Peter Borschberg, *Hugo Grotius "Commentarius in Theses XI": An Early Treatise on Sovereignty, the Just War, and the Legitimacy of the Dutch Revolt*, 201–83. Berne: Peter Lang.
———. 2004. *The Free Sea*. Edited by David Armitage. Indianapolis: Liberty Fund.
———. 2005. *The Rights of War and Peace*. Edited by Richard Tuck. Indianapolis: Liberty Fund.
———. 2006. *Commentary on the Law of Prize and Booty*. Edited by Marine Julia van Ittersum. Indianapolis: Liberty Fund.
Gryphius, Andreas. 1991. *Dramen*. Edited by Eberhard Mannack. Frankfurt am Main: Deutscher Klassiker Verlag.
Guicciardini, Francesco. 1984. *The History of Italy*. Translated by Sidney Alexander. Princeton, NJ: Princeton University Press.
———. 1991. *Ricordi. Storie Florentine*. Edited by Emanuella Scarano. Milan: Editori Associati.
———. 1994. *Dialogue on the Government of Florence*. Translated by Alison Brown. Cambridge: Cambridge University Press.
Gundling, Nicolaus Hieronymus. 1734. *Ausführlicher Discours über das Natur- und Völcker-Recht*. Frankfurt: Spring.
Gurr, Andrew. 2004. *Playgoing in Shakespeare's London*. Cambridge: Cambridge University Press.
Haakonssen, Knud. 1996. *Natural Law and Moral Philosophy from Grotius to the Scottish Enlightenment*. Cambridge: Cambridge University Press.
Habermas, Jürgen. 1990. *Der Strukturwandel der Öffentlichkeit*. Frankfurt am Main: Suhrkamp.
Hacking, Ian. 2006. *The Emergence of Probability*. 2nd ed. Cambridge: Cambridge University Press.
Hamilton, Alexander, James Madison, and John Jay. 1999. *The Federalist Papers*. Edited by Clinton Rossiter. New York: Mentor.
Hamilton, Keith, and Richard Langhorne. 2011. *The Practice of Diplomacy*. London: Routledge.
Hammerstein, Notker. 1972. *Jus und Historie. Ein Beitrag zur Geschichte des historischen Denkens an deutschen Universitäten im späten 17. und 18. Jahrhundert*. Göttingen: Vandenhoeck & Ruprecht.

Hampton, Timothy. 2009. *Fictions of Embassy: Literature and Diplomacy in Early Modern Europe*. Ithaca, NY: Cornell University Press.
Hardie, Philip. 1986. *Virgil's "Aeneid": Cosmos and Imperium*. Oxford: Clarendon Press.
Harsdörffer, Georg Philipp. 1648–53. *Poetischer Trichter*. Nürnberg: Wolfgang Endter.
Hartbecke, Karin, ed. 2008. *Zwischen Fürstenwillkür und Menschheitswohl—Gottfried Wilhelm Leibniz als Bibliothekar*. Frankfurt am Main: Vittorio Klostermann.
Hart, H. L. A. 1994. *The Concept of Law*. 2nd ed. Oxford: Oxford University Press.
Healy, Christina. 2006. "'A Perfect Retreat Indeed': Speculation, Surveillance, and Space in Defoe's Roxana." *Eighteenth Century Fiction* 21: 493–512.
Heliodorus. 1989. *An Ethiopian Story*. In *Collected Ancient Greek Novels*, edited by B. P. Reardon, 349–588. Berkeley: University of California Press.
Heller-Roazen, Daniel. 2009. *The Enemy of All: Piracy and the Law of Nations*. New York: Zone Books.
Herbert, Sir Percy. 1661. *The Princess CLORIA*. London: Ralph Wood.
Hesiod. 1988. *Theogony* and *Works and Days*. Translated by M. L. West. Oxford: Oxford University Press.
Hill, Charles. 2010. *Grand Strategies*. New Haven, CT: Yale University Press.
Hinsley, F. H. 1986. *Sovereignty*. 2nd ed. Cambridge: Cambridge University Press, 1986.
Hobbes, Thomas. 1994. *The Elements of Law: Human Nature and De Corpore Politico*. Edited by John C. A. Gaskin. Oxford: Oxford University Press.
———. 1996. *Leviathan*. Edited by Richard Tuck. Cambridge: Cambridge University Press.
———. 1998. *On the Citizen*. Edited and translated by Richard Tuck and Michael Silverthorne. Cambridge: Cambridge University Press.
Hochstrasser, T. J. 2000. *Natural Law Theories in the Early Enlightenment*. Cambridge: Cambridge University Press.
Homer. 1996. *The Odyssey*. Translated by Robert Fagles. New York: Penguin.
———. 2011. *The Iliad*. Translated by Richmond Lattimore. With a new Introduction by Richard Martin. Chicago: The University of Chicago Press.
Hont, Istvan. 2005. *Jealousy of Trade: International Competition and the Nation-State in Historical Perspective*. Cambridge, MA: Harvard University Press.
Höpfl, Harro. 2004. *Jesuit Political Thought*. Cambridge: Cambridge University Press.
Hopkins, Lisa. 2008. *The Cultural Uses of the Caesars on the English Renaissance Stage*. Aldershot: Ashgate.
Hotman de Villiers, Jean. 1603. *L'Ambassadeur*. s.l.: s.n.
Hoxby, Blair. 2010. "Allegorical Drama." In *The Cambridge Companion to Allegory*, edited by Riter Copeland, 191–209. Cambridge: Cambridge University Press.
———. 2015. *What Was Tragedy: Theory and the Early Modern Canon*. Oxford: Oxford University Press.
Huet, Pierre Daniel. 1715. *The History of Romances*. Translated by Stephen Lewis. London: Hooke.
Hulme, Peter. 1986. *Colonial Encounters: Europe and the Native Caribbean, 1492–1797*. London: Methuen.
Hulme, Peter, and William Sherman, eds. 2000. *The Tempest and Its Travels*. Philadelphia: University of Pennsylvania Press.

Hume, David. 1987. *Essays, Moral, Political and Literary*. Edited by Eugene Miller. Indianapolis: Liberty Fund.

———. 2007. *A Treatise of Human Nature*. Edited by David Fate Norton and Mary J. Norton. Oxford: Clarendon Press.

Hüning, Dieter. 2000. "'Inter arma silent leges': Naturrecht, Staat und Völkerrecht bei Thomas Hobbes." In *Der Leviathan*, edited by Rüdiger Voigt, 145–67. Baden-Baden: Nomos.

Hunt, Lynn. 2007. *Inventing Human Rights: A History*. New York: Norton.

Hutcheson, Francis. 2004. *An Inquiry into the Original of Our Ideas of Beauty and Virtue*. Edited by Wolfgang Leidhold. Indianapolis: Liberty Fund.

Ijsewijn, Joseph. 1983. "John Barclay and His Argenis. A Scottish Neo-Latin Novelist." *Humanistica Lovaniensia* 32: 1–27.

Iser, Wolfgang. 1991. *Das Fiktive und das Imaginäre: Perspektiven literarischer Anthropologie*. Frankfurt am Main: Suhrkamp.

Ittersum, Martine Julia van. 2006. *Profit and Principle: Hugo Grotius, Natural Rights Theories and the Rise of Dutch Power in the East Indies, 1595–1615*. Leiden: Brill.

———. 2016. "Hugo Grotius: The Making of a Founding Father of International Law." In *The Oxford Handbook of the Theory of International Law*, edited by Anne Orford, Florian Hoffmann, and Martin Clark, 82–100. Oxford: Oxford University Press.

James I, King of England (James VI, King of Scotland). 1994. *Political Writings*. Edited by Johann P. Sommerville. Cambridge: Cambridge University Press.

James, Heather. 1997. *Shakespeare's Troy: Drama, Politics, and the Translation of Empire*. Cambridge: Cambridge University Press.

Jhering, Rudolf von. 1887. "Die Gastfreundschaft im Alterthum." *Deutsche Rundschau* 51: 357–97.

Jodelle, Étienne. 1968. *Cléopâtre captive*. In *Œuvres Complètes* II, edited by Enea Balmas, 91–147. Paris: Gallimard.

Jong, Jan de. 2013. *The Power and the Glorification*. University Park: Pennsylvania State University Press.

Jordheim, Helge. 2007. *Der Staatsroman im Werk Wielands and Jean Pauls*. Tübingen: Niemeyer.

Jouannet, Emmanuelle. 1998. *Emer de Vattel et l'émergence doctrinale du droit internationale classique*. Paris: Pedone.

———. 2012. *The Liberal-Welfarist Law of Nations: A History of International Law*. Cambridge: Cambridge University Press.

Jowitt, Claire. 2011. "Pirates and Politics in John Barclay's *Argenis* (1621)." *The Yearbook of English Studies* 41 (1): 56–172.

Justinian. 1985. *The Digest of Justinian*. 4 Vols. Edited by Alan Watson. Philadelphia: University of Pennsylvania Press.

———. 1987. *Justinian's Institutes*. Translated by Peter Birks and Grant McLeod. Ithaca, NY: Cornell University Press.

Kahn, Victoria. 2004. *Wayward Contracts: The Crisis of Political Obligation in England, 1640–1674*. Princeton, NJ: Princeton University Press.

———. 2008. "Disappointed Nationalism: Milton in the Context of Seventeenth-Century Debates about the Nation-State." In *Early Modern Nationalism and Mil-

ton's England, edited by David Loewenstein and Paul Stevens, 249–72. Toronto: University of Toronto Press.

Kant, Immanuel. 1977. *Kritik der Urteilskraft*. Werkausgabe, vol. 10. Edited by Wihelm Weischedel. Frankfurt am Main: Suhrkamp.

———. 1991a. "Idea for a Universal History With a Cosmopolitan Purpose." In *Political Writings*, edited by Hans Reiss, translated by H. B. Nisbet. Cambridge: Cambridge University Press, 41–53.

———. 1991b. "Perpetual Peace: A Philosophical Sketch." In *Political Writings*, edited by Hans Reiss, translated by H. B. Nisbet. Cambridge: Cambridge University Press, 93–130.

Kantorowicz, Ernst. 1957. *The King's Two Bodies: A Study in Medieval Political Theology*. Princeton, NJ: Princeton University Press.

———. 1961. "The Sovereignty of the Artist: A Note on Legal Maxims and Renaissance Theories of Art." In *De artibus opuscula XL*, edited by Millard Meiss, 267–79. New York: New York University Press.

Kaser, Max. 1993. *Ius gentium*. Cologne: Böhlau.

Kaulbach, Hans-Martin. 1998. "The Portrayal of Peace Before and After 1648." In *1648: War and Peace in Europe*, edited by Klaus Bussmann and Heinz Schilling, vol. 2, 593–603. Münster: Bruckmann.

Kay, Carol. 1988. *Political Constructions: Defoe, Richardson, and Sterne in Relation to Hobbes, Hume, and Burke*. Ithaca, NY: Cornell University Press.

Kelsen, Hans. 1967. *Pure Theory of Law*. Translated by Max Knight. Berkeley: University of California Press.

Kempe, Michael. 2010. *Fluch der Weltmeere: Piraterie, Völkerrecht und internationale Beziehungen 1500–1900*. Frankfurt am Main: Campus Verlag.

Kerényi, Károly. 1973. *Die griechisch-orientalische Romanliteratur in religionsgeschichtlicher Beleuchtung*, 3rd ed. Darmstadt: Wissenschaftliche Buchgesellschaft.

Kermode, Frank. 2000. *The Sense of an Ending*. Oxford: Oxford University Press.

Keymer, Thomas, ed. 2009. *The Cambridge Companion to Laurence Sterne*. Cambridge: Cambridge University Press.

Kibbie, Ann Louise. 1995. "Monstrous Generation: The Birth of Capital in Defoe's Moll Flanders and Roxana." *PMLA* 110: 1023–34.

Kiefer, Frederick. 2003. *Shakespeare's Visual Theater*. Cambridge: Cambridge University Press.

Kissinger, Henry. 2014. *World Order*. New York: Penguin.

Kitzinger, Martin. 2012. "From the Middle Ages to the Peace of Westphalia." In *The Oxford Handbook of the History of International Law*, edited by Bardo Fassbender and Anne Peters, 607–27. Oxford: Oxford University Press.

Klabbers, Jan. 2005. "The Concept of Legal Personality." *Ius Gentium* 11: 35–66.

Kleingeld, Pauline. 2012. *Kant and Cosmopolitanism: The Philosophical Ideal of World Citizenship*. Cambridge: Cambridge University Press.

Konstan, David. 2009. "Cosmopolitan Traditions." In *A Companion to Greek and Roman Political Thought*, edited by Ryan K. Balot, 473–84. Chichester: Wiley-Blackwell.

Korowicz, Marek St. 1956. "The Problem of the International Personality of Individuals." *American Journal of International Law* 50: 533–62.

Koschorke, Albrecht. 1999. *Körperströme und Schriftverkehr: Mediologie des 18. Jahrhunderts*. Munich: Fink.

———. 2012. *Wahrheit und Erfindung: Grundzüge einer allgemeinen Erzähltheorie*. Frankfurt am Main: Fischer.

Koschorke, Albrecht, Thomas Frank, Ethel Matala de Mazz, and Susanne Lüdemann. 2007. *Konstruktionen des politischen Körpers in der Geschichte Europas*. Frankfurt am Main: Fischer.

Koselleck, Reinhart. 1973. *Kritik und Krise: Eine Studie zur Pathogenese der bürgerlichen Welt*. Frankfurt am Main: Suhrkamp.

Koskenniemi, Martti. 2001. *The Gentle Civilizer of Nations: The Rise and Fall of International Law 1870–1960*. Cambridge: Cambridge University Press.

———. 2010. "International Law and *Raison d'état*: Rethinking the Prehistory of International Law." In *The Roman Foundations of the Law of Nations*, edited by Benedict Kingsbury and Benjamin Straumann, 297–339. Oxford: Oxford University Press.

Kraft, Stephan. 2004. *Geschlossenheit und Offenheit der "Römischen Octavia" von Herzog Anton Ulrich*. Würzburg: Königshausen und Neumann.

Krings, Hermann. 1982. *Ordo: Philosophisch-historische Grundlegung einer abendländischen Idee*. Hamburg: Meiner.

Lake, Peter. 2016. *How Shakespeare Put Politics on the Stage: Power and Succession in the History Plays*. New Haven, CT: Yale University Press.

Lamberty, Guillaume de. 1724–1740. *Mémoires pour servir à l'histoire du XVIII siècle [. . .]*. The Hague: Scheurleer.

La Rochefoucauld, François de. 2007. *Collected Maxims and Other Reflections*. Translated by E. H. and A. A. M. Blackmore and Francine Giguère. Oxford: Oxford University Press.

Las Casas, Bartolomé de. 1974. *In Defense of the Indians*. Translated by Stafford Poole. DeKalb: Northern Illinois University Press.

Lauterpacht, Hersch. 1932. "The Nature of International Law and General Jurisprudence." *Economica* 37: 301–20.

———. 1946. "The Grotian Tradition in International Law." *British Yearbook of International Law* 23: 1–53.

———. 1947. "The Subjects of the Law of Nations." *Law Quarterly Review* 63: 438–69.

Legendre, Pierre. 1985. *L'inestimable objet de la transmission: Étude sur le principe généalogique en Occident*. Paris: Fayard.

———. 1988. *Le désir politique de Dieu*. Paris: Fayard.

———. 1997. *Law and the Unconscious*. Edited by Peter Goodrich. New York: St. Martin's Press.

Lehmann, Hans-Thies. 2013. *Tragödie und dramatisches Theater*. Berlin: Alexander Verlag.

Leibniz, Gottfried Wilhelm. 1963a. *Caesarini Fürstenerii de Jure Suprematus ac Legationis Principum Germaniae*. In *Sämtliche Schriften und Briefe. Vierte Reihe, zweiter Band*, 3–270. Berlin: Akademie Verlag.

———. 1963b. *Entretien de Philarete et d'Eugene sur la question du temps agitée à Nimwegue touchant la droit d'ambassade des Electeurs et Princes de l'Empire*. In *Sämtliche Schriften und Briefe. Vierte Reihe, zweiter Band*, 278–338. Berlin: Akademie Verlag.

———. 1988. *Political Writings*. Edited by Patrick Riley. 2nd ed. Cambridge: Cambridge University Press.
———. 1996. *Die Theodizee*. Vol. 2 of *Philosophische Schriften*. Frankfurt am Main: Suhrkamp.
———. 1998a. *Discourse on Metaphysics*. In *Philosophical Texts*, translated by Richard Francks and R. S. Woolhouse, 53–93. Oxford: Oxford University Press.
———. 1998b. *Monadology*. In *Philosophical Texts*, translated by Richard Francks and R. S. Woolhouse, 267–81. Oxford: Oxford University Press.
———. 2004. *Codex juris gentium diplomaticus* (Praefatio). In *Schriften und Briefe zu Geschichte*, edited by Malte-Ludolf Babin and Gerd van den Heuvel, 131–217. Hannover: Verlag Hahnsche Buchhandlung.
———. 2005. *Confessio philosophi: Papers Concerning the Problems of Evil, 1671–1678*. Translated and edited by Robert C. Sleigh. New Haven, CT: Yale University Press.
Leibniz, Gottfried Wilhelm, and Anton Ulrich von Braunschweig-Wolfenbüttel. 1888. *Leibnizens Briefwechsel mit dem Herzoge Anton Ulrich von Braunschweig-Wolfenbüttel*. Edited by Eduard Bodemann, 73–244. *Zeitschrift des historischen Vereins für Niedersachen 1888*. Hannover: Hahnsche Buchhandlung.
Lesaffer, Randall. 2000. "The Medieval Canon Law of Contract and Early Modern Treaty Law." *Journal of the History of International Law* 2: 178–98.
———. 2002. "The Grotian Tradition Revisited: Change and Continuity in the History of International Law." *British Yearbook of International Law* 73: 103–39.
———. 2004. "Peace Treaties from Lodi to Westphalia." In *Peace Treaties and International Law in European History*, edited by Randall Lesaffer, 9–44. Cambridge: Cambridge University Press.
———. 2012. "Peace Treaties and the Formation of International Law." In *The Oxford Handbook of the History of International Law*, edited by Bardo Fassbender and Anne Peters, 71–94. Oxford: Oxford University Press.
Lesser, Zachary. 2007. "Tragical-Comical-Pastoral-Colonial: Economic Sovereignty, Globalization, and the Form of Tragicomedy." *ELH* 74: 881–908.
Lessing, Gotthold Ephraim. 1985. *Hamburgische Dramaturgie*. In *Werke und Briefe in zwölf Bänden*, vol. 6, edited by Klaus Bohnen, 81–694. Frankfurt am Main: Deutscher Klassiker Verlag.
Lévi-Strauss, Claude. 1966. *The Savage Mind*. London: Weidenfeld and Nicolson.
———. 1969. *The Elementary Structures of Kinship*. Translated by James Bell. Boston: Beacon Press.
Lipsius, Justus. 2004. *Politica: Six Books of Politics or Political Instructions*. Edited by Jan Waszink. Assen: Royal van Gorcum.
Lisska, Anthony. 1996. *Aquinas' Theory of Natural Law*. Oxford: Clarendon Press.
Littlewood, C. A. J. 2004. *Self-Representation and Illusion in Senecan Tragedy*. Oxford: Oxford University Press.
Liu, Lydia. 2009. *Clash of Empires: The Invention of China in Modern World Making*. Cambridge, MA: Harvard University Press.
Livermore, H. V. 1973. *Epic and History in the "Lusiads."* Lisbon: Comissão Executiva do IV Centenário da Publicação de "Os Lusídas".
Livy. 2006. *Hannibal's War*. Books 21–30 of *Ab urbe condita*. Translated by J. C. Yardley. Oxford University Press.

Locke, John. 1988. *Two Treatises of Government*. Cambridge: Cambridge University Press.
Lockey, Brian. 2006. *Law and Empire in English Renaissance Literature*. Cambridge: Cambridge University Press.
Loewenstein, David, and Paul Stevens, eds. 2008. *Early Modern Nationalism and Milton's England*. Toronto: University of Toronto Press.
Lohenstein, Daniel Caspar von. 1970. *Sophonisbe*. Edited by Rolf Tarot. Stuttgart: Reclam.
———. 2008. *Cleopatra*. Edited by Volker Meid. Stuttgart: Reclam.
Long, A. A., and D. N. Sedley, eds. 1987. *The Hellenistic Philosophers. Vol. 1: Translations of the Principal Sources*. Cambridge: Cambridge University Press.
Lossky, Andrew. 1970. "International Relations in Europe." In *The New Cambridge Modern History*, vol. 6, edited by J. S. Bromley, 154–92. Cambridge: Cambridge University Press.
Louvat, Bénédicte, and Marc Escola. 1998. "Le statut de l'épisode dans la tragédie classique: Œdipe de Corneille ou le complexe de Dircé." *XVIIe Siècle* 50: 453–70.
Lünig, Johann Christian. 1719–20. *Theatrum Ceremoniale Historico-Politicum, oder Historisch- und Politischer Schau-Platz aller Ceremonien*. Leipzig: Weidmann.
Lupton, Julia. 2000. "Creature Caliban." *Shakespeare Quarterly* 51: 1–23.
Luther, Martin. 2007. "The Freedom of a Christian." In *Selected Writings of Martin Luther*, edited by Theodore Tappert, vol. 2, 3–53. Minneapolis: Fortress Press.
Mably, Gabriel Bonnot de. 1748. *Le droit public de l'Europe, fondé sur les traités*. Nouvelle Edition. Geneva: Compagne des Libraires.
———. 1757. *Des principes des négociations pour servir d'introduction au droit public d'Europe*. The Hague: s.n.
Macedo, Helder. 1983. *The Purpose of Praise*. London: King's College.
Machiavelli, Niccolò. 1965. *The Chief Works and Others*. Translated by Allan Gilbert. Durham, NC: Duke University Press.
———. 1988. *The Prince*. Edited by Quentin Skinner and Russell Price. Cambridge: Cambridge University Press.
———. 2003. *The Discourses*. Translated by Leslie J. Walker. London: Penguin.
McCabe, Richard. 1993. *Incest, Drama and Nature's Law, 1550–1700*. Cambridge: Cambridge University Press.
MacLean, Ian. 1999. "Legal Fictions and Fictional Entities in Renaissance Jurisprudence." *Legal History* 20, no. 3: 1–24.
Malcolm, Noel. 2002. *Aspects of Hobbes*. Oxford: Oxford University Press.
———. 2007. *Reason of State, Propaganda, and the Thirty Years' War: An Unknown Translation by Thomas Hobbes*. Oxford: Oxford University Press, 2007.
Manger, Klaus, 1996. "Wielands Kosmopoliten." In *Europäische Sozietätsbewegung und demokratische Tradition*, edited by Klaus Garber, Heinz Wisman, and Winfried Siebers, vol. 2, 1637–67. Tübingen: Niemeyer.
Mann, William-Edward. 1916. *Robinson Crusoe en France*. Paris: Davy.
Marcus, Leah. 1988. *Puzzling Shakespeare: Local Reading and Its Discontents*. Berkeley: University of California Press.
Marlowe, Christopher. 2003. *Tamburlaine the Great, Part One* and *Part Two*. In *The Complete Plays*, edited by Frank Romany and Robert Lindsey, 69–240. London: Penguin Books.

Martens, Georg Friedrich von. 1796. *Einleitung in das positive europäische Völkerrecht auf Verträge und Herkommen gegründet.* Göttingen: Dieterich.
Mattingly, Garrett. 1962. *Renaissance Diplomacy.* London: Cape.
Maultrot, Gabriel Nicolas. 1788. *Examen des décrets du Concile de Trente, et de la jurisprudence Françoise sur la marriage.* Tome premier. s.l.: s.n.
May, Larry. 2013. *Limiting Leviathan: Hobbes on Law and International Affairs.* Oxford: Oxford University Press.
McGowan, Margaret, ed. 2013. *Dynastic Marriages 1612/1615.* Farnham: Ashgate.
McKeon, Michael. 1987. *The Origins of the English Novel 1600–1740.* Baltimore: Johns Hopkins University Press.
——. 2005. *The Secret History of Domesticity: Public, Private, and the Division of Knowledge.* Baltimore: Johns Hopkins University Press.
McMurran, Mary Helen. 2009. *The Spread of Novels: Translation and Prose Fiction in the Eighteenth Century.* Princeton, NJ: Princeton University Press.
Mégret, Frédéric. 2012. "International Law as Law." In *The Cambridge Companion to International Law*, edited by James Crawford and Martti Koskenniemi, 64–92. Cambridge: Cambridge University Press.
Meinecke, Friedrich. 1963. *Die Idee der Staatsräson in der neueren Geschichte.* 3rd ed. Munich: Oldenbourg.
Merkelbach, Reinhold. 1962. *Roman und Mysterium in der Antike.* Munich: Beck.
Merlin, Hélène. 1994. *Public et littérature en France au XVIIe siècle.* Paris: Les belles lettres.
Merlin-Kajman, Hélène. 2000. *L'absolutisme dans les lettres et la théorie des deux corps.* Paris: Champion.
Milton, John. 1991. *The Major Works.* Edited by Stephen Orgel and Jonathan Goldberg. Oxford: Oxford University Press.
Mohamed, Feisal. 2011. *Milton and the Post-Secular Present: Ethics, Politics, Terrorism.* Stanford: Stanford University Press.
Mohnhaupt, Heinz. 1972. "Potestas legislatoria und Gesetzesbegriff im Ancien Régime." *Ius Commune* 4: 188–239.
Möllers, Christoph. 2015. *Die Möglichkeit der Normen: Über eine Praxis jenseits von Moralität und Kausalität.* Berlin: Suhrkamp.
Montesquieu, Charles de Secondat. 1989. *The Spirit of Laws.* Edited by Anne M. Collier, Basia Miller, and Harold Stone. Cambridge: Cambridge University Press.
Morgan, J. R. 1989. "A Sense of the Ending: The Conclusion of Heliodorus' *Aithiopika*." *Transactions of the American Philological Association* 119: 299–320.
Moritz, Karl Philip. 1793. *Die große Loge oder der Freimaurer mit Wage und Senkblei.* Berlin: Ernst Felisch.
Moser, Johann Jakob. 1750. *Grund-Sätze des jetzt-üblichen Europäischen Völcker-Rechts in Fridens-Zeiten.* Hanau: s.n.
——. 1752. *Grund-Sätze des jetzt-üblichen Europäischen Völcker-Rechts in Kriegs-Zeiten.* Tübingen: Cotta.
——. 1777–80. *Versuch des neuesten europäischen Völkerrechts in Friedens- und Kriegszeiten.* Frankfurt am Main: Varrentrapp.
Mulagk, Karl-Heinz. 1973. *Phänomene des politischen Menschen im 17. Jahrhundert.* Berlin: Erich Schmidt.

Muldoon, James. 2013. "Rights, Property, and the Creation of International Law." In *Bridging the Medieval-Modern Divide: Medieval Themes in the World of the Reformation*, edited by James Muldoon, 175–204. Farnham: Ashgate Publishing.
Naudé, Gabriel. 1907. *News from France Or a Description of the Library of Cardinal Mazarin, Preceded by The Surrender of the Library*. Chicago: McClurg.
———. 1950. *Advice on Establishing a Library*. Berkeley: University of California Press.
———. 2004. *Considérations politiques sur les coups d'État*. Edited by Frédérique Marin and Marie-Odile Perulli. Paris: Gallimard.
Nandrea, Lorri. 2015. *Misfit Forms: Paths Not Taken by the British Novel*. New York: Fordham University Press.
Neff, Stephen. 2005. *War and the Law of Nations*. Cambridge: Cambridge University Press.
———. 2014. *Justice Among Nations*. Cambridge, MA: Harvard University Press.
Newman, Jane. 2000. *The Intervention of Philology: Gender, Learning, and Power in Lohenstein's Roman Plays*. Chapel Hill: University of North Carolina Press.
Niefanger, Dirk. 2005. *Geschichtsdrama der Frühen Neuzeit*. Tübingen: Niemeyer.
———. 2010. "Lohensteins *Sophonisbe* als Metadrama." *Wolfenbütteler Barock-Nachrichten* 37: 33–46.
Nietzsche, Friedrich. 1967. *The Will to Power*. Translated by Walter Kaufman. New York: Vintage Books.
Niggl, Günter. 1977. *Geschichte der deutschen Autobiographie im 18. Jahrhundert*. Stuttgart: Metler.
Nijman, Janne Elisabeth. 2004. *The Concept of International Legal Personality*. The Hague: Asser Press.
Novak, Maximilian. 1963. *Defoe and the Nature of Man*. Oxford: Oxford University Press.
Novalis. 1968. *Schriften*. Edited by Richard Samuel. Darmstadt: Wissenschaftliche Buchgesellschaft.
Noyes, John. 2006. "Goethe on Cosmopolitanism and Colonialism: *Bildung* and the Dialectic of Critical Mobility." *Eighteenth-Century Studies* 39: 443–62.
Nussbaum, Martha. 1997. "Kant and Stoic Cosmopolitanism." *Journal of Political Philosophy* 5: 1–25.
O'Hara, James. 1990. *Death and the Optimistic Prophecy in Vergil's Aeneid*. Princeton, NJ: Princeton University Press.
Olivier, Pierre J. J. 1975. *Legal Fictions in Practice and Legal Science*. Rotterdam: Rotterdam University Press.
Opitz, Martin. 1970. *Buch von der Deutschen Poeterey*. Edited by Herbert Jaumann. Stuttgart: Reclam.
Ovid. 1987. *Metamorphoses*. Translated by A. D. Melville. Oxford: Oxford University Press.
Pagden, Anthony. 1987. "Dispossessing the Barbarian." In *The Languages of Political Theory in Early-Modern Europe*, edited by Anthony Padgen, 79–98. Cambridge: Cambridge University Press.
Parfitt, Rose. 2016. "Theorizing Recognition and International Personality." In *The Oxford Handbook of the Theory of International Law*, edited by Anne Orford, Florian Hoffmann, and Martin Clark, 583–99. Oxford: Oxford University Press.

Parry, Adam. 1963. "The Two Voices of Virgil's *Aeneid.*" *Arion* 2: 66–80.
Parry, John. 2014. "What is the Grotian Tradition in International Law?" *University of Pennsylvania Journal of International Law* 35: 299–377.
Pascale, Blaise. 1995. *Pensées and Other Writings*. Translated by Honor Levi. Oxford: Oxford University Press.
Patterson, W. B. 1997. *King James VI and I and the Reunion of Christendom*. Cambridge: Cambridge University Press.
Pecquet, Antoine. 1737. *Discours Sur l'Art de Negocier*. Paris: Nyon fils.
Pennington, Kenneth. 1993. *The Prince and the Law, 1200–1600*. Berkeley: University of California Press.
Plazenet, Laurence. 1997. *L'ébahissement et la délectation: réception comparée et poétique du roman grec en France et en Angleterre au XVIe et au XVIIe siècle*. Paris: Champion.
Plutarch. 1914. *Lives*. Translated by Bernadotte Perrin. Cambridge, MA: Harvard University Press.
Pocock, J. G. A. 1975. *The Machiavellian Moment*. Princeton, NJ: Princeton University Press.
Polloczek, Dieter. 1999. *Literature and Legal Discourse: Equity and Ethics from Sterne to Conrad*. Cambridge: Cambridge University Press.
Porras, Ileana. 2006. "Constructing International Law in the East Indian Seas: Property, Sovereignty, Commerce and War in Hugo Grotius's *De iure praedae*." *Brooklyn Journal of International Law* 31: 741–804.
Portmann, Roland. 2010. *Legal Personality in International Law*. Cambridge: Cambridge University Press.
Posner, Richard. 2009. *Law and Literature*, 3rd ed. Cambridge, MA: Harvard University Press.
Preiß, Klaus. 2006. *Unbekanntere Bausteine der Freimaurerei*. Frankfurt am Main: Haag und Herchen Verlag.
Prigent, Michel. 1986. *Le héros et l'Etat dans la tragédie de Pierre Corneille*. Paris: Presses universitaires de France.
Pufendorf, Samuel. 1927. *De officio hominis et civis juxta legem naturalem libri duo*. Translated by Frank Gardner Moore. New York: Oxford University Press.
———. 1934. *De Jure Naturae et Gentium Libri Octo*. Translated by C. H. Oldfather and W. A. Oldfather. Oxford: The Clarendon Press.
———. 2007. *The Present State of Germany*. Translated by Edmund Bohum. Indianapolis: Liberty Fund.
———. 2013. *An Introduction to the History of the Principal Kingdoms and States of Europe*. Translated by Jodocus Crull. Indianapolis: Liberty Fund.
Putnam, Michael. 1965. *The Poetry of the "Aeneid."* Cambridge, MA: Harvard University Press.
Quint, David. 1993. *Epic and Empire*. Princeton, NJ: Princeton University Press.
Quintilian. 2001. *Institutio Oratoria*. Edited and translated by Donald Russell. Cambridge, MA: Harvard University Press.
Rachel, Samuel. 1916. *De jure naturae et gentium dissertationes*. Translated by John Pawley Bate. Washington: Carnegie Institution.
Racine, Jean. 1999. *Œuvres complètes*. Edited by Georges Forestier (Bibliothèque de la Pléiade). Paris: Gallimard.

REFERENCES

Raman, Shankar. 2001. *Framing "India": The Colonial Imaginary in Early Modern Culture*. Stanford: Stanford University Press.

Raymond of Penyafort, Saint. 2005. *Summa on Marriage*. Translated by Pierre Payer. Ontario: Pontifical Institute of Mediaeval Studies.

Reardon, B. P., ed. 1989. *Collected Ancient Greek Novels*. Berkeley: University of California Press.

———. 1991. *The Form of Greek Romance*. Princeton, NJ: Princeton University Press.

Recueil des traittez de paix, treves et neutralité entre des couronnes d'Espagne et de France. 1660. 2nd ed. s.l.: s.n.

Redfield, James. 1994. *The Nature and Culture in the "Iliad": The Tragedy of Hector*. Durham, NC: Duke University Press.

Reeve, Clara. 1785. *The Progress of Romance, Through Times, Countries and Manners [...]*. Colchester: Keymer.

Repgen, Konrad. 2015. *Dreißigjähriger Krieg und Westphälischer Friede*, 3rd ed. Paderborn: Ferdinand Schöningh.

Richards, Anna. 2006. "Forgetting the Dead in Gellert's *Das Leben der Schwedischen Gräfin von G****." *Oxford German Studies* 35: 165–75.

Richetti, John, ed. 1996. *The Cambridge Companion to the Eighteenth-Century Novel*. Cambridge: Cambridge University Press.

Riley, Patrick. 1976. "Three 17th-Century German Theorists of Federalism: Althusius, Hugo and Leibniz." *Publius* 6: 7–41.

———. 1996. *Leibniz' Universal Jurisprudence*. Cambridge, MA: Harvard University Press.

Ripa, Cesare. 1603. *Iconologia overo descrittione di diverse imagini cavate dell'antichità et di propria inventione*. Roma: Faci.

———. 1709. *Iconologia, or Moral Emblems*. London: Motte.

Rist, Johann. 1967. *Irenaromachia, Das ist eine newe Tragico-comœdia von Fried und Krieg*. In *Sämtliche Werke*, edited by Eberhard Mannack, vol. 1, 1–115. Berlin: Walter de Gruyter.

Rivère de Carles, Natalie, ed. 2016. *Early Modern Diplomacy, Theater and Soft Power*. London: Palgrave Macmillan.

Rivers, Isabel. 2005. *Reason, Grace, and Sentiment. Vol. 2: Shaftesbury to Hume*. Cambridge: Cambridge University Press.

Robortello, Franceso. 1548. *In librum Aristotelis De arte poetica explicationes*. Florence: In officina Laurentii Torrentini.

Rohan, Henri de. 1995. *De l'intérêt des princes et des Etats de la chrétienté*. Edited by Christian Lazzeri. Paris: Presses Universitaires de France.

Roosen, William. 1976. *The Age of Louis XIV: The Rise of Modern Diplomacy*. Cambridge, MA: Schenkman.

———. 1980. "Early Modern Diplomatic Ceremonial: A Systems Approach." *Journal of Modern History* 52: 452–76.

———. 1986. *Daniel Defoe and Diplomacy*. London: Associated University Press.

Rösch, Gertrud Maria. 2004. *Clavis Scientiae. Studien zum Verhältnis von Faktizität und Fiktionalität am Fall der Schlüsselliteratur*. Tübingen: Niemeyer.

Rousseau, Jean-Jacques. 1997. *The Social Contract and Other Later Political Writings*. Edited and translated by Victor Gourevitch. Cambridge: Cambridge University Press.

———. 2005. *The Plan for Perpetual Peace, On the Government of Poland, and Other Writings on History and Politics*. Vol. 11 of *The Collected Works of Rousseau*, translated by Christopher Kelly and Judith Bush. Hannover, NH: Dartmouth College Press.

Rousset de Missy, Jean. 1728–55. *Recueil historique d'actes, négociations, mémoires et traitez [. . .]*. The Hague: Scheurleer.

———. 1739. *Le cérémonial diplomatique des cours de l'Europe*. Amsterdam: Janssons.

———. 1746. *Mémoires sur le rang et la préséance entre les souverains de l'Europe et entre leurs ministres répresentans suivant leurs différens caractères*. Amsterdam: L'Honoré.

Russell, Joycelyne. 1986. *Peacemaking in the Renaissance*. Philadelphia: University of Pennsylvania Press.

Saavedra Fajardo, Diego de. 1700. *The Royal Politician Represented in One Hundred Emblems*. Translated by J. Astry. London: Gylliflower and Meredith.

Sahmland, Irmtraut. 1991. *Christoph Martin Wieland und die deutsche Nation*. Tübingen: Niemeyer.

Saint-Pierre, Charles Irénée Castel de. 1717. *Project de traité pour rendre la paix perpétuelle entre les souverains chrétiens, [. . .] Proposé autre fois par Henry le Grand, Roy de France*. Utrecht: Schouten.

———. 1981. *Projet pour rendre la Paix perpétuelle en Europe*. Edited by Simone Goyard-Fabre. Paris: Garnier.

Saint-Prest, Jean Yves de. 1725. *Histoire des traités de paix, et autres negotiations du dix-septième siècle [. . .]*. Amsterdam: Bernard.

Salisbury, John of. 1595. *Policraticus*. Lugduni Batavorum: apud Franciscum Raphelengium.

Sauer, Elizabeth. 2014. *Milton, Toleration, and Nationhood*. Cambridge: Cambridge University Press.

Scaliger, Julius Caesar. 1994–2011. *Poetices libri septem*. Edited by Luc Deitz and Gregor Vogt-Spira. Stuttgart-Bad Cannstatt: Fromann-Holzboog.

Scattola, Merio. 1999. *Das Naturrecht vor dem Naturrecht*. Tübingen: Max Niemeyer.

———. 2001. "Models in History of Natural Law." *Ius Commune* 28: 91–159.

———. 2017. "Jean Bodin on International Law." In *System, Order and International Law: The Early History of International Legal Thought from Machiavelli to Hegel*, edited by Stefan Kadelbach, Thomas Kleinlein, and David Roth-Isigkeit, 78–91. Oxford: Oxford University Press.

Schechner, Richard. 1988. *Performance Theory*. New York: Routledge.

Schiesaro, Alessandro. 2003. *The Passions in Play: Thyestes and the Dynamics of Senecan Drama*. Cambridge: Cambridge University Press, 2003.

Schiller, Friedrich. 1988. "Wie kann eine gute stehende Schaubühne eigentlich wirken? (Die Schaubühne als eine moralische Anstalt betrachtet)." In *Werke und Briefe in zwölf Bänden*, edited by Otto Dann et al. vol. 8, 185–200. Frankfurt am Main: Deutscher Klassiker Verlag, 1988.

Schings, Hans-Jürgen. 1983. "*Constantia* und *Prudentia*. Zum Funktionswandel des barocken Trauerspiels." *Daphnis* 12: 403–39.

Schmidgen, Wolfram. 2002. *Eighteenth-Century Fiction and the Law of Property*. Cambridge: Cambridge University Press.

Schmidt, Frank-Steffen. 2007. *Praktisches Naturrecht zwischen Thomasius und Wolff: Der Völkerrechtler Adam Friedrich Glafey (1692–1753)*. Baden-Baden: Nomos.

Schmitt, Carl. 1997. *Der Nomos der Erde im Völkerrecht des Jus Publicum Europaeum*, 4th ed. Berlin: Duncker und Humblot.
Schnelhase, Kenneth. 1977. *Tacitus in Renaissance Political Thought*. Chicago: University of Chicago Press.
Schönborn, Sibylle, and Vera Viehöver, eds. 2009. *Gellert und die empfindsame Aufklärung*. Berlin: Erich Schmidt.
Schofield, Malcolm. 1991. *The Stoic Idea of the City*. Cambridge: Cambridge University Press.
Schonhorn, Manuel. 1991. *Defoe's Politics: Parliament, Power, Kingship and "Robinson Crusoe."* Cambridge: Cambridge University Press.
Schröder, Jan. 2000. "Die Entstehung des modernen Völkerrechtsbegriffs im Naturrecht der frühen Neuzeit." *Jahrbuch für Recht und Ethik* 8: 47–71.
Schröder, Peter. 2001. "Reich versus Territorien? Zum Problem der Souveränität im Heiligen Römischen Reich nach dem Westfälischen Frieden." In *Altes Reich, Frankreich und Europa*, edited by Olaf Asbach, 123–43. Berlin: Duncker und Humblot.
Schwab, Dieter. 1967. *Grundlagen und Gestalt der staatlichen Ehegesetzgebung in der Neuzeit bis zum Beginn des 19. Jahrhunderts*. Bielefeld: Gieseking.
Seelmann, Kurt. 1979. *Die Lehre des Fernando Vazquez de Menchaca vom Dominium*. Cologne: Heymanns.
———. 2007. "Selbstherrschaft, Herrschaft über die Dinge und individuelle Rechte in der spanischen Spätscholastik." In *Politische Metaphyisk*, edited by Matthias Kaufmann, 43–57. Frankfurt am Main: Peter Lang.
Segal, Charles. 1994. *Singers, Heroes, and Gods*. Ithaca, NY: Cornell University Press, 1994.
Seidel, Michael. 1981. "Crusoe in Exile." *PMLA* 96: 363–74.
Seneca. 1932. *De Otio*. In *Moral Essays II*, edited and translated by John Basore, 180–201. Cambridge, MA: Harvard University Press.
———. 2002. *Hercules*. In *Tragedies I*, edited and translated by John Fitch, 48–159. Cambridge, MA: Harvard University Press.
———. 2004. *Thyestes*. In *Tragedies II*, edited and translated by John Fitch, 230–323. Cambridge, MA: Harvard University Press.
Serjeantson, R. W. 2009. "*Samson Agonistes* and 'Single Rebellion.'" In *The Oxford Handbook of Milton*, edited by Nicholas McDowell and Nigel Smith, 613–32. Oxford: Oxford University Press.
Seznec, Jean. 1972. *The Survival of Pagan Gods*. Princeton, NJ: Princeton University Press.
Sfez, Gérald. 2000. *Les doctrines de la raison d'État*. Paris: Armand Colin.
Shaftesbury, Anthony Ashley Cooper, 3rd Earl of. 1999. *Characteristics of Men, Manners, Opinions, Times*. Edited by Philip Ayres. Oxford: Oxford University Press.
Shakespeare, William. 1982. *Henry V*. Edited by Gary Taylor. Oxford: Oxford University Press.
———. 1987. *The Tempest*. Edited by Stephen Orgel. Oxford: Oxford University Press.
———. 1989. *The Life and Death of King John*. Edited by A. R. Braunmuller. Oxford: Oxford University Press.
———. 1996. *The Winter's Tale*. Edited by Stephen Orgel. Oxford: Oxford University Press.

———. 1998. *Cymbeline*. Edited by Roger Warren. Oxford: Oxford University Press.
———. 2003. *Pericles, Prince of Tyre*. Edited by Roger Warren. Oxford: Oxford University Press.
Sheeran, Paul. 2007. *Literature and International Relations*. Aldershot: Ashgate.
Shell, Alison. 2010. *Shakespeare and Religion*. London: Bloomsbury.
Shelley, Percy. 2003. *The Major Works*. Edited by Zachary Leader and Michael O'Neill. Oxford: Oxford University Press.
Sidnell, Michael, ed. 1991. *Sources of Dramatic Theory*. Cambridge: Cambridge University Press.
Sidney, Algernon. 1763. *Discourses Concerning Government*. London: Millar.
Sidney, Philip. 1890. *The Defense of Poesy*. Edited by Albert Cook. Boston: Ginn and Company.
Siegl-Mocavini, Susanne. 1999. *John Barclays "Argenis" und ihr staatstheoretischer Kontext*. Tübingen: Niemeyer.
Silvestrini, Gabriella. 2010. "Rousseau, Pufendorf and the Eighteenth-Century Natural Law Tradition." *History of European Ideas* 36: 280–301.
Simon, Thomas. 2005. "Geltung: Der Weg von der Gewohnheit zur Positivität des Rechts." *Rechtsgeschichte* 7: 100–137.
Simpson, Gerry. 2015. "Sentimental Life of International Law." *London Review of International Law* 3: 3–29.
Skinner, Gillian. 1999. *Sensibility and Economics in the Novel, 1740–1800*. New York: St. Martin's Press.
Skinner, Quentin. 1978. *The Foundations of Modern Political Thought*. Cambridge: Cambridge University Press.
———. 2002. *Visions of Politics*. Cambridge: Cambridge University Press.
Slaughter, Joseph. 2007. *Human Rights, Inc. The World Novel, Narrative Form, and International Law*. New York: Fordham University Press.
Smith, Adam. 1976. *The Theory of Moral Sentiments*. Edited by D. D. Raphael and A. L. Macfie. Oxford: Oxford University Press.
———. 1978. *Lectures on Jurisprudence*. Edited by R. L. Meek, D. D. Raphael, and P. G. Stein. Oxford: Oxford University Press.
Snyder, Jon. 2009. *Dissimulation and the Culture of Secrecy in Early Modern Europe*. Berkeley: University of California Press.
Sommerville, J. P. 1991. "Absolutism and Royalism." In *The Cambridge History of Political Thought, 1450–1700*, edited by J. H. Burns, 347–73. Cambridge: Cambridge University Press.
Sophocles. 1991. *Oedipus the King, Oedipus at Colonus, Antigone*. Translated by David Greene. 2nd ed. Chicago: University of Chicago Press.
Soto, Domingo de. 1967. *De Iustitia et Iure Libri Decem*. Madrid: Instituto de Estudios Políticos.
———. 1995. *Relectio Sapientissimi Magistri Fratris Dominici de Soto, Qvam Habvit Primam in Qvartvm Sententiarvm et Inscripsit de Dominio*. In *Relecciones y Opusculos*, edited by Jaime Brufau Prats, vol. 1, 79–191. Salamanca: Editorial San Esteban.
Spacks, Patricia. 2006. *Novel Beginnings: Experiments in Eighteenth-Century English Fiction*. New Haven, CT: Yale University Press.
Spahr, Blake Lee. 1966. *Anton Ulrich und Aramena*. Berkeley: University of California Press.

Spinoza, Benedictus de. 2002. *Theological-Political Treatise*. In *Complete Works*, edited by Michael Morgan, 383–583. Indianapolis: Hackett.
Stach, Reinhard. 1991. *Robinson und Robinsonaden in der deutschsprachigen Literatur*. Würzburg: Königshausen und Neumann.
Steiger, Heinhard. 2010. *Die Ordnung der Welt: Eine Völkerrechtsgeschichte des karolingischen Zeitalters (741 bis 840)*. Cologne: Böhlau.
Sterne, Laurence. 1968. *A Sentimental Journey Through France and Italy by Mr. Yorick*. Oxford: Oxford University Press.
Stieve, Gottfried. 1715. *Europäisches Hoff-Ceremoniel [. . .]*. Leipzig: Gleditsch.
Stolleis, Michael. 1988–2012. *Geschichte des öffentlichen Rechts in Deutschland*. Munich: Beck.
Stone, Lawrence. 1990. *Road to Divorce: England, 1530–1987*. Oxford: Oxford University Press.
Straumann, Benjamin. 2015. *Roman Law in the State of Nature*. Cambridge: Cambridge University Press.
Strayer, Joseph. 1970. *On the Medieval Origins of the Modern State*. Princeton, NJ: Princeton University Press.
Strong, Roy. 1984. *Art and Power: Renaissance Festivals 1450–1650*. Berkeley: University of California Press.
Suárez, Francisco. 1944. *A Treatise on Laws and God the Lawgiver*. In *Selections from Three Works*, translated by Gwladys L. Williams, 3–865. Oxford: Clarendon Press.
Subrahmanyam, Sanjay. 1998. *The Career and Legend of Vasco da Gama*. Cambridge: Cambridge University Press.
Sueur, Philippe. 2001. *Histoire du droit public français XVe–XVIIIe siècle*, 3rd ed. Paris: Presses Universitaires de France.
Sully, Maximilien de Béthune, duc de. 1767. *Mémoires de Maximilien de Béthune, duc de Sully, Principal Ministre de Henri le Grand. Mise en order, avec des Remarques par M. D. L. D. L*. New edition. Vol. 8. London: s.n.
———. 1921. *Grand Design of Henry IV*. London: Sweet and Maxwell.
Tacitus. 2008. *The Annals*. Translated by J. C. Yardley. Oxford: Oxford University Press.
Tang, Chenxi. 2010. "Re-imagining World Order: From International Law to Romantic Poetics." *Deutsche Vierteljahresschrift für Literaturwissenschaft und Geistesgeschichte* 84: 526–79.
———. 2011a. "Theatralische Inszenierung der Weltordnung. Völkerrecht, Zeremonialwissenschaft und Schillers *Maria Stuart*." *Jahrbuch der deutschen Schillergesellschaft* 55: 142–68.
———. 2011b. "Die Tragödie der Zivilisation. Völkerrecht und Ästhetik des Tragischen im 19. Jahrhundert." *Forum Vormärz-Forschung Jahrbuch* 17: 87–136.
———. 2011c. "Travel Literature and Modern Natural Law." *Colloquium Helveticum* 42: 19–39.
———. 2012. "The Transformation of the Law of Nations and the Reinvention of the Novella: Legal History and Literary Innovation from Boccaccio's *Decameron* to Goethe's *Unterhaltungen deutscher Ausgewanderten*." *Goethe Yearbook* 19: 67–92.
———. 2014. "International Legal Order and Baroque Tragic Play: Andreas Gryphius's *Catharina von Georgien*." *Deutsche Vierteljahresschrift für Literaturwissenschaft und Geistesgeschichte* 88: 141–71.

Tans, Olaf. 2014. "The Imaginary Foundation of Legal Systems: A Mimetic Perspective." *Law and Literature* 26, no. 2: 127–43.
Tasso, Torquato. 1582. *Il Messagiero*. s.l.: s.n. www.classicitaliani.it/tasso/prosa/Tasso_messagiero.htm.
———. 2000. *Jerusalem Delivered*. Translated by Anthony Esolen. Baltimore: Johns Hopkins University Press.
Tatum, James, ed. 1994. *The Search for the Ancient Novel*. Baltimore: Johns Hopkins University Press.
Thomasius, Christian. 1688–90. *Freimütige, lustige und ernsthafte, jedoch vernunftmässige Gedanken oder Monatsgespräche über allerhand, fürnemlich aber neue Bücher*. Halle: Christoph Salfelden.
———. 2003. *Grund-Lehren des Natur- und Völcker-Rechts, nach dem sinnlichen Begriff aller Menschen vorgestellet*. Hildesheim: Georg Olms.
———. 2006. *Höchstnöthige Cautelen welche ein Studiosus Juris, der sich zur Erlernung der Rechts-Gelahrheit auff eine kluge und geschickte Weise vorbereiten will/ zu beobachten hat*. Hildesheim: Georg Olms.
Tierney, Brian. 1963. "'The Prince is Not Bound by the Laws': Accursius and the Origins of the Modern State." *Comparative Studies in Society and History* 5: 378–400.
———. 1997. *The Idea of Natural Rights: Studies on Natural Rights, Natural Law, and Church Law 1150–1625*. Atlanta: Scholars Press.
———. 2007. "Vitoria and Suarez on *Ius Gentium*, Natural Law, and Custom." In *The Nature of Customary Law*, edited by Amanda Perreau-Saussine and James Murphy, 101–24. Cambridge: Cambridge University Press.
Toyoda, Tetsuya. 2011. *Theory and Practice of the Law of Nations: Political Bias in International Law Discourse of Seven German Court Councilors in the Seventeenth and Eighteenth Centuries*. Leiden: Martinus Nijhoff.
Toze, Eobald. 1752. *Die allgemeine Christliche Republik in Europa: Nach den Entwürfen Heinrichs des Vierten, Königs von Frankreich, des Abts von St. Pierre, und anderer vorgestellet*. Göttingen: Vandenhoek.
Trissino, Giovan Giorgio. 1997. *Sofonisba*. In *Teatro del Cinquecento. La Tragedia*, vol. 1, edited by Renzo Cremante, 29–162. Milan: Riccardo Ricciardi Editore.
Truman, Ronald. 1999. *Spanish Treatises on Government, Society and Religion in the Time of Philip II*. Leiden: Brill.
Tuck, Richard. 1979. *Natural Rights Theories*. Cambridge: Cambridge University Press.
———. 1987. "The 'Modern' Theory of Natural Law." In *The Languages of Political Theory in Early-Modern Europe*, edited by Anthony Pagden, 99–122. Cambridge: Cambridge University Press.
———. 1993. *Philosophy and Government 1572–1651*. Cambridge: Cambridge University Press.
———. 2001. *The Rights of War and Peace*. Oxford: Oxford University Press.
Turner, Victor. 1969. *The Ritual Process*. Ithaca, NY: Cornell University Press.
———. 1982. *From Ritual to Theater: The Human Seriousness o Play*. New York: PAJ Publications.
Vasari, Giorgio. 1852. *Lives of the Most Eminent Painters, Sculptors, and Architects*. London: Bohn.
Vattel, Emer de. 1916. *Le droit des gens. Ou Principles de la loi naturelle, appliqué à la conduit et aux affaires des nations et des souverains*. Washington: The Carnegie Institution.

Vázquez de Menchaca, Fernando. 1572. *Controversiarum illustrium, aliarumque usu frequentium libri tres.* Frankfurt am Main: Feyerabend.

Vec, Miloš. 1998. *Zeremonialwissenschaft im Fürstenstaat: Studien zur juristischen und politischen Theorie absolutischer Herrschaftsrepräsentation.* Frankfurt am Main: Klostermann.

Vera y Zuñiga, Juan Antonio de. 1635. *Le parfait ambassadeur.* Translated by Le Sieur Lancelot. Paris: Anthoine de Sommaville.

Vernant, Jean-Pierre, and Pierre Vidal-Naquet. 1990. *Myth and Tragedy in Ancient Greece.* New York: Zone Books, 1990.

Virgil. 2010. *The Aeneid.* Translated by Robert Fagles. New York: Penguin.

Viroli, Maurizio. 1992. *From Politics to Reason of State.* Cambridge: Cambridge University Press.

Vismann, Cornelia. 2011. *Medien der Rechtsprechung.* Frankfurt am Main: Fischer.

Vitoria, Francisco de. 1934–35. *De justitia.* Edited by Vicente Beltrán de Heredia. Madrid: Associación Francisco de Vitoria.

———. 1992. *Political Writings.* Edited and translated by Anthony Pagden and Jeremy Lawrance. Cambridge: Cambridge University Press.

———. 1995–97. *Vorlesungen (Relectiones).* Edited by Ulrich Horst, Heinz-Gerhard Justenhoven, and Joachim Stüben. Stuttgart: Kohlhammer.

Voges, Michael. 1987. *Aufklärung und Geheimnis: Untersuchungen zur Vermittlung von Literatur- und Sozialgeschichte am Beispiel der Aneignung des Geheimbundmaterials im Roman des späten 18. Jahrhunderts.* Tübingen: Niemeyer.

Vogl, Joseph. 2004. *Kalkül und Leidenschaft: Poetik des ökonomischen Menschen.* Berlin: Diaphanes.

Vollhardt, Friedrich. 2001. *Selbstliebe und Geselligkeit: Untersuchungen zum Verhältnis von naturrechtlichem Denken und moraldidaktischer Literatur im 17. und 18. Jahrhundert.* Tübingen: Niemeyer.

Vondel, Joost van den. 1996. *Mary Stuart or Tortured Majesty.* Translated by Kristiaan P. Aercke. Ottawa: Dovehouse Editions.

Waith, Eugene. 1962. *The Herculean Hero in Marlowe, Chapman, Shakespeare and Dryden.* New York: Columbia University Press.

Waldron, Jeremy. 2010. "Ius gentium: A Defence of Gentili's Equation of the Law of Nations and the Law of Nature." In *The Roman Foundations of the Law of Nations*, edited by Benedict Kingsbury and Benjamin Straumann, 283–96. Oxford: Oxford University Press.

Walton, Kendall. 1993. *Mimesis as Make-Believe.* Cambridge, MA: Harvard University Press.

Warburg, Aby. 2010. "Die Theaterkostüme für die Intermedien von 1589." In *Werke in einem Band*, edited by Martin Treml, Sigrid Weigel, and Perdita Ladwig, 124–67. Berlin: Suhrkamp.

Warren, Christopher. 2010. "Gentili, the Poets, and the Laws of War." In *The Roman Foundations of the Law of Nations*, edited by Benedict Kingsbury and Benjamin Straumann, 146–62. Oxford: Oxford University Press.

———. 2015. *Literature and the Law of Nations, 1580–1680.* Oxford: Oxford University Press.

Watkins, John. 2017. *After Lavinia: A Literary History of Premodern Marriage Diplomacy.* Ithaca, NY: Cornell University Press.

Watt, Ian. 1957. *The Rise of the Novel: Studies in Defoe, Richardson and Fielding*. Berkeley: University of California Press.

Weber, Max. 1978. *Economy and Society*. Edited by Guenther Roth and Claus Wittich. Berkeley: University of California Press.

Welch, Ellen. 2017. *A Theater of Diplomacy: International Relations and the Performing Arts in Early Modern France*. Philadelphia: University of Pennsylvania Press.

Weinberg, Bernard. 1961. *A History of Literary Criticism in the Italian Renaissance*. Chicago: University of Chicago Press.

Werner, Wouter, and Geoff Gordon. 2016. "Kant, Cosmopolitanism, and International Law." In *The Oxford Handbook of the Theory of International Law*, edited by Anne Orford, Florian Hoffmann, and Martin Clark, 505–25. Oxford: Oxford University Press.

Whitmarsh, Tim, ed. 2008. *The Cambridge Companion to the Greek and Roman Novel*. Cambridge: Cambridge University Press.

———. 2011. *Narrative and Identity in the Ancient Greek Novel: Returning Romance*. Cambridge: Cambridge University Press.

Wicquefort, Abraham van. 1682. *L'Ambassadeur et ses Fonctions*. The Hague: Maurice George Veneur.

Wichert, Adalbert. 1991. *Literatur, Rhetorik und Jurisprudenz im 17. Jahrhundert: Daniel Casper von Lohenstein und sein Werk*. Tübingen: Niemeyer.

Wieland, Christoph Martin. 1788. "Das Geheimniss des Kosmopolitenordens." *Der Teutsche Merkur* 1788 (August): 97–115.

———. 1794. *Geschichte des Agathon*. Third Version. In *Sämmtliche Werke*, vol. 1–3. Leipzig: Göschen.

———. 2008. *Geschichte des Agathon*. First Version. In *Wielands Werke: Historisch-kritische Ausgabe*, edited by Klaus Manger and Jan Philipp Reemtsma, vol. 8.1, 1–461. Berlin: Walter de Gruyter.

———. 2009. *Geschichte des Agathon*. Second Version. In *Wielands Werke: Historisch-kritische Ausgabe*, edited by Klaus Manger and Jan Philipp Reemtsma, vol. 10.1/2, 1–553. Berlin: Walter de Gruyter.

Wight, Martin. 1977. *Systems of States*. Leicester: Leicester University Press.

Wilks, Michael. 1963. *The Problem of Sovereignty in the Later Middle Ages*. Cambridge: Cambridge University Press.

Wilson, Eric. 2008. *The Savage Republic: De Indis of Hugo Grotius, Republicanism and Dutch Hegemony within the Early Modern World-System (c. 1600–1619)*. Leiden: Martinus Nijhoff.

Winkler, John. 1999. "The Mendacity of Kalasiris and the Narrative Strategy of Heliodorus' Aithiopika." In *Oxford Readings in the Greek Novel*, edited by Simon Swain, 286–350. Oxford: Oxford University Press.

Wisner, David. 1997. *The Cult of the Legislator in France, 1750–1830*. Oxford: Voltaire Foundation.

Wokler, Robert. 2012. *Rousseau, the Age of Enlightenment, and Their Legacies*. Princeton, NJ: Princeton University Press.

Wolff, Christian. 1934. *Jus Gentium Methodo Scientifica Pertractatum*. Translated by Joseph Drake. Oxford: The Clarendon Press.

Womersley, David. 2010. *Divinity and State*. Oxford: Oxford University Press.

Wyduckel, Dieter. 1979. *Princeps Legibus Solutus*. Berlin: Duncker und Humblot.

Yan, Xuetong. 2013. *Ancient Chinese Thought, Modern Chinese Power*. Princeton, NJ: Princeton University Press.
Zanger, Aby. 1997. *Scenes from the Marriage of Louis XIV*. Stanford: Stanford University Press.
Zatti, Sergio. 2006. *The Quest for Epic*. Toronto: University of Toronto Press.
Zetzel, James. 1996. "Natural Law and Poetic Justice: A Carneadean Debate in Cicero and Virgil." *Classical Philology* 91: 297–319.
Ziegler, Karl-Heinz. 2004. "The Influence of Medieval Roman Law on Peace Treaties." In *Peace Treaties and International Law in European History*, edited by Randall Lesaffer, 147–61. Cambridge: Cambridge University Press.
Zimmermann, Reinhard. 1996. *The Law of Obligations: Roman Foundations of the Civilian Tradition*. Oxford: Oxford University Press.
Zurcher, Amelia. 2007. *Seventeenth-Century English Romance*. New York: Palgrave Macmillan.
Zurcher, Andrew. 2010. *Shakespeare and Law*. London: Methuen Drama.
Zwantzig, Zacharias. 1709. *Theatrvm Præcedentiæ, oder eines theils Illvstrer Rang-Streit, andern theils Illvstre Rang-Ordnung*. Frankfurt: Fritsch.

Index

Note: Page numbers in *italics* indicate illustrations.

absolutism, 23, 156, 205; John Barclay on, 174, 176; William Barclay on, 172, 174; Jean Bodin on, 116; marriage alliances and, 152–53; normative order and, 15; Roman law and, 108; tragedy and, 111, 161
advice books for princes, 46–48, 176
Aeschylus, 16, 149
Agamben, Giorgio, 30, 100
Aithiopika (Heliodorus), 170, 176–81, 184, 189, 272
Alciato, Andrea, 12
Alexander the Great, 51
allegory, 150, 206; peace treaties and, 67–74, 69–71, *75*; in political romance, 194; of Shakespeare's romances, 140
ambassadors, 99–100, 224. *See also* diplomacy
Amelot de La Houssaie, Abraham Nicholas, 223
Amerindians: Las Casas on, 33; Sepúlveda on, 32–33; Vitoria on, 33–37, 55
Amiens, Treaty of (1527), 68, *70*
anagnorisis, 167
Andromaque (Racine), 206, 216–18
Anglo-Dutch War (1652–1654), 195
animal rights, 30–31
anomie, 81, 143
Anton Ulrich. *See* Braunschweig-Lüneburg, Anton Ulrich von
Apuleius, Lucius, 198
Aquinas, Thomas, 26, 30–31; on *ius gentium*, 35; on natural law, 29–30; on private property, 89
arcana imperii, 219–22
Argenis (Barclay), 2, 14, 23–24, 128, 170–76, 180–91
Aristotle, 56, 104, 151; on mimesis, 16, 168; on plot, 174; on poetic fiction, 13, 14, 168, 242; on tragedy, 109–10, 206

Attila (Corneille), 112, 154, 164, 166–67, 215
Aubignac, François Hédelin d', 110
Aubigné, Théodore Agrippa d', 187
Augustine of Hippo, 29, 95

Bakhtin, Mikhail, 38, 300n19
Baldus de Ubaldis, 12, 72, 76, 93
Barbeyrac, Jean, 223
Barclay, John, 188, 300n23; *Argenis*, 2, 14, 23–24, 128, 170–76, 180–91; Grotius and, 172; Leibniz and, 200
Barclay, William, 105, 172, 187
Baricave, Jean, 105
Bartelson, Jens, 283n17
Barthes, Roland, 216
Bartolus of Saxoferrato, 35–36, 76, 93
Benjamin, Walter, 145, 167
Bentham, Jeremy, 3, 16
Bernard, Jacques, 220, 223
Bildungsroman (novel of educational development), 2, 24, 233, 266; cosmopolitanism and, 271–78
Birken, Sigmund von, 197–99
Blanckenburg, Friedrich von, 241, 273
Blumenberg, Hans, 201
Bodin, Jean, 4, 98, 113, 116, 217
Bodmer, Johann Jacob, 242–43
Bossuet, Jacques-Bénigne, 157
Botero, Giovanni, 27, 146; advice books by, 47; *Delle cause della grandezza e magnificienza della città*, 51; on reason of state, 49, 51, 148, 188
Bourbon dynasty, 103, 195, 200
Bourriaud, Nicolas, 284n36
Braunschweig-Lüneburg, Anton Ulrich von, 3, 81–82, 84–87, 96; death of, 172, 203; *Die durchleuchtige Syrerinn Aramena*, 191–92, 197–200; *Die römische Octavia*, 191–92, 203–4

335

Brett, Annabel, 290n108
Bruner, Jerome, 15, 18

Callières, François de, 224, 265
Calvinism, 105, 144, 174. *See also* Reformation
Camden, William, 187
Camões, Luíz Vaz de, 2, 42–45, 48; on reason of state, 22, 27, 37–38, 51–52, 55
Carey, Daniel, 304n49
Carolus Stuardus (Gryphius), 24, 206–9, 218
Castelvetro, Lodovico, 110
Catharina von Georgien (Gryphius), 112, 140, 141, 143, 145
ceremonial theater, 97–100, 107–8
Cervantes, Miguel de, 186, 242
Charles I of England, 192, 194–96; Gryphius on, 24, 205–9, 218
Charles II of England, 192, 196, 254, 255
Charles II of Spain, 200
Charles V, Holy Roman Emperor, 32, 68–71, 71, 73–74
Charles VIII of France, 26
Charron, Pierre, 146
Chénier, André, 285n58
chronicles, 187, 197–98
Cicero, 40, 49, 269; Grotius and, 62; on natural law, 28–29, 88–89
civitas maxima (supreme state), 12–13
Cleopatra (Lohenstein), 112, 140–45, 150–52
Codex Iuris Civilis, 12
colonialism, 137, 138, 248, 304n49
commonwealth, 31, 88–92
Confucius, 203
Constantine I, Roman emperor, 51
Conti, Natale, 101
Copernicus, Nicolaus, 54
Corneille, Pierre, 2, 19, 149; marriage alliance tragedies of, 112–13, 152–67, 171, 215
Corneille, Pierre, works of: *Attila*, 112, 154, 164, 166–67, 215; *Le Cid*, 163; *Nicomède*, 163; *Œdipe*, 112–13, 153–61, 163, 215; *Rodogune*, 163; *Sophonisbe*, 112, 154, 164, 165, 299n133; *La Toison d'Or*, 100–103, 108, 112, 153–54, 163–66; *Les trois discours sur le poème dramatique*, 168
corpus mysticum, state as, 27–28, 157
cosmopolitanism, 233, 266–78; *Bildungsroman* and, 271–78; of Kant, 2, 9, 233, 266; Stoicism and, 233, 268–71, 275–78; of Wieland, 268–72
coups d'État, 147–49
Cover, Robert, 11

Crucé, Éméric, 16, 183, 202
Curtius, Ernst Robert, 22

David, Jacques-Louis, 14
De jure belli ac pacis (Grotius), 12, 62–64, 75–78, 87–88, 111–12, 227
Defence of Poesie (Sidney), 13, 110, 186, 190
"Defence of Poetry" (Shelly), 14
Defoe, Daniel, 232, 244–46, 278–79
Defoe, Daniel, works of: *Memoirs of a Cavalier*, 245; *Moll Flanders*, 239; *Robinson Crusoe*, 232, 238–39, 245–50, 304n49; *Roxana*, 232, 246, 250–55
DeGabriele, Peter, 304n43
Deleuze, Gilles, 95
Devolution, War of (1667–1668), 153, 154
Diderot, Denis, 229, 230, 242, 273
Dilthey, Wilhelm, 266
Diogenes of Sinope, 268, 269
diplomacy, 50, 60, 188, 224; by ambassadors, 99–100; manuals of, 265; sentimentalism and, 264–66
dissimulation, 141–49, 151
divine right, 105, 167, 171, 248
Dumont, Jean, 221–24
Dutch East India Company (VOC), 60, 84
Dworkin, Ronald, 17, 19

Elizabeth I of England, 107, 188
embassy: ambassadors of, 99–100, 224; law of, 58–60, 290n115
English Civil War (1642–1651), 171, 192, 210
English Revolution (1688), 24
epic, 26; classical, 26–27, 37–42, 52; definitions of, 38; Renaissance, 2, 21–23; tragedy and, 110
Euripides, 150

Fairfax, Thomas, 207
Federalist Papers, 285n63
Ficino, Marsilio, 53
fictionalization, 187–91, 300n21
Fielding, Henry, 239, 243, 273
Flaccus, Valerius, 103
Foucault, Michel, 48; on *coups d'État*, 147, 149; on Greek romance, 175; on reason of state, 289n76; on Sophocles, 155
founding narratives: of Grotius, 77–81, 87–88; of Hobbes, 79–81, 235, 236; of Leibniz, 88; of Pufendorf, 235–36
François I of France, 68–71, 71, 73–74
free trade, Grotius on, 90–93
Freemasonry, 275–76
Frye, Northrop, 106, 109

INDEX 337

Gama, Paulo da, 52
Gama, Vasco da, 27, 42–46, 52
Garatus, Martinus, 72
Gedichtgeschicht (poetic history), 198
Gellert, Christian Fürchtegott, 233, 259–64, 267
genealogical principle, 156
Gentili, Alberico, 12, 28, 111, 124, 290n115; *De armis Romanis*, 58, 111; *De iure belli libri tres*, 58, 111; on international law, 58–60, 113, 142; on reason of state, 58–60
Geschichtgedicht (historical poem), 197–98
Glafey, Adam Friedrich, 227–28
globalization, 236, 244–46, 250
Godefroy, Denys, 102
Godefroy, Théodore, 99, 159–60, 187
Goethe, Johann Wolfgang von, 38; *Wilhelm Meisters Lehrjahre*, 233, 266, 274–77
Goldast, Melchior, 219
Goodrich, Peter, 284n36
Gracián, Baltasar, 148
Greenblatt, Stephen, 114
Greene, Thomas, 288n57
Greiffenberg, Catharina Regina von, 300n36
Grewe, Wilhelm, 26
Gringore, Pierre, 69
Grotius, Hugo, 5, 26, 67, 124; Barclay and, 172; Cyclops figure in, 39; on emergence of property, 87–93; on free trade, 90–93; on international law, 60–64, 75–77, 226–27; Kant on, 281; Lauterpacht on, 291n41; on natural law, 60–64, 76, 77, 226–28, 232; on origin of states, 77–81; on rebellion, 78–79; Roman law and, 76–77, 92; on sovereignty, 81; on voluntary consent, 73
Grotius, Hugo, works of: *Annales et Historiæ de Rebus Belgicis*, 83; *De Indis*, 61, 64, 77–78; *De jure belli ac pacis*, 12, 62–64, 75–78, 87–88, 111–12, 227; *Sophompaneas*, 78–79
Grundling, Nicolaus Hieronymus, 238–39
Gryphius, Andreas, 2, 143; *Carolus Stuardus*, 24, 206–9, 218; *Catharina von Georgien*, 112, 140, 141, 143, 145
Guicciardini, Francesco, 27, 49, 148; *Dialogo del reggimento di Firenze*, 49; *Storia d'Italia*, 46, 68
Gustavus Adolphus, Swedish king, 12–13

Habsburg dynasty, 72, 103, 150, 200
hamartia (tragic flaw), 212, 213, 215
Hamilton, Alexander, 285n63

Happel, Eberhard Werner, 240
Harsdörffer, Georg Philipp, 110–11
Hart, H. L. A., 6–9, 14–15, 168
Heliodorus, 198; *Aithiopika*, 170, 176–81, 184, 189, 272
Henri IV of France, 183, 189, 202
Herbert, Percy, 171, 192–96
Hesiod, 89–91
historiography, 45–48, 197–98
Hobbes, Thomas, 15, 64, 67; on colonialism, 248; *De Cive*, 80; on international law, 79.112, 236; Leibniz and, 94, 95; *Leviathan*, 5–6, 209, 234; on natural law, 226, 228, 232; on origin of states, 79–81, 235–36; on sovereignty, 84–86; translation of Thucydides by, 267
höfisch-historischer Roman, 171, 191–92
Homer, 27, 198; *Iliad*, 119, 120; *Odyssey*, 37–39, 42
homo œconomicus, 247–48
Horace, 241
hospitality: in ancient world, 38–40; in Camões, 43–45
Huet, Pierre Daniel, 175
Huguenots, 251
human rights, 233, 278
humanitarian interventions, 34
Hume, David, 237, 238, 240, 256–58
Hunt, Lynn, 279
Hutcheson, Francis, 247

Iconologia (Ripa), 74, 75, 146
Illuminati, 275
intermezzi, 102, 112
International Court of Justice, 282
international law, 3–9, 23, 202, 223–24, 232, 281–82; as academic discipline, 218–29, 231; Bentham's definition of, 3; deniers of, 6; as dissimulation, 141–49; Gentili on, 58–60, 113, 142; Grotius on, 60–64, 75–77, 226–27; history of European literature and, 20–24; Hobbes on, 79.112, 236; Kant on, 277–78, 281; Meinecke on, 142–43; natural law and, 236–37; in Neoscholastic jurisprudence, 54–57; poetic constitution of, 9–13; poetic literature and, 206; public, 54–64; public law and, 224–25; Pufendorf on, 236; recognition narratives of, 81–82; Suárez on, 55–57; tragedy and, 111–13, 206; Wolff on, 228–29
international legal personality, 77–87, 92–93
international order. *See* world order
international social drama, 103–6

INDEX

ius civile (municipal law), 3, 37; Grotius on, 63; Suárez on, 57

ius gentium (law of nations), 3–4, 281; Aquinas on, 35; customary law and, 57; Grotius on, 61, 63–64; Kant on, 277–78; Leibniz on, 86; natural law and, 33–37, 76, 233–38, 240; Pufendorf on, 226; Suárez on, 55–57; Ulpian on, 34; Vásquez de Menchaca on, 36; Vitoria on, 26, 34–37, 55

ius naturae. *See* natural law

ius publicum europaeum, 25, 138, 219, 222–25

James I of England, 105, 107, 128, 133, 172; *Basilicon Doron*, 176, 187; *The Trew Law of Free Monarchies*, 187

Jhering, Rudolf von, 39

Jodelle, Étienne, 141

Justinian, Byzantine emperor, 221, 222

Kahn, Victoria, 300n31

Kant, Immanuel, 235–36; on cosmopolitanism, 2, 9, 233, 266, 277–78; on genius, 14; on international law, 277–78, 281

Kantorowicz, Ernst, 76

Kay, Carol, 304n24

Kelsen, Hans, 6–7

La Calprenède, Gautier de Costes de, 191

La Rochefoucauld, François de, 166

Lamberty, Guillaume de, 222

Las Casas, Bartomomé de, 32, 33, 287n22

Launoy, Jean, 162

Lauterpacht, Hersch, 8, 291n41

Legendre, Pierre, 100, 102

Lehmann, Hans-Thies, 107

Leibniz, Gottfried Wilhelm, 13, 67, 84–87, 148, 220, 226; on *ius gentium*, 86; on justice, 88; on "poem of the universe," 97; on relative sovereignty, 81–82, 85–88, 95; on theodicy, 171, 201, 202; on world order as romance, 200–202

Lessing, Gotthold Ephraim, 229–30

Lévi-Strauss, Claude, 8, 130

Lipsius, Justus, 27, 48, 188; advice books by, 47, 48; on *prudentia mixta*, 146

Livy, 11, 141, 299n133

Locke, John, 247, 248

Lohenstein, Daniel Casper von, 2, 112; Gryphius and, 143; on *mundus ludens*, 149–50

Lohenstein, Daniel Casper von, works of: *Cleopatra*, 112, 140–45, 150–52; *Großmüthiger Feldherr Arminius*, 191–92; *Sophonisbe*, 112, 140–45, 149–52

Long, Kingsmill, 188

Lorenzetti, Ambrogio, 74

Louis XII of France, 68, 69

Louis XIII of France, 12–13, 172; marriage of, 153, 195

Louis XIV of France, 24, 99–103; marriage of, 153, 164, 195; Racine and, 215

Lünig, Johann Christian, 221

Lutheranism, 32, 144. *See also* Reformation

Lycurgus, 11, 14

Mably, Gabriel Bonnot de, 224–25, 229

Machiavelli, Niccolò, 27; on diplomacy, 50; *Discorsi*, 48, 50; on dissimulation, 146; on fortune, 150; *Il Principe*, 47–48

Madrid, Treaty of (1526), 219

magna universitas (great society of states), 12–13, 76, 87, 95

Mark Antony, 141

Marlowe, Christopher, 2, 39; Seneca and, 118; *Tamburlaine the Great*, 111, 113–21, 126–27, 168

marriage alliances, 127, 192; absolutism and, 152–53, 161; in Barclay's *Argenis*, 170, 180–81, 184–86; ceremonies of, 100–103, 108; Corneille's plays of, 112–13, 152–67, 171, 215; in Herbert's *Princess Cloria*, 171, 192–96; James I on, 176; Shakespeare's plays of, 130, 132–38; in Ulrich's *Aramena*, 197–200

Mary Stuart, 140

Mary Tudor, 68, 69

Mazarin, Jules, 148, 195

Medici, Catherine de, 101

Meinecke, Friedrich, 142–43, 289n76

Milton, John: *Eikonoklastes*, 207; *Samson Agonistes*, 24, 206, 209–15, 218, 301n16; *The Tenure of Kings and Magistrates*, 207

mimesis, 154, 205–6; Aristotle on, 16, 168; verisimilitude and, 168, 242–43

mirror-for-princes genre, 46–48, 176

Molina, Luis de, 289n86

Möllers, Christoph, 8

moral sentimentalism, 256–59

Moritz, Karl Philip, 275

mos italicus, 28, 58

Moser, Johann Jakob, 225

municipal law. *See ius civile*

mythological spectacles, 100–103, 108

natural law, 3, 12, 64; Aquinas on, 29–30; Cicero on, 28–29, 88–89; Grotius on,

60–64, 76, 77, 226–28, 234; Hobbes on, 226, 228, 234; international law and, 236–37; *ius gentium* and, 33–37, 76, 233–38, 240; in New World, 30–33; novel and, 21–22, 304n24; positive law and, 226–27; Pufendorf on, 24, 226–28, 232, 234–38; subject of, 28–33; Thomasius on, 240; Ulpian on, 29; Vitoria on, 26–27, 31–32, 54–55
natural rights: Grotius on, 28; Hobbes on, 79; individual, 78, 232; Suárez on, 62; subjective, 26
Naudé, Gabriel, 146–49
Neoscholasticism, 26, 27, 30; Grotius and, 82; jurisprudence of, 28–37, 54–58, 73, 234–35
Netherlands, 153; United Dutch East India Company of, 60, 84; wars with England of, 194–95
Newton, Isaac, 94
Nice, Peace of (1538), 73–74
Nietzsche, Friedrich, 114–15
Nijmegen, Peace Congress of (1676), 81–82, 84–87
Novalis (Friedrich von Hardenberg), 277
novel, 15, 24, 231–33; *Bildungsroman*, 2, 24, 233, 266; chain, 17–18; definition of, 231; development of, 232; natural law and, 21–22, 304n24; poetics of, 238–44; sentimental, 233, 255–66, 279
Nuremberg, 220

oaths, 100, 127
Œdipe (Corneille), 112–13, 153–61, 163, 215
opera, 102, 230
Opitz, Martin, 110
origin stories. *See* founding narratives
Os Lusíadas. *See* Camões, Luíz Vaz de
Ovid, 89–91

Pascal, Blaise, 145, 166
Paul III, pope, 68, 71, 73–74
peace treaties, 67–74, 69–71, 75, 142
Pecquet, Antoine, 265
Philip II of France, 122–25
Philip II of Spain and Portugal, 83
Philip IV of Spain and Portugal, 99, 100, 153
Pistoia, Cino da, 12, 13
Plato, 53, 273
Plutarch, 141, 158
poetic jurisdiction, 9, 15–20
poetic lawmaking, 9, 13–15
political romance, 170–72, 187–205, 240, 244
préciosité, 158

private property, emergence of, 87–93
public law, 23; of Europe, 25, 138, 219, 222–25; Grotius on, 63–64
Pufendorf, Samuel von, 15, 24, 64, 212; on colonialism, 248; on commercial society, 232; on human nature, 240; on international law, 112, 226, 236–37; Kant on, 281; Leibniz and, 95, 226; on modern history, 218; on natural law, 24, 226–28, 232, 234–38; on sovereignty, 84–86, 236; on world order, 138
Pyrenees, Treaty of (1659), 153, 219
Pythagoras, 269

Quintilian, 10

Rachel, Samuel, 227
Racine, Jean, 19, 24, 149, 215–18, 229; *Andromaque*, 206, 216–18; *Bérénice*, 218
reason of state, 48–52, 249; Botero on, 49, 51, 148, 188; Camões on, 22, 27, 37–38, 51–52, 55; Foucault on, 289n76; Gentili on, 28, 58–60; Grotius on, 60–64; Guicciardini on, 49; Lipsius on, 48, 188; Lohenstein on, 112, 150; Meinecke on, 289n76; Naudé on, 146–47; tragedy of, 140–52
rebellion, 104–5; Grotius on, 78–79
recognition narratives, 81–82
Reformation, 25, 105, 174; natural law and, 32; sacrifice and, 144–45
res nullius, 90
respublica christiana, 72, 124
Richard I, English king, 124
Richardson, Samuel, 258, 305n66; *Clarissa*, 242; Diderot on, 242
Ripa, Cesare, 74, 75, 146
Rist, Johan, 112
Robinson Crusoe (Defoe), 232, 238–39, 245–50, 304n49
Robortello, Francesco, 109
Rohan, Henri de, 147–48
roman à clef, 192, 244. *See also* romance genre
Roman Empire, 41, 48
roman héroïque, 171, 191. *See also* romance genre
Roman law, 108; Grotius and, 76–77, 92; *ius gentium* in, 3; marriage in, 162
romance genre, 23–24, 96; Greek, 128, 175–76, 189–90, 272, 299n3; novels and, 231; political narratives of, 170–72, 187–205, 240, 244; Shakespeare's works in, 112, 128–40
Rousseau, Jean-Jacques, 39, 237–38, 240, 273

INDEX

Rousset de Missy, Jean, 222, 223
Roxana (Defoe), 232, 246, 250–55
Rymer, Thomas, 220

Saavedra Fajardo, Diego de, 150
sacrifice, 144–45; in Barclay's *Argenis*, 184, 189; Bossuet on, 157; in Corneille's *Œdipe*, 157; martyrological, 151–52
Saint-Pierre, Charles-Irénée Castel de, 16, 96, 183, 202, 223, 244
Saint-Prest, Jean Yves de, 220
Samson Agonistes (Milton), 24, 206, 209–15, 218, 301n16
Santa Catarina, seizure of, 60–62, 81–84, 111–12
Scaliger, Julius Caesar, 109–10
Schiller, Friedrich, 18; on "aesthetic state," 20; on epic poetry, 38
Schmitt, Carl, 138, 225; on "global linear thinking," 25; *Nomos der Erde*, 3, 25; on "war in due form," 289n98
Scudéry, Madeleine de, 158, 191
Sebastião, Portuguese king, 46, 47, 51
secret histories, 274
secret societies, 275–76
Seneca, 118, 146–47, 269
sentimental novel, 233, 255–66, 279
Sepúlveda, Juan Ginés, 32
Shaftesbury, Anthony Ashley Cooper, 3rd Earl of, 247, 256
Shakespeare, William, 2, 112, 149; audiences of, 19; romances of, 112, 128–40
Shakespeare, William, works of: *Cymbeline*, 112, 128, 129, 133, 135–36, 138, 139; *Hamlet*, 134; *King John*, 111, 113–14, 121–27, 168; *Pericles*, 112, 128–31, 133, 135, 138, 139; *The Tempest*, 39, 112, 128–30, 132–39; *The Winter's Tale*, 112, 128–35, 137–40
Shelly, Percy Bysshe, 14
Sidney, Algernon, 205
Sidney, Philip, 198; *Defence of Poesie*, 13, 110, 186, 190
Simpson, Gerry, 279
simulation, 144–49, 151
Skinner, Quentin, 105, 209
Smith, Adam, 238, 257–58
Solon, 11, 14
Sophocles, 149, 153–55, 161
Sophonisbe (Corneille), 112, 154, 164, 165, 299n133
Sophonisbe (Lohenstein), 112, 140–45, 149–52

Soto, Domingo de, 30, 37
sovereignty, 232; Bodin on, 116, 217; divine right and, 105, 167, 171, 248; divisible, 81; Hobbes on, 84–86; in Marlowe's *Tamburlaine*, 111, 113–21; Pufendorf on, 84–86, 236; relative, 81–82, 85–88, 95; in Shakespeare's *King John*, 121–27; tragedy and, 109–11, 113–114
Spanish Succession, War of (1701–14), 153, 200, 221, 244
spectacles: of marriage alliances, 100–103, 108; of world order, 97–103
Spinoza, Benedict de, 112
Staatsroman, 273–74
Sterne, Laurence, 233, 255, 264–66
Stieve, Gottfried, 221
Stoicism, 28, 233, 268, 271; cosmopolitanism and, 233, 268–71, 275–78
Strayer, Joseph, 283n9
Suárez, Francisco, 11, 27–28, 54–58, 62, 124

Tacitus, 46, 48, 83
Talon, Denis, 162–63
Tamburlaine the Great (Marlowe), 111, 113–21, 126–27, 168
Tasso, Torquato, 59, 289n83
Ten Commandments, 11
Thirty Years' War, 12–13, 80, 245
Thomasius, Christian, 227, 240–41
Thucydides, 80, 267
Tilly, Charles, 283n9
Toison d'Or, La (Corneille), 100–103, 108, 112, 153–54, 163–66
Tordesillas, Treaty of (1494), 25
tragedy, 2, 23–24; absolutism and, 111; Aristotle on, 109–10, 206; audiences of, 19; Benjamin on, 145, 167; bourgeois, 229; classical, 16, 21, 107, 118, 126–27; Corneille on, 112–13, 152–67; epic and, 110; Frye on, 106, 109; Grotius on, 78–79; Harsdörffer on, 110–11; international law and, 111–13, 206; Milton on, 210; of reason of state, 140–52; renaissance of, 107–9; Scaliger on, 109–10; Sidney on, 110; sovereignty and, 109–11, 113–114
Trissino, Giovan Giorgio, 141
Tuck, Richard, 290n104
Turner, Victor, 103–4

Ulpian (Roman jurist), 29, 34
United Dutch East India Company (VOC), 60, 84
United Nations, 282

universal law, 22–23, 28–37, 40–41, 268, 275
universitas, 76, 87. See also *magna universitas*
Utrecht, Peace of (1713), 200–202

Valois dynasty, 72
van den Vondel, Joost, 140
Vasari, Giorgio, 74; *Universal Peace*, 68, 71
Vattel, Emer de, 11, 228–29, 233, 237, 263, 281
Vázquez de Menchaca, Fernando, 36, 62
Verenigde Oostindische Compagnie (VOC), 60, 84
verisimilitude, 168, 242–43. See also mimesis
Vernant, Jean-Pierre, 118
Vienna, Congress of (1814–1815), 225, 281
Virgil, 27, 38, 46–48, 198; *Aeneid*, 37, 40–42, 288n57
Vismann, Cornelia, 97
Vitoria, Francisco de, 22, 30–31, 55; on Amerindians, 33–37, 55; on commonwealth, 30; on *ius gentium*, 26, 34–37, 54; on natural law, 26–27, 31–32, 54–55
Voltaire, 273

Walton, Kendall, 12
war, 40–41; in "due form," 60, 289n98; "just," 34, 82; law of, 58–60, 111

Warburg, Aby, 103
Warren, Christopher, 286n81
Watt, Ian, 273, 303n2
Westphalia, Peace of (1648), 60, 127, 219, 220, 293n101; Mably and, 224–25; Shakespeare and, 138
Wicquefort, Abraham van, 99–100
Wieland, Martin Christoph, 233, 243, 266–75
Wilhelm Meisters Lehrjahr (Goethe), 233, 266, 274–77
William II, prince of Orange, 192, 194, 196
William III of England, 196
Winkler, John, 299n15
Wolff, Christian, 11; *Jus gentium methodo scientifica pertractatum*, 12, 228–29
world order, 107–9; canonistic-papal versus secularized view of, 26; cosmopolitan, 233, 266–78; Hume on, 237; imaginary, 187–91; literary approaches to, 9–20; in Marlowe's *Tamburlaine*, 117–18; novel and, 231–33, 278–79; as romance, 200–202; spectacles of, 97–103; through tragic experience, 167–69; transnational commercial, 236, 244–46, 250–52

Zeno of Citium, 268
Zetzel, James, 288n50

CPSIA information can be obtained
at www.ICGtesting.com
Printed in the USA
BVHW030115071118
531826BV00002B/25/P

9 781501 716911